JANE FEARNLEY-WHITTINGSTALL'S

GARDEN PLANTS
MADE EASY

JANE FEARNLEY-WHITTINGSTALL'S

GARDEN PLANTS MADE EASY

500 PLANTS WHICH GIVE THE
BEST VALUE IN YOUR GARDEN

PHOENIX ILLUSTRATED

CONTENTS

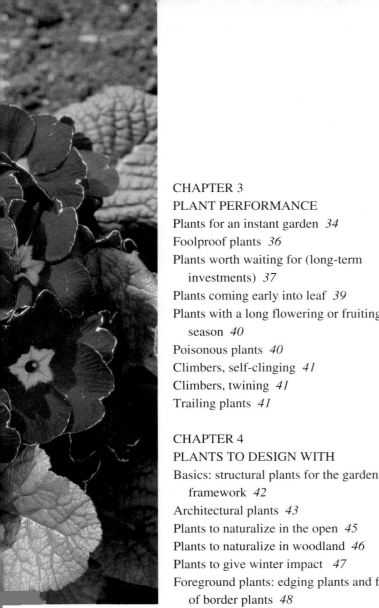

for Sophy

Text © Jane Fearnley-Whittingstall, 1997
Photographs © George Weidenfeld &
Nicolson Ltd, 1997 and Harry Smith
Horticultural Photographic Collection, 1997

The right of Jane Fearnley-Whittingstall to
be identified as the Author of this Work has
been asserted by her in accordance with the
Copyright, Designs & Patents Act, 1988

First published in 1997 by George
Weidenfeld & Nicolson Ltd

This paperback edition first published
in 1999 by Phoenix Illustrated
Orion Publishing Group, Orion House
5, Upper St. Martin's Lane
London WC2H 9EA

A CIP catalogue record for this book is
available from the British Library

ISBN 0 75380 691 6

Designed and produced by Blackjacks
Original plant photography by John Freeman
Illustrations by Ian Sidaway
Edited by Casey Horton
Horticultural editing by Lin Hawthorne and
Katy Sparrow
Colour reproduction by Scanners, London
Printed and bound in Italy

Acknowledgements
I would like to thank Carole Way for her invaluable help with research; Ian Sidaway
for his beautiful illustrations; John Freeman for his photographs and Lynne Woods
and Anthony Gardiner for helping him; Lin Hawthorne and Casey Horton for editing
the book, and especially everyone at Blackjacks for producing it.

INTRODUCTION

There has never been such a wide variety of plants available in garden centres, nurseries and mail order catalogues as there is today. The problem is knowing how to choose the right ones for your garden, as it is only too easy to be disappointed because you have made the wrong choice.

You may, for example, pick a plant that looks wonderful for two or three weeks when it is flowering, but is a drab tenant of valuable space for the other forty-nine weeks of the year. Or you may select one with glossy green leaves that gradually turn yellow and drop off because the soil in your garden is too alkaline; or one on which the buds become so badly infested with aphids that the plant never reaches the flowering stage. Faced with such problems you will probably begin to wonder whether you are at fault.

Similarly, when plants die or just fail to thrive, you may feel you are guilty of neglect or ill-treatment – pruning in the wrong way at the wrong time, perhaps, or overfeeding or underfeeding, giving too much water or too little. Any or all of these things may be bad for the plants, but worrying about them is bad for the gardener: it takes the enjoyment out of gardening.

Garden Plants Made Easy is intended to restore and increase your enjoyment of gardening by helping you choose the right plants for your garden's soil and climate. It also tells you how to keep the plants healthy – how to plant, prune, feed and water them.

Comprehensive plant encyclopedias can be difficult to find your way around in order to select a few plants for a particular spot in your garden. My aim is to make choosing easy by pre-selecting plants that perform well and are easy to grow. From the many thousands of plants available I have arrived at a list of about five hundred that are truly garden worthy. All the plants listed give good value in the garden, either because they have a long flowering season or because they have additional features, such as ornamental fruit, autumn colour or evergreen leaves.

My philosophy is that gardening is one of life's greatest pleasures, and I believe that the pleasure comes mainly from the creative process of growing and nurturing plants. I hope this book will contribute to your pleasure by making the process easier.

How to use this book

Whether you are creating a garden from scratch, renewing a neglected garden or replanting an unsatisfactory corner in an established garden, you should be able to find suitable plants for your situation within these pages.

Part I, 'Choosing Plants for Your Garden', lists plants for different situations and different purposes. To find the plants you are looking for, you will probably want to consult more than one list. For example, you may be looking for plants that will attract bees and butterflies and will thrive in a limestone area with alkaline soil. When you have arrived at a list of suitable and desirable plants for your purpose, you should turn to the plant index in Part II for a detailed description of each plant and its cultural requirements.

Part II gives additional information that may be useful at the planning stage. It includes a section on good companions, which will help you to compose colour schemes or contrasting and harmonizing foliage effects, and wherever appropriate gives alternative varieties of different sizes and colours.

Most of the plants listed are fairly readily available from garden centres, local nurseries or nurseries with mail order services. However I have included some plants which, although they are not easy to find, are worthwhile plants. Tracking down these less popular plants has become far easier with the publication of *The RHS Plant Finder*, which contains a very comprehensive list of plants and where to purchase them. The information, including current plant classification and the correct botanical names of plants, is updated annually.

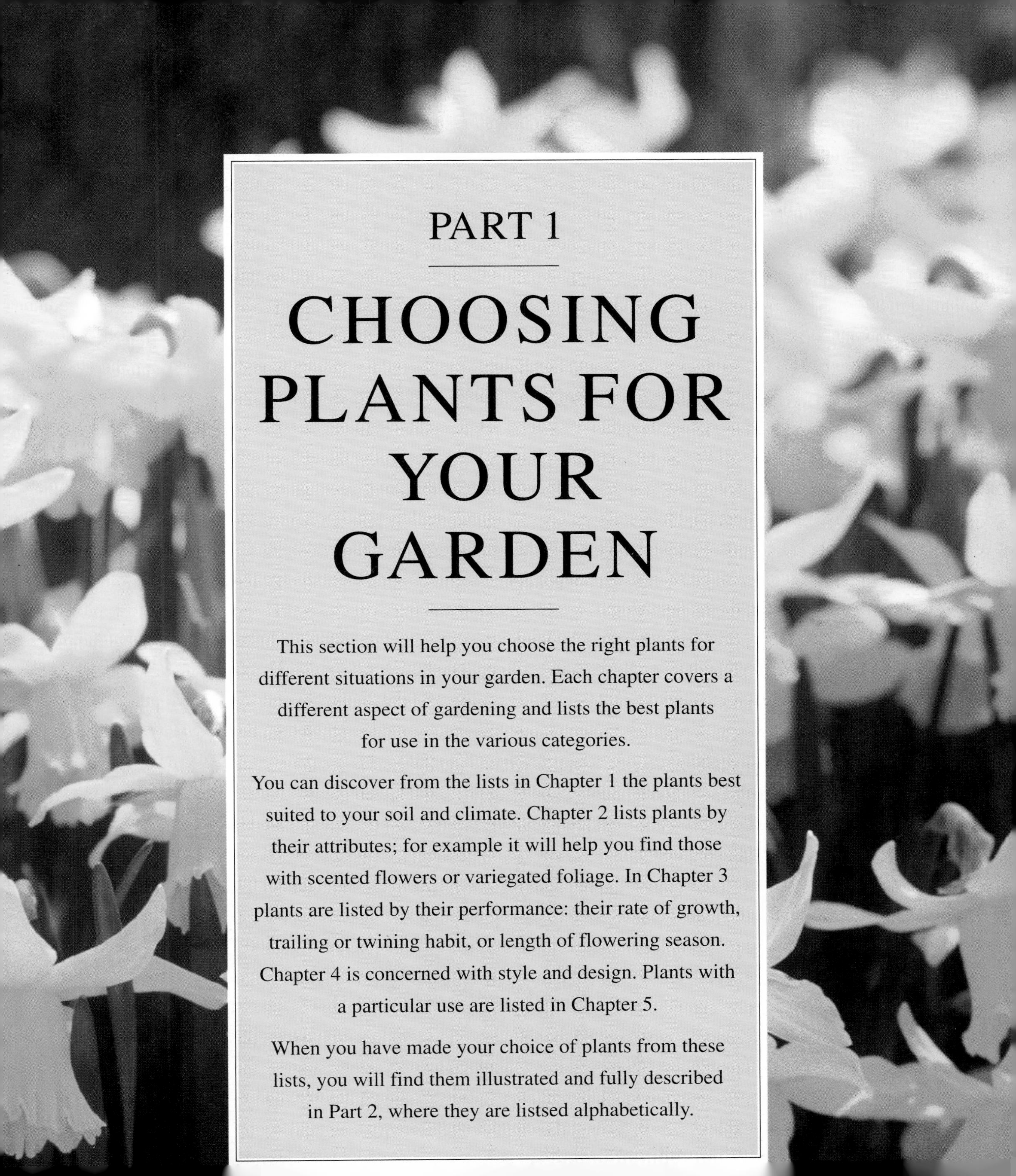

PART 1

—

CHOOSING PLANTS FOR YOUR GARDEN

—

This section will help you choose the right plants for different situations in your garden. Each chapter covers a different aspect of gardening and lists the best plants for use in the various categories.

You can discover from the lists in Chapter 1 the plants best suited to your soil and climate. Chapter 2 lists plants by their attributes; for example it will help you find those with scented flowers or variegated foliage. In Chapter 3 plants are listed by their performance: their rate of growth, trailing or twining habit, or length of flowering season. Chapter 4 is concerned with style and design. Plants with a particular use are listed in Chapter 5.

When you have made your choice of plants from these lists, you will find them illustrated and fully described in Part 2, where they are listsed alphabetically.

1 | Plants for Different Soils and Climates

In nature, plants have evolved to thrive in widely different soils and climates. It follows that, in the garden, there are plants to suit even the most unpromising conditions. The choice of plants will be strictly limited if, for example, your garden is on clay on a seaside cliff-top exposed to gale force winds. But even in such a place, if you choose your plants carefully they will reward you by growing strong and healthy and producing a good display of flowers and fruit.

Plants for clay soil

Soil with a high proportion of clay is dense, heavy and sticky. The same qualities that make it an ideal material for pottery make it difficult to dig when wet and, when dry, cause it to bake so hard that it is almost impossible to get a spade or fork into it. It is slow to warm up in spring. In it's favour, clay is usually high in plant nutrients.

Oak and ash trees, an underlayer of hazel, thorn and bramble and a carpet of wood anemones, primroses, bluebells and foxgloves are all components of a typical clay landscape.

If in doubt as to what plants will do well, look for those with robust root systems. Delicate fibrous roots have difficulty in forcing their way through the dense clay.

Trees
Acer platanoides, Aesculus, Alnus, Betula pendula, Carpinus, Crataegus laevigata, Eucalyptus gunnii, Fraxinus, Ilex aquifolium, Laburnum, Malus, Metasequoia glyptostroboides, Picea breweriana, Pinus nigra austriaca, Prunus, Pyrus, Quercus, Salix, Sorbus, Taxus baccata, Thuja plicata 'Atrovirens', Tilia

Climbers
Campsis, Clematis, Euonymus fortunei 'Silver Queen', Hedera, Humulus lupulus, Hydrangea petiolaris, Lathyrus latifolius, Lonicera, Parthenocissus, Passiflora, Vitis coignetiae, Wisteria

Shrubs
Abelia, Aesculus, Amelanchier, Aralia, Aucuba, Berberis, Chaenomeles, Choisya, Cornus alba 'Sibirica', Corylus, Cotoneaster, Garrya, Hypericum, Kerria, Lonicera, Mahonia, Osmanthus, Philadelphus, Potentilla, Prunus laurocerasus, Pyracantha, Ribes, Rosa,

Rubus, Salix, Sambucus racemosa, Symphoricarpus, Syringa, Taxus baccata, Viburnum opulus, Vinca, Weigela

Perennials
Astilbe, Caltha, Cardamine pratensis, Filipendula ulmaria, Gunnera manicata, Hemerocallis, Hosta, Lysichiton, Lysimachia, Lythrum, Matteucia struthiopteris, Osmunda regalis, Phormium, Primula, Rheum, Rodgersia

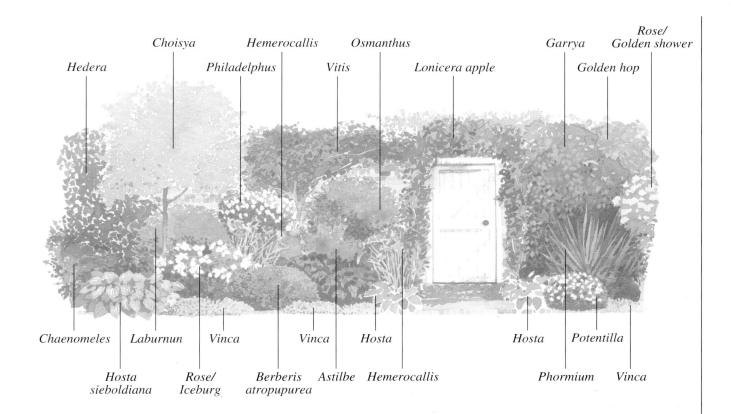

Hedera

Choisya

Philadelphus

Hemerocallis

Vitis

Osmanthus

Lonicera apple

Garrya

Golden hop

*Rose/
Golden shower*

Chaenomeles

Laburnun

Vinca

Vinca

Hosta

Hosta

Potentilla

*Hosta
sieboldiana*

*Rose/
Iceburg*

*Berberis
atropupurea*

Astilbe

Hemerocallis

Phormium

Vinca

Plants for alkaline soil, chalk or limestone

Most plants will grow happily in a moderately alkaline soil. The exceptions are camellias, most rhododendrons and azaleas, and most heathers; they must have acid soil to do well. In Britain, chalk downland supports a wonderfully diverse wild flower population. In limestone areas, field maple, hawthorn, blackthorn and hazel are typical hedgerow components with bluebells, cowslips, cranesbill, ox-eye daisies, scabious and yarrow in road verges.

Alkaline soil is usually open textured with good drainage, so that nutrients tend to get washed away. Many herbs and Mediterranean plants such as lavenders and cistuses enjoy these conditions provided they are planted in full sun.

Trees
Acer campestre, Acer griseum, Acer negundo, Aesculus, Alnus, Amelanchier, Arbutus unedo, Betula, Caragana, Carpinus betulus, Catalpa, Cercis siliquastrum, Chamaecyparis lawsoniana, Crataegus, Cupressocyparis leylandii, Fagus sylvatica, Fraxinus, Gleditsia, Juglans, Juniperus, Laburnum, Malus, Morus nigra, Prunus avium, Prunus sargentii, Pyrus, Quercus cerris, Quercus robur, Robinia, Sorbus aria, Taxus baccata, Thuja, Tilia tomentosa

Climbers
Actinidia kolomikta, Akebia quinata, Clematis, Hedera, Hydrangea petiolaris, Jasminum officinale, Lathyrus latifolius, Lonicera, Parthenocissus tricuspidata, Passiflora caerulea, Solanum crispum, Trachelospermum jasminoides, Vitis, Wisteria sinensis

Shrubs
Aesculus parviflora, Aucuba, Berberis, Brachyglottis, Buddleja davidii, Buxus, Ceanothus, Choisya ternata, Cistus, Corylus, Cotoneaster, Cytisus (some), *Deutzia, Elaeagnus, Escallonia, Euonymus, Fuchsia, Hebe, Hydrangea villosa, Hypericum, Ilex aquifolium, Kerria, Kolkwitzia, Ligustrum, Lonicera, Mahonia aquifolium, Osmanthus, Paeonia, Philadelphus, Phlomis fruticosa, Potentilla, Prunus laurocerasus, Pyracantha, Ribes, Romneya, Rosa rugosa, Rosmarinus, Sambucus, Santolina, Sinarundinaria, Syringa, Viburnum tinus, Vinca, Weigela, Yucca*

Perennials
Acanthus spinosus, Achillea, Aconitum, Anchusa, Anemone x hybrida, Aubrieta, Bergenia, Brunnera, Campanula lactiflora,

Centranthus, Clematis, Corydalis lutea, Dianthus, Doronicum, Eryngium, Geranium pratense, Gypsophila, Helleborus, Heuchera, Kniphofia, Linum narbonense, Lychnis chalcedonica, Origanum, Paeonia, Pulsatilla, Salvia nemorosa, Saxifraga (some), *Scabiosa caucasica, Sedum, Stachys, Thymus, Verbascum, Veronica spicata*

Annuals and Biennials
Antirrhinum, Calendula officinalis, Cosmos, Dianthus, Erysimum, Lavatera, Matthiola (Brompton Series), *Tropaeolum*

Cercis siliquastrum
Wisteria
Vitis
Lonicera japonica
Diitalis
Juniperus
Lavender
Cistus pupureus
Bay
Scabiosa
Basil
Iris
Tarragon
Achillea
Nasturtium
Santolina
Thymes
Cistus
Sage

Plants for sandy soil

A high proportion of visible sand makes this soil type easy to identify. It is very free draining, therefore dry and usually acid. A local landscape of silver birch, broom, gorse and bracken indicates sandy soil. The more manure and compost you can add to sandy garden soil the better. Sand is an insatiable consumer of organic material, but however much you provide, dry conditions still prevail. An ability to survive drought is an essential requirement for plants to thrive in sandy soil.

Trees

Acer negundo, Alnus cordata, Arbutus menziesii, Betula pendula, Caragana, Castanea sativa, Cercidiphyllum japonicum, Cercis siliquastrum, Cryptomeria, Fraxinus ornus, Gleditsia triacanthos, Juniperus, Picea (most), *Quercus ilex, Robinia, Thuja occidentalis*

Shrubs

Amelanchier larmarckii, Artemisia arborescens, Ballota pseudodictamnus, Berberis, Brachyglottis, Calluna vulgaris, Ceanothus thyrsiflorus, Ceratostigma, Cistus, Convolvulus cneorum, Corylus, Cotoneaster, Cytisus scoparius, Elaeagnus, Erica, Fuchsia magellanica, Genista tinctoria, Helianthemum, Helichrysum, Hypericum, Lavandula, Olearia, Perovskia, Phlomis, Phormium, Potentilla, Romneya, Rosmarinus, Salvia, Spartium junceum, Symphoricarpus, Yucca gloriosa

Climbers

Parthenocissus, Passiflora, Solanum crispum 'Glasnevin'

Perennials

Acaena, Acanthus spinosus, Achillea, Alchemilla, Armeria, Centranthus, Echinops ritro, Epimedium, Eryngium tripartitum, Gaillardia x grandiflora, Gypsophila repens, Helleborus, Limonium platiphyllum, Nepeta faassenii, Origanum vulgare 'Aureum', *Papaver orientale, Romneya coulteri, Sedum, Sisyrinchium*

Annuals and Biennials

Anchusa, Calendula officinalis, Centaurea cyanus, Helichrysum, Impatiens, Lavatera, Limnanthes douglasii, Osteospermum, Papaver somniferum, Rudbeckia, Verbascum,

Plants for waterlogged soil

These are plants that do not mind having their feet in water. If the right conditions do not exist in your garden, it is possible to create a bog artificially. (*See also* 'Plants for the water garden and bog garden' in Chapter 4).

Shrubs
Aralia, Berberis, Chaenomeles, Cornus alba, Cotoneaster, Mahonia x media, Salix, Sambucus, Viburnum opulus

Perennials
Caltha, Gunnera manicata, Hemerocallis, Lysichiton, Mimulus guttatus, Myosotis scorpiodes, Persicaria affine, Primula (several), *Zantedeschia*

Viburnum opulus

Gunnera

Primula

Cornus alba

Lysichiton

Astilbe

Alnus cordata

Sambucus

Iris

Zantedeschia

Primula

Plants that need acid soil

Many plants have a preference for acid soil (below pH 5.5) but will tolerate slightly alkaline conditions. There are a few plants that are lime-haters (calcifuge) and will not survive at all in limey (alkaline) soil. They must be planted in acid soil. If you want to grow them, but are uncertain whether your soil is acid or alkaline, check the pH level. Most garden shops sell inexpensive, easy-to-use kits for this purpose.

Trees and Shrubs
Arbutus menziesii, Azalea, Calluna, Camellia, Cryptomeria, Erica, Hamamelis, Hydrangea (blue-flowered kinds), *Liquidambar, Magnolia* (most), *Picea pungens glauca* 'Koster', *Pieris, Rhododendron, Skimmia*

Plants for damp soil

Some plants will thrive in moisture-retentive soil, usually with a high organic content such as peat or, sometimes, clay. The soil around the roots of these plants should not be allowed to dry out, but neither should it be permanently swampy.

Trees
Alnus, Amelanchier, Betula, Crataegus oxyacantha, Mespilus germanica, Metasequoia glyptostroboides, Pyrus communis (pear), *Salix, Sorbus aucuparia*

Shrubs
Cornus alba, Photinia, Salix, Sambucus, Spiraea, Symphoricarpus, Viburnum opulus

Perennials
Alchemilla mollis, Aster, Astrantia, Campanula lactiflora, Euphorbia griffithii, Filipendula, Gunnera, Hemerocallis, Iris pseudacorus, Ligularia, Lythrum, Miscanthus, Narcissus, Persicaria, Rheum, Rudbeckia

Plants that will tolerate air pollution

In spite of clean air regulations, unfortunately there are still areas of industrial pollution. If you are unlucky enough to live in one, the following plants stand a reasonable chance of strong and healthy growth.

Trees
Acer platanoides, Aesculus hippocastanum, Alnus cordata, Betula pendula, Carpinus betulus, Catalpa bignonioides, Crataegus, Gingko biloba, Ilex x altaclarensis, Magnolia grandiflora, Malus, Pyrus, Robinia, Salix, Sorbus, Taxus baccata

Climbers
Clematis, Hedera, Hydrangea petiolaris, Parthenocissus, Vitis

Shrubs
Aucuba, Berberis, Buddleja davidii, Camellia, Cotoneaster, Elaeagnus, Fatshedera lizei, Fuchsia magellanica, Garrya elliptica, Ilex altaclarensis, Ilex aquifolium, Leycesteria formosa, Ligustrum, Mahonia aquifolium, Philadelphus, Salix, Spiraea, Viburnum

Perennials
Aconitum napellus, Aquilegia vulgaris, Aubrieta, Bergenia cordifolia, Campanula poscharskyana, Dicentra formosa, Euphorbia amygdaloides, Geranium endressii, Helleborus niger, Helleborus orientalis, Hemerocallis, Heuchera, Hosta, Iris, Lamium, Polemonium, Polygonatum, Pulmonaria, Rudbeckia, Sedum, Sisyrinchium striatum, Symphytum, Thalictrum, Tiarella, Veronica gentianoides, Veronica spicata

Fast-growing plants for a windbreak or hedge

Hedges or belts of trees make more effective windbreaks than solid walls and fences: a solid barrier tends to create turbulence on the leeward side, whereas a dense hedge allows the wind to enter and entraps it. If a formal, clipped hedge is not your style, make an informal belt of shrubs from the lists below.

Trees
Abies grandis, Alnus cordata, Chamaecyparis lawsoniana, x Cupressocyparis leylandii, Thuja plicata

Shrubs
Cotoneaster simonsii, Elaeagnus x ebbingei, Ligustrum ovalifolium, Pyracantha x watereri, Rosa 'Charles de Mills', *Rosa rugosa*

OTHER PLANTS RESISTANT TO COLD WINDS

Trees
Acer negundo, Acer platanoides, Betula pendula, Crataegus x lavallei, C. monogyna, Cryptomeria japonica, Fraxinus excelsior, Ginkgo biloba, Gleditsia triacanthos, Ilex aquifolium, Laburnum, Picea breweriana, Quercus robur, Salix alba, Sorbus, Taxus baccata, Tilia cordata

Shrubs
Berberis, Brachyglottis, Buddleia davidii, Calluna vulgaris, Chaenomeles, Cornus alba, Corylus avellana, Cotinus coggyria, Cotoneaster horizontalis (and other low-growing kinds), *Deutzia, Elaeagnus, Erica, Escallonia, Euonymus fortunei, Fuchsia magellanica, Genista, Helianthemum, Ilex aquifolium, Juniperus, Kerria, Lavatera, Mahonia aquifolium, Philadelphus, Potentilla, Pyracantha, Rhododendron, Rosa, Salix, Spartium, Viburnum opulus, Yucca*

Perennials
Anaphalis, Artemisia absinthium, Campanula portenschlagiana, Centranthus ruber, Eryngium, Euphorbia characias, Festuca glauca, Kniphofia, Limonium platiphyllum, Phlomis russeliana, Sedum, Stachys byzantina, Yucca filamentosa

Annuals and Biennials
Borago officinalis, Calendula, Centaurea cyanus, Dianthus barbatus, Lavatera episymum, Limnanthes, Lunaria, Papaver somniferum

Bulbs
Anemone, Chionodoxa, Colchicum, Crocus, Cyclamen, Fritillaria, Galanthus, Iris reticulata, Muscari, Narcissus (dwarf kinds), *Ornithogalum, Scilla, Tulipa* (dwarf kinds)

1 Hedges catch the wind and slow it down.

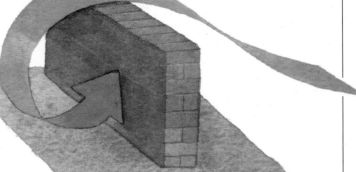

2 When wind hits a wall or other solid barrier, it leaps over it, causing turbulence on the leeward side.

Plants for the seaside

Like the plants listed on the previous page, these can stand up to strong winds. In addition they are not affected by the salt carried on winds from the sea.

Trees
Arbutus unedo, Crataegus, x Cupressocyparis leylandii, Fraxinus, Ilex aquifolium, Laburnum, Quercus ilex, Salix, Sorbus aria, Sorbus aucuparia

Shrubs
Calluna vulgaris, Choisya ternata, Cistus, Cotoneaster, Elaeagnus, Escallonia, Euonymus fortunei, Fuchsia magellanica, Garrya elliptica, Genista, Hebe, Helianthemum, Helichrysum, Hydrangea, Ilex aquifolium, Juniperus, Laurus nobilis, Lavandula, Lavatera, Leycesteria formosa, Olearia, Phlomis, Phormium, Pyracantha, Rosa, Rosmarinus, Salix, Sambucus racemosa, Santolina, Sinarundinaria, Spartium junceum, Spiraea, Viburnum, Yucca

Perennials
Agapanthus, Anaphalis, Artemisia absinthium, Centranthus ruber, Eryngium, Euphorbia characias, Festuca glauca, Kniphofia, Phormium, Sedum spectabile, Stachys byzantina

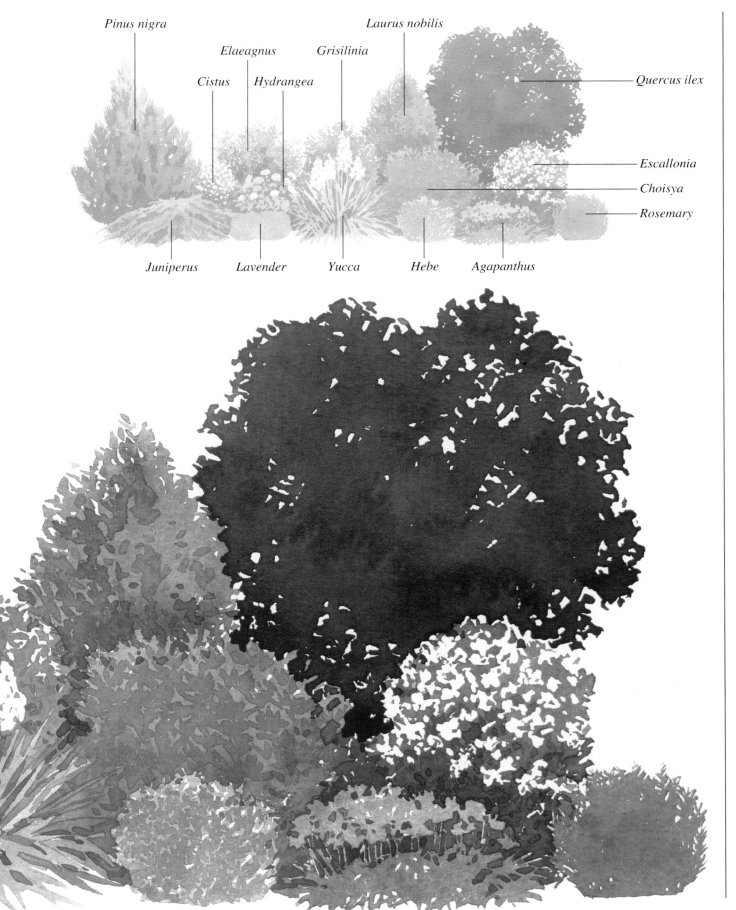

Pinus nigra

Elaeagnus

Cistus   *Hydrangea*

Grisilinia

Laurus nobilis

Quercus ilex

Escallonia

Choisya

Rosemary

Juniperus   *Lavender*   *Yucca*   *Hebe*   *Agapanthus*

Plants for heavy shade

It is unlikely that the whole of your garden is in dense shade. But if it is, or if you have a dark corner, make a virtue of necessity by emphasizing the mysterious gloom. Place a statue, urn or broken column where it is half hidden by evergreens. Allow no colour except for a touch of light, provided by a strand of variegated ivy.

Shrubs

Aucuba japonica, Buxus sempervirens, Camellia japonica, Elaeagnus, Euonymus fortunei, Fatshedera lizei, Hedera helix, Hypericum calycinum, Ilex x altaclarensis, Ilex aquifolium, Juniperus x media 'Pfitzeriana', *Ligustrum, Lonicera nitida, Mahonia aquifolium, Prunus laurocerasus, Prunus lusitanica, Rhododendron, Rubus tricolor, Sinarundinaria, Skimmia, Symphoricarpos, Taxus baccata, Viburnum davidii, Vinca*

Plants for dry shade

This is a situation that has most gardeners in despair, yet because the opportunities are so limited, planting schemes for dry shade usually have a pleasing quality of simplicity.

Trees
Alnus, Betula, Crataegus prunifolia, Sorbus aucuparia

Shrubs
Amelanchier, Aucuba, Buxus sempervirens, Cotoneaster, Euonymus fortunei, Fatsia japonica, Hedera, Ilex aquifolium, Juniperus x media, Lonicera pileata, Mahonia, Prunus laurocerasus, Ribes, Rubus tricolor, Sambucus, Symphoricarpos, Vinca

Perennials
Acanthus mollis, Aconitum, Ajuga, Alchemilla mollis, Anaphalis, Anemone x hybrida, Aquilegia vulgaris, Asplenium scolopendrium, Aubrieta, Bergenia, Brunnera macrophylla, Campanula poscharskyana, Convallaria majalis, Dicentra, Digitalis grandiflora, *Epimedium, Euphorbia amygdaloides, Geranium* (some), *Gypsophila repens, Helleborus foetidus, Helleborus orientalis, Heuchera* 'Pewter Moon' and others, *Iris foetidissima, Lamium maculatum, Polygonatum x hybridum, Pulmonaria, Saxifraga umbrosa, Saxifraga x urbium, Symphytum, Tellima grandiflora, Tiarella cordifolia, Viola labradorica*

Annuals and Biennials
Digitalis purpurea, Matthiola bicornis

Bulbs
Anemone blanda, Anemone nemorosa, Arum italicum 'Pictum', *Cyclamen coum*, etc., *Galanthus, Hyacinthoides non-scripta*

Ilex aquifolium

Fatsia japonica

Prunus laurocerasus

Polygonatum x hybridum

Brunnera

Tiarella cordifolia

Iris foetidissima

Cycianthem coum

Viola labradorica

Plants for moist shade

In dappled shade under trees or in a north-facing border, there is plenty of choice provided the ground is not too dry. The type of plants that thrive in these conditions have a distinctive character, and many of them look their best in a woodland garden.

Trees
Acer griseum, Acer negundo, Acer platanoides, Alnus, Betula pendula, Crataegus, Fraxinus, Quercus, Salix, Sorbus aucuparia

Shrubs
Aucuba, Buxus sempervirens, Camellia japonica, Cercidiphyllum japonicum, Cornus alba, Daphne odora 'Aureomarginata', *Elaeagnus, Euonymus, Fatshedera lizei, Fuchsia magellanica* 'Versicolor', *Hedera helix, Hydrangea, Ilex aquifolium, Ligustrum, Lonicera pileata, Mahonia aquifolium, Osmanthus, Prunus laurocerasus, Rhododendron, Rubus, Salix, Sambucus, Skimmia, Symphoricarpos, Viburnum davidii, Viburnum rhytidophyllum, Vinca*

Perennials
Alchemilla mollis, Aruncus dioicus, Astilbe, Astrantia major, Bergenia, Brunnera, Caltha palustris, Convallaria, Cyclamen hederifolium, Dicentra formosa, Gentiana asclepiadea, Helleborus, Hemerocallis, Hosta, Melissa officinalis 'Aurea', *Monarda, Myrrhis odorata* (sweet cecily), *Persicaria affine* 'Superba', *Phlox paniculata, Platycodon, Primula, Rumex acetosa* (sorrel), *Tanacetum parthenium, Thalictrum, Tiarella cordifolia*

Annuals and Biennials
Angelica archangelica, Digitalis purpurea, Impatiens, Matthiola bicornis, Primula vulgaris, Viola x wittrockiana, Viola labradorica

Bulbs
Allium schoenoprasum (chives), *Anemone blanda, Arum italicum, Corydalis, Eranthis, Erythronium, Galanthus, Leucojum, Lilium* (some), *Narcissus cyclamineus, Narcissus triandrus, Scilla bifolia, Trollius, Tulipa sylvestris*

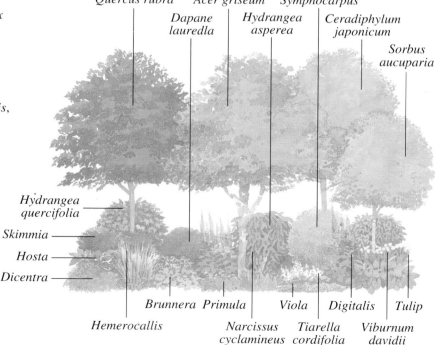

Quercus rubra   Acer griseum   Symphocarpus
Dapane lauredla   Hydrangea asperea   Ceradiphylum japonicum
Sorbus aucuparia
Hydrangea quercifolia
Skimmia
Hosta
Dicentra
Hemerocallis   Brunnera   Primula   Viola   Digitalis   Tulip
Narcissus cyclamineus   Tiarella cordifolia   Viburnum davidii

Climbers and wall plants for north- and east-facing walls

The soil at the base of a wall is usually dry. Make sure climbing plants get adequate moisture by planting them at least 45cm (18in) away from the wall.

Akebia quinata, Azara microphylla, Camellia, Chaenomeles, Clematis alpina, Clematis macropetala, Clematis montana, Clematis 'Comtesse de Bouchaud', *Clematis* 'Edith', 'Hagley Hybrid', 'Jackmanii', 'Margot Koster', 'Marie Boisselot', 'Perle d'Azur', 'William Kennet', *Euonymus fortunei* 'Silver Queen', *Garrya elliptica, Hedera, Humulus lupulus, Hydrangea petiolaris, Jasminum nudiflorum, Lathyrus latifolius, Parthenocissus, Pyracantha, Rosa* 'Alberic Barbier', 'Félicité et Perpetué', 'Gloire de Dijon', 'Golden Showers', 'Kathleen Harrop', 'Mme Alfred Carrière', 'Mme Grégoire Staechelin', 'Maigold', 'May Queen', 'New Dawn', 'Paul's Scarlet', 'Zéphirine Drouhin', *Vitis coignetiae*

1 Plant climbers at least 45cm (18in) out from a wall to avoid the dry soil at its base.

2 Lean the plant against the wall with the main shoots fanned out and tied to canes.

2 | Plant Attributes

This chapter introduces some of the attributes and characteristics of plants that can be used to make a wide variety of garden pictures and experiences, adding new dimensions to your enjoyment of the garden. If you are planning a colour scheme, use these lists to find plants with foliage that will harmonize or contrast with the flowers.

Scented flowers

The scent of many flowers is strongest at the beginning and the end of the day; plant them near a door that you use regularly, under windows so that the scent can waft indoors, and around the area where you sit in the garden to enjoy the evening sun.

Trees
Aesculus, Crataegus monogyna, Laburnum vossii, Magnolia kobus, Malus coronaria 'Charlottae', *Malus floribunda, Malus* 'Profusion', *Prunus* 'Amanogawa', *Prunus shirotae, Prunus x yedoensis, Tilia*

Climbers
Akebia quinata, Clematis armandii, Clematis flammula, Clematis montana 'Elizabeth', *Jasminum officinale, Lathyrus odoratus, Lonicera x americana, Lonicera japonica* 'Halliana', *Lonicera periclymenum, Rosa* (many), *Trachelospermum, Wisteria*

Shrubs
Azara microphylla, Buddleia alternifolia, Buddleia davidii, Choisya, Cytisus battandieri, Elaeagnus, Hamamelis 'Pallida', *Lonicera, Mahonia japonica, Osmanthus delavayi, Osmanthus burkwoodii, Philadelphus, Pyracantha, Rhododendrons* (many, including *R.* 'Fragrantissima', *R. luteum*), *Romneya, Rosa* (many), *Spartium junceum, Syringa, Viburnum x bodnantense, Viburnum x burkwoodii, Viburnum carlesii*

Perennials
Centranthus ruber, Convallaria majalis, Crambe cordifolia, Dianthus 'Brympton Red', 'Doris', 'Little Jock', 'Nyewood's Cream', 'White Ladies', and others, *Filipendula ulmaria, Hemerocallis lilio-asphodelus, Hosta* 'Honeybells', *Hosta plantaginea* 'Grandiflora', *Iris, Paeonia lactiflora* 'Duchesse de Nemours', *Paeonia lactiflora* 'Laura Dessert', 'President Poincare', 'Sarah Bernhardt', *Phlox maculata, Phlox paniculata* (those with pale colours),

Primula florindae, Primula vulgaris 'Dawn Ansell', *Viola* 'Maggie Mott', 'Moonlight'

Annuals and Biennials
Antirrhinum, Calendula officinalis, Erisymum, Heliotropum, Hesperis matronalis, Lathyrus odoratus, Matthiola bicornis, Nicotiana sylvestris

Bulbs
Crocus chrysanthus, Hyacinthus, Lilium candidum, Lilium regale and others, *Narcissus jonquilla* 'Baby Moon', 'Trevithian' and others, *Narcissus tazetta* 'Cheerfulness', 'Yellow Cheerfulness', 'Minnow', *Tulipa* 'Bellona', 'Prince of Austria', 'Orange Favourite'

Scented leaves

Aromatic leaves release their fragrance when you brush against them, or when you rub a leaf in your fingers. Plant them beside paths and seats, or in the herb garden.

Shrubs
Artemisia abrotanum, Artemisia arborescens, Caryopteris, Choisya ternata, Cistus x cyprius, Cistus x purpureus, Escallonia, Helichrysum angustifolium, Juniperus, Laurus nobilis, Lavandula, Perovskia, Rosa eglanteria (sweet brier), *Rosmarinus, Salvia, Santolina, Thuja, Thymus*

Perennials
Chamaemelum nobile, Foeniculum vulgare, Geranium macrorrhizum, Mentha, Myrrhis odorata, Origanum, Tanacetum parthenium

Plants with red, purple or coppery leaves

Foliage in this colour range is an invaluable foil to strong flower colours, taking the 'sting' out of scarlet and orange and giving depth to crimsons and purples. A hedge of copper beech makes an unusual boundary to a rose garden.

Use the soft greyish-purple foliage of *Rosa glauca* or purple sage to soften the transition from stronger red-purples to plain grey. When planning spring colour schemes, remember that many Hybrid Tea and Floribunda roses have dark red or coppery leaves on their new young shoots, and that peony shoots start copper-red before turning green.

I have left out *Acer platanoides* 'Crimson King', a very large tree, all too often planted in quite small gardens. Its large, dark brown-purple leaves look heavy and oppressive at midsummer. Perversely, I have included the copper beech, *Fagus sylvatica* 'Purpurea', just as large, but both majestic and graceful.

Trees
Fagus sylvatica 'Purpurea', *Malus* 'Profusion', *Malus* 'Royalty', *Prunus pissardii* 'Nigra'

Climbers
Vitis vinifera 'Purpurea'

Shrubs
Acer palmatum 'Bloodgood', *Berberis thunbergii* 'Red Chief' and others, *Corylus maxima* 'Purpurea', *Cotinus coggyria* 'Notcutt's Variety', *Phormium tenax* 'Purpureum', *Rosa glauca*, *Salvia officinalis* 'Purpurascens'

Perennials
Ajuga reptans 'Atropurpurea', *Astilbe* 'Fanal' and others, *Foeniculum vulgare* 'Bronze', *Heuchera micrantha* 'Palace Purple', *Sedum maximum* 'Atropurpureum', *Sedum* 'Vera Jameson'

Plants with yellow leaves

Yellow-leaved plants need placing with care: grouped together they can look glaring and brassy. However, a single blob of, say, yellow privet in an otherwise green group stands out too strongly. 'Gold and silver', that is, yellow foliage mixed with grey, is also an uneasy combination.

I like yellow shrubs best mixed with one or two variegated shrubs and others in various shades of green, all grouped against a dark background. Most yellow leaves tend to scorch in full sun, so plant them where they have some shade at midday. In denser shade they will be a colour somewhere between yellow and lime green, giving a sunlit appearance to a dark corner. For me the golden forms of spiraea, ribes and many heathers are spoilt by the combination of yellow leaves with harsh mauve-pink flowers.

Trees
Chamaecyparis lawsoniana 'Lanei Aurea', *x Cupressocyparis leylandii* 'Castlewellan', *Cupressus macrocarpa* 'Gold Crest', *Gleditsia triacanthos* 'Sunburst', *Robinia pseudacacia* 'Frisia', *Thuja occidentalis* 'Sunkist'

Shrubs
Acer japonicum 'Aureum', *Catalpa bignonioides* 'Aurea', *Hedera helix* 'Buttercup', *Juniperus communis* 'Depressa Aurea', *Juniperus media* 'Old Gold', *Ligustrum ovalifolium* 'Aureum', *Lonicera nitida* 'Baggesen's Gold', *Philadelphus coronarius* 'Aureus', *Sambucus racemosa* 'Plumosa Aurea', *Spiraea japonica* 'Goldflame', *Taxus baccata* 'Fastigiata Aurea', *Taxus baccata* 'Summergold'

Perennials
Carex hachijoensis, *Filipendula ulmaria* 'Aurea', *Hosta fortunei* 'Gold Standard', *Humulus lupulus* 'Aureus', *Lamium maculatum* 'Aureum', *Lysimachia nummularia* 'Aurea', *Melissa officinalis* 'Aurea', *Milium effusum aureum*, *Origanum vulgare* 'Aureum', *Tanacetum parthenium* 'Aureum'

Plants with white or cream variegated leaves

Some variegated plants look, from a distance, as though they were covered in white or creamy flowers. Others are just what is needed to set off orange, crimson or violet flowers. White and cream variegations colour well in shade, and plants such as hostas, variegated irises, ivies and vincas are invaluable for making groups to lighten gloomy areas.

Trees
Acer negundo 'Flamingo' (pinkish-white), *Ilex aquifolium* 'Argenteo-marginata'

Climbers
Hedera canariensis 'Variegata', *Hedera helix* (numerous varieties)

Shrubs
Cornus alba 'Elegantissima', *Euonymus fortunei* 'Emerald Gaiety' and 'Silver Queen', *Hebe x franciscana* 'Variegata', *Philadelphus coronarius* 'Variegatus', *Phormium cookianum* 'Cream Delight', *Prunus lusitanica* 'Variegata', *Weigela florida* 'Variegata'

Perennials
Astrantia 'Sunningdale Variegated', *Eryngium variifolium*, *Hosta undulata albomarginata*, *Iris foetidissima* 'Variegata', *Lamium maculatum* 'Album', 'Beacon Silver', 'White Nancy', *Mentha suaveolens* 'Variegata', *Miscanthus sinensis* 'Variegatus', *Phalaris arundinacea* 'Picta', *Pulmonaria officinalis* 'Sissinghurst White', *Sisyrinchium striatum* 'Aunt May', *Symphytum grandiflora* 'Variegatum'

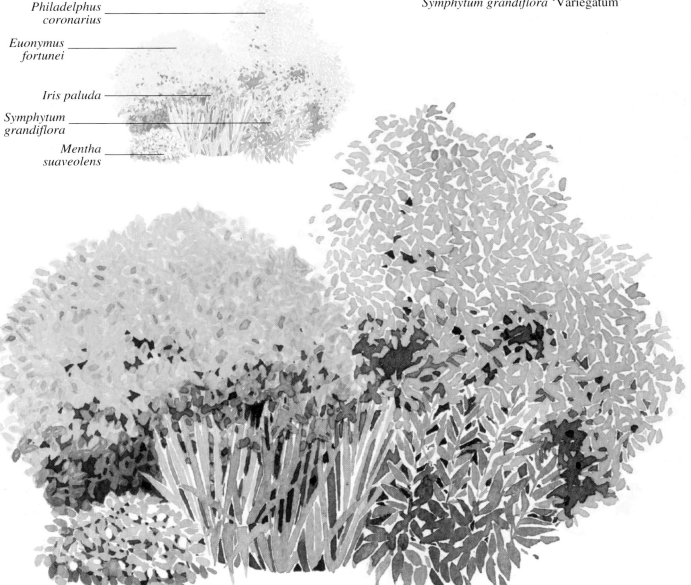

Philadelphus coronarius

Euonymus fortunei

Iris paluda

Symphytum grandiflora

Mentha suaveolens

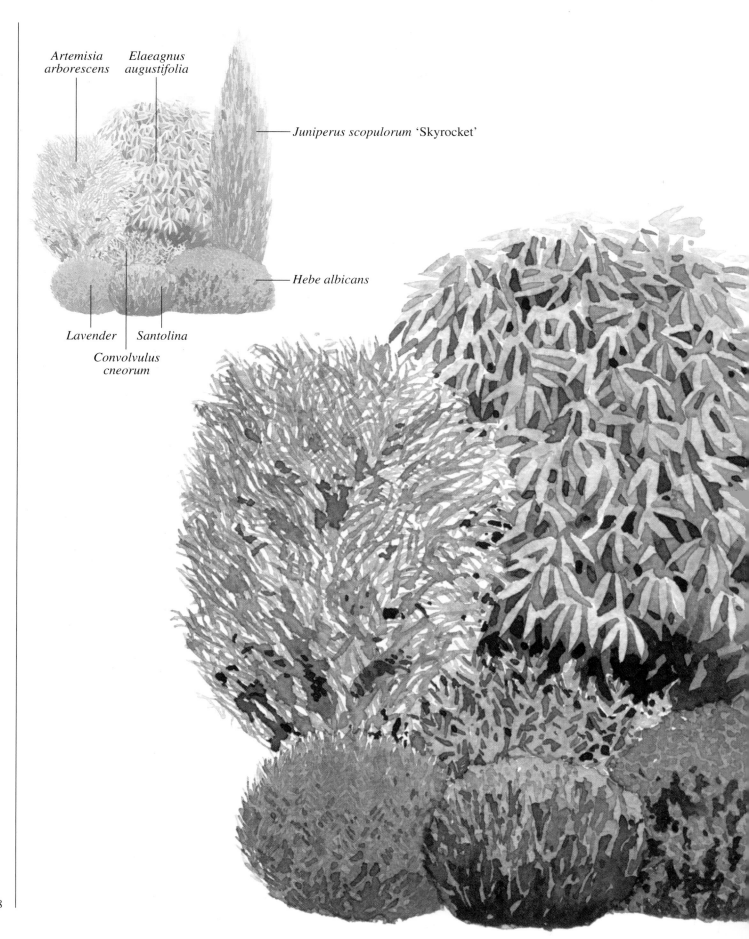

*Artemisia
arborescens*

*Elaeagnus
augustifolia*

Juniperus scopulorum 'Skyrocket'

Hebe albicans

Lavender

Santolina

*Convolvulus
cneorum*

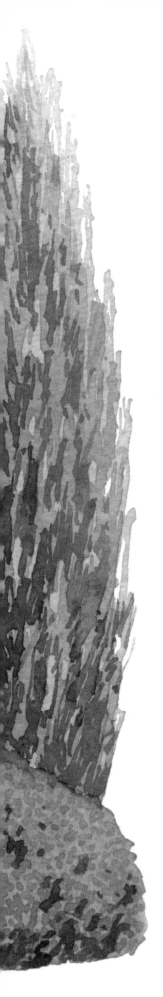

Plants with grey or silver leaves

Grey-leaved plants are sun lovers and most of them will thrive in poor, stony soil provided it is well-drained. They bring great variety of form and texture to foliage schemes, from the fine spikey leaves of lavender to the huge thistle-like leaves of the cardoon, and they are an essential component of soft summer colour schemes. Grey leaves make a satisfying contrast against warm red brick walls and paving, but they are just as appropriate against stone of all shades of grey, buff and brown.

Trees
Juniperus scopulorum 'Skyrocket', *Pyrus salicifolia* 'Pendula', *Salix alba* 'Sericea', *Sorbus aria*

Shrubs
Abutilon vitifolium 'Veronica Tennant', *Artemisia arborescens*, *Brachyglottis*, *Buddleia alternifolia* 'Argentea', *Buddleia x* 'Lochinch', *Caryopteris clandonensis*, *Convolvulus cneorum*, *Cytisus battandieri*, *Elaeagnus angustifolia*, *Hebe albicans*, *Juniperus virginiana* 'Grey Owl', *Lavandula*, *Perovskia*, *Romneya coulteri*, *Salix elaeagnos*, *Salvia officinalis*, *Santolina chamaecyparissus*, *Santolina neapolitana*

Perennials
Achillea 'Moonshine', *Anaphalis triplinervis*, *Artemisia ludoviciana*, *Cynara cardunculus*, *Dianthus* (most), *Dicentra formosa*, *Galanthus*, *Geranium renardii*, *Iris germanica*, *Lychnis coronaria*, *Macleaya cordata*, *Nepeta faassinnii*, *Nepeta* 'Six Hills Giant', *Sedum spectabile*, *Stachys byzantina*

Annuals and Biennials
Onopordium acanthium, *Senecio cineraria* 'White Diamond', *Verbascum olympicum*

Plants with yellow variegated leaves

The variegated shrubs are easier to accommodate than their all-yellow counterparts. Evergreens such as the aucuba and elaeagnus are invaluable for brightening a gloomy winter day; phormium and irises provide splendid vertical accents; and the ivies are great stand-bys for walls, pillars and along the ground.

Climbers
Hedera colchica 'Dentata Variegata', *Hedera colchica* 'Sulphur Heart', *Hedera helix* 'Goldheart' and others

Shrubs
Aucuba japonica 'Picturata', *Cornus alba* 'Spaethii', *Elaeagnus pungens* 'Maculata', *Euonymus fortunei* 'Emerald 'n' Gold', *Ilex x altaclarensis* 'Golden King', *Ilex aquifolium* 'Golden van Tol', *Phormium tenax* 'Yellow Wave', *Salvia officinalis* 'Icterina'

Perennials
Aquilegia vulgaris 'Aureovariegata', *Hosta fortunei* 'Albopicta', *Hosta fortunei* 'Areomarginata', *Iris pallida* 'Variegata', *Miscanthus sinesis* 'Zebrinus', *Saxifraga x urbium* 'Aureopunctata'

Plants with glaucous blue-grey leaves

These plants enjoy the same conditions as the grey-leaved plants; the borderline between the two categories as far as colour is concerned is fairly indistinct. But the rather steely blue of blue-grey plants separates them from the greys when it comes to planning colour schemes. Their natural complements are orange or soft yellow flowers; they do nothing for the mauves and violets of such plants as the grey-leaved catmint, salvia or lavender.

Trees
Chamaecyparis lawsoniana 'Pembury Blue', *Eucalyptus gunnii*

Shrubs
Hebe pinguifolia 'Pagei', *Juniperus chinensis* 'Pyramidalis', *Juniperus squamata* 'Blue Carpet', *Picea pungens glauca* 'Hoopsii', *Ruta graveolens* 'Jackman's Blue'

Perennials
Dianthus (some), *Dicentra formosa* 'Langtrees', *Festuca glauca*, *Hosta sieboldiana* and others

Plants with leaves that colour in autumn

When planning a small or medium sized garden I would never choose a plant for its autumn colour alone. However, the fiery colours of autumn are a wonderful bonus, and given a choice between two plants equal in other respects, I would choose the one with the autumn leaves. To get full value from such plants, make sure they are in a sheltered situation where the leaves will not blow off before you have had time to enjoy them.

Trees
Acer griseum (scarlet), *Amelanchier lamarckii* (orange, red), *Betula* (yellow), *Cercidiphyllum* (pinky-orange on lime-free soil), *Crataegus prunifolia* (orange, scarlet), *Fagus sylvatica* (russet), *Ginkgo biloba* (yellow), *Liquidambar* (crimson, gold), *Liriodendron* (yellow), *Malus coronaria* 'Charlottae', 'Dartmouth', 'Evereste' (red, gold), *Metasequoia glyptostroboides* (bronze, gold), *Parrotia persica* (red, orange, gold), *Prunus avium* (red-orange), *Prunus x hillieri* 'Spire' (red), *Prunus sargentii* (scarlet), *Prunus Taihaku* (yellow and orange), *Pyrus calleryana* 'Chanticleer' (maroon red), *Sorbus aucuparia* 'Aspleniifolia', *Sorbus cashmiriana*, *Sorbus* 'Embley' (red shades), *Sorbus* 'Joseph Rock'

Climbers
Parthenocissus (scarlet, crimson, orange), *Vitis* 'Brandt' (orange, pink), *Vitis coignetiae* (orange, crimson), *Vitis vinifera* 'Purpurea' (dark crimson)

Shrubs
Acer palmatum (red, orange, yellow), *Aesculus parviflora* (yellow), *Berberis thunbergii* and most others (brilliant red), *Cotoneaster divaricatus*, *Cotoneaster horizontalis*, *Cotoneaster rotundifolius*, *Cotoneaster simonsii* (all scarlet), *Euonymus alata*, *Euonymus europaeus* (scarlet, crimson), *Rosa rugosa* (yellow), *Viburnum opulus* (orange, red), *Viburnum plicatum* 'Lanarth' (purple)

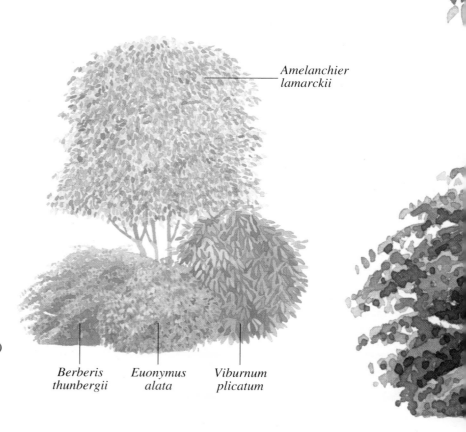

Amelanchier lamarckii

Berberis thunbergii *Euonymus alata* *Viburnum plicatum*

Plants with decorative fruit, berries or seed pods

By choosing plants with attractive fruit you can not only prolong the season of colour in the garden but also do the birds of the neighbourhood a favour by supplying them with winter food.

If you can, give these plants a position where the low winter sun will catch their colours when seen from the house windows. Most of the berries come at a season when you will not be spending much time outdoors just standing about and staring.

Trees
Aesculus hippocastanum, Aesculus indica, Castanea sativa, Catalpa bignonioides, Crataegus persimilis 'Prunifolia' and others, *Ilex altaclarensis, Ilex aquifolium, Malus*, most, especially 'Crittenden', 'Dartmouth', 'Evereste', 'Red Sentinel', 'Golden Hornet', *Mespilus germanica, Morus nigra, Pyrus, Sorbus aria, Sorbus aucuparia*

Climbers
Actinidia deliciosus, Akebia quinata, Clematis orientalis, Clematis tangutica, Passiflora, Vitis

Shrubs
Arbutus, Berberis, Chaenomeles, Colutea arborescens, Corylus avellana, Cotoneaster, Euonymus europaeus, Hippophäe rhamnoides, Pyracantha, Rosa moyesii, Rosa macrophylla, Rosa webbiana and others, *Sambucus, Skimmia, Symphoricarpus, Viburnum davidii, Viburnum opulus*

Perennials
Agapanthus, Allium christophii, Aquilegia, Arum italicum, Iris foetidissima, Pulsatilla vulgaris

Annuals and Biennials
Lunaria, Nigella

3 | Plant performance

The plants listed in this chapter give exceptionally good value. Many of them are those we have come to think of as cottage garden plants – tried and trustworthy favourites which can be relied on to flower prolifically year after year with comparatively little attention. Others are good investments and will still be performing in twenty years or more.

Plants for an instant garden

Most people are in a hurry to see results in the garden. They may want to screen an ugly view as quickly as possible, or achieve privacy. They may simply be excited about the project and yearn to enjoy the sight and scent of their plants. People move house more frequently than they once did, and it may not be worth waiting twelve years or so for a newly planted magnolia to produce its glorious blooms.

Whatever the reason, there is always a demand for fast-growing plants: creepers that cover the ground almost while you watch, and leapers that rush up to the first floor windows almost overnight.

Most fast-growing plants are short-lived; they reach maturity quickly and then decline with equal rapidity. So it is just as well to mix a few tortoise-like plants among the hares to get a good long-term result.

All the fast-growing plants listed on page 17, plus the following.

Trees

Acer negundo, Acer platanoides, Acer saccharinum, Alnus rubra, Castanea sativa, Eucalyptus, Fraxinus excelsior, Juglans regia, Metasequoia glyptostroboides, Prunus avium, Prunus cerasifera, Salix alba, Salix chrysocoma, Tilia americana

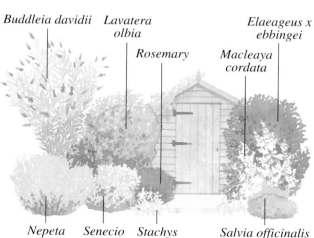

Buddleia davidii Lavatera olbia Rosemary Elaeageus x ebbingei Macleaya cordata

Nepeta Senecio Stachys Salvia officinalis

Climbers

Actinidia deliciosa, Akebia quinata, Clematis montana, Clematis tangutica, Hedera colchica 'Dentata Variegata', *Hedera helix* 'Cristata', *Hedera helix* 'Goldheart', *Humulus lupulus, Jasminum officinale, Lathyrus latifolius, Lonicera periclymenum* 'Belgica', *Parthenocissus henryana, Parthenocissus quinquefolia, Parthenocissus tricuspidata* 'Veitchii', *Passiflora caerulea, Rosa, Vitis vinifera* 'Purpurea', *Vitis* 'Brant', *Vitis coignetiae, Wisteria sinensis*

Shrubs

Abelia x grandiflora, Berberis darwinii, Berberis x stenophylla, Berberis thunbergii, Brachyglottis, Buddleia davidii, Caryopteris x clandonensis, Ceanothus 'Blue Mound', *Cistus laurifolius, Cornus alba* 'Elegantissima', *Cotoneaster* 'Cornubia', *Cotoneaster* 'Skogholm', *Cytisus scoparius, Cytisus x*

praecox, Escallonia 'Crimson Spire', *Escallonia* 'Donard Seedling', *Eucalyptus gunnii, Forsythia* 'Beatrix Farrand', *Hebe* 'Midsummer Beauty', *Hydrangea* 'Preziosa', *Hypericum, Juniperus x media* 'Pfitzeriana', *Juniperus* 'Grey Owl', *Kerria japonica* 'Pleniflora', *Lavatera olbia* 'Rosea', *Leycesteria formosa, Lupinus arboreus, Mahonia aquifolium, Mahonia japonica, Philadelphus coronarius, Photinia x fraseri* 'Red Robin', *Prunus laurocerasus* 'Zabeliana', *Pyracantha, Ribes sanguineum* 'Splendens', *Rosa, Rosmarinus officinalis* 'Miss Jessopp's Upright', *Salvia officinalis* 'Purpurascens', *Sambucus nigra*

Perennials

Alchemilla mollis, Anthemis cupaniana, Aruncus sylvester, Aubrieta, Campanula lactiflora, Campanula poscharskyana, Crambe cordifolia, Cynara cardunculus, Euphorbia amygdaloides, Euphorbia characias, Geranium macrorrhizum, Helianthemum, Lamium maculatum, Macleaya cordata, Malva moschata, Nepeta 'Six Hills Giant', *Phlox subulata, Phormium tenax, Pulmonaria, Romneya coulteri, Stachys byzantina*

Foolproof plants

If you are an inexperienced gardener, or a nervous one, these are plants you can trust. It is no coincidence that many of them are found in almost every garden – laburnum and lilac for example. They seem to thrive on neglect and, with one or two exceptions (forsythia, hardy fuchsias), once they are established, they need no feeding or pruning.

The herbaceous plants listed here grow like weeds; they come up year after year and reproduce themselves without help from the gardener, either seeding themselves around or colonizing the ground around them by making ever wider clumps. Once you have them, gardening becomes a matter of pulling out plants where they are not wanted.

I have not listed trees separately, as almost all trees are foolproof provided they are carefully planted and have enough water during their first few years.

Shrubs
Abelia, Berberis, Daphne odora 'Aureomarginata', *Elaeagnus, Euonymus fortunei, Fatsia japonica, Forsythia, Fuchsia, Genista, Hebe, Ilex, Lonicera, Philadelphus, Phormium, Potentilla, Rosa* (species roses, rugosa types, modern shrub roses), *Syringa, Viburnum* (most kinds), *Yucca*

Herbaceous, Biennials and Annuals
Angelica archangelica, Antirrhinum, Aquilegia vulgaris, Aubrieta, Borago officinalis, Calendula officinalis, Campanula persicifolia, Centaurea cyanus, Centranthus ruber, Digitalis purpurea, Euphorbia wulfenii, Galanthus, Hesperis matronalis, Hyacinthoides hispanica, Limnanthes douglasii, Lunaria annua, Muscari, Myosotis, Nigella, Onopordium acanthum, Papaver somniferum, Primula vulgaris, Silybum marianum, Tanacetum parthenium, Tropaeolum majus, Verbascum, Viola

Digitalis   *Philadelphus*   *Papaver somniferum*   *Berberis*

Euphorbia   *Verbascium*   *Aquilegia vulgaris*   *Onopordium acanthum*

Plants worth waiting for (long-term investments)

These are the 'tortoise' plants. They grow slowly but they will catch up with the 'hares' eventually. Most of them are choice specimens; they include many conifers, the Japanese acers, and magnolias. It is a pleasure to watch their gradual development and their maturity is well worth waiting for. Because they are slow, it is worth paying extra for the largest specimen you can find. Nevertheless, they take up very little room when first planted compared to the space they will occupy eventually. To avoid leaving empty space around them, fill it with expendable plants – herbaceous plants that can be moved as necessary or annuals renewed each season.

Trees
Acer pseudoplatanus 'Brilliantissimum', *Alnus*, *Chamaecyparis lawsoniana* 'Broomhill Gold', *Chamaecyparis lawsoniana* 'Pembury Blue', *Fagus sylvatica* 'Pendula', *Ginkgo biloba*, *Gleditsia triacanthos* 'Ruby Lace', *Picea breweriana*, *Picea pungens* 'Hoopsii', *Quercus ilex*, *Taxus baccata* 'Fastigiata'

Shrubs
Acer palmatum, *Arbutus*, *Buxus suffruticosa*, *Camellia*, *Catalpa bignonioides* 'Aurea', *Chamaecyparis lawsoniana* (dwarf varieties), *Choisya ternata*, *Cryptomeria japonica*, *Daphne mezereum*, *Ilex altaclarensis*, *Ilex aquifolium*, *Juniperus* (prostrate varieties), *Magnolia*, *Osmanthus delavayi*, *Pinus mugo*, *Skimmia*, *Thuja* (dwarf varieties), *Viburnum carlesii*

Plants coming early into leaf

Bring spring into your garden early by including a few plants with the first buds to break. Their branches are bare for such a short time in winter that these shrubs and trees are almost as good as evergreens for screening and providing shelter. The perennials get their ground cover established before many weeds emerge after the winter.

Trees
Alnus cordata, Caragana arborescens, Cercidiphyllum japonicum, Crataegus monogyna, Mespilus germanica, Prunus pissardii 'Nigra', *Salix alba, Salix chrysocoma*

Shrubs
Berberis thunbergii 'Atropurpurea', *Cytisus battandieri, Daphne mezereum, Paeonia, Rosa, Sambucus, Spiraea, Viburnum opulus, Viburnum plicatum* 'Mariesii'

Perennials
Aconitum, Allium schoenophrasum, Aquilegia, Corydalis, Dicentra formosa, Fritillaria imperialis, Geranium, Helleborus, Hemerocallis, Lilium candidum, Myrrhis odorata, Paeonia, Persicaria affine 'Superba', *Primula, Sedum spectabile, Symphytum*

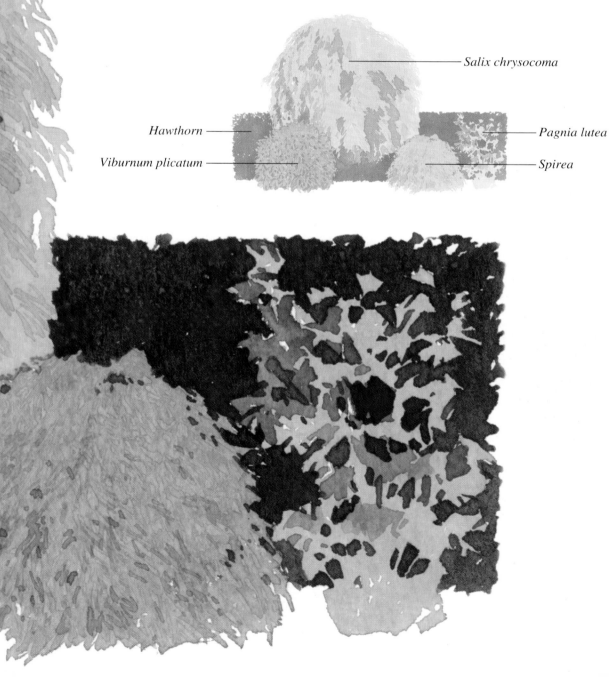

Salix chrysocoma

Hawthorn

Viburnum plicatum

Pagnia lutea

Spirea

Plants with a long flowering or fruiting season

Much of the disappointment gardeners experience occurs because some plants have flowers or fruit that are here today, gone tomorrow. They are often acquired as impulse buys when in full flower. We plant them, the flowers fade and they do nothing for fifty weeks. Some we can forgive: the flowering cherries may, in a windy spring, carry their blossom for a mere two weeks or less, but we value them all the more because their beauty is so fleeting.

If plants with a short flowering season are on your 'must have' list, look for varieties that have a second attribute – autumn colour, ornamental fruit or perhaps coloured winter bark.

The plants on the following lists bear their flowers (or in some cases their berries) for at least six weeks.

Trees
Crataegus x lavallei (fruit), *Crataegus prunifolia* (fruit), *Malus* 'Crittenden' (fruit), *Malus* 'Golden Hornet'(fruit), *Malus* 'Red Sentinel' (fruit), *Sorbus esserteauana* (berries), *Sorbus vilmorinii* (berries)

Climbers
Jasminum nudiflorum, Lonicera periclymenum 'Graham Thomas', *Pyracantha* (berries), *Rosa* (numerous climbers)

Shrubs
Abelia, Abutilon, Buddleia, Camellia, Ceanothus 'Gloire de Versailles', *Chaenomeles, Colutea, Cotoneasters* (berries), *Erica carnea, Fuchsia, Hebe, Helianthemum, Hibiscus, Hippophae rhamnoides, Hydrangea, Hypericum, Ilex* (berries), *Lavatera, Mahonia, Photinia x fraseri* 'Red Robin', *Potentilla fruticosa, Pyracantha* (berries), *Romneya coulteri, Rosa* (Hybrid Teas, Floribundas, Hybrid Musks, *R. rugosa*), *Skimmia* (berries), *Spartium junceum, Symphoricarpos* (berries), *Viburnum x bodnantense* 'Dawn', *Viburnum tinus, Vinca*

Perennials
Achillea millefolium, Ajuga, Aster ericoides, Astilbe, Astrantia, Aubrieta, Campanula lactiflora, Campanula persicifolia, Campanula poscharskyana, Centranthus ruber, Dianthus, Dicentra formosa, Dicentra eximia, Echinops ritro, Eryngium oliverianum, Euphorbia, Gaillardia 'Burgundy', *Gaillardia* 'Kobold', *Geranium endressii, Geranium* 'Johnson's Blue', *Geranium macrorrhizum, Geranium x riverslianum* 'Russell Pritchard', *Geum, Gypsophila paniculata, Helleborus orientalis, Hemerocallis* 'Stella d'Oro', *Iberis, Knautia macedonica, Lysimachia punctata, Monarda* 'Cambridge Scarlet', *Nepeta, Oenothera missouriensis, Penstemon, Phlox maculata, Potentilla, Primula vulgaris, Pulmonaria, Rudbeckia fulgida* 'Goldsturm', *Salvia superba* 'May Night', *Scabiosa caucasica, Sedum, Thalictrum delavayi, Veronica teucrium* 'Crater Lake Blue', *Viola*

Annuals and Biennials
Most

Poisonous plants

It is just as well to know which plants are poisonous, especially if you have small children. Very few plants have deadly components, such as laburnum seeds, but some plants can cause an uncomfortable stomach ache, diarrhoea, or cramp if eaten, and others give rise to an irritating skin rash if touched. But keep a sense of proportion: we don't take our lives in our hands every time we go into the garden. But it is sensible to avoid putting any part of any plant into your mouth unless you are sure it is edible.

Trees
Fagus sylvatica, Laburnum, Quercus, Taxus

Shrubs
Buxus, Cotoneaster, Daphne mezereum, Hedera, Hippophae rhamnoides, Juniperus, Ruta graveolens

Perennials
Aconitum, Aquilegia, Caltha, Helleborus, Iris, Polygonatum, Primula, Pulsatilla

Climbers, self-clinging

In the wild these species hoist themselves towards the light by clinging to tree trunks. In the garden they will cling almost as tenaciously to walls, pillars or posts. If you want to train them on wooden trellis or wire mesh you will need to tie their branches to the structure initially.

Euonymus fortunei, Hedera canariensis, Hedera colchica, Hedera helix, Hydrangea petiolaris, Parthenocissus

Climbers, twining

Plants that climb by twining their tendrils around the branches of other plants need either a host plant in the garden or a substitute in the form of trellis, wire mesh or horizontal wires spaced at 30cm (12in) intervals.

Actinidia deliciosa, Actinidia kolomikta, Akebia quinata, Clematis, Lonicera, Passiflora, Solanum crispum, Solanum jasminoides, Vitis, Wisteria

Trailing plants

Ivies and some other climbers will trail gracefully if they are planted in a pot or at the top of a retaining wall. The shrubs listed here are also happy in the dry conditions on top of a wall or in a rock garden, and will drape themselves over ledges and over the rims of pots and tubs.

Shrubs
Anthemis cupaniana, Cotoneaster microphyllus, Cytisus kewensis, Euonymus fortunei, Fuchsia, Hebe pinguifolia 'Pagei', *Helianthemum, Helichrysum petiolare, Juniperus conferta, Juniperus horizontalis* (several varieties), *Rosa* (ground cover varieties, 'Grouse', 'Nozomi' etc.), *Salvia officinalis, Vinca*

Climbers
Clematis (small-flowered varieties), *Euonymus fortunei, Hedera* (most), *Jasminum nudiflorum*

Perennials
Acaena 'Blue Haze', *Aubrieta, Campanulas* (low-growing kinds), *Dianthus, Erigeron mucronatum, Erysimum, Euphorbia myrsinites, Gypsophila repens, Lysimachia nummularia* 'Aurea', *Phlox subulata*

Annuals and Biennials
Lobelia, Petunia, Tropaeolum majus

41

4 | Plants to Design With

This chapter offers guidance to gardeners who want to combine plants to achieve different effects. As you plan your garden, you will soon come to recognize what the design requires: a strong statement here, an informal effect there; vertical exclamation marks to liven up a prosy group of plants; carpeting plants to cover an expanse of gravel. There are plants for all these purposes, and others for background or foreground planting to make the best possible setting for the jewels of the garden.

Basics: structural plants for the garden framework

A firm framework of trees and shrubs or formal hedges to contain luxuriant planting is one of the hallmarks of English gardening. Such a framework provides shelter from the wind and privacy for the occupants. Framework plants are also useful to divide up the space within a garden.

TALL HEDGING FOR BOUNDARIES AND DIVISIONS

Buxus sempervirens, Berberis thunbergii, Carpinus betulus, Chamaecyparis lawsoniana, Crataegus monogyna, x Cupressocyparis leylandii, Escallonia, Fagus sylvatica, Ilex aquifolium, Ligustrum, Lonicera nitida, Pyracantha, Rosa rugosa, Taxus baccata, Thuja plicata

LOW HEDGING FOR DIVISIONS WITHIN THE GARDEN OR FOR KNOTS

Artemisia abrotanum, Berberis thunbergii atropurpurea 'Nana', *Buxus suffruticosa, Hyssopus officinalis, Lavandula, Rosmarinus* 'Miss Jessopp's Upright', *Salvia officinalis, Santolina*

EVERGREEN SHRUBS FOR MIXED BACKGROUND PLANTING

Berberis x stenophylla, Camellia, Choisya ternata, Elaeagnus x ebbingei, Garrya elliptica, Ilex x altacarensis, Ilex aquifolium, Laurus nobilis, Ligustrum, Osmanthus x burkwoodii, Prunus laurocerasus, Prunus lusitanica, Pyracantha, Rhododendron, Taxus baccata, Viburnum rhytidophyllum, Viburnum tinus

EARLY-FLOWERING SHRUBS FOR BACKGROUND PLANTING

After flowering in spring these shrubs provide the background to summer-flowering plants: *Berberis thunbergii, Ceanothus, Chaenomeles, Corylus maxima* 'Purpurea', *Cytisus, Forsythia, Kerria japonica, Spiraea thunbergii, Syringa, Viburnum x bodnantense, Viburnum burkwoodii*

Architectural plants

Using plants with dramatic form or foliage you can build up sculptural groups of plants which will be satisfying quite independently of their flowers and fruit. Plants with a strong vertical shape (spikes) can be used to contrast with rounded mounds of foliage (buns) and with plants with strong horizontal lines.

SPIKES

Trees

Chamaecyparis lawsoniana 'Kilmacurragh' and others, *Crataegus monogyna* 'Stricta', *Fagus sylvatica* 'Dawyck', *Metasequoia*, *Taxus baccata* 'Fastigiata', *Salix* (stooled plants), *Thuja plicata*

Shrubs

Juniperus (several), *Phormium*, *Rubus thibetanus*, *Sinarundinaria*, *Yucca*

Perennials including Bulbs

Acanthus (flower spikes), *Aconitum* (flower spikes), *Ajuga* (flower spikes), *Alcea rosea* (flower spikes), *Allium*, *Camassia* (flower spikes), *Campanula latiloba* (flower spikes), *Campanula persicifolia*, *Crocosmia*, *Delphinium* (flower spikes), *Dianthus* (leaves), *Digitalis grandiflora* (flower spikes), *Festuca glauca*, *Helictotrichon*, *Hemerocallis*, *Hyacinthoides*, *Iris*, *Kniphofia*, *Lupinus* (flower spikes), *Miscanthus*, *Narcissus*, *Persicaria bistorta* 'Superba' (flower spikes), *Phalaris arundinacea*, *Schizostylis*, *Sisyrinchium*, *Stipa gigantea*, *Verbascum* (flower spike)

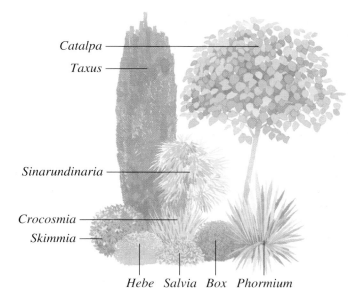

Catalpa

Taxus

Sinarundinaria

Crocosmia

Skimmia

Hebe Salvia Box Phormium

43

BUNS: ROUNDED OR ARCHING SHAPES

Weeping Trees and Shrubs

Betula pendula 'Tristis', *Caragana arborescens* 'Pendula', *Fagus sylvatica* 'Pendula', *Ilex aquifolium* 'Pendula', *Malus* 'Red Jade', *Morus alba* 'Pendula', *Prunus* 'Cheal's Weeping', *Prunus subhirtella* 'Pendula', *Pyrus salicifolia* 'Pendula', *Salix caprea* 'Kilmarnock', *Salix x chrysocoma*

Rounded Shrubs

Ballota pseudodictamnus, Berberis rubrostilla, Berberis x stenophylla, Brachyglottis 'Sunshine', *Buddleia alternifolia* 'Argentea', *Buxus, Ceanothus thyrsiflorus* 'Repens', *Cistus* 'Silver Pink', *Choisya ternata, Daphne odora* 'Aureomarginata', *Genista lydia, Hebe albicans, Hebe rakaensis, Hypericum* 'Hidcote', *Hyssopus officinalis, Lavandula angustifolia, Olearia x haastii, Osmanthus delavayi, Phlomis fruticosa, Potentilla fruticosa, Rosmarinus officinalis, Ruta graveolens, Salvia officinalis, Santolina, Skimmia, Spiraea arguta, Viburnum davidii, Viburnum rhytidophyllum, Vinca minor*

Perennials

Alchemilla mollis, Armeria maritima, Astrantia major 'Sunningdale Variegated', *Aubrieta, Calaminta nepeta, Chamaemelum nobile* 'Flore Pleno', *Corydalis lutea, Dianthus* (some kinds), *Dicentra formosa, Epimedium, Erisymum, Euphorbia polychroma, Festuca glauca, Geranium* (most kinds), *Iberis sempervirens, Melissa officinalis* 'Aurea', *Milium effusum* 'Aureum', *Miscanthus sinensis, Nepeta faassenii, Nepeta* 'Six Hills Giant', *Ophiopogon planiscapus, Origanum vulgare* 'Aureum', *Saxifraga moschata, Sedum* (most kinds), *Tanacetum parthenium, Thalictrum delavayi*

PLANTS WITH HORIZONTAL FORM

Trees and Shrubs

Cornus controversa 'Variegata', *Cotoneaster horizontalis, Cotoneaster salicifolius, Mespilus germanica, Parrotia persica, Viburnum plicatum* 'Mariesii'

PLANTS WITH LARGE LEAVES

Trees

Aesculus, Castanea sativa, Catalpa bignonioides, Juglans regia, Magnolia grandiflora, Sorbus aria 'Michellii', *Tilia americana*

Climbers

Actinidia deliciosa, Clematis armandii, Hedera algeriensis, Hedera colchica, Humulus lupulus 'Aureus', *Vitis coignetiae*

Shrubs,

Aralia elata, Fatshedera lizei, Ficus, Hydrangea villosa, Mahonia 'Charity', *Paeonia, Phormium, Prunus laurocerasus, Rhododendron* (some kinds), *Sambucus racemosa* 'Plumosa Aurea', *Viburnum rhytidophyllum, Yucca*

Perennials

Acanthus spinosus, Anemone x hybrida, Angelica archangelica, Arum italicum 'Pictum', *Bergenia, Brunnera macrophylla, Canna, Crambe cordifolia, Cynara cardunculus, Digitalis, Echinops, Eryngium giganteum, Fritillaria imperialis, Gunnera manicata, Helleborus corsicus, Hosta, Ligularia, Lysichiton americanus, Macleaya cordata, Onopordum acanthium, Phormium tenax, Rheum palmatum, Rodgersia, Romneya coulteri, Verbascum, Zantedeschia aethiopica*

PLANTS WITH TACTILE, FINE-TEXTURED LEAVES

Trees

Gleditsia, Robinia, Sorbus cashmiriana

Shrubs

Acer palmatum 'Dissectum', *Artemisia* (several), *Azara microphylla, Ballota pseudodictamnus, Convolvulus cneorum, Crypotomeria, Juniperus* (most kinds), *Lavandula, Rosa webbiana, Rosa willmottiae, Rosmarinus officinalis, Sambucus nigra* 'Laciniata', *Sambucus racemosa* 'Tenuifolia', *Santolina neapolitana, Spiraea x arguta*

Perennials

Achillea, Aconitum, Anthemis punctata ssp. *cupaniana, Argyranthemum frutescens, Asplenium, Astilbe, Athyrium, Corydalis, Dicentra formosa, Filipendula, Foeniculum vulgare, Myrrhis odorata, Tanacetum parthenium, Thalictrum delavayi, Thymus*

Annuals and Biennials

Cosmos, Nigella, Pulsatilla

Plants to naturalize in the open

All plants originated in the wild, and if we can provide conditions in the garden that mirror those in their original natural habitats, they will form natural colonies, seeing off competition from weeds and grasses. This style of planting has an appealing informality and is very labour-saving. Plant in broad swathes of at least nine of a kind. Alternatively, in areas where the soil is poor enough to exclude coarse, competitive grasses (on chalky grassland for example), dot your plants singly for a flowery meadow effect. The following should be tough enough to look after themselves in an open, sunny position.

Perennials

Acanthus, Achillea, Alchemilla, Aruncus dioicus, Asphodeline, Aster, Astrantia, Campanula lactiflora, Crambe cordifolia, Crocosmia, Euphorbia griffithii, Euphorbia polychroma, Filipendula, Foeniculum, Geranium (some), *Hemerocallis* (some), *Kniphofia, Lunaria, Lupinus, Lythrum, Macleaya, Paeonia, Papaver orientale, Salvia superba, Verbascum*

Bulbs

Camassia, Colchicum, Crocus, Galanthus, Lilium (some), *Narcissus* (most), *Scilla, Tulipa*

Kniphofia — *Achillea* — *Aster* — *Alchemilla* — *Campanula* — *Lupinus* — *Papaver* — *Aster*

Plants to naturalize in woodland

The leafy, dappled shade of deciduous woodland is in itself a satisfying garden experience. The type of plants that flourish beneath the trees also have a distinctive character. Most have broad leaves to take full advantage of the filtered light. The flowers tend to be pale, delicate and widely spaced. Imitate nature by planting foxgloves, aquilegias and other tall plants in positions where they can colonize open glades. Plant ajugas, hardy cyclamens, dicentras, hederas, lamiums and vincas to make pools of soft colour around the base of tree trunks and between the roots of the trees.

Perennials

Aconitum, Ajuga, Anemone nemorosa, Aquilegia, Arum italicum, Astrantia, Cardamine, Dicentra, Digitalis purpurea, Epimedium, Euphorbia amygdaloides, Filipendula ulmaria, Gentiana asclepiadea, Geranium macrorrhizum, Helleborus, Hosta, Lamium, Lunaria, Polygonatum, Primula vulgaris, Pulmonaria, Symphytum, Tellima, Tiarella, Vinca, Viola labradorica

Bulbs

Cyclamen, Erythronium

Plants to give winter impact

For winter effect, think in terms of structure and shape: tall, cone-shaped conifers contrast with others of spreading, horizontal habit; evergreen shrubs can be clipped to form dense mounds or fantastic topiary shapes.

In winter the skeletal forms of deciduous trees and shrubs become apparent, some graceful, some robust and some, like the corkscrew hazel, bizarre. On winter's restricted palette, the colours of stems and twigs come into their own. They range from the silver and white of birch bark to the warm, purple-brown or russets of twiggy shrubs.

TALL CONIFERS

Chamaecyparis lawsoniana 'Columnaris Glauca' and others, *Cryptomeria japonica* 'Elegans', *Cupressocyparis leylandii*, *Juniperus communis* 'Hibernica' and others, *Juniperus scopulorum* 'Skyrocket', *Taxus baccata* 'Fastigiata', *Thuja plicata*

HORIZONTAL CONIFERS

Juniperus horizontalis 'Hughes', *Juniperus x media* 'Pfitzeriana', *Juniperus squamata* 'Blue Carpet', *Taxus baccata* 'Dovastonii Aurea'

EVERGREENS THAT RESPOND WELL TO CLIPPING

Buxus sempervirens, *Choisya ternata*, *Cotoneasters* (several), *Cupressocyparis leylandii*, *Elaeagnus x ebbingei*, *Hebe albicans* and others, *Hedera canariensis* 'Gloire de Marengo' and most other ivies, *Hyssopus officinalis*, *Ilex x altaclarensis* and other hollies, *Laurus nobilis*, *Lavandula angustifolia* 'Hidcote', *Lonicera nitida*, *Pyracantha*, *Skimmia japonica*, *Taxus baccata*

SHAPELY SKELETONS

Cornus alternifolia 'Variegata', *Corylus avellana* 'Contorta', *Cotoneaster* (numerous varieties), *Fraxinus excelsior* 'Pendula', *Parottia persica*, *Pyrus salicifolia* 'Pendula', *Rosa omoensis pteracantha*

COLOURED BARK OR STEMS

Acer griseum (peeling bark), *Acer davidii* (snakebark), *Arbutus menziesii* (red-brown mottled bark), *Betula utilis jacquemontii* (white peeling bark), *Betula* papyrifera (papery bark),

Cornus alba 'Sibirica Westonbirt' (red stems) and 'Spaethii' (red stems), *Cornus stolonifera* 'Flaviramea' (yellow stems), *Cytisus x praecox* 'Warminster' (green stems), *Deutzia* (peeling stems), *Eucalyptus gunnii* (blue-white stems), *Hydrangea petiolaris* (red-brown bark), *Kerria japonica* (green stems), *Leycesteria formosa* (green stems), *Prunus serrula* (mahogany peeling bark), *Rubus cockburnianus* (stems with white bloom), *Salix alba* 'Chermesina' (red stems) and 'Vitellina'(yellow stems)

AUTUMN LEAVES OR FRUIT HELD THROUGHOUT THE WINTER

Acanthus (seed heads), *Carpinus betulus* (leaves), *Cotoneaster* 'Rothschildianus' (fruit), *Cotoneaster watereri* (fruit), *Fagus sylvatica* (leaves), *Hedera* (fruit of adult forms), *Iris foetidissima* (seed heads), *Lunaria rediviva* (seed heads), *Malus* 'Red Sentinel' (fruit)

PLANTS THAT HOLD THEIR LEAVES LATE INTO WINTER

Buddleia, *Carpinus betulus*, *Cercis siliquastrum*, *Clematis montana*, *Cotoneaster horizontalis* and others, *Fagus sylvatica*, *Quercus robur* and other oaks, *Rosa* (many)

PLANTS THAT FLOWER IN WINTER

Trees
Prunus subhirtella 'Autumnalis'

Shrubs
Camellia, *Daphne mezereum*, *Erica carnea*, *Erica x darleyensis*, *Garrya elliptica* 'James Roof', *Hamamelis mollis* 'Pallida', *Jasminum nudiflorum*, *Mahonia japonica*, *Viburnum x bodnantense*, *Viburnum tinus*

Perennials
Bergenia cordifolia, *Helleborus niger*, *Iris unguicularis*, *Pulmonaria*

Bulbs
Crocus, *Eranthis hyemalis*, *Galanthus nivalis*

EVERGREEN PERENNIALS

Arum italicum 'Pictum', *Bergenia*, *Festuca glauca*, *Heuchera* 'Palace Purple', *Iris foetidissima* 'Variegata', *Lamium maculatum*, *Phormium*, *Stachys byzantina*, *Vinca*

Foreground plants: edging plants and front of border plants

Planted in bold sweeps in the front row and drifting back beneath larger perennials and shrubs, these plants give unity to planting schemes and pull them together. Mix foliage of similar colour but different texture.

Shrubs

Berberis thunbergii 'Atropurpurea Nana', *Buxus suffruticosa*, *Erica carnea*, *Hebe pinguifolia*, *Hebe rakaensis*, *Hedera* (small-leaved ground cover varieties), *Helianthemum*, *Santolina chamaeyparissus* 'Nana', *Thymus vulgaris*, *Vaccinium*

Perennials

Acaena, Ajuga, Alchemilla, Allium schoenoprasum, Anthemis punctata ssp. *cupaniana, Armeria maritima, Artemisia stelleriana, Aubrieta, Bergenia, Calaminta nepeta, Campanula* (low growing kinds), *Cerastium tomentosum* var. *columnae, Chaemaemelum nobile, Convallaria majalis, Corydalis, Dianthus, Diascia, Dicentra, Euphorbia cyparissias, Festuca glauca, Geranium cinereum, Geranium macrorrhizum, Geranium renardii, Gypsophila repens, Heuchera, Hosta, Iberis, Knautia macedonica, Lamium maculatum, Lysimachia nummularia, Nepeta faassinii, Omphaloides cappadocica, Ophiopogon planiscapus* 'Nigrescens', *Origanum, Primula vulgaris, Pulmonaria, Pulsatilla vulgaris, Saxifraga, Sedum* 'Vera Jameson', *Stachys byzantina, Tiarella, Vinca minor, Viola*

Annuals and Biennials

Impatiens, Limnanthes, Myosotis, Nasturtium, Nemisia

Plants for the water garden and bog garden

Just as the idea of a desert conjures up images of cacti, spikey yuccas and plants with dry, grey leaves, so water, whether it is contained in a still pond or gurgling through a rocky stream bed, suggests lush greenery.

Some plants grow naturally with their roots underwater or in waterlogged soil. They tend to produce the broad, emerald green leaves you might expect to see. Many, such as astilbes, ferns, gunnera, primulas and lysichitum, do best in light shade, so try to choose a site for your water garden that is partly shaded by a tree or by tall shrubs. If you need to create shade, salix (willow) and sambucus (elder) species will grow quickly in swampy conditions. In moist but not waterlogged soil, plant alnus, crataegus or pyrus where there is room for a tree. Plant philadelphus, spiraea, *viburnum opulus* or *v. rhytidophyllum* if a fast-growing shrub is needed.

Arranging water and marginal plants to make the most of their contrasting shapes and textures is a delightful occupation. Most have leaves that fall easily into the categories of horizontal, vertical or gracefully arching. The fine-cut leaves of astilbes and ferns contrast strongly with the smooth blades of irises and reeds.

I have found that two problems crop up again and again when planting water gardens. The first is that, if there are ducks on a pond (and if you do not introduce them they are likely to colonize your pond uninvited), they will gobble up the succulent shoots as they emerge until there are no plants left. The only way to prevent this is to put a fence around the plants or around the ducks. To be duck-proof the fence should reach to at least 15cm (6in) above water level, so it

Ferns   *Typhalatifolia*

Acorus calamus   *Ligolaria*   *Zantedeshia*

cannot be invisible. The most unobtrusive material is galvanized chicken wire, held in place by thin timber or metal posts painted black. Once the plants are established the fence can be removed.

Another recurrent problem concerns planting the banks of a pond or watercourse. Unless the bog areas are part of the design, water cannot seep from the pond into the marginal ground. Far from being waterlogged, the banks of artificial ponds or streams are often unusually dry. The moisture-loving plants that look appropriate beside the water simply will not grow in such conditions. The answer is to choose plants such as hostas that thrive in dry conditions but look as if they enjoy a damp spot (some of which are listed below).

Most of the following water plants are not included in the Plant A-Z in Part II because of lack of space, but they are described fully in my previous book *Gardening Made Easy*.

OXYGENATING PLANTS

Callitriche palustris (water starwort), *Ceratophyllum demersum* (thornwort), *Myriophyllum aquaticum* syn. *M. proserpinacoides*

FLOATING PLANTS

Hottonia palustris (water violet), *Hydrocharis morsus-ranae* (frogbit), *Stratiotes aloides* (water soldier)

DEEP WATER: 60cm (24in) and over

Water lilies, including the following: *Nymphaea* 'James Brydon' AGM, *Nymphaea* 'Marliacea Chromatella' AGM, *Nymphaea* 'Escarboucle' AGM, *Sagittaria sagittifolia*

DEPTH 30-60cm (12-24in)

Aponogeton distachyos, Butomus umbellatus, Nymphaea 'Laydekeri Fulgens', *Nymphaea* 'Laydekeri Lilacea'

DEPTH 15-30cm (6-12in)

Acorus calamus 'Variegatus', *Menyanthes trifoliata, Orontium aquaticum, Pontederia cordata, Schoenoplectus lacustris* 'Zebrinus', *Zantedeschia aethiopica* AGM

DEPTH 5-15cm (2-6in)

Acorus gramineus 'Variegatus', *Calla palustris, Iris laevigata* AGM, *Iris pseudacorus* 'Variegata' AGM, *Nymphaea* 'Pygmaea Alba', *Nymphaea x helvola* AGM

SHALLOW WATER AND MARGINAL MUD

Caltha palustris 'Flore pleno' AGM, *Cardamine pratensis* 'Flore Pleno' AGM, *Myosotis scorpioides, Mimulus cardinalis* AGM

DRY BANKS

Acanthus spinosus, Ajuga reptans, Alchemilla mollis, Bergenia, Brunnera macrophylla, Carex hachijoensis, Cotoneaster (prostrate varieties), *Crambe cordifolia, Geranium, Hedera, Hosta, Iris sibirica, Oenothera, Phormium, Pulmonaria, Sisyrinchium striatum, Stipa, Symphoricarpos*

Protect young plants from water-fowl with a simple-to-make mesh barrier.

Plants for containers

If your garden is a roof, balcony or paved yard, it will be impossible to dig a hole for a plant. In that case you must grow everything in pots, tubs, boxes or other containers – and I do mean 'everything', for even trees can be grown in this way, provided the container is a reasonable size, the compost or other growing medium is suitable and the plant is fed and watered.

On a roof or balcony it is a wise precaution to get a surveyor to check its load-bearing capacity: large pots full of wet soil are very heavy.

In larger gardens, pots provide an opportunity to ring the changes on patios and terraces from season to season and from year to year. Orange and lemon trees and other tender plants can be grown in containers and moved indoors for the winter at the first threat of frost. If your garden is on alkaline soil and you yearn for camellias and azaleas, they can be planted in containers filled with acid soil.

Climbers
Most will succeed. Grow annual climbers in 25cm (12in) pots, perennials in 45cm (18in) and vigorous woody plants (e.g. wisteria) in pots a minimum of 50cm (20in) tall and deep.

Plant in soil-based compost John Innes No. 2 with a slow-release fertilizer. Top dress in spring with slow-release fertilizer.
Clematis, Convolvulus, Hedera, Jasminum, Lathyrus, Lonicera, Passiflora, Tropaeolum

Trees and Shrubs
Slow-growing species take longer to outgrow their pots, but it is worth experimenting with almost any plant. Restriction of root growth within a container has a 'big bonsai' effect, resulting in restricted growth above, as well as below, the soil.
Acer palmatum, Buxus sempervirens, Convolvulus cneorum, Crataegus laevigata, Euonymus fortunei, Fatshedera, Fuchsia, Hebe, Hydrangea arborescens 'Annabelle', *Hydrangea macrophylla, Ilex aquifolium, Juniperus, Laurus nobilis, Lavandula, Malus, Myrtus communis, Phormium, Pinus mugo, Rhododendron* (most), *Rosa* (most), *Salvia officinalis, Santolina, Senecio cineraria* 'Silver Dust', *Sorbus cashmiriana, Vinca, Yucca, Viburnum tinus*

Perennials
Agapanthus, Bergenia, Campanula, Dianthus, Geranium, Helianthemum, Hemerocallis, Hosta, Penstemon, Saxifraga

Bulbs
All

Annuals and Perennials
Most

Plants for topiary

Buxus sempervirens, Crataegus monogyna, Hedera helix, Hyssops officinalis, Ilex aquifolium, Juniperus chinensis, Laurus nobilis, Ligustrum ovalifolium, Lonicera nitida, Prunus lusitanica, Rosmarinus officinalis, Santolina chamaecyparissus, Taxus baccata

Plants to grow as standards

Plants trained as standards are the ultimate example of humans taming nature. If that idea is what appeals to you most about gardening, there are all sorts of opportunities to experiment with unlikely subjects. Commercial producers make standards by grafting buds on to the sturdy stem of a more robust relation of the plant in question. DIY enthusiasts may also like to have a go at grafting, but the easy way is to train a long, strong stem of the subject to a vertical cane.

Remove all side shoots at the bud stage and pinch out the tips of shoots that appear at the top, to encourage bushy growth.

Shrubs and Climbers
Buddleia alternifolia, Buxus sempervirens, Cotoneaster, Hedera, Hydrangea paniculata, Ilex, Laurus nobilis, Ligustrum ovalifolium, Lonicera, Rosa (especially ramblers as weeping standards), *Vitis vinifera, Wisteria*

Plants to grow in paving or rock gardens or on the tops of walls

These are plants that are at home in very free draining positions and are not fussy about soil, indeed some will grow in pure rubble. Good drainage enables some doubtfully hardy plants such as *Convolvulus cneorum* to come through quite harsh winters: it is frozen wet soil around their roots that kills. Many alpine plants thrive in paving, in gravel or on top of a wall; it is not necessary to create a separate rock garden.

Perennials
Acaena, Alchemilla, Aubrieta, Campanula poscharskyana, Cerastium, Convolvulus cneorum, Dianthus, Diascia, Erysimum, Gypsophila repens, Helianthemum, Origanum, Phlox douglasii, Sedum (dwarf kinds), *Stachys byzantina, Thymus, Viola*

5 | Useful Plants

The earliest gardens in history were made with plants collected in the wild for their usefulness: food plants, medicinal herbs, herbs to flavour food, to keep fleas away, even to cure a broken heart. Such uses are mentioned in the plant descriptions. Over the next few pages I have listed plants to encourage wildlife into the garden; plants to make weed-smothering mulches; and flowers to pick fresh or to dry for indoor decoration. A few food plants that taste better from the garden than from the supermarket are described in the alphabetical list under their English name, for example apple, bean.

Plants for wildlife

FOOD, SHELTER FOR BIRDS

Plants with berries, hedges, ivy and dense, twiggy shrubs for shelter and nesting sites.

NECTAR PLANTS FOR BEES

Trees
Acer negundo, Aesculus, Catalpa bignonioides, Crataegus, Malus, Prunus avium and other flowering cherries, *Pyrus communis, Sorbus*

Shrubs
Berberis thunbergii, Buddleia, Buxus, Ceanothus, Cercis siliquastrum, Chaenomeles speciosa, Cistus, Colutea arborescens, Cotoneaster, Cytisus Escallonia, Fuchsia, Hedera helix (adult flowering form), *Helianthenmum, Hyssopus, Ilex, Laurus nobilis, Lavandula, Lavatera, Perovskia, Potentilla, Prunus laurocerasus, Syringa, Viburnum x bodnantense, Viburnum opulus, Viburnum tinus, Weigela*

Perennials
Achillea, Allium, Alstroemeria, Alyssum, Anthemis, Calamintha, Campanula, Delphinium, Echinops, Eryngium, Filipendula ulmaria, Geranium pratense, Malva, Nepeta, Origanum, Papaver, Phlox, Polemonium, Pulmonaria, Romneya, Salvia, Saxifraga, Scabiosa, Sedum, Verbascum, Veronica, Viola

NECTAR PLANTS FOR BUTTERFLIES

Shrubs
Buddleia, Hyssopus, Lavandula, Ligustrum, Syringa

Perennials
Achillea, Ajuga, Anaphalis, Aster novi-belgii, Aubrieta, Calamintha, Centranthus, Dianthus deltoides, Echinops, Erysimum, Knautia, Lunaria, Malva moschata, Muscari, Nepeta, Phlox, Primula veris, Primula vulgaris, Scabiosa, Sedum spectabile, Solidago, Tanacetum parthenium

Annuals and Biennials
Alyssum, Calendula officinalis, Centaurea cyanus, Cheiranthus, Dianthus barbatus, Hesperis matronalis, Matthiola, Papaver somniferum

WILD FOOD PLANTS FOR BUTTERFLY CATERPILLARS

Stinging Nettle – *Urtica dioica* (Comma, Peacock, Red Admiral, Small Tortoiseshell), Bird's-foot Trefoil – *Lotus corniculatus* (several including Common Blue), Restharrow – *Ononis repens* (Common Blue), Toadflax – *Linaria vulgaris* (Spotted Fritillary), Mullein – *Verbascum thapsus* (Mullein Moth), Heather – *Calluna vulgaris* (Silver-studded Blue, Mottled Beauty), Honeysuckle – *Lonicera periclymenum* (several including White Admiral), Horseshoe Vetch – *Hippocrepis comosa* (Adonis Blue, Dingy Skipper), Lady's Smock – *Cardamine pratensis* (Orange Tip), Purple Loosestrife – *Lythrum salicaria* (Emperor moth, Small Elephant Hawkmoth), Sweet Violet – *Viola odorata* (High Brown Fritillary, Pearl-bordered Fritillary), White Clover – *Trifolium repens* (several including Common Blue)

Weed-smothering plants

FOR SHADE

Shrubs and Climbers
Arundinaria, Aucuba, Choisya ternata, Cotoneaster (prostrate kinds), *Euonymus fortunei, Gaultheria, Hedera* (lots), *Hydrangea anomala* ssp. *petiolaris, Hypericum, Mahonia aquifolium, Prunus laurocerasus, P.l.* 'Otto Luyken', *P.l.* 'Zabeliana', *Rubus tricolor, Schizophragma hydrangeoides, Viburnum plicatum* 'Lanarth', *Vinca minor*

Perennials
Acanthus, Ajuga, Alchemilla mollis, Anaphalis, Astrantia, Aubrieta, Bergenia (most), *Brunnera macrophylla, Dicentra, Epimedium perralderianum, Euphorbia amygdaloides* ssp. *robbiae, Geranium macrorrhizum, Hemerocallis, Heuchera, Hosta* (most), *Lamium, Polygonum, Prunella grandiflora, Pulmonaria, Saxifraga x urbium, Symphytum grandiflorum, Tellima grandiflora* 'Purpurea', *Tiarella cordifolia*

FOR SUN

Shrubs and Climbers
Ceanothus thyrsiflorus 'Repens', *Choisya ternata, Cistus, Cotoneaster* (prostrate kinds), *Elaeagnus, Erica carnea, Hebe, Hypericum, Juniperus, Lathyrus latifolius, Lonicera japonica* 'Halliana', *Mahonia aquifolium, Origanum vulgare* 'Aureum', *Phlomis, Potentilla, Rosa* (ground cover kinds), *Rosmarinus officinalis, Rubus tricolor, Salvia, Santolina, Senecio, Thymus, Viburnum davidii, Vinca, Vitis coignetiae*

Perennials
Acaena, Acanthus, Achillea, Anaphalis, Anthemis punctata ssp. *cupaniana, Armeria maritima, Artemisia, Aubrieta, Ballota, Campanula poscharskyana, Crambe, Dianthus, Diascia, Dicentra, Epimedium, Euphorbia polychroma, Geranium* (most), *Gypsophila* 'Rosy Veil', *Helianthemum, Iberis sempervirens, Nepeta, Pulmonaria, Rheum palmatum, Salvia, Sedum, Stachys, Viola*

Plants for flower arranging

Trees and Shrubs
Aesculus, Artemisia, Camellia, Chaenomeles, Choisya, Cotoneaster, Erica, Forsythia, Kerria, Kolkwitzia, Lavandula, Lonicera, Mahonia, Malus, Philadelphus, Pyracantha, Ribes, Rosa, Rosmarinus, Salix, Skimmia, Spartium, Spiraea, Symphoricarpus, Syringa, Viburnum, Vinca, Weigela

Perennials
Acanthus, Achillea, Aconitum, Agapanthus, Alchemilla mollis, Allium, Alstroemeria, Anaphalis, Anchusa, Anemone x hybrida, Anthemis tinctoria, Aquilegia, Aster, Astrantia, Campanula, Crambe, Crocosmia, Cynara, Dahlia, Delphinium, Dianthus, Dicentra, Doronicum, Echinops, Eryngium, Euphorbia, Geum, Gypsophila, Helichrysum, Helleborus, Heuchera, Iris, Kniphofia, Lychnis, Lythrum, Macleaya, Miscanthus, Monarda, Nerine, Paeonia, Papaver orientale, Penstemon, Persicaria, Phlox, Polygonatum, Primula, Pulmonaria, Pulsatilla, Salvia x superba, Scabiosa, Schizostylis, Sisyrinchium, Stachys byzantina, Stipa, Tanacetum parthenium, Thalictrum, Zantedeschia

Annuals and Biennials
Angelica, Centaurea cyanus, Cosmos, Digitalis, Erysimum, Lathyrus odoratus, Matthiola, Myosotis, Nigella

Bulbs
Most, especially *Lilium, Narcissus, Tulipa*

Flowers for drying

Pick the flowers on a dry day, just before they reach their peak.

To Air Dry

Tie the stems together in a bunch and hang upsidedown in a warm, dry place away from direct sunlight, for example in an airing cupboard. They will take a week or more to dry. With some flowers the heads only should be picked and speared on florists' wire before drying; others can be left to dry in a vase of water (see list).

To Microwave

You need silica gel, obtainable from chemists. Place the flowers on a 6mm (¹/₄in) layer of gel in an ovenproof dish or jug; cover with another layer of gel. Put in the microwave with the power full on for two to three minutes. Trial and error will show you the correct timing for different species. Leave for twenty minutes before removing the flowers from the silica gel. The gel can be re-used. Flowers stripped of their foliage can be microwaved without the gel on several layers of kitchen paper. Cook them, uncovered, on a medium setting for two to three minutes. If the paper becomes damp, replace it and repeat the process.

Acanthus mollis (dry in water), *Achillea*, *Alchemilla mollis*, *Allium* (pick in bud), *Anaphalis*, *Argyranthemum frutescens* syn. *Chrysanthemum frutescens* (marguerite), *Aster* (wire heads), *Astilbe* (dry in water), *Astrantia major*, *Calendula*, *Centaurea cyanus* (wire heads or dry in water), *Crocosmia* (dry in water), *Cynara*, *Dahlia*, *Delphinium* (dry in water), *Digitalis*, *Echinops* (pick in bud), *Eryngium*, grasses, *Gypsophila*, *Helleborus*, *Hydrangea* (wire, or dry in water), *Helichrysum bracteatum* (pick in bud), *Lavandula* (pick in bud, dry in water), *Limonium*, *Lunaria*, *Monarda*, *Nepeta* (dry in water), *Nigella*, *Origanum* (pick in bud), *Paeonia* (wire heads), *Pansies*, *Papaver*, *Physalis* (Chinese lanterns), *Polygonum*, *Poppies* (poisonous), *Phlomis russelliana*, *Rosa* (dry in water), *Salvia horminum*, *Santolina* (dry in water), *Sedum spectabile*, *Solidago* (dry in water)

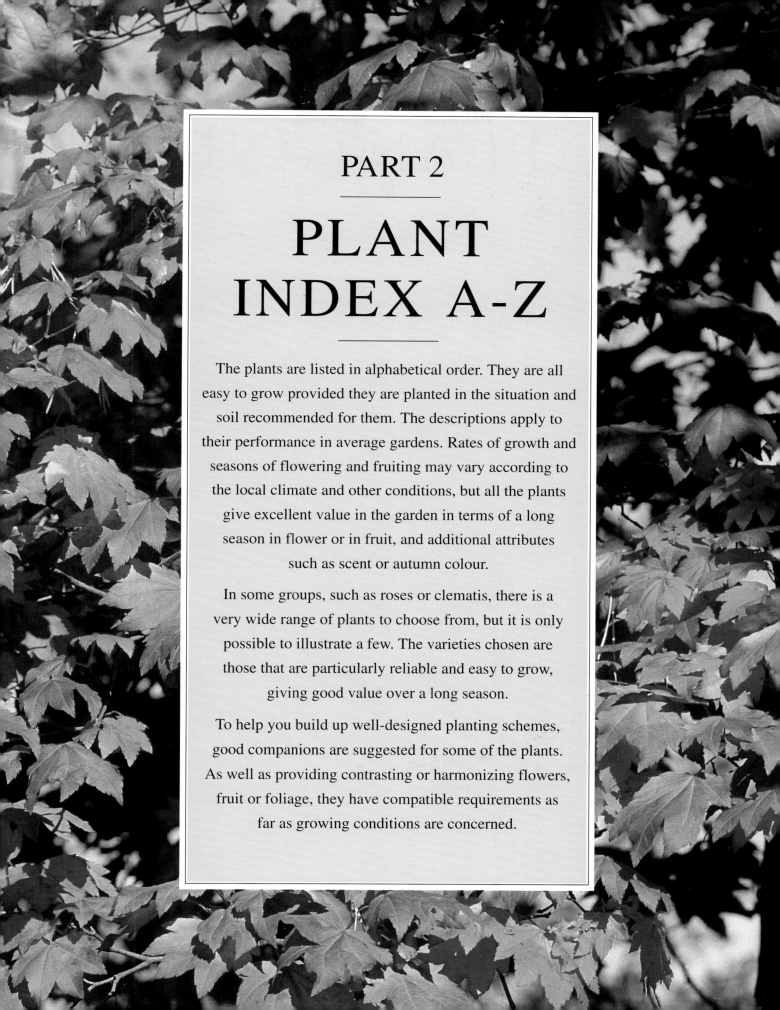

PART 2

PLANT INDEX A-Z

The plants are listed in alphabetical order. They are all easy to grow provided they are planted in the situation and soil recommended for them. The descriptions apply to their performance in average gardens. Rates of growth and seasons of flowering and fruiting may vary according to the local climate and other conditions, but all the plants give excellent value in the garden in terms of a long season in flower or in fruit, and additional attributes such as scent or autumn colour.

In some groups, such as roses or clematis, there is a very wide range of plants to choose from, but it is only possible to illustrate a few. The varieties chosen are those that are particularly reliable and easy to grow, giving good value over a long season.

To help you build up well-designed planting schemes, good companions are suggested for some of the plants. As well as providing contrasting or harmonizing flowers, fruit or foliage, they have compatible requirements as far as growing conditions are concerned.

GUIDE TO USING THE PLANT INDEX

To help you find the plants you want, the alphabetical entries are colour-coded:

TREES

SHRUBS

CLIMBING PLANTS

PERENNIALS

BULBS

BIENNIALS

ANNUALS

Plants with evergreen leaves have a calendar coloured green:

Plants with deciduous leaves have a calendar coloured white:

J	F	M	A	M	J	J	A	S	O	N	D

Plants that are semi-evergreen or have evergreen and deciduous varieties have a calendar coloured both green and white:

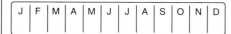

The Latin, or scientific plant names used are those in the most recent edition of *The RHS Plant Finder*. Sometimes the plants are reclassified and put in a different group, and the official names are changed. Where this has happened recently the old name is given as a synonym (syn.). If you only know a plant by its old name or its English name, look it up in the index of synonyms and common names on page 252.

In a Latin name, the first word tells you which genus, or family, the plant belongs to, for example **Potentilla**. The second word tells you the species or wild form of the plant, for example *Potentilla **fruticosa***. The third word tells you which variety, or garden form it is, for example *Potentilla fruticosa* **'Abbotswood'**. There are a few variations on this basic formula, such as *Euphorbia characias* ssp. (subspecies) *wulfenii*, or *Amenone x hybrida*, or *Viola cornuta* Purpurea Group. These complications exist for the sake of botanical accuracy.

The plant's Latin name and synonym is followed by:

⊛ the common name in English, if one exists

⊛ type of plant (i.e. tree, shrub, etc.)

⊛ the country or area of origin

⊛ the date of its introduction to Britain if it is known

⊛ approximate height and spread of a mature specimen. This will vary according to local conditions. In the case of slow-growing trees and shrubs, two sizes are usually given, one after five or ten years (shrubs) and after twenty years (trees), and the other the size of the plant at maturity.

⊛ AGM tells you the plant has the Royal Horticultural Society's Award of Garden Merit. The award is given to plants that have proved their worth over a period of years and under varied growing conditions. Some awards were made several decades ago, therefore in some cases the plants are not necessarily the best of their type available today, but the award does indicate the plant is of good quality and gives value for money.

The codes, chart and calendar at the base of each entry provide 'at-a-glance' information about the plant:

PREFERRED SOIL
acid or alkaline
dry or wet

For example, this would indicate a plant that does not like heavily alkaline soils, nor soil that is dry.

POSITION
● = Prefers a a position in shade
◗ = Prefers a position in partial sunlight
○ = Prefers a position in direct sunlight

FAST- OR SLOW-GROWING
🐇 = Fast-growing plant
🐢 = Slow-growing plant

CAN BE CONTAINER GROWN
⊞ = This plant can be grown in a container

PRUNING
Best month(s) for pruning are marked thus:

FLOWERS
Best month(s) for flowers are marked thus:

FOLIAGE
Best month(s) for foliage are marked thus:

FRUITS OR BERRIES
Best month(s) for fruit and/or berries are marked thus:

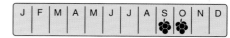

ABELIA X GRANDIFLORA

Syn. A rupestris of gardens, semi-evergreen shrub, a garden hybrid between A. chinensis (China, 1816) and A. uniflora (China, 1845). Mature at 10 years: 1.2-1.8m x 1.5m (4-6ft x 5ft); taller against a wall and in mild climates. AGM

A graceful, arching shrub with pointed, glossy, dark green leaves. The young branches contribute warm red-brown colouring to the winter scene. Profuse, faintly scented, pale pink and white bell-shaped flowers appear from midsummer to autumn. Frost hardy and stronger than either of its parents, but in very harsh winters may be cut to the ground; it usually sprouts again if given a deep dry winter mulch.

USES For late summer interest, plant against a south- or west-facing wall, or in a mixed border where neighbouring shrubs provide shelter. In mild climates it can be used as a hedge.

CULTIVATION Plant in autumn or spring, in well-drained soil, in a position protected from cold winds, preferably against a wall. Remove dead, diseased or frost-damaged wood in late spring.

PROPAGATION Take semi-ripe cuttings in midsummer. Place in pots of sandy soil in a propagator with gentle bottom heat.

PESTS AND DISEASES Generally trouble free.

OTHER VARIETIES A. 'Edward Goucher' AGM is similar, with darker, mauve-pink flowers. A. schumannii has purplish stems and rose-pink flowers.

COMPANIONS Use spire-shaped conifers such as *Juniperus scopulorum* 'Skyrocket', or Irish yew (*Taxus baccata* 'Fastigiata' AGM) to contrast with the abelia's arching form. The purple foliage of *Viola labradorica* at ground level will set off the delicate, pale pink flowers.

ABELIA GRANDIFLORA

ABUTILON VITIFOLIUM VAR. ALBUM

Frost hardy, deciduous shrub (Chile, 1836). Mature at 5 years: 4 x 2.5m (12 x 8ft).

A fast-growing shrub with handsome, vine-like leaves. The leaves and young shoots are covered with whitish down giving an overall effect of soft grey-green. From late spring to late summer the plant is covered with large, single, mallow-like white flowers. It may outgrow its strength and die suddenly, but luckily it comes true from seed.

USES In mild areas it will thrive in the open, but it is safest to plant it against a south- or west-facing wall, where it will give good value for nearly three-quarters of the year.

CULTIVATION Plant in late spring or early autumn, in well-drained soil in a sheltered site. In all but the mildest districts, protect in winter with straw or bracken. Prune in early spring only to remove dead or frosted wood, or to keep overall growth within bounds.

PROPAGATION Cuttings are difficult to root. Sow seed in late spring at 15-18°C (59-64°F).

PESTS AND DISEASES Scale insects and mealy bugs sometimes infest the leaves and stems, leaving sticky excretions and, in the case of mealy bugs, tufts of white wool. Spray when symptoms first appear.

OTHER VARIETIES A. vitifolium 'Veronica Tennant' AGM has large, blue-mauve flowers. A. megapotamicum AGM is rather tender, but worth trying on a sheltered wall.

COMPANIONS The pale grey-green of A. vitifolium blends well with the foliage of other plants that enjoy the same warm, free-draining conditions: *Ballota pseudodictamnus*, *Phlomis fruticosa* and *Stachys byzantina* 'Primrose Heron'. Neighbours on a wall could include the dark red, velvet rose 'Guinée' and *Solanum crispum* 'Glasnevin'.

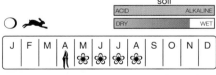

ABUTILON VITIFOLIUM

ACAENA SACCATICUPULA 'BLUE HAZE'

Syn. A. 'Pewter'. New Zealand burr, evergreen perennial. Mature at 3 years: 10 x 75cm (4 x 30in) and more.

A vigorous, prostrate plant forming a flat mat of tiny steel-blue leaflets. Spherical, brownish-red flower heads develop in late summer into dark crimson burrs with pinkish-red spines.

USES Acaena will hug the contours of a stone in the rock garden, but don't allow it to smother choicer, less bold specimens. It makes impenetrable low ground cover among shrubs and other, taller perennials, and will happily colonize the cracks between paving slabs.

CULTIVATION Plant at any time from early autumn to spring, in well-drained soil, in sun or partial shade.

PROPAGATION Divide and replant in early spring, or sow seeds in an open frame or cold greenhouse between early autumn and spring.

PESTS AND DISEASES Generally trouble free.

OTHER VARIETIES A. buchananii is even neater and more ground hugging, but not as blue. The grey-green, pinnate leaves are no higher than 5cm (2in) and the burrs are yellow-green. A. microphylla has bronze-green leaves and crimson burrs. Cultivars with self-descriptive names include A. microphylla 'Kupferteppich' (syn. 'Copper Carpet') and 'Pewter Carpet'.

COMPANIONS A carpet of acaena is the ideal background for snowdrops, white or yellow crocuses, *Iris danfordiae*, species tulips and other small bulbs, but avoid using those with blue, mauve or violet-purple flowers. Red-purple, however, looks rather good against glaucous leaves. Orange flowers, too, are set off well: try acaenas in front of *Euphorbia griffithii* 'Fireglow', or *Lilium* 'Enchantment' AGM.

ACAENA CAESIIGLAUCA

A

ACANTHUS SPINOSUS

Bear's breeches, herbaceous perennial. (S. Europe, 1629). Mature at 3 years: 120 x 60cm (4 x 2ft). AGM

Acanthus are among the most sculptural of garden plants, idealized by stone masons on the capitals of stone columns. The huge glossy, spine-tipped leaves are dark green and deeply cut. They arch and overlap to form total ground cover. Robust spikes arise in midsummer, covered in white flowers with mauve-purple bracts that are palest green at the base, giving soft and subtle colour effects.

USES Acanthus make excellent ground cover. They can be used singly, or in a group of three where a strong sculptural focus is needed. They may be grouped in a colony by themselves, and can even be naturalized successfully in grass. Acanthus can be invasive, so beware of planting them near any special treasure. The flowers are good for cutting and drying.

CULTIVATION Acanthus grow in sun or shade, but flower better in sun. Plant in spring in deep, fertile well-drained soil and protect with mulch for the first winter. Cut the stems back almost to ground level after flowering.

PROPAGATION Sow seed in spring or take root cuttings in winter. The easiest way is to divide the roots at any time between autumn and early spring.

PESTS AND DISEASES Generally trouble free.

OTHER VARIETIES Avoid planting *A. mollis latifolius*. It is shy of flowering and can be very invasive.

COMPANIONS Bergenias with their big, bold leaves are among the few herbaceous plants that hold their own with acanthus. The leaves of *Rosa glauca*, syn. *R. rubrifolia*, AGM, have subtle colouring similar to acanthus flowers, and are a good foil.

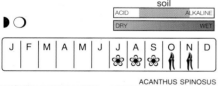

J	F	M	A	M	J	J	A	S	O	N	D

ACANTHUS SPINOSUS

ACER GRISEUM

Paperbark maple, deciduous tree. (C. China, 1901). Mature at 50 years: 5m (15ft) high, after 20 years; 10 x 8m (30 x 26ft) at maturity. AGM

Slow-growing, but worth waiting for. A straight trunk and ascending branches carry a rounded crown of triple leaves. In autumn, they turn vibrant scarlet or orange. The smooth, papery bark curls away from the trunk like flaking paint, revealing new cinnamon-coloured bark, an effect to enjoy in winter.

USES Give *A. griseum* pride of place in a position where it can be seen from the house. It is compact enough to be used in this way in quite small gardens. In a large mixed border, take care not to hide the stem from view.

CULTIVATION Plant in cool, well-drained but moist soil, in sun or dappled shade. *A. griseum* is tolerant of lime and even of chalk, but must have shelter from cold winds and late frosts followed by early morning sun. Shelter from prevailing autumn winds.

PROPAGATION Not easy. Try sowing the seed as soon as ripe – just as the 'keys' begin to colour – in a seed bed outdoors or in an open frame.

PESTS AND DISEASES Sadly, a rather daunting list but don't let it put you off. Aphids make the foliage sticky and sooty. Coral spot causes shoot die-back. Scorching, tar spot and verticillium wilt can affect the leaves. Honey fungus may strike.

OTHER VARIETIES Snakebark maples, notable for their striated bark, are similar in size and requirements. Most have colourful autumn leaves. They include: *A. davidii* and its variants, *A. capillipes* AGM, and *A. pensylvanicum* AGM.

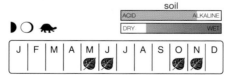

J	F	M	A	M	J	J	A	S	O	N	D

ACER GRISEUM

ACER NEGUNDO

Ash-leaved maple, box elder, deciduous tree (N. America). Mature at 40 years: 9m (28ft) after 20 years; 15 x 8m (50 x 26ft) at maturity.

A quite handsome tree forming a wide, rather open, irregular dome. Its ash-like leaves are unremarkable and it is only included here because it is very fast, very hardy and will grow almost anywhere.

USES The box elder can cope with industrial pollution, poor drainage, chalk and clay. As a bonus it provides food for bees.

CULTIVATION As *Acer griseum*, but easier.

PROPAGATION Sow seeds in autumn in an open frame or outdoors.

PESTS AND DISEASES As *Acer griseum*, but more tolerant of honey fungus.

OTHER VARIETIES *A. negundo* 'Flamingo' AGM, a pretty tree with white-variegated leaves that are tinged pink at the margins when young.

OTHER SPECIES There are other acers which are useful because they are fast-growing, but many, such as the common sycamore (*A. pseudoplatanus*) and Norway maple (*A.platanoides*) are so big that they are more useful to landscapers than to gardeners. *Acer saccharinum*, syn. *A. dasycarpum* AGM, the silver maple, is a borderline case: fast growing and large (25 x 15m/ 80 x 50 ft), it has a graceful, spreading shape, and the white down on the undersides of the leaves gives a silvery effect when stirred by the wind. The branches are rather brittle, so it is best planted in a fairly sheltered situation. In autumn the leaves turn yellow or red. *A. saccharinum* f. *laciniatum* has finely-cut leaves, which give an even more elegant effect.

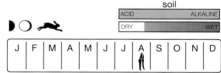

J	F	M	A	M	J	J	A	S	O	N	D

ACER NEGUNDO

ACER PALMATUM F. ATROPURPUREUM

Syn. **A. palmatum** *'Atropurpureum', deciduous shrub or small tree (Japan, Korea, China, 1857). Mature at 20 years: 1.8 x 1.8m (6 x 6ft) after 10 years; 4 x 4m (13 x 13ft) at maturity; to twice this height in the wild.*

Japanese maples slowly develop rounded crowns, often wider than they are high. *A. palmatum* has typically lobed maple leaves, with five or seven 'fingers'. The subspecies *f. atropurpureum* is one of several valued for the colour and finely dissected shape of their leaves. Its red-purple foliage turns brilliant red in autumn. *A. p.* 'Bloodgood' is similar but smaller, to 5m (15ft), with richer autumn colour.

USES Invaluable components of schemes planned for autumn colour. Their distinctive and elegant habit has always been greatly valued by Japanese gardeners, who garden with restraint and attach more importance to form and texture than to colour. Slow-growing and compact, they are excellent in pots in patio or courtyard gardens.

CULTIVATION Although hardy, these acers are susceptible to late spring frosts and to desiccating winds when the leaves are unfolding. Provide shelter to the north and east. They dislike chalk or limestone; the ideal soil is a moist, but well-drained, leafy loam. Although tolerant of partial shade, they grow best in sun.

PROPAGATION Named cultivars are propagated by grafting on to rootstocks of the parent species.

PESTS AND DISEASES As described for other acer species.

OTHER VARIETIES *Acer palmatum*, the species, is more tolerant of lime than the rest. An enormous number of cultivars is available. Among them, *A. p.* var. *dissectum* AGM and *A. p.* 'Garnet' AGM have intricately dissected feathery leaves. *A. p.* 'Sango-kaku' syn. 'Senkaki', the coral bark maple, is very beautiful but difficult. To date, three have died on me. *A. japonicum* 'Vitifolium' is fully hardy.

COMPANIONS Dark green and bluish conifers, irises and hostas contrast well with the acers' fiery autumn leaves.

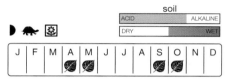

ACER PALMATUM 'DISSECTUM ATROPUREUM'

ACER JAPONICUM 'VITIFOLIUM'

Syn. **A. aegyptica** *of gardens, herbaceous perennial. Mature at 2 years: 60 x 50cm (24 x 20in).*

This member of the yarrow family has feathery, silver-grey leaves and flat heads of tiny, pale yellow flowers on strong stems from mid to late summer.

USES This and other achilleas are well-behaved border plants, flowering over a long period. They are good as cut flowers and dry well.

CULTIVATION A fairly retentive but well-drained soil is ideal, but achilleas are not fussy. They do, however, need plenty of sun. Plant or transplant in spring, in groups of at least three plants. Cut flowered stems down to ground level in autumn or winter.

PROPAGATION Divide and replant in early spring, or sow seeds in a cold frame or greenhouse in early spring.

PESTS AND DISEASES Generally trouble free.

OTHER VARIETIES *A.* 'Moonshine' AGM is easier to find and similar, but the flowers are a harsher shade of yellow. Other varieties with grey-green rather than silver leaves include *A. millefolium* 'Cerise Queen' and 'Lilac Queen', and *A.* 'Lasschönheit' syn. 'Salmon Beauty'. The Summer Pastels Group are a pretty mix of soft peach and buff shades: they look good sown in drifts through a big border.

COMPANIONS The grey-green and pale yellow colouring of *A.* 'Taygetea' contrasts beautifully with violet and blue salvias, and with the purple-leaved *Salvia officinalis* Purpurascens Group AGM. Also exciting with scarlet *Lychnis chalcedonica* AGM, or the magenta-flowered *Geranium psilostemon* AGM.

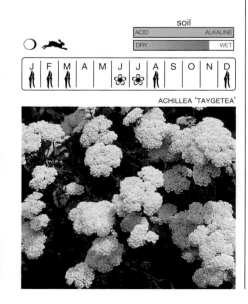

ACHILLEA 'TAYGETEA'

A

ACONITUM CARMICHAELII

Syn. A. fischeri of gardens, monkshood, helmet flower, wolf's bane, herbaceous perennial (Kamtchatka, China, 1886). Mature at 3 years: 120 x 30cm (4 x 1ft).

All parts of these plants are poisonous. The rich green foliage is glossy and deeply divided. It is attractive from early spring onwards. Hooded mauve-blue flowers cover stout spiky stems in early autumn. The seed heads are attractive in their early stages when they are green.

USES A stalwart component of the herbaceous or mixed border, and a good cut flower.

CULTIVATION As the plants start into growth very early, autumn or late winter planting is best. Plant the tuberous roots 12cm (5in) deep, in any soil that does not dry out, in sun or shade. They are best in groups of at least five. Flower stems may need staking. To keep them sturdy, thin out and replant every few years. Cut stems down to the ground after flowering.

PROPAGATION Divide and replant the roots in autumn or winter, handling with care because they are poisonous. Or sow seeds in spring in a cold frame or greenhouse.

PESTS AND DISEASES Generally trouble free.

OTHER VARIETIES *A. anglicum* (1.2m/4ft) is a robust British native with mauve-blue flowers; it is the earliest to flower, starting in late spring. 'Bressingham Spire' AGM, (90cm/3ft) has violet-blue flowers in late summer. *A. lycoctonum* ssp. *vulparia* has pale straw-yellow flowers on floppy spikes that need support.

COMPANIONS *A. anglicum* is early enough to grow with yellow shrub and species roses such as 'Frühlingsgold' AGM and *Rosa xanthina* f. *hugonis* or 'Canary Bird' AGM. *A. carmichaelii* contrasts well with kniphofias or crocosmias.

ACONITUM

ACTINIDIA DELICIOSA

Syn. A. chinensis. Chinese gooseberry, kiwi fruit, deciduous climber (China, Japan, 1900). At maturity, 9-10m (28-30ft); 3 x 3m (10 x 10ft) after 5 years.

A vigorous, woody, twining climber with exceptionally large, heart-shaped, brownish green leaves. Leaves, stems and shoots are entirely covered with shaggy, red-brown hairs. In midsummer, small, fragrant, creamy flowers appear mainly on spurs of older wood, followed, on female plants, by edible fruit, if male and female plants are grown together.

USES Plant it to cover large expanses of south- or west-facing walls, or to sprawl over a low wall or bank. It will also clothe a large tree, but make sure that the host can stand the weight.

CULTIVATION *A. deliciosa* grows in any but chalky or badly drained soil, but prefers a fertile loam. Plant between autumn and spring, at least 45cm (18in) out from the base of a wall or tree. Pinch out the growing point when young to encourage a spreading habit. On a wall, provide horizontal wires for support, at 30cm (12in) spacing. In the early stages tie the new shoots to the wires using soft string. Prune in winter if it outgrows its position.

PROPAGATION Sow seeds in autumn in a cold greenhouse. Root semi-ripe cuttings in sandy soil, with bottom heat.

PESTS AND DISEASES Trouble free.

OTHER VARIETIES *Actinidia kolomikta* is less robust and can be temperamental. Grown for its pretty heart-shaped leaves; they are pink at the tip, fading into white, and green at the stem.

COMPANIONS The handsome, hirsute leaves of *A. deliciosa* are an antidote to the prettiness of climbing and rambling roses.

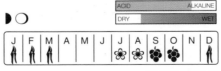

ACTINIDIA DELICIOSA

AESCULUS FLAVA

Syn. A. octandra. Sweet buckeye, yellow buckeye, deciduous tree. (Southeastern USA, 1764). Mature at 50 years: 9m (30ft) after 20 years; 15 x 8m (50 x 25ft) at maturity.

This handsome tree shares many features with the horse chestnut, *A. hippocastanum*, but is a more manageable size. It carries a tall, rounded head of glossy dark green leaves that turn bright orange-red in autumn. The upright panicles of yellow flowers are typical chestnut 'candles' and appear in late spring and early summer, followed by smooth rounded fruit. The flowers are scented.

USES Where there is enough space it makes a fine specimen tree on a lawn, with plenty of room to develop to maturity. Branches of 'sticky buds' cut in spring and brought inside will open in water.

CULTIVATION The main requirement is a good, deep soil, not too limy. Like all trees and shrubs with colourful autumn leaves, if they are to last at all, a position sheltered from the prevailing autumn wind is needed.

PROPAGATION The seeds should be collected and sown as soon as they fall in autumn. They should not be planted too deep.

PESTS AND DISEASES Leaf spot can be a problem. Small discoloured spots gradually spread, turning the leaf brown all over so that it withers.

OTHER VARIETIES The most reliable horse chestnut for chalky soil is *Aesculus indica* AGM. It grows to about 9m (30ft) and flowers at midsummer. The flowers are white, flushed with pink and yellow, and the fruit are smooth-coated conkers. The leaves are a soft orange when they first unfurl. Where conkers are a nuisance, the barren, pink-flowered *A. x carnea* 'Plantierensis' is the one to choose.

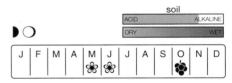

AESCULUS FLAVA

AESCULUS PARVIFLORA

Bottlebrush buckeye, deciduous shrub (Southeastern USA, 1785). Mature at 15 years: 4 x 5m (13 x 16ft).

This shrub spreads by means of suckers from the base, so it usually ends up considerably wider than it is high. The leaves are bronze when young, dark green in summer and yellow in autumn. Panicles of scented, red-centred white flowers appear from mid- to late summer. In spite of its suckering habit it is a graceful shrub. It very occasionally forms a single trunk, making a small tree. Its fruit seldom ripens in Britain.

USES Planted as a single specimen on a lawn, it always attracts attention. It provides food for bees.

CULTIVATION It will grow in clay soil in sun or partial shade.

PROPAGATION It is easily increased by division. Just dig up a sucker with a good bit of root on it.

PESTS AND DISEASES
It is sometimes affected by leaf spot, which spreads until the entire affected leaf withers.

AESCULUS PARVIFLORA

AGAPANTHUS CAMPANULATUS

A

African Blue Lily, deciduous fleshy-rooted perennial (S. Africa c.1870). Mature at 3 years: 60-150cm x 46-60cm (2-5ft x 18-24in).

Headbourne Hybrids, syn. Palmer Hybrids are light and dark blue forms of *A. campanulatus*, and are among the hardiest. They were originally distributed during the 1950s and 1960s from the Hon. Lewis Palmer's garden at Headbourne Worthy in Hampshire. The greyish-green, narrowly strap-shaped leaves have rounded tips and arch slightly. The flowers appear in late summer. They are like numerous small blue trumpets loosely arranged to form a sphere at the top of a tall, smooth stem. They give way to attractive globular green seeds. The name Headbourne Hybrids is now often misapplied to cover a range of seedling stock that varies in colour and quality.

USES Agapanthus are often planted in tubs, where they can remain undisturbed, giving a fine display year after year. In very cold areas the tubs can be brought in during the winter, just to be on the safe side. They look good growing informally out of gravel on a sunny terrace. They also make excellent cut flowers.

CULTIVATION Agapanthus need full sun and shelter, and soil that is reliably moist but nevertheless well drained. In enclosed gardens they tend to lean towards the sun, so if you want them facing forwards, give them a south-facing position. Plant them in groups with about 5cm (2in) of soil above the crowns. Cut flower stems to the ground after flowering.

PROPAGATION The thick fleshy roots increase slowly and can be divided and replanted in spring 5cm (2in) deep. Seeds germinate readily, but seedlings may take two to three years or more to reach flowering size.

PESTS AND DISEASES Generally trouble free.

OTHER VARIETIES There are numerous named cultivars and the best way to choose is to see them in flower. If you intend to grow them outdoors, check that they come from hardy stock. 'Bressingham White' is popular; 'Isis' has flowers of darker blue than many hybrids. The more compact 'Midnight Blue' (to 45cm/18in) is, as its name suggests, one of the darkest.

COMPANIONS
A late summer display of crimson fuchsias alternating with blocks of blue agapanthus stays in my mind. They contrast well with crocosmias, both the orange 'Emily McKenzie' and yellow 'Golden Fleece', syn. 'George Davison', and with kniphofias.

AGAPANTHUS HEADBOURNE HYBRIDS

AJUGA REPTANS, 'ATROPURPUREA'

Bugle, evergreen perennial (Europe, Caucasus to Iran). Mature at 2 years: 15-38 x 45-60cm (6-15 x 18-24in). AGM

For once, 'Atropurpurea' (black-purple) is an accurate description of the leaf colour. The leaves are long and glossy, forming neat, ground-hugging rosettes. In spring and early summer each rosette produces one or more dense spikes of small, blue, tubular flowers with protruding lower lips. Each plant puts out several trailing stems above ground from which new plants grow.

USES Ajugas are among the top dozen ground cover plants, making a complete carpet of leaves.

CULTIVATION Plant in ordinary soil at any time when the ground is not waterlogged or frozen. Ajugas prefer a moist position and will grow in shade. Avoid dry, sunny sites.

PROPAGATION Divide and replant at any time when the soil is in a workable condition.

PESTS AND DISEASES Generally trouble free.

OTHER VARIETIES *A. reptans* 'Catlin's Giant' AGM is a handsome variation on 'Atropurpurea', twice its size and with the same depth of colour. *A. pyramidalis* 'Metallica Crispa' is a very choice variety: the leaves have a metallic sheen and crimped edges. There are several variegated forms including *A. reptans* 'Burgundy Glow' AGM.

COMPANIONS One of the most effective ways to use ajuga is in interlocking drifts of its own cultivars, plain and variegated. They mingle happily with other ground cover: *Lysimachia nummularia* 'Aurea' for a strong contrast with purple-leaved ajugas, *Viola labradorica* to harmonize. The small cultivars are low enough to allow crocuses, species tulips and other small bulbs to grow up through them.

	soil	
	ACID	ALKALINE
	DRY	WET

J	F	M	A	M	J	J	A	S	O	N	D

AJUGA REPTANS 'CATLIN'S GIANT'

AKEBIA QUINATA

Chocolate vine, semi-evergreen climber (Japan, China, Korea, 1845). Mature at 5 years: height 10m (30ft) or more.

The elegant, smooth pale green leaves are carried in a circle of five leaflets. Small dark maroon flowers appear in late spring and have a strong vanilla scent. If more than one plant is grown for pollination, after a hot summer purplish, sausage-shaped fruit will develop.

USES Akebia's vigorous twining habit is well adapted for growing over pergolas and arches, on trellises, fences and wired walls, or rambling over other shrubs or trees. It will flower on a north or east wall, but not so profusely as in full sun.

CULTIVATION Plant in fertile loamy soil, placing a cane to guide the shoots towards their support. The stems will twine around any cane, wire, or small branch they come into contact with. Initially, coax them in the right direction to give good coverage. Once established akebias resent disturbance of their roots. If necessary, prune after flowering to reduce rampant growth.

PROPAGATION Akebias root easily from layers made in winter. They can also be grown from seeds sown in autumn or spring, or from semi-ripe cuttings taken in summer and raised in gentle heat.

PESTS AND DISEASES Trouble free.

	soil	
	ACID	ALKALINE
	DRY	WET

J	F	M	A	M	J	J	A	S	O	N	D

AKEBIA QUINATA

ALCEA ROSEA

Syn. Althaea rosea. Hollyhock, biennial or short-lived perennial (Probably Western Asia, before 1573). Mature at 2 years: up to 2.4m x 60cm (8 x 2ft).

Tall erect stems emerge from clumps of large rounded, rough-textured leaves. Single or very double flowers in a range of colours, including pink, yellow, cream and almost black, appear all the way up the stems in summer and early autumn.

USES Hollyhocks are an indispensable component of the traditional cottage garden. The tall flowering stems make them useful as a temporary screen, or to give height at the back of a new border until more permanent plants have developed.

CULTIVATION Hollyhocks do well in heavy but well-drained soil and in full sun. In a really sheltered position you may get away without staking, but it is wise to do so as a precaution. Mulch with well-rotted manure or compost and water well in dry periods.

PROPAGATION Sow seeds outdoors in a seed bed in the summer and move plants to their final position in autumn. Hollyhocks can be treated as annuals by sowing in early spring in heat, or directly in the site in late spring, thinning the seedlings to 38cm (15in) apart.

PESTS AND DISEASES Caterpillars and capsid bugs can nibble the leaves. Rust is often a serious problem even on plants grown from seed described as 'from rust-free stock'. Rusty spots disfigure the leaves, which sometimes shrivel up. In the worst cases the plant dies. Reduce the risk of infection by growing new plants each year. Young plants flower best in any case.

COMPANIONS Assuming the worst, plant *Crambe cordifolia*, or groups of other plants with large or dense leaves in front of your hollyhocks to hide rust-infested leaves.

	soil	
	ACID	ALKALINE
	DRY	WET

J	F	M	A	M	J	J	A	S	O	N	D

ALCEA ROSEA

A

(handwritten note overlaid at top left: "Hollyhock Althaea rosea P.66 any — Moe")

P.66

ians,
re at
). AGM

Alchemilla
ans with
mounded
ny lime-
mmer.

ground cover
or edging
f space,
seed itself
vel paths and
ants to which
er arrangers' is
an also be dried.

or shade in any
ss you want it to
the flowering
. Tidy the plants
ng by cutting the
se.

s in spring, or
divide a_____ y time from early
autumn until spring, transplant self-sown
seedlings when small; they rapidly develop
a deep root.

PESTS AND DISEASES Trouble free.

COMPANIONS The leaves enhance virtually
any neighbour and are particularly
satisfying with white, yellow, blue and
purple flowers.

OTHER VARIETIES *A. alpina*, 15 x 60cm
(6 x 24in), is a pretty miniature version of
A. mollis. *A. conjuncta* is a small treasure
with darker green leaves edged with the
narrowest possible thread of silver. Both of
these have fine silver, silky hair on the
undersides of the leaves.

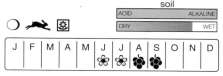

		soil	
ACID			ALKALINE
DRY			WET

J	F	M	A	M	J	J	A	S	O	N	D

ALCHEMILLA MOLLIS

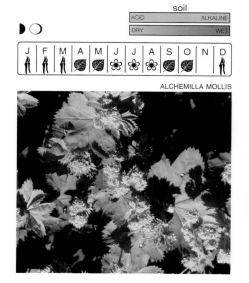

ALLIUM CHRISTOPHII

Syn. **A. albopilosum, A. christophii,
bulbous perennial (Turkestan, 1901).
Mature at 1 year: 30-60 x 15-20cm
(12-24 x 6-8in). AGM**

A summer-flowering bulb with rather
untidy, hairy grey strap-shaped leaves that
droop at their tips. Luckily they go
un-noticed once the spectacular spherical
flower heads are in bloom. The flower
globes are composed of numerous close-
packed metallic pinkish-mauve stars, each
with six long narrow points.

USES Like most alliums *A. cristophii* is an
excellent cut flower and dries well, both at
the flowering stage and after the seeds have
developed.

CULTIVATION Alliums do best in well-
drained soil in full sun. Plant the bulbs in
autumn, covering them with soil to three or
four times their own depth.

PROPAGATION After several years flowering
performance deteriorates and clumps can be
lifted and divided, either in autumn or as
growth starts in the spring. Replant each
bulb immediately and keep the soil moist, or
sow seeds from autumn through to spring.

PESTS AND DISEASES Generally trouble free,
but young shoots, leaves and stems may be
eaten by slugs. White rot may cause the
leaves to turn yellow and die back, the roots
to rot and a white fluffy fungus to form on
the bulb's base.

OTHER VARIETIES The allium family
includes leeks, onions, shallots, garlic and
chives (see *A. schoenoprasum*). Worthwhile
hardy species with ornamental flowers
include *A. aflatunense*, with 100cm (3ft 3in)
stems and purple flower heads the size of
tennis balls, *A. cernuum*, with 45cm (18in)
stems bearing hanging clusters of bright
purple-pink flowers, and *A. flavum* AGM, to
35cm (14in) tall, with rosettes of grey-blue
leaves and yellow bell-shaped flowers.

COMPANIONS Plant with grey-leaved
dicentras for similar colouring, but
contrasting shape and texture. The
colouring and strong shape of alliums make
them good companions for shrub roses.

		soil	
ACID			ALKALINE
DRY			WET

J	F	M	A	M	J	J	A	S	O	N	D

ALLIUM CHRISTOPHII

A

ALLIUM SCHOENOPRASUM

Chives, bulbous perennial (Europe, Asia, N. America). Mature at 1 year: 12-25 x 5-10cm (5-10 x 2-4in).

A clump-forming, summer-flowering bulb with very narrow hollow, grass-like dark green leaves. Bare stems hold the pale purple flowers just above the leaves in numerous densely packed little pompons.

USES Chives are one of the most useful kitchen herbs. Using scissors, the fresh, raw leaves can be snipped into salads and soups. The tidy leaves and pretty flowers make chives good front row or edging plants, especially for a herb garden. They do well in window boxes and pots and the flowers are well worked by bees.

CULTIVATION Plant in any reasonable soil in sun or partial shade. In containers, use loam-based or loamless compost. Chives need frequent watering during dry spells. To encourage fresh young leaves to sprout, cut one or two plants to the ground before they flower, and do the same to other plants when the flowers start to fade. The leaves die during winter but reappear the following spring. Clumps protected by cloches throughout the winter will produce leaves by early spring.

PROPAGATION Sow seeds outdoors in spring, or divide overgrown clumps.

PESTS AND DISEASES Generally trouble free, but rust sometimes attacks the leaves.

COMPANIONS The distinctive vertical leaves are invaluable as a contrast to most other foreground plants, especially violas with blue, violet, or pale yellow flowers. Plant chives in front of *Nepeta racemosa*.

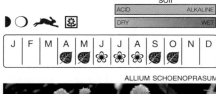

ALLIUM SCHOENOPRASUM

ALNUS CORDATA

Italian alder, deciduous tree (S. Italy, 1820). Mature at 30 years: 12m (40ft) after 20 years; 20 x 10m (65 x 33ft). AGM

A fast-growing pyramidal tree, *A. cordata* is one of the best alders, with lustrous heart-shaped, deep green leaves and clusters of yellow catkins in late winter and early spring. The rough-textured, egg-shaped fruit are held erect and stay on the tree throughout winter.

USES The Italian alder will grow almost anywhere, in wet and dry soils, in sun and shade, on chalk, clay or sand and on both acid and alkaline soils. As it is also fast-growing it is invaluable for planting in industrial or polluted areas, and on sites consolidated by machines and then reclaimed. It fixes nitrogen in the soil. Like all alders, it looks very at home by the waterside.

CULTIVATION Plant in autumn in any of the situations described above.

PROPAGATION Surface sow seed as soon as it is ripe in late autumn, in an open frame. Take hardwood cuttings in winter.

PESTS AND DISEASES May suffer from *Phytophthera* root rot.

OTHER SPECIES *Alnus rubra*, the red alder, imported from Western North America in the 19th century, shares many of the qualities of *A. cordata*.

COMPANIONS Other plants that will tolerate difficult conditions almost as well, besides other alders, include birch, hawthorn, cotoneasters, elder, willow and any of the shrubby potentillas.

ALNUS CORDATA

ALOYSIA TRIPHYLLA

Syn Lippia citriodora. Lemon verbena, vervain, tender deciduous shrub (Argentine, Chile late 18th century). Mature at 15 years: up to 3 x 2.5m (10 x 8ft).

Although it will only survive winter out of doors in very mild climates, I include lemon verbena for the sake of the refreshing lemon scent of the leaves when they are crushed. They are pale green, long and pointed, with a pronounced central vein. They grow on a fairly open branched bush. In late summer tiny mauve-pink flowers are borne in loose clusters at the ends of the stems.

USES Fresh or dried leaves can be infused to make herbal tea, or to flavour cakes and sweets. They are a useful ingredient of potpourri. Lemon verbena can be grown in a pot indoors or out. Plant it in a position where you can pinch a leaf to release the fragrance as you pass.

CULTIVATION Lemon verbena can only be grown out of doors in areas that are almost frost free, and even then it needs the protection of a south-facing wall. It must have good drainage and the growth will be hardier in quite poor alkaline soil. Otherwise it should be grown in a pot, in general purpose compost, and watered sparingly. Bring it into a frost-free greenhouse or room for the winter and in spring prune the branches back by one third to a half, and spray the plant with warm water to encourage new growth.

PROPAGATION Take softwood cuttings during the summer.

PESTS AND DISEASES Generally trouble free except for the usual greenhouse pests such as whitefly.

COMPANIONS Grow a cocktail of fruity scents together: lemon verbena, pineapple broom, pineapple sage, cherry pie and apple-scented sweetbrier.

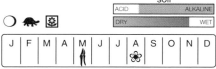

ALOYSIA TRIPHYLLA

ALSTROEMERIA LIGTU HYBRIDS

A

Peruvian lily, tuberous perennial (Chile, mid 18th century). Mature at 3 years: 120 x 45cm (4ft x 18in). AGM

Bare wiry stems with heads of lily-like flowers at their tips are borne above twisted, strap-shaped leaves. The flowers come in varying shades of pink, yellow and soft orange, often spotted or streaked with contrasting colours.

USES A valuable component of herbaceous or mixed borders, flowering from early to midsummer, and essential in a cutting border. They can also be grown in pots as a terrace or conservatory plant.

CULTIVATION Plant in late summer or spring, in a sunny position sheltered from wind, in well-drained soil. Leave undisturbed for several years. Damage to the roots on planting is a common cause of failure. Plant pot grown plants carefully, taking care not to disturb the roots. They can be planted in a hollow and earthed up as they develop. They look best in groups of at least seven; set at 30 cm (12 in) apart. Protect with a thick mulch for the first winter or two. Support with twiggy pea sticks, or with horizontal mesh.

PROPAGATION Sow seeds in early spring in sandy compost in a cold frame; plant out the following spring. Alternatively divide in spring or autumn and replant immediately. To obtain greater numbers, carefully separate individual roots, pot them up and grow on in a cold frame; plant out about one year later.

PESTS AND DISEASES Slugs may eat the tender young shoots. Swift moth caterpillars may damage the roots and the growing points. Virus diseases cause yellow mottling and distortion.

OTHER VARIETIES *A. aurea*, syn. *A. aurantiaca*, has flamboyant orange flowers.

COMPANIONS The Ligtu Hybrids associate well with roses of similar shades such as 'Buff Beauty' AGM, 'Cornelia' AGM, and 'Apricot Nectar'. They also show to great advantage next to *Philadelphus* 'Sybille' and 'Belle Etoile', both AGM, or *Nepeta* 'Six Hills Giant'.

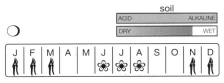

ALSTROEMERIA AUREA

ALSTROEMERIA LIGTU HYBRIDS

AMELANCHIER LAMARCKII

Snowy mespilus, June berry, deciduous tree or shrub (N. America, late 16th century). Mature at 15 years: 5 x 4m 17 x 13ft) after 10 years; 6 x 5m (20 x 17ft) at maturity. AGM

A large shrub or small tree, usually multi-stemmed, but it can be trained as a standard. The leaves are silky and coppery when young, becoming smooth and mid-green. They turn to glowing orange-red in autumn. Profuse star-shaped flowers, white, or slightly flushed with pink, are borne in spring, followed by round black, sweet-tasting berries, which ripen in midsummer.

CULTIVATION Plant in autumn in any good garden soil that does not dry out, in a sunny or partially shaded position. To train as a single stemmed tree, remove all side shoots gradually during the first few years.

PROPAGATION Remove suckers from the base of the shrub, or layer shoots from near the base by pegging them down in spring. By autumn the layered shoots should have made sufficient roots to sever them from the parent, then plant out and grow on.

PESTS AND DISEASES Generally trouble free. Fireblight can cause blackening and shrivelling on the flowers.

COMPANIONS Amelanchier coincides in its flowering time with spring bulbs. The slight pinkish tinge to both leaves and flowers is better complemented by an underplanting of blue scillas, chionodoxas, or *Anemone blanda*, than by yellow narcissus.

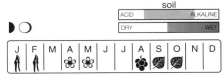

AMELANCHIER LAMARCKII

A

ANAPHALIS TRIPLINERVIS 'SOMMERSCHNEE'

Syn. 'Summer Snow'. Pearl everlasting, herbaceous perennial. Mature at 3 years: 38 x 60cm (15 x 24in). AGM

The plants form compact, slowly spreading mounds of short spear-shaped grey leaves covered with white woolly hairs, giving an overall silvery effect. Small clusters of white everlasting flowers, papery in texture, are carried at the top of the stems from late summer onwards.

USES Anaphalis is the only grey-leaved plant I know of that is happy growing in shade as well as sun. It is an invaluable edging or foreground plant in a shady border. If cut for the house it will last through the winter, or it can be dried.

CULTIVATION Plant in sun or shade, in any moisture-retentive but well-drained soil. Cut the flower stems to the ground in autumn or spring. If they become untidy during summer, or grow too tall for their neighbours, they can be cut back hard and will produce fresh foliage.

PROPAGATION Divide the clumps at any time between autumn and spring, or take cuttings of basal shoots in spring. Anaphalis species can also be raised from seeds sown in spring and placed in a cold frame.

PESTS AND DISEASES Generally trouble free.

COMPANIONS Use anaphalis in grey foliage schemes, contrasting its texture with *Stachys byzantina*, syn. *S. olympica*, santolina and artemisia. In the shade, plant it to contrast with the shiny dark evergreen leaves of bergenias, or as a foreground to foxgloves and *Campanula persicifolia*.

soil

ACID	ALKALINE
DRY	WET

J	F	M	A	M	J	J	A	S	O	N	D

ANAPHALIS TRIPLINERVIS

ANCHUSA AZUREA

A. anchusa, syn. A. italica, hardy perennial (S. Europe, N. Africa, W. Asia, 1597). Mature at 3 years: 90 x 60cm (3ft x 2ft).

A. anchusa 'Loddon Royalist' AGM, is one of the few flowers of true royal blue without a hint of mauve or purple. The flat single, deep blue flowers are born on upright, branching spikes in early summer. The lance-shaped leaves are coarse and hairy and grow mainly at the base of the plant, so the brilliance of the flowers is not obscured.

USES This species of anchusa is an almost obligatory component of the traditional herbaceous border.

CULTIVATION Plant in full sun, in any reasonable soil. Provide support soon after the leaves emerge in spring, using pea sticks or netting pegged out horizontally. Removing the upper halves of the stems after flowering may result in a second crop of flowers. In autumn, cut the whole plant down to the ground. Young plants produce the best flowers, so propagate new stock every few years.

PROPAGATION Take root cuttings during the dormant season between autumn and spring.

PESTS AND DISEASES Cucumber mosaic virus sometimes disfigures the leaves with yellow spots.

OTHER VARIETIES 'Little John' is a compact form, 45 x 30cm (18 x 12in), with deep blue flowers. 'Opal' has sky blue flowers.

COMPANIONS Plant with pale yellow lupins and/or *Achillea* 'Taygetea' for a very pure, clear contrast.

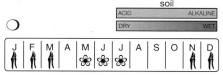

soil

ACID	ALKALINE
DRY	WET

J	F	M	A	M	J	J	A	S	O	N	D

ANCHUSA AZUREA

ANEMONE BLANDA 'ATROCAERULEA'

Tuberous perennial (S.E. Europe and Turkey). Mature at 1 year: 5-10 x 10-15cm (2-4 x 4-6in).

The clear blue flowers with pale cream-yellow stamens appear in early spring. They are like wide-open, blue daisies with many narrow petals. The green leaves have three deeply toothed lobes.

USES If planted in sparse grass under deciduous trees or shrubs, *A. blanda* will gradually spread to form a dense colony. It can also be used to underplant roses and other shrubs in more formal situations, providing interest before the shrubs get into their stride.

CULTIVATION Plant in autumn in any good well-drained soil in sun or partial shade. Bury the knobbly tubers 5cm (2in) deep. It is impossible to tell which way up they should go and it does not matter.

PROPAGATION Separate the offsets, or divide the tubers after the top growth has died down in late summer. Sow seeds in late summer or simply allow the plants to seed themselves; cultivars may produce offspring of variable colour.

PESTS AND DISEASES Flea beetles sometimes attack young seedlings. Older plants may be eaten by caterpillars, various cutworms, aphids or slugs. Several virus diseases can cause problems, including arabis mosaic and cucumber mosaic. Cluster-cup rust causes malformation of the leaves.

OTHER CULTIVARS 'Radar' AGM has showy, deep pink petals with white centres; 'White Splendour' AGM is all white except for the yellow stamens. *A. nemorosa* can be naturalized in wooded areas.

COMPANIONS Best planted alone in large groups or drifts.

ANEMONE BLANDA 'ATROCAERULEA'

ANEMONE NEMOROSA

ANEMONE X HYBRIDA 'HONORINE JOBERT'

A

Syn. A. japonica 'Honorine Jobert', perennial (1858). Mature at 3 years: 150 x 60cm (5ft x 2ft). AGM

One of the most beautiful plants for late summer and early autumn, this Japanese anemone makes a clump of large handsome vine-like leaves. The flower buds are smooth, grey-green buttons poised on smooth, slender but strong, branching stems which seldom need staking in spite of their height. The saucer-shaped, pristine white flowers have yellow stamens.

USES Plant Japanese anemones in herbaceous borders or between shrubs. They are also ideal for transitional areas between fairly formal plantings and the woodland or wild garden. They make good cut flowers.

CULTIVATION Plant in fertile, well-drained but moisture-retentive soil. The seed heads and leaves are attractive until the frost shrivels and browns them, then you can cut them down to the ground. Japanese anemones are slow starters; there is no need to worry if they don't do much in the first year or two.

PROPAGATION Divide and replant from autumn to spring, or take root cuttings during the winter.

PESTS AND DISEASES May suffer leaf spots and powdery mildew in dry summers.

OTHER CULTIVARS There are various single and double-flowered variants in white and shades of purplish pink. *A. x hybrida* 'Königin Charlotte', 120 x 60cm (4 x 2ft) AGM, has large, rose-pink, semi-double flowers with rounded petals.

COMPANIONS Japanese anemones overlap with Michaelmas daisies and with the second burst of flowers of the hybrid musk roses 'Buff Beauty', 'Cornelia' and 'Felicia'. The white-flowered cultivars look good with *Crocosmia masonorum*.

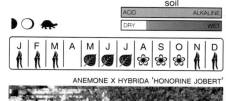

ANEMONE X HYBRIDA 'HONORINE JOBERT'

ANGELICA ARCHANGELICA

Angelica, Holy Ghost, short-lived perennial usually grown as a biennial (Europe). Mature at 2 years: 2 x 1m (6 x 3ft).

A statuesque plant with large deeply divided bright green leaves. In the second year, large umbels of tiny green-white flowers are carried on smooth, ridged stems in late summer.

USES The stems can be used to flavour sweets and drinks, and crystallized for decorating cakes. The flowers and seed heads are good for cutting and for drying.

CULTIVATION Plant in spring in sun or light shade, in moist humus-rich soil.

PROPAGATION The plants usually die after flowering and producing seeds, but the seeds germinate easily and plenty of seedlings spring up around each plant. If you make two initial plantings in consecutive years, you will never be without a few plants. If you don't want to leave it to chance, buy or gather seed and sow it outdoors in spring. Move the young plants to their final planting position when they are sturdy.

PESTS AND DISEASES Generally trouble free.

COMPANIONS Where there is plenty of space, angelica associates well with other umbelliferous herbs such as fennel and dill. It can hold its own with big, bold plants such as hostas and acanthus.

soil		
ACID		ALKALINE
DRY		WET

J	F	M	A	M	J	J	A	S	O	N	D

ANGELICA ARCHANGELICA

ANTHEMIS PUNCTATA SSP. CUPANIANA

Perennial (Italy, Sicily). Mature at 3 years: 30 x 30cm (12 x 12in). AGM

A fast-growing evergreen, carpeting perennial with finely-cut foliage, silver-grey in summer, grey-green in winter. White daisy flower heads with yellow centres are borne singly on short, bare stems in early summer and intermittently until autumn.

USES An excellent plant to give quick cover in newly planted areas, especially in poor stony soil, in gravel or on rocky terrain. Good for cutting.

CULTIVATION Plant in full sun in any well-drained soil. After the first flush of flowering clip over the plants to keep them dense and tidy and to encourage another crop of flowers.

PROPAGATION Take cuttings of young basal shoots in late spring or early summer, or divide and replant the roots between early autumn and spring.

PESTS AND DISEASES Generally trouble free.

COMPANIONS Many other plants that like a sunny well-drained position are also grey-leaved: lavenders, santolinas, *Convolvulus cneorum* AGM. Avoid monotony by adding some dark-leaved cistus.

soil		
ACID		ALKALINE
DRY		WET

J	F	M	A	M	J	J	A	S	O	N	D

ANTHEMIS PUNCTATA SPP. CUPANIANA

ANTHEMIS TINCTORIA

Dyer's camomile, ox-eye chamomile, golden marguerite, perennial (Europe, 1561). Mature at 2 years: 1 x 1m (3 x 3ft).

The cultivar *A. tinctoria* 'E.C. Buxton' makes a dense mound of finely-cut, ferny green leaves. Masses of pale yellow daisies are borne singly on slim stems from mid-summer until the first frosts.

USES This is quite the best shade of yellow for mixing with other colours in beds and borders and in cut flower arrangements.

CULTIVATION Plant in autumn or spring, in full sun in ordinary soil. The flowering stems tend to flop around, so provide support with pea sticks or wire netting stretched horizontally. To save staking, when the new season's growth is about 30cm (12in) high cut it to the ground. The second crop of stems will be just as sturdy and flower just as well but they will remain shorter. If you cut the stems and leaves right back after flowering it encourages a clump of evergreen leaves for the winter.

PROPAGATION Divide or take basal cuttings of new young shoots in spring.

PESTS AND DISEASES Usually trouble free.

OTHER CULTIVARS The flowers of *A. tinctoria* 'Wargrave' are a paler, more creamy yellow.

COMPANIONS Use the pale yellow flowers to cool the strong crimsons and magentas of border phlox and to complement *Campanula lactiflora*, eryngiums and salvias.

soil

| ACID | | | | | | | | | ALKALINE |
| DRY | | | | | | | | | WET |

| J | F | M | A | M | J | J | A | S | O | N | D |

ANTHEMIS TINCTORIA 'E.C. BUXTON'

ANTIRRHINUM MAJUS

Snapdragon, half-hardy to hardy perennial, usually treated as an annual (Mediterranean, naturalized in some parts of Britain). Mature at 4 months: they are grouped according to height: tall 60-90 x 30-45cm (24-36 x 12-18in); intermediate 45 x 45cm (18 x 18in); dwarf 20-30 x 30cm (8-12 x 12in).

The ease with which antirrhinums can be grown, their prolific flowers, long season and the wide range of sizes and colours make them popular and much-loved plants. Children love the individual snapdragon flowers which can be manipulated to 'bite' one's finger. The flower shape can be regular (tubular); penstemon (trumpet-shaped); irregular (tubular) or double. The flower petals are velvety; colours include white, pink, red, purple, yellow, orange and salmon. The flowers are borne from spring until autumn in branching spires. The stout stems rise out of a cluster of narrow lance-shaped leaves.

USES Antirrhinums are popular and useful bedding plants. They can also be grown in the greenhouse as pot plants to flower at any time of the year. If they are grown outdoors in pots they can be planted out to fill mid- to late summer gaps in beds and borders.

CULTIVATION Plant in spring, in ordinary garden soil in a sunny position. Well-drained, light to medium soil enriched with well-rotted manure gives the very best

results, but antirrhinums tolerate dry conditions and will even seed themselves in cracks in walls. When the plants are settled in their growing position, pinch out the tips to encourage bushy growth. Dead-head regularly.

PROPAGATION Sow seeds under glass at 16-18°C (61-64°F) in early spring, or in late summer and early autumn for greenhouse pot plants.

PESTS AND DISEASES Aphids may infest the young shoots. Plants can be susceptible to damping-off, downy mildew, rust and other fungal diseases.

soil

| ACID | | | | | | | | | ALKALINE |
| DRY | | | | | | | | | WET |

| J | F | M | A | M | J | J | A | S | O | N | D |

ANTIRRHINUM

ANTIRRHINUM

A

APPLE

Malus sylvestris var. domestica, *grafted, deciduous tree. Forms grown for orchard fruit are described here; for ornamental crab apples, see* Malus. *Mature at 20 years.*

Orchard apple trees are usually grown for their fruit, but are also in the first rank for their prolific, pink-and-white spring blossom. Grown as dwarf bush forms, columns or 'step-over' cordons, they are strong candidates for inclusion in even the smallest of gardens. A standard tree will reach about 4.5-6 m (15-20ft), by as much across; half standards to 3.6-4.5m (12-15ft), depending on soil type and rootstock.

USES Apples are usually described as cookers (used in pies, tarts, compôtes and sauces), or as eaters (dessert apples). They are amenable to training as tunnels, free-standing ornamental shapes or as espaliers and cordons.

CULTIVATION Plant from autumn to spring in almost any but shallow, chalky or water-logged soil. Apples grow and fruit best in sun, in deep well-drained but retentive soil, in a site sheltered from spring frosts and strong winds. Avoid coastal sites. Prune trained trees to maintain shape by shortening side shoots by 10-15cm (4-6in), in late summer, further reducing them to 2-5cm (1-2in) in winter. Prune bushes and standards in winter to keep the centre open and remove dead, diseased and crossing branches. Mulch apple trees in spring with farmyard manure or top-dress them with a general fertilizer.

PROPAGATION By budding or grafting on to an appropriate rootstock.

PESTS AND DISEASES Birds, codling moth, apple sawfly larvae, aphids and caterpillars can all be troublesome, and diseases include canker, mildew and scab. The cultivars recommended are generally trouble free.

GOOD VARIETIES These will cross-pollinate and are recommended for their healthy, robust growth and for their flavour. Cookers: 'Bramley' is still unbeatable. It needs two pollinators chosen from the following eaters: 'Discovery', 'Fiesta', 'Greensleeves', 'James Grieve', 'Sunset'.

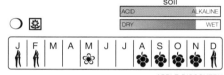

APPLE DISCOVERY

APPLE DISCOVERY

AQUILEGIA ALPINA

Alpine columbine, hardy perennial (Europe). Mature at 2 years: 45x 15cm (18 x 6in).

Wonderfully versatile, although short-lived, flowering prolifically in sun or shade in early summer. The smooth rounded finely divided basal leaves are beautiful in themselves. Above them, slender but strong stems carry clear blue or violet-blue flowers with short spurs.

USES Plant in mixed or herbaceous borders to bridge the gap between tulips and roses, or naturalize in thin grass under trees, or under a hedge. They make good cut flowers.

CULTIVATION Plant in sun or light shade, in ordinary soil, ideally rich, moist but well-drained. If possible choose a position where they can be left to self-seed. Otherwise, cut down the stems immediately after flowering, and the leaves in autumn.

PROPAGATION Move self-sown seedlings or sow seeds in a cold frame in late summer or early spring. Divide at any time between autumn and spring.

OTHER VARIETIES The elegant *A. longissima*, an American native, has exceptionally long-spurred yellow flowers. *A. vulgaris*, the 'Granny's bonnet' of cottage gardens, seeds promiscuously, producing variable flowers in a colour range from black-purple through mauve, or crimson to pink and white. 'Nora Barlow' AGM, has very double, shaggy heads of pink, white and green petals. The Vervaeneana Group have cream and gold mottled leaves. Taller hybrid strains, to 90cm (3ft), have long-spurred, two-coloured flowers: white with blue or purple; yellow with red or pink.

COMPANIONS Columbines make their own colour combinations by hybridizing and self-seeding. If planted among roses, their flowers will fade as the roses begin to bloom, and can then be cut.

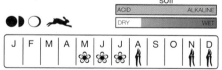

AQUILEGIA

ARALIA ELATA 'VARIEGATA'

Syn. A. chinensis 'Variegata'. Japanese angelica tree, deciduous shrub (Japan, Korea, Manchuria and Russia, 1830). Mature at 10 years: 3 x 3m (10 x 10ft) after 10 years; 3.5 x 3m (11.5 x 10ft) at maturity.

This is a very choice shrub and, because it is difficult to propagate, is expensive to buy. Spectacular leaves up to 90cm (3ft) long are composed of numerous paired leaflets with creamy-white margins. They unfold in late spring on thick spiny stems. In late summer and autumn huge panicles, 30-60cm (1-2ft) long, of fluffy cream-white flowers are carried at the top of each stem. The ultimate size depends on the site; in ideal growing conditions aralias can become small trees.

USES To make the most of their architectural shape, use aralias as focal points in a shrub border, or as single specimens on a lawn. The green-leaved type can withstand industrial pollution.

CULTIVATION Variegated forms are only moderately hardy, so plant in spring rather than autumn, in fertile soil. The huge leaves can be badly torn and scorched by cold winds, so choose a sheltered position. Green stems may shoot from the rootstock. They are more vigorous than the variegated stems and may dominate the plant; remove them as soon as they appear. Avoid pruning as this can stimulate suckers around the base, which will be the plain green leaved type.

PROPAGATION Variegated forms can only be propagated by grafting on to the species rootstock.

OTHER VARIETIES *A. elata*, the plain green species, is fast-growing. It makes a dramatic impact where there is plenty of space. 'Aureovariegata' has yellow margins to the leaves.

soil

ACID		ALKALINE
DRY		WET

J	F	M	A	M	J	J	A	S	O	N	D
							❀	❀			

ARALIA ELATA

ARALIA ELATA

ARBUTUS UNEDO

A

Killarney strawberry tree, evergreen tree (Mediterranean and S.W. Ireland). Mature at 30 years: 2.5 x 1.5m (8 x 5ft) after 10 years; 4.5-6 x 3-5M (15-20 x 10-16.5ft) at maturity. AGM

This is the hardiest and most versatile of the genus *Arbutus*. It is slow-growing and usually forms a shrub rather than a tree in the garden, but, in time, develops a wide spreading crown of glossy rich green leaves on branches with rough, peeling brown bark. The small pendent, urn-shaped white flowers appear in autumn and winter, at the same time as the previous season's strawberry-like red fruit.

USES *A. unedo* makes a good seaside screen or windbreak, as it withstands salt-laden winds. It will grow in areas that are affected by industrial pollution.

CULTIVATION Plant in spring in fertile loam, with shelter from cold north and east winds. Young plants are rather tender so protect them for the first few winters by wrapping them in bracken or straw. They become hardier as they mature. *A. unedo* is lime-tolerant, as are *A. x andrachnoides*, and the slightly more tender *A. andrachne*.

PROPAGATION Sow seeds in spring in sandy compost, or take heeled semi-ripe cuttings in late summer.

PESTS AND DISEASES Leaf spot shows as small brown spots on the foliage.

OTHER VARIETIES *A. x andrachnoides* has the bonus of decorative red-brown stems revealed by the peeling bark. *A. menziesii*, which needs acid soil, has silky smooth, golden-olive stems beneath flaking, chestnut-red bark. Both have received an AGM.

COMPANIONS Keep underplanting low so that the shape of the tree can be appreciated.

soil

ACID		ALKALINE
DRY		WET

J	F	M	A	M	J	J	A	S	O	N	D
❀	❀	🍃	🍃	🍃	🍃	🍃	🍃	🍃	🍃	❀	❀

ARBUTUS ANDRACHNOIDES

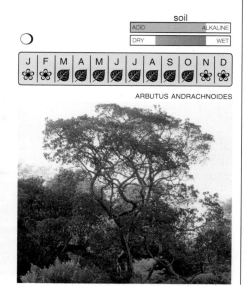

A

ARGYRANTHEMUM

Syn. Chrysanthemum frutescens. Marguerite, Paris daisy, evergreen shrub (Canary Islands, 1699). Mature at 5 years: 90 x 90cm (3 x 3ft).

This compact bush has elegantly divided leaves and is covered throughout summer and most of autumn with pretty pink, white or yellow daisies held up well above the leaves on slender leafless stalks.

USES Marguerites are among the most trustworthy summer bedding plants for pots and tubs. If they are dead-headed regularly they seldom fail to provide a long and colourful display. In autumn when frost threatens them in the garden they can be brought indoors and will continue to flower for a few weeks. In very mild areas they may survive the winter in a sheltered corner.

CULTIVATION In early summer when there is no danger of frost, set out young plants in ordinary soil in beds or borders, or in general purpose compost in containers. Water them in dry spells, adding a liquid feed every two weeks or so. Cut off all dead flower stems regularly. At the end of the season the plants can either be discarded or potted up, cut back and overwintered in a cold frame or frost-free greenhouse. Use them for cuttings or plant them out in summer for a second season.

PROPAGATION Take cuttings in winter in a mixture of half compost, half sand, at a temperature of 10-13°C (50-55°F).

PESTS AND DISEASES Generally trouble free. However the flowers sometimes attract aphids.

GOOD VARIETIES Several double and single named varieties are available, including the following: 'Snowstorm' (white); 'Jamaica Primrose' AGM; 'Cornish Gold' and 'Penny' (single yellow); 'Vancouver' AGM (single pale pink), and 'Mary Wootton' (double pale pink).

COMPANIONS In pots and tubs mix marguerites with trailing petunias and lobelias.

		soil		
ACID				ALKALINE
DRY				WET

J	F	M	A	M	J	J	A	S	O	N	D

ARGYRANTHEMUM 'JAMAICA PRIMROSE'

ARGYRANTHEMUM 'VANCOUVER'

ARMERIA MARITIMA

Sea pink, thrift, hardy evergreen perennial (coastal and mountain habitats, northern hemisphere). Mature at 3 years: 10 x 15cm (4 x 6in).

Thrift is a brave little plant. In its native habitats the tufts of coarse grassy, dark green leaves hug the ground tenaciously on windswept, rocky cliffs. Stiff stems carry round heads of many small white or pink flowers in summer.

USES A trusty plant for open, exposed situations, thrift makes a neat edging plant. It will colonize stony banks or gravel areas.

CULTIVATION Avoid a rich diet; good drainage and full sun are the prerequisites. Plant from autumn to spring. After flowering clip over to remove the faded flower heads and tidy up the grassy clumps.

PROPAGATION Divide in spring, or sow seeds in spring in a cold frame. Cuttings can be rooted in the summer and grown in a cold frame, and large cuttings often root if planted *in situ* in spring or autumn.

PESTS AND DISEASES Generally trouble free, although the plants may sometimes be attacked by rust.

OTHER VARIETIES *A. juniperifolia* 'Bevan's Variety' AGM, is a pretty little plant for the rock garden: little tussocks of darkish grey-green leaves bear almost stemless pink flowers 5cm (2in) high. *A. maritima* 'Alba' has pure white flowers in midsummer; 'Vindictive' AGM, has spheres of dark pink flowers all summer long.

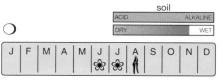

		soil		
ACID				ALKALINE
DRY				WET

J	F	M	A	M	J	J	A	S	O	N	D

ARMERIA MARITIMA

ARTEMISIA ABSINTHIUM

Wormwood, frost-hardy evergreen shrubby perennial (S. Europe). Mature at 3 years: 80 x 50cm (32 x 20in).

'Lambrook Silver' AGM, is one of the best garden cultivars. Masses of finely-divided, aromatic, silvery-grey leaves are held on upright branches from a woody base. Plumes of tiny, yellow and silver flower heads appear in summer.

USES Like most grey-leaved plants, artemisias help to bring a Mediterranean atmosphere to sunny courtyards and terraces. They are useful background plants in flower arrangements, and most artemisias dry well.

CULTIVATION Plant artemisias in any sunny well-drained site that is reasonably sheltered. They are excellent plants for sandy soil. In cold areas, do not cut down the stems until spring.

PROPAGATION Take softwood or semi-ripe cuttings with a heel, in summer.

PESTS AND DISEASES Aphids sometimes attack the roots, and rust may be a problem occasionally.

OTHER SPECIES *A. abrotanum* AGM, southernwood, lad's love, old man. The sage-green feathery leaves have an aroma that is not to everyone's taste, hence the unflattering English name. The plants soon get leggy if they are not cut back hard every spring, but if this is done, they make a good low hedge about 45cm (18in) high. *A. stelleriana* is low growing with finely-cut, silver-grey leaves. *A.* 'Powis Castle' AGM, is a substantial subshrub, 1 x 1.2m (3 x 4ft) tall, with finely-cut grey-white leaves.

COMPANIONS These silvery-leaved plants are very pretty with old-fashioned roses and with pink and cerise cistus. They are also a good foil for orange flowers: *Lilium* 'Enchantment', or orange poppies.

	soil	
ACID		ALKALINE
DRY		WET

J	F	M	A	M	J	J	A	S	O	N	D

ARTEMISIA STELLERIANA

ARTEMISIA ABSINTHIUM 'LAMBROOK SILVER'

ARUM ITALICUM 'MARMORATUM'

A

Cuckoo pint, lords and ladies, hardy tuberous perennial (S. Europe). Mature at 2 years: 15-25 x 20-30cm (6-10 x 8-12in). AGM

Broad arrowhead leaves, glossy green netted with white or cream veins, emerge in late autumn and remain poised on smooth stems all winter and spring, surviving the frosts. The leaves die down in summer, and in early autumn creamy white flower spathes appear, ripening to provide spikes of shiny red berries. WARNING The berries are poisonous.

USES This arum is one of those invaluable plants that will tolerate quite dense shade, making glossy green and white ground cover in the winter months, just when there is little else to catch the eye. Arums can be naturalized in sparse grass or at the base of hedges. The leaves are useful in winter flower arrangements.

CULTIVATION Plant the tubers in autumn or spring, in any reasonable soil in shade or partial shade.

PROPAGATION In autumn, detach offset tubers. Alternatively, wearing gloves, rub the flesh from the seeds and sow them in a cold frame.

PESTS AND DISEASES Generally trouble free.

OTHER SPECIES *Arum creticum* is a beautiful arum for moist, rich soil in a sheltered sunny position, but it is not reliably hardy. The glossy green leaves are typical of arums and the flower spathes are clear yellow and scented.

COMPANIONS Use the Italian arum to make bold foliage compositions with other shade-tolerant plants; such as bergenias, *Brunnera macrophylla* AGM, *Euphorbia amygdaloides* var. *robbiae* AGM, ivies and pulmonarias.

	soil	
ACID		ALKALINE
DRY		WET

J	F	M	A	M	J	J	A	S	O	N	D

ARUM CRETICUM

A

ARUNCUS DIOICUS

Syn. A. sylvester, Spiraea aruncus, goat's beard, hardy perennial (northern hemisphere, 1633). Mature at 3 years: 2 x 1.2m (6 x 4ft). AGM

The large deeply cut, ferny leaves grow in big clumps. At midsummer the clumps throw up tall, loosely branching plumes of fluffy cream flowers. Male and female plants differ slightly; the males usually have more showy, feathery flowers, but females carry long-lasting ornamental seed heads. Unfortunately, as with so many white and cream coloured flowers, they fade to an unattractive brown.

USES These statuesque plants look right beside water, in ditches and in the bog garden. They can also be used to add height at the back of herbaceous borders.

CULTIVATION *A. dioicus* will grow in almost any soil, dry or moist, and in sun or shade, but it gives its best performance in moist, rich soil and partial shade. The self-sown seedlings of females can be a nuisance, so cut the flower branches down before they set seed unless you are hoping the plants will naturalize.

PROPAGATION Divide and replant in autumn or spring.

PESTS AND DISEASES The larvae of a saw-fly species eat holes in the leaves.

OTHER VARIETIES *A. dioicus* 'Kneiffii' 90 x 50cm (3ft x 20in) is smaller and more elegant with very finely-cut, feathery leaves and smaller flower plumes.

COMPANIONS Tall campanulas, especially in shade, *C. latiloba* and Solomon's Seal (*Polygonatum x hybridum*) contrast well being of almost equal stature. Aruncus is also a good companion for shrub roses of strong pink, red or violet colouring.

ARUNCUS DIOICUS

ASPARAGUS OFFICINALIS

Asparagus, hardy perennial. Maturing after 3 years and remaining productive for between 8 and 20 years.

Asparagus plants are crowns with a fringe of pale, fleshy roots. The edible parts are the new young shoots or spears, which are harvested while they are still tightly in bud.

USES When it was only available for a very short season, asparagus was considered a great delicacy. Even today, when imported asparagus extends the season, it is something of a treat. The spears can be boiled or steamed.

CULTIVATION Asparagus does best on neutral or slightly alkaline soil; acid soils should have lime added. As asparagus is a long term crop, it is worth taking trouble to prepare the ground by thorough weeding, digging and manuring. In early spring dig trenches and set the crowns 30-45cm (12-18in) apart, each on a small mound with the top of the crown 10cm (4in) deep. One-year-old crowns are easiest to handle. Cut only a very few, if any, spears in the first two years so the plants can build up their strength. Cut at least 2.5cm (1in) below the surface. Stop cutting after six weeks in the first spring, and after eight weeks in subsequent years.

PROPAGATION Sow seeds under glass in late winter or outdoors in spring.

PESTS AND DISEASES Slugs and asparagus beetles can do serious damage. Worse still, violet root rot and *Fusarium* root rot may kill the plants and spread to other vegetable crops. If this happens, burn all infected plants and start again on a new site.

GOOD VARIETIES 'Lucullus' is a well-flavoured general purpose variety. 'Giant Mammoth' is recommended for clay soil and 'Connover's Colossal' for light soil.

ASPARAGUS

ASPHODELINE LUTEA

Asphodel, king's spear, hardy perennial (Sicily, 1596). Mature at 3 years: 1-1.2m x 0.6-1m (3-4 x 2-3ft).

Whorls of narrow grassy, grey-green leaves send up thick spikes densely set with star-shaped, fragrant yellow flowers in late spring. After the petals fall the stems are studded with shiny, bright green seed pods.

USES The grassy clumps of glaucous leaves contribute to ground cover schemes and the stems give a strong vertical line in mixed plantings, when in seed as well as when they are in flower.

CULTIVATION Plant in a sunny sheltered position, in fairly dry soil, and even so, be prepared to lose your plants to frost in a hard winter.

PROPAGATION Divide the thick, fleshy roots in early spring, taking care not to damage them. Plants can also be raised from seed sown in autumn or spring.

OTHER VARIETIES *A. liburnica*, which grows to 1m (3ft) tall, has blue-green leaves and pale yellow flowers.

COMPANIONS *A. lutea* and *A. liburnica* associate particularly well with *Thalictrum aquilegifolium*, forming fine foliage contrasts.

ASPHODELINE LUTEA

soil

| ACID | ALKALINE |
| DRY | WET |

| J | F | M | A | M | J | J | A | S | O | N | D |

ASPLENIUM SCOLOPENDRIUM

Syn. **Phyllitis scolopendrium,** **Scolopendrium vulgare.** *Spleenwort, hart's tongue fern, evergreen fern (Europe including Britain). Mature at 3 years: 45-60cm (18-24in).*

A sculptural plant with a fascination out of all proportion to its status as a common wild plant. You can hardly go for a country walk without seeing it in woodland, on a shady bank or even in a wall crevice, but it is always a delight to see how the tightly scrolled young fronds unfurl into shiny broad green straps with slightly ruffled margins.

USES Not only is the hart's tongue fern extremely handsome, but it will even grow in dry shade, a situation where so few plants succeed. Plant it on stony banks or between the roots of trees.

CULTIVATION Plant at any time from autumn to spring in ordinary soil, dry or damp, in partial or full shade. Although they grow well in dry shade once established, water regularly during their first season, and mulch with leaf mould or garden compost. Cut down the dead fronds in autumn.

PROPAGATION When new crowns have formed around the original one, separate them up at any time from autumn to spring. Or sow spores as soon as ripe, on moist compost.

PESTS AND DISEASES Generally trouble free.

OTHER VARIETIES *A. s.* 'Crispum' has exceptionally frilly margins to its fronds. The plants are usually sterile, and can therefore only be vegetatively propagated, which makes them relatively expensive.

COMPANIONS Hart's tongue ferns contrast well with more feathery ferns, including, for positions in dry shade, *Dryopteris* (the Buckler fern) and *Polypodium* cultivars.

	soil	
ACID		ALKALINE
DRY		WET

J	F	M	A	M	J	J	A	S	O	N	D

ASPLENIUM SCOLOPENDRIUM

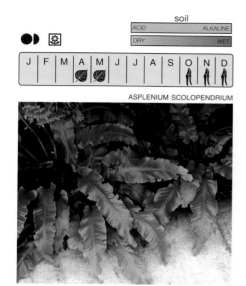

ASTER ERICOIDES

Syn. **A. multiflorus,** *hardy perennial (N. America, 1732). Mature at 3 years: 75 x 30cm (30 x 12in).*

A bushy, upright plant with dull green lance-shaped leaves and wiry branching stems. In autumn the plant produces sprays carrying a multitude of small, long-lasting daisy-like flower heads in white or pale colours.

USES Like other forms of Michaelmas daisy, this aster is an invaluable plant for autumn effect in herbaceous and mixed borders, and is a useful cut flower.

CULTIVATION Plant in spring in sun or partial shade, in any reasonable soil. Keep diseases at bay by keeping the plants fed and watered, and by dividing and replanting them frequently.

PROPAGATION Divide overgrown clumps in the spring.

PESTS AND DISEASES Tarsonemid mites, slugs and caterpillars are occasionally a nuisance. *A. ericoides* is less susceptible than some other asters to fungal diseases such as black root rot, rhizoctonia, powdery mildew and *Verticillium* wilt.

GOOD CULTIVARS 'Blue Star' AGM, 'Brimstone' AGM, 'Erlkönig', 'Golden Spray' AGM, 'Pink Cloud' AGM.

OTHER SPECIES The taller, traditional Michaelmas daisies are tempting, but you may want to rule them out as they are prone to mildew. It is less likely to be a problem if you grow them in rich, moist soil and divide the plants every year. However, if you want to play safe, stick to the following shorter kinds; they are usually disease-free and don't need staking. *Aster amellus* 'King George' AGM, 60 x 50cm (24 x 20in) has large mauve-blue flowers with yellow centres. 'Pink Zenith', 60cm (24in) tall, is clear pink and 'Violet Queen' AGM, is shorter at 30cm (12in), with violet flowers.

COMPANIONS *Agapanthus, Caryopteris x clandonensis,* fuchsias, nerines, sedums.

	soil	
ACID		ALKALINE
DRY		WET

J	F	M	A	M	J	J	A	S	O	N	D

ASTER ERICOIDES

A

A

ASTER X FRIKARTII 'MONCH'

Hardy perennial (Switzerland, 1920). Mature at 3 years: 90 x 38cm (36 x 15in). AGM

Sometimes recommended as the best of all Michaelmas daisies, this one has many excellent qualities. It is in flower continuously from late summer through autumn. Rosettes of rough, oblong dark green leaves produce stems of large bright lavender blue daisy flowers with bright yellow centres.

USES Plant it for its reliable long flowering season and for its charm as a cut flower.

CULTIVATION Plant in spring in a sunny position in good soil. When the flowering stems finally wither, cut them right down to the base.

PROPAGATION Increase by dividing established clumps in spring.

PESTS AND DISEASES Usually trouble free. One of the few Michaelmas daisies that is generally not attacked by mildew.

OTHER VARIETIES *A. x frikartii* 'Wunder von Stäfa' AGM has flowers that are deep violet blue.

COMPANIONS Combined with *Lavatera* 'Rosea', syn. *L. olbia* 'Rosea' AGM, Japanese anemones, penstemons and sedums, asters will keep your garden in colour right up to the first hard frost.

			soil								
			ACID			ALKALINE					
			DRY			WET					

J	F	M	A	M	J	J	A	S	O	N	D

ASTER X FRIKARTII MONCH

ASTILBE X ARENDSII

Hardy perennial (China, Japan, 1933). Mature at 3 years: 60-90 x 60-90cm (2-3ft x 2-3ft).

Astilbes have finely-cut fern-like leaves, either green or reddish bronze. Tiny flowers are carried in loose upright panicles, giving the effect of feathery plumes, lasting from mid-to late summer. In autumn they turn rusty brown and remain on the stems, contributing to the winter scene. Flower colours range from dark crimson-red, through salmon-pink and mauve-pink, to cream and white.

USES Although astilbes are familiar plants in bog gardens and at the water's edge, they can also make a valuable contribution to the herbaceous or mixed border.

CULTIVATION Plant in autumn or spring, in any soil except excessively chalky or clay soils, provided it can be kept damp. Cut the flowered stems down to ground level in autumn, unless you want to leave them for winter effect.

PROPAGATION Divide every three years or so in autumn or spring.

PESTS AND DISEASES Generally trouble free.

GOOD VARIETIES 'Bressingham Beauty' is free-flowering and one of the tallest, with rich pink flowers 90cm (3ft) tall; 'Fanal' AGM, 60 x 90cm (2 x 3ft), has crimson-red flowers; 'Venus', 90cm (3ft) tall, has handsome, pale pink flower trusses. 'Snowdrift', 60cm (2ft), and 'Weisse Gloria', 90cm (3ft), are good whites.

OTHER SPECIES *A. simplicifolia* 'Aphrodite', 35cm (15in), has deep pink flowers and glossy bronze leaves; *A. s.* 'Sprite', 25cm (9in), also has dark foliage with shell pink flowers. *A. s.* 'William Buchanan' has crimson leaves and cream flower spikes. *A.* 'Feuer' is another good species.

COMPANIONS Combine astilbes with hostas and border phlox, which both like the same damp, lightly shaded conditions.

			soil								
			ACID			ALKALINE					
			DRY			WET					

J	F	M	A	M	J	J	A	S	O	N	D

ASTILBE 'FEUER'

ASTRANTIA MAJOR

Masterwort, Hatty's pincushion, hardy perennial (Europe, late 16th century). Mature at 3 years: 60 x 45cm (24 x 18in).

Astrantias are very well-behaved plants; the leaves make handsome, weed-smothering clumps and the stems don't need staking. The mid-green leaves are divided into five serrated fingers and are well poised above the crown. At midsummer several flowers are held upright on smooth branching stems. In close-up, each flower consists of tiny green and white florets radiating from a crimson centre, like pins in a pincushion. Each head is surrounded by a ruff of pink- or green-tipped, off-white bracts.

USES Astrantias are good ground cover plants and make excellent cut flowers.

CULTIVATION Plant at any time between autumn and spring, in groups of three or more 35cm (15in) apart, in ordinary garden soil in sun or partial shade. Water during dry spells if the leaves wilt. After flowering cut the whole plant down to the ground; this will encourage a neat mound of fresh leaves to develop.

PROPAGATION Divide mature clumps in autumn or spring.

PESTS AND DISEASES Generally trouble free.

GOOD CULTIVARS 'Sunningdale Variegated' AGM is one of the best of all variegated plants. In spring the emerging leaves are splashed with rich yellow-cream, making a light, bright mound. The variegation fades to white as the leaves mature. The flowers are white, tinged with green and pink. *A. major var. rubra*, 45cm (18in), has the darkest flowers, which are wine-red, and *A. maxima* AGM has the largest flowers.

COMPANIONS Plant *Viola labradorica* in front of *A. m.* 'Sunningdale Variegated' AGM for a pleasing contrast of purple and cream foliage. *A. m.* var. *rubra* and *A. maxima* mix well with old roses in understated colour schemes.

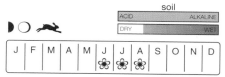

ASTRANTIA MAJOR 'SUNNINGDALE VARIEGATED'

ATHYRIUM FILIX-FEMINA

A

Lady fern, hardy deciduous fern (Europe, including Britain). Mature at 3 years: 45cm-1.2m (18-48in). AGM

The lacy fronds radiating from the central crown are fresh green. They vary in length from 45cm (18in) to 1.2m (4ft), according to the conditions in which they are grown.

USES Ferns are a great standby for shady places, preferably with a mossy rock or gnarled tree root to nestle beside.

CULTIVATION Plant during early autumn or spring in partial or full shade, in moist humus-rich soil. Contrary to popular belief, most ferns do not need acid soil, but most do need moisture. Don't allow the soil to dry out, and mulch every spring with leaf mould or garden compost. The top growth may be cut down to ground level in autumn. Lift and replant every third or fourth year.

PROPAGATION Sow spores in damp compost as soon as ripe, or divide and replant in spring once a few crowns have formed.

PESTS AND DISEASES Generally trouble free.

OTHER VARIETIES *A. niponicum* var. *pictum* AGM, 38cm (15in), displays its fronds horizontally, showing a silver-grey surface with a pinky-maroon flush spreading from the central vein. There are also forms of *A. filix-femina* with variously crimped and crested fronds, which will interest those who want to start a fern collection. In that case, it's best to visit a specialist nursery to select the plants.

COMPANIONS Plant ferns with other quietly green or variegated shade lovers: hostas, hellebores, ivies, bergenias.

ATHYRIUM FILIX-FEMINA

A

ATRIPLEX HORTENSIS 'RUBRA'

Red mountain spinach, red orach, half hardy annual (Central Asia). Mature at 3 months: 120 x 30cm (4 x 1ft).

This plant makes a tall spire of dusky crimson triangular leaves. In late summer the top part of the stem is covered with small, insignificant flowers of similar colouring, followed by papery seeds.

USES Orach was originally grown as a cure for gout and jaundice and as a food crop; the young leaves can be added to salads and the older, coarser leaves can be cooked and eaten like spinach. It is sometimes planted in rows to make a quick temporary hedge to protect more delicate crops, and the leaves of red orach are decorative enough to be used in ornamental planting schemes.

CULTIVATION Sow the seeds in late spring or early summer in good ordinary garden soil, either in rows 60cm (2ft) apart, or in blocks or drifts in the intended final site. Water the seedlings during dry spells and keep them free of weeds. If you are growing the plants for food, pinch out the tips to prevent them flowering and to encourage plenty of leafy growth. In autumn either leave the plants to self-seed before cutting them down, or collect the seed for use next season.

PESTS AND DISEASES Generally trouble free.

OTHER VARIETIES The parent species is plain green and there is also a yellow-leaved form, but the red one is much the most attractive.

COMPANIONS Plant red orach as background to scarlet and orange dahlias.

		soil	
	ACID		ALKALINE
	DRY		WET

J	F	M	A	M	J	J	A	S	O	N	D

ATRIPLEX HORTENSIS 'RUBRA'

AUBRIETA

Hardy evergreen perennial (S. Europe, Asia Minor). Mature at 3 years: 5-10 x 15-30cm (2-4 x 6-12in).

Very easy and obliging plants, aubrietas make dense low mounds of small, grey-green leaves spreading horizontally or, on walls and steep banks, vertically. From early spring to midsummer the plants are covered in small single or double flowers. The colour range is from mauve-blue to purplish-red.

USES Aubrietas thrive in dry stony positions. They love limestone and quickly colonize dry stone walls and rocky banks. Use them in paving crevices, to soften the margins of gravel paths or as ground cover under roses and other shrubs.

CULTIVATION Plant at any time from autumn to spring in well-drained, preferably limy soil. Aubrieta flowers best in sun, but I find it does well in shade, flowering rather less prolifically. After flowering, cut back hard to encourage dense, compact new cushions. Plants in walls should be lightly clipped to remove the flowered stems, if they are within reach.

PROPAGATION Sow seeds in early spring, or take cuttings in summer. You can also divide the plant in autumn.

PESTS AND DISEASES White blister or downy mildew occasionally attacks the plants.

GOOD CULTIVARS There are numerous named cultivars, nearly all of them reliable, including some with variegated leaves. The best way to choose the colours you prefer is to visit a nursery when they are in flower.

COMPANIONS In limestone areas the effect of aubrieta in every crevice on every wall can be too dazzling, particularly when partnered by bright yellow alyssums. Avoid the blue and yellow contrast and mix a few red and purple cultivars in with the blue ones. They go well with the lime-green of *Euphorbia polychroma*, or with *Euphorbia a.* var. *robbiae*.

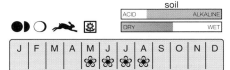

		soil	
	ACID		ALKALINE
	DRY		WET

J	F	M	A	M	J	J	A	S	O	N	D

AUBRIETA

AUCUBA JAPONICA

Evergreen shrub (Japan, 1850s). Mature at 15 years: 2 x 2m (7 x 7ft).

Aucubas, like the laurels which they resemble, thrive in the most unprepossessing sites, forming dank shrubberies under dripping trees in Victorian suburban driveways. By association, they have become unfairly despised. This species has smooth-edged, glossy green leaves and makes a tidy, rounded bush, even under beech trees where nothing else will grow. The olive-green, star-shaped flowers produced in spring are inconspicuous. On female plants clusters of bright scarlet berries often persist from autumn to spring.

USES Invaluable for dry shade, especially in the variegated form (see below) which, seen from a distance, can bring an impression of sunlight to a dark corner. Aucubas will grow in containers on town balconies and in shady yards, and they withstand industrial pollution well. They provide food and shelter for birds.

CULTIVATION Among the most easily grown evergreen shrubs. Plant in autumn or spring in ordinary soil, in sun or shade. To ensure berries, grow both male and female plants – one male to three female. Fruit is more abundant in sun. No pruning is necessary, but you can keep the plants bushy and in good shape by cutting old stems back to 60-90cm (2-3ft) in spring. Feed plants in containers with a weak liquid feed every 2-3 weeks in summer.

PROPAGATION In late summer, take cuttings of lateral shoots 10-15cm (4-6in) long, preferably with a heel.

PESTS AND DISEASES Generally trouble free.

OTHER VARIETIES Variegated aucubas (spotted laurel) were introduced from Japan in 1783 before the plain species. 'Crotonifolia' AGM is heavily spotted and mottled with butter yellow. The leaves of 'Picturata' are bright green with a central yellow blotch.

AUCUBA JAPONICA 'CROTONIFOLIA'

AZARA MICROPHYLLA

Evergreen shrub or small tree (Chile, 1861). Mature at 15 years: 6 x 4m (20 x 13ft). AGM

This elegant plant, taller than it is wide, has numerous slightly pendulous branchlets closely set with small, shining dark green leaves. Although there are masses of green flowers they are so tiny they are visually insignificant. The significance lies in the scent – strong, good-enough-to-eat vanilla – in late winter or early spring.

USES Plant this azara where you will get the benefit of the scent, beside a door or path that you use frequently in winter.

CULTIVATION It will grow in ordinary well-drained soil and in sun or shade but, although generally hardy, it can suffer in severe winters. Give protection by planting in spring, rather than in autumn, and by training it against a sheltered south- or west-facing wall.

PROPAGATION Take semi-ripe cuttings during the summer.

PESTS AND DISEASES Generally trouble free.

OTHER VARIETIES *A. m.* 'Variegata' is a plant of great elegance and distinction, but less reliably hardy.

COMPANIONS Azara has given of its best by the time spring arrives, so it makes sense to let it share its position with a later flowering climber, such as honeysuckle or *Trachelospermum*. Alternatively make use of it later in the year as a host for a clematis.

AZARA MICROPHYLLA

B

BALLOTA PSEUDODICTAMNUS

Evergreen subshrub (Eastern Mediterranean). Mature at 5 years: 60 x 90cm (2 x 3ft). AGM

This is one of the very best foliage plants. Lots of soft stems covered in fine white fur grow from a woody base to form a mound of rounded, heart-shaped leaves. It is tempting to group ballota with grey-leaved plants, but its colour is distinct and unique; the pale green leaves being overlaid with the same layer of fine white hairs as the stems. At midsummer the stems are encircled by small, tubular, two-lipped mauve-pink flowers that have pale green calyces.

USES One of those few valuable plants that will grow in the shallowest, poorest of soils. All it needs is sun. Plant it as part of a group of foliage plants, or as a foil to colourful herbaceous or annual flowers.

CULTIVATION Plant in late spring in poor or ordinary well-drained soil in full sun. It is susceptible to wet conditions in winter and may need the protection of an open-ended cloche. Prune to shape the plants in late spring, cutting back the previous season's growth by half or more.

PROPAGATION Take cuttings of non-flowering, lateral shoots in summer and insert them in equal parts of peat and sand in a cold frame. The rooted cuttings can be planted out in their permanent positions in early summer the following year.

PESTS AND DISEASES Generally trouble free.

COMPANIONS The soft green-white leaves are a good foil to plants with crimson or violet flowers.

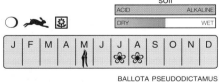

BALLOTA PSEUDODICTAMUS

BEANS

Broad bean, hardy annuals. Mature at 4 months: to 90cm (3ft) tall. French beans, tender annual twining climbers

Very few vegetables are described in this book because most taste almost as good when bought from a greengrocer as they do when home grown. Broad beans are an exception: you have to grow them yourself if you want to harvest them when the beans are still deliciously small. I include climbing French beans because, like runner beans, they are ornamental as well as edible.

USES French beans have edible seeds and seed pods. The climbing beans can provide quick and unusual cover for bare walls or fences, arches and arbours, and for bamboo wigwams as well.

CULTIVATION Sow broad bean seeds 15cm (6in) apart in rows or blocks in any reasonable soil in late autumn or early spring. After harvesting the crop cut down the stems leaving the roots in the ground to release nitrogen. French beans must be sown in a greenhouse or indoors in spring or outdoors in late spring.

PESTS AND DISEASES Both types of bean may be attacked by various pests and diseases, particularly bean aphids, which infest the young growing tips of the shoots. Either spray against them or pinch out the leading shoots as soon as the aphids appear.

GOOD VARIETIES Broad beans with excellent flavour include 'Aquadulce Claudia' and 'Exhibition Longpod'. 'Blue Lake' and 'Climbing Purple' are good French beans.

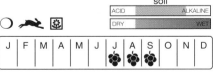

RUNNER BEANS

BEGONIA

Tender evergreen or deciduous perennials and annuals. Mature at 3 years.

The Semperflorens and Tuberohybrida groups are most often used in the garden. They have fleshy, succulent stems and single or double flowers with semi-transparent petals in shades of red, pink, yellow, orange, apricot and white.

USES Begonias range from house plants grown for their dramatic foliage (*B. rex* and others) to summer bedding plants in numerous sizes and flower colours. The latter are a traditional component of 'carpet bedding' and are relied upon by parks departments charged with the heavy responsibility of creating a floral clock. In gardens, the most useful are probably those with a pendulous habit (pendula begonias) planted in pots and hanging baskets.

CULTIVATION Plant out in early summer when all risk of frost has passed. Begonias prefer dappled shade and loamless compost if grown in containers. Add slow-release fertilizer to the compost when planting or administer liquid feed once a week. After flowering gradually reduce the amount of watering to none. Store in pots laid on their sides in frost-free conditions during winter. In early spring, start into growth by watering, sparingly at first.

PROPAGATION Take basal cuttings in spring or sow seeds on the surface of sandy compost.

GOOD VARIETIES There is a huge range available, and this is one of the cases where a selection is best made by looking at what is on offer in your local garden centre.

COMPANIONS Begonias have an exotic, tropical look to them. Plant them with Canna lilies, which share this characteristic, or dress pots and tubs with two kinds of begonia: an upright variety in the centre and trailing kinds around the edge.

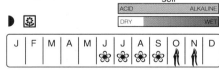

BEGONIA

BELLIS PERENNIS

Double daisy, Bachelor's button, hardy perennial, often grown as a biennial (Europe, including Britain, Asia). Mature at 12 months: 15 x 15cm (6 x 6in)

The double cultivars of a familiar lawn weed, *Bellis perennis* has a rosette of mid-green leaves and a sunburst of narrow white (sometimes pink- or red-tipped) ray-like petals. Flowers are also sometimes entirely red or pink. It has a very long flowering season, and is hardly ever out of flower from early spring till autumn.

USES Double daisies make neat edging to small-scale formal beds, or margins to narrow paths. They can also be used as part of a carpet bedding pattern and, in the smallest gardens, in pots and window boxes.

CULTIVATION In autumn, set out young plants raised from seed or bought as small plants, at 8-12cm (3-5in) apart. They will thrive in any garden soil provided it is well drained, in sun or partial shade. They flower very prolifically on alkaline soil. If you can find the time, regular dead-heading keeps the flowers coming and prevents inferior self-sown seedlings occurring.

PROPAGATION Sow seeds in early summer to flower the following year.

PESTS AND DISEASES Generally trouble free.

GOOD CULTIVARS Choose whatever appeals to you from a mail order seed catalogue or choose by the picture on the seed packet.

COMPANIONS Double daisies associate best with other cottage garden plants such as campanulas, pansies, stocks, sweet williams and snapdragons.

BELLIS PERENNIS

BERBERIS 'RUBROSTILLA'

Syn. B. x rubrostilla. Barberry, deciduous shrub (raised from a seedling in the Royal Horticultural Society's garden at Wisley, 1916). Mature at 15 years: 1.2 x 2m (4 x 7ft)

There are so many good berberis that it is difficult to choose typical examples. On this compact, gracefully arching mound, the brassy yellow flowers are followed by exceptionally beautiful oval berries of translucent coral-red: they are prolific, hanging from the branches in small clusters. The leaves are small and narrow, densely covering prickly stems.

USES Berberis come top of the municipal landscaper's list of vandal-proof shrubs. Their dense, thorny habit does indeed make them invaluable for use where a stock-proof and people-proof barrier is needed. They make effective ground cover in almost any situation and soil.

CULTIVATION Plant from late autumn to spring, in sun or light shade. They tolerate shallow and thin soils, limestone and clay. No regular pruning is necessary, but to renovate old plants, remove the oldest stems at the base and cut back all branches to healthy young shoots in late winter.

PROPAGATION Sow seed in a seed bed in early winter; seedlings may not come true. Alternatively, take cuttings of lateral shoots in late summer.

PESTS AND DISEASES Generally trouble free.

OTHER VARIETIES *B. x ottawensis* 'Superba' AGM, 2 x 1.8m (7 x 6ft), has the darkest red-purple leaves. Many *B. thunbergii* cultivars have crimson leaves that colour brilliant red in autumn to coincide with red berries; 'Atropurpurea Nana', 60 x 60cm (2 x 2ft), is almost thornless. This, and the even smaller 'Bagatelle' AGM, make good formal or informal edging plants. Of the taller forms, 'Red Chief' AGM, 1.8 x 1.5m (6 x 5ft), AGM, is upright and arching; 'Rose Glow' 1.5 x 1.2m (5 x 4ft) has young leaves mottled with silver-pink and bright pink.

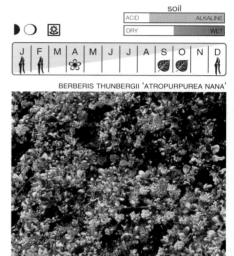

BERBERIS THUNBERGII 'ATROPURPUREA NANA'

BERBERIS 'RUBROSTILLA'

B

BERGENIA

Elephant's ears, evergreen perennials. Mature at 3 years: 23 x 30cm (9 x 12in), to 60 x 60cm (2 x 2ft).

Bergenias are grown mainly for their bold evergreen foliage. Thick-textured, glossy rounded leaves, often turning red or purple in autumn, grow from rough rhizomes which, in old plants, sprawl above ground. The leaves colour best on poor soil in full sunlight. In spring, thick fleshy stems bear heads of open cup-shaped flowers in colours from dark magenta-pink to white.

USES Bergenias make good ground cover in almost any situation, including dry shade, limy soil and clay. Both flowers and leaves are good for flower arranging.

CULTIVATION Plant between autumn and spring, in sun or shade. Weed until the plants have joined up to make ground cover. The only further attention needed is to tidy up dead leaves and any other debris from time to time.

PROPAGATION Divide overcrowded clumps in late spring after flowering.

PESTS AND DISEASES Generally trouble free.

GOOD CULTIVARS For the best winter colour, plant *B. cordifolia* 'Purpurea' AGM, 50 x 50cm (20 x 20in), *B. purpurascens* AGM, 45 x 30cm (18 x 12in), with beetroot-red leaves held erect, or 'Sunningdale', 60 x 30cm (24 x 12in). If the rather coarse pink flowers of these forms

are too much for you, you must forgo the autumn colour of the leaves and plant 'Bressingham White' AGM, or 'Silberlicht' (Silverlight) AGM, for their white flowers.

COMPANIONS The autumn-colouring cultivars are set off well by the creamy variegated leaves of *Hedera canariensis* 'Variegata', or *Euonymus fortunei* 'Emerald and Gold' AGM.

BERGENIA CORDIFOLIA

BERGENIA 'SUNNINGDALE'

BETULA UTILIS VAR. JACQUEMONTII

Syn. B. jacquemontii. W. Himalayan birch, deciduous tree (Himalaya, Kumaon region, late 19th century). Mature at 30 years: 7m tall after 20 years, 15 x 7m (50 x 23ft) at maturity. AGM

Of all birch trees in cultivation, this one usually has the whitest bark, although there are individuals with light ochre or pinkish-brown bark. The small serrated and pointed leaves are mid-green and turn clear yellow in autumn.

USES For winter effect, three or more should be planted close together against a dark background where the stems catch the rays of the low winter sun. Like many birches they tolerate some shade and exposure and, once established, dry conditions.

CULTIVATION Plant in autumn in sun or shade on light soil, either acid or alkaline. Birches have wide-spreading surface roots, so do not plant close to borders or fences where the roots will encroach on neighbouring property.

PROPAGATION Sow seeds in early spring in a cold frame; seed collected from the garden may produce hybrids. Take softwood cuttings in early summer.

PESTS AND DISEASES Aphids sometimes infest the leaves; caterpillars and the larvae of sawflies feed on the leaves. Honey fungus may kill the trees.

OTHER SPECIES The silver birch, *B. pendula* AGM, is delicate and graceful in appearance and tough as old boots in constitution: very fast-growing and able to cope with almost any difficult conditions. An even more elegant version, *B. p.* 'Laciniata' (syn. 'Dalecarlica') has deeply cut leaves giving a soft, feathery effect. *B. papyrifera*, paper birch, has gleaming white bark which peels in large strips on old trees.

BETULA UTILIS JACQUEMONTII

B

BORAGO OFFICINALIS

Borage, hardy annual (Europe). Mature at 4 months: 75 x 30cm (30 x 12in).

Borage's corrugated, pointed oval leaves lie flat against the ground. From midsummer until autumn, stout hollow stems arise, producing much-branched heads of drooping intensely blue star-shaped flowers. The whole plant is covered with rough grey hairs.

USES Borage has a long history as a culinary and medicinal herb. The young leaves have a cucumber flavour. They are used with the flowers to flavour and decorate salads and cold drinks, especially Pimms No. 1. The flowers can also be candied to decorate cakes and sweets. The plants provide food for bees and, if planted near strawberries, are said to stimulate their growth. Borage will quickly colonize poor, stony soil.

CULTIVATION Sow seeds in virtually any soil in sun. The stems will flop with the weight of the flowering heads but it is hardly worth staking them. Cut them down as the flowers fall.

PROPAGATION Sow seeds in spring and make further sowings at intervals throughout the summer for a continuous supply of young leaves. Seeds sown in early autumn will flower the following spring. Borage is a very prolific self-seeder; the seeds remain viable for many years, so it can be left to fend for itself in very informal planting schemes.

PESTS AND DISEASES Generally trouble free.

COMPANIONS Borage associates well with other herbs, and can be planted in large groups or drifts in herbaceous borders or among old-fashioned roses.

BRACHYGLOTTIS DUNEDIN GROUP 'SUNSHINE'

Syn. Senecio 'Sunshine'. Hardy evergreen shrub (New Zealand). Mature at 10 years: 75cm x 1.5m (2ft 6in x 5ft). AGM

This grey-leaved shrub, familiar to many gardeners, nurserymen and garden centre managers as *Senecio* 'Sunshine', has undergone a confusing name change. It is difficult to know under which name you should ask for it, but it is certainly worth asking for. It makes a low mound of quite large, leathery, rounded silver-grey leaves. In early summer, silver-white globular buds are held at the tips of white felted stalks. They will open into slightly brassy yellow daisies, which some gardeners prefer to remove.

USES Excellent evergreen ground cover on sandy or chalky soil, *Brachyglottis* stands up well to seaside conditions and to industrial pollution, provided it is grown in full sun and has shelter from cold winds. It can provide a solid block of grey foliage to give structure to groups of shrubs of indefinite shape such as roses.

CULTIVATION Plant in spring in free-draining soil in a sunny, sheltered position. If the yellow flowers are not wanted, cut them off as they open. To prevent the shrubs becoming leggy, cut them back in spring to within a few centimeters of the old wood. Rejuvenate old plants by cutting them down to a stump.

PROPAGATION Take semi-ripe cuttings in late summer or detach and plant any rooted layers you can find.

PESTS AND DISEASES Generally trouble free.

OTHER VARIETIES *B. monroi* (syn. *Senecio monroi*) AGM is another good evergreen foliage shrub. It will grow to 1.2 x 1.2m (4 x 4ft) and has dark grey-green, wavy-edged leaves with white undersides. It needs the same conditions as *B.* 'Sunshine' and has similar yellow daisy flowers.

BRIZA MAXIMA

Greater quaking grass, pearl grass, annual grass (Mediterranean). Mature at 3 months: 50 x 10cm (20 x 4in).

The narrow, mid-green pointed leaves form small tufts. In early summer they produce erect stems terminating in loose panicles of pendent, heart-shaped purplish green spikelets. They tremble in the lightest breeze, hence the name quaking grass.

USES We are beginning to get away from the idea that any grass not growing in a lawn is a weed. Ornamental grasses are easy to grow and provide a good foil for other, more colourful plants. If the dried stems are not cut, but are left on the plants, they also make a valuable contribution to the winter scene. If cut and dried, they are useful in flower arrangements.

CULTIVATION Sow the seeds directly into their permanent position in autumn or spring, in ordinary, well-drained soil in a sunny position. Cut stems for drying in sunny weather when the spikelets are fully developed, but before the seeds set. Hang in bunches to dry in a cool place.

PROPAGATION Sow seeds in autumn or spring, or simply allow an established clump to seed itself.

PESTS AND DISEASES Generally trouble free.

OTHER VARIETIES Britain's native quaking grass, *Briza media*, is a smaller plant with denser flowering panicles.

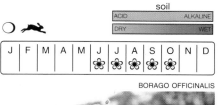

soil
| ACID | | ALKALINE |
| DRY | | WET |

| J | F | M | A | M | J | J | A | S | O | N | D |

BORAGO OFFICINALIS

soil
| ACID | | ALKALINE |
| DRY | | WET |

| J | F | M | A | M | J | J | A | S | O | N | D |

BRACHYGLOTTIS 'SUNSHINE'

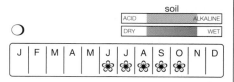

soil
| ACID | | ALKALINE |
| DRY | | WET |

| J | F | M | A | M | J | J | A | S | O | N | D |

BRIXA MAXIMA

B

BRUNNERA MACROPHYLLA

Syn. Anchusa myostidiflora, hardy perennial (W. Caucasus, 1800). Mature at 3 years: 45 x 60cm (18 x 24in). AGM.

Handsome clumps of large, heart-shaped leaves last throughout the summer. From late spring to midsummer, before the leaves have fully developed, branching stems of blue flowers, similar to forget-me-nots, are held well above the leaves.

USES Brunneras are a great standby as ground cover under trees and in other places where dry shade predominates. Even if they were not so obliging, one would still want to grow them for their good looks.

CULTIVATION Plant between autumn and spring in any ordinary soil, in sun or shade. If they are grown in sun they are less drought tolerant and should not be allowed to dry out at the roots. Cut the stems and leaves down to the ground when they turn brown in autumn.

PROPAGATION Divide and replant the roots of crowded clumps in autumn or early spring. Alternatively, take root cuttings in autumn and grow on in a cold frame; plant out the rooted cuttings in a nursery bed in early summer. They should be sturdy enough to transfer to a permanent position in the autumn.

PESTS AND DISEASES Generally trouble free: the fact that the leaves do not appeal to slugs gives brunneras the edge over hostas for shade beds.

OTHER VARIETIES *B. m.* 'Langtrees' is an improved form, with large leaves discreetly

decorated at the margins with a pattern of silvery spots. There are several variegated forms, of which 'Hadspen Cream' AGM is the easiest to grow, but it does need to be planted in damp soil.

COMPANIONS The flowers will coincide prettily with the young leaves of variegated hostas, or *Astrantia major* 'Sunningdale Variegated'.

BRUNNERA MACROPHYLLA

BRUNNERA MACROPHYLLA

BUDDLEIA ALTERNIFOLIA

Deciduous shrub (China 1880). Mature at 15 years: 4 x 3m 15 x 10ft. AGM.

This shrub is unlike other buddleias in several respects: it is slow growing, it has elegant, willow-like leaves and long graceful arching branches. At midsummer the flowering branches are smothered almost along their entire length by small, sweet-scented lavender-blue flowers. It is seen at its very best when trained as a standard tree. The form 'Argentea' has leaves covered in silky hairs.

USES In its multi-stemmed, shrubby form, it will make good ground cover, sprawling over banks or retaining walls. As a standard it makes a very beautiful little weeping tree, far more appealing than the ubiquitous weeping silver pear and a far more manageable size in small gardens.

CULTIVATION Plant in autumn or spring, in loamy soil in full sun. All buddleias are lime tolerant. The flowers are produced on wood made the previous summer, so the plants should not be pruned in spring. Simply remove the stems that have flowered immediately after flowering, and carry out any pruning needed to improve the shape at the same time.

PROPAGATION If suckers appear, dig them up and transplant them. Cuttings of 10-15cm (4-5in) with a heel strike easily. Take them from half-ripe lateral shoots in summer.

PESTS AND DISEASES Generally trouble free, but cucumber mosaic virus sometimes affects the leaves.

COMPANIONS Mix it with other summer-flowering shrubs, especially roses. If you grow it as a tree, keep the planting around it low so that its graceful habit can be well appreciated. A carpet of *Viola labradorica* would be attractive and trouble free.

BUDDLEIA ALTERNIFOLIA

BUDDLEIA 'LOCHINCH'

Deciduous shrub (garden origin). Mature at 3 years: 2 x 1.8m (7 x 6ft). AGM.

Fast-growing, with slightly arching branches, the stems and large, lance-shaped leaves are covered in white hairs giving them a silver-grey appearance. Long panicles of densely-packed, fragrant, lavender-blue flowers are borne in profusion on the current year's growth, from late summer to autumn.

USES Buddleias are invaluable for producing quick results. The flowers are almost smothered with butterflies on sunny summer days.

CULTIVATION Plant in autumn or spring in any well-drained soil in sun; they thrive on chalk and limestone. This one needs a sheltered position. The panicles turn brown as they fade, so dead-head to improve appearance and to keep flowers coming. Prune hard in spring; cut back all shoots to within 15cm (6in) of a framework.

PROPAGATION In summer, root heeled, semi-ripe cuttings of lateral shoots 10-12cm (4-5in) long in a cold frame. Take hardwood cuttings 20-30cm (8-12in) long in autumn.

PESTS AND DISEASES As for *B. alternifolia*.

OTHER VARIETIES Cultivars of *B. davidii*, 3 x 1.8m (10 x 6ft), are more reliable in cold or exposed conditions. The flowers of 'Black Knight' AGM are vibrant violet-purple; 'Royal Red' AGM, is an equally strong shade of purple red; 'Pink Delight' AGM is more compact with greyish leaves. The best for small gardens is the elegant 'Nanho Blue'; 1.5 x 1.5m (5 x 5ft). 'Nanho Purple' is a similar form. *B. globosa* and *B. x weyeriana* are completely different and grow to 6 x 6m (15 x 15ft). Both produce balls of orange flowers and crinkled, dull dark green leaves.

COMPANIONS For an instant garden, plant with other shrubs from the list of quick-growing plants on page 34.

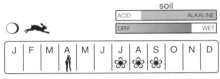

BUDDLEIA GLOBOSA

BUDDLEIA 'NANHO PURPLE'

BUXUS SEMPERVIRENS

B

Common box, evergreen shrub or small tree (Europe including Britain, Turkey, N. Africa). Mature at 20 years: 2 x 2m (6 x 6ft) after 10 years; up to 3 x 3m (10 x 10ft) at maturity. AGM

Left untrimmed, box forms an irregularly shaped, much-branched bush densely covered in small oblong glossy leaves, yellow-green in spring, darkening with age. The pale green unisexual flowers of late spring are inconspicuous.

USES Its dense, tidy leaves and slow growth make box one of the very best plants for hedging and screening, up to 1.5m (5ft) high, and for topiary. For instant gardening, bushes can be bought (at a price) trained into pyramids, cones, peacocks and so on. They can also be clipped more informally into mounds and irregular clumps to give solid bulk.

CULTIVATION Plant box in early autumn or spring in any ordinary soil. It thrives on chalk. For hedging, use plants 25-30cm (9-12in) high, spaced 30-40cm (12-5in) apart. Plant *B. s.* 'Suffruticosa' for edging, 10cm (4in) apart. Cut back leading shoots by one-third after planting, or in spring to promote bushy growth. Clip hedges and topiary in spring or late summer.

PROPAGATION Take cuttings 8-10cm (3-4in) long in late summer or early autumn, in sandy soil in a cold frame. Line out in nursery rows in early summer the following year and grow on for two years.

PESTS AND DISEASES Generallly trouble free but can suffer leaf spot, physiological disorders and rust.

OTHER VARIETIES *B. balearica* does better in Southern European gardens. *B. s.* 'Suffruticosa' AGM is the dwarf box traditionally used for edging and for knots.

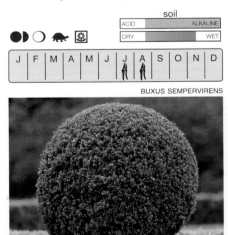

BUXUS SEMPERVIRENS

C

CALAMINTHA GRANDIFLORA

Syn. Clinopodium grandiflorum, a hardy perennial (S. Europe, Caucasus, Crimea to Iran). Mature at 3 years: 30 x 30cm (12 x 12in).

Calamint makes a tidy mound of dull greyish-green, mint-like leaves, the stems turning woody at the base as they mature. In spite of the name 'grandiflora' the pale pinkish-mauve flowers are very small, but seen from a distance they give the impression of a pale mist over the plants. They have a long flowering season.

USES Calamint is a good plant to colonize poor stony soil provided the place is open and sunny. As a herb it has a history of medicinal use; an infusion of the leaves is thought to relieve flatulent colic and act as a tonic. The leaves can also be used in cough syrup or, picked fresh and crushed, as a poultice for bruises.

CULTIVATION Plant in spring in sun or dappled shade, in any free-draining soil. Calamint is happiest on chalk or limestone, but will look after itself almost anywhere. In autumn, cut the flower and leaf stems down to the ground.

PROPAGATION If you are aiming at a natural, informal effect, just allow calamint to seed itself and pull out any seedlings that appear where you don't want them. Alternatively, divide, sow seeds or take cuttings of the young shoots in spring.

OTHER VARIETIES 'White Cloud' and 'Blue Cloud' have flowers with a much more pronounced colouring.

COMPANIONS Plant calamint among grey-leaved plants as a gentle colour contrast. It associates well with other herbs of quiet colouring, such as horehound, rosemary, hyssop and rue, and contributes to the restful atmosphere of a herb garden.

CALAMINTHA GRANDIFLORA

CALENDULA OFFICINALIS

Pot marigold, a hardy annual (S. Europe). Mature at 3 months: 30cm (12in).

An archetypal cottage garden plant. The stems and leaves are a fresh light green. The daisy-like flowers of pure orange or yellow are freely produced from early summer until the first frosts. The seed heads are an attractive circle of green incurved sickles, fading as they dry out.

USES Marigolds make good cut flowers and are edible, so they can be used to decorate salads and to colour rice and fish dishes. The flowers and leaves have numerous medicinal uses, being apparently antiseptic.

CULTIVATION Marigolds thrive with little or no attention in the poorest soils and the worst conditions. If they are grown for flower arranging or as a herbal crop, a sunny position in ordinary garden soil will suit. Pinch out the stem tips to encourage branching. Dead-head regularly to keep flowers coming and to prevent self-seeding.

PROPAGATION Sow the seeds *in situ*, in early spring for summer flowering, or in late summer to flower the following spring.

PESTS AND DISEASES Generally trouble free. If powdery mildew, rust, or smut appear, pull up and burn affected plants.

OTHER VARIETIES Single- and double-flowered hybrids have been bred in new colours ranging from red-orange to pale cream, but I prefer the simplicity of form and the purity of colour of the species.

COMPANIONS Many gardeners find orange a difficult colour to place, but the pure clear orange of pot marigolds is quite versatile. It makes a light-hearted contrast with forget-me-nots in early summer, or later with blue hyssop in the herb garden. Marigolds growing haphazardly among white flowers, or plants with cream-variegated foliage lighten a dull day amazingly.

CALENDULA OFFICINALIS 'ORANGE KING'

CALTHA PALUSTRIS 'FLORE PLENO'

Double marsh marigold, king cup, a hardy perennial (Europe, including Britain). Mature at 3 years: 25 x 25cm (10 x 10in). AGM

The double-flowered version of this familiar waterside plant has glossy, deep green rounded leaves, slightly toothed at the edges. Flowers resembling large double buttercups with glossy, vibrant yellow petals, are held on branching succulent green stalks in early spring.

USES The leaves are dense enough to make good ground cover in damp conditions or in shallow water at the margins of streams, ponds or lakes.

CULTIVATION Like all water plants, marsh marigolds are best planted in late spring. Although they are by nature waterside or bog plants, they will grow happily in sun or shade in beds and borders, provided the soil is kept fairly moist at all times. Towards the end of the summer, remove any unsightly leaves to keep the plants looking tidy.

PROPAGATION Divide and replant the roots in early summer immediately after flowering. If you lift each plant carefully with a fork and wash the soil away from its roots you will find the crowns divide quite easily into separate pieces. You can cut back any long, straggly roots in order to make planting easier.

PESTS AND DISEASES Generally trouble free, but leaves can be disfigured by rust.

OTHER VARIETIES *C. palustris* AGM has single flowers which do not last as long as the double ones. *C. p.* var. *alba*, the white form, has beautiful flowers but is nothing like as robust as the yellow forms.

soil

ACID										ALKALINE
DRY										WET

J	F	M	A	M	J	J	A	S	O	N	D

CALTHA PALUSTRIS

CAMASSIA LEICHTLINII

Quamash, a bulbous perennial (N. America, 1850s). Mature at 1 year: 90 x 20cm (36 x 8in).

All camassias make clumps of mid-green, strap-shaped pointed leaves. This, one of the most reliable of the species, produces strong, erect leafless stems that are covered in star-shaped white or blue flowers in the early summer.

USES Camassias provide a vertical element in mixed borders, without any staking. They inhabit damp meadows in the wild, and look appropriate growing in an informal colony beside a pond or stream. They can be naturalized in grass, where they will seed themselves if they like the site. If not they may survive for a few years. Plant enough bulbs each year to keep the group going.

CULTIVATION Heavy moist soil that does not dry out during spring and early summer is ideal. Plant the bulbs in autumn, about 10cm (4in) deep, and leave them for several years until they become crowded. Remove the stems after flowering unless you want to collect seeds.

PROPAGATION Dig up established bulbs in late summer, remove offsets and replant them immediately. They will take from one to three years to grow to flowering size. They can also be propagated from seed sown in autumn, but it is a slow business.

PESTS AND DISEASES Generally trouble free.

OTHER VARIETIES *C. quamash*, the common quamash, is a much more variable plant, reaching a height anywhere between 20cm and 80cm (8in and 32in). There are some good named forms of *C. leichtlinii*, including 'Electra', which has large rich blue flowers.

GOOD COMPANIONS They provide a striking vertical contrast to mound-forming plants such as *Nepeta* 'Six Hills Giant'.

soil

ACID										ALKALINE
DRY										WET

J	F	M	A	M	J	J	A	S	O	N	D

CAMASSIA LEICHTLINII

C

CAMASSIA LEICHTLINII

C

CAMELLIA X WILLIAMSII

C. japonica x C. saluenensis, a hardy evergreen shrub (hybrids raised in Cornwall). Mature at 15 years: 2-2.5 x 1-1.2m ((6-8 x 4-6ft) after 10 years; 4 x 2.5m (12 x 8ft) at maturity.

Camellias slowly form dense mounds of dark glossy evergreen leaves. Their showy flowers appear in late winter and early spring, a rare treat at that time. An enormous number of cultivars with single, semi-double or double flowers, 2.5-10cm (1-4in) across, is available, with red, pink, white, or striped petals and yellow stamens.

USES They thrive against north- or west-facing walls in town gardens or courtyards, and are perfect for woodland gardens. After flowering their foliage makes an excellent backdrop to other plants. The compact root balls make them ideal for growing in containers.

CULTIVATION Camellias must have lime-free, humus-rich, moisture-retentive soil and shelter from wind. Grow in shade or in sun if roots can be kept cool. Avoid east-facing positions – early morning sun after frost damages the flowers. Mulch annually with leaf mould. Plant in containers slightly bigger than the rootball and pot on every few years. Use lime-free compost; replace the top 1cm (½in) annually after flowering. Prune only occasionally after flowering to improve the shape or reduce size.

CAMELLIA X WILLIAMSII 'DONATION'

PROPAGATION Take 10cm (4in) semi-ripe cuttings in summer, or layer in early autumn. Leaf-bud cuttings are sometimes also used to increase stock.

PESTS AND DISEASES Birds sometimes peck at the flowers. Scale insects, mealy bugs and aphids may be a problem under glass. Dry soil and frost cause bud drop.

GOOD CULTIVARS *C. x williamsii* 'Anticipation', deep rose-pink double; 'Donation', semi-double pink; and 'J.C.Williams', single pale pink. All of these are AGM plants.

COMPANIONS Underplant camellias with the earliest bulbs – snowdrops, aconites, crocuses. Later, use the dark green leaves to advantage as background to azaleas, *Smilacina racemosa*, or pale-flowered lilies.

CAMELLIA JAPONICA 'ANEMONIFLORA'

soil		
ACID		ALKALINE
DRY		WET

J	F	M	A	M	J	J	A	S	O	N	D

CAMELLIA JAPONICA 'TRICOLOR'

CAMPANULA COCHLEARIFOLIA

Syn. **C. pusilla.** *Fairy thimbles, a hardy perennial (European Alps). Mature at 3 years: 8cm (3in) tall, spread indefinite. AGM*

This prostrate campanula is one of the easiest to grow. From a central rosette of small round toothed leaves, runners produce secondary rosettes of the same fresh bright green. The pale mauve-blue bell-shaped flowers are like small thimbles, held up in clusters on thin stems.

USES *C. cochlearifolia* will make a tidy carpet in the border, under shrubs and between groups of herbaceous plants. It is equally at home in rock gardens or draping the face of a retaining wall.

CULTIVATION Plant between early autumn and spring in any well-drained soil, in sun or partial shade. After flowering, clip over with shears or scissors to keep tidy.

PROPAGATION Sow seeds in autumn or early spring in a cold frame. When the seedlings are large enough prick out and grow on. Plant out in early spring or early autumn. Divide in autumn or spring.

PESTS AND DISEASES Slugs, snails, or rabbits can feed on the plants and cause them to disappear overnight. Rust sometimes attacks the plants in autumn.

OTHER SPECIES *C. poscharskyana* is the rampant thug among prostrate campanulas, sending long runners in all directions. *C. portenschlagiana* AGM is better, but still vigorous, with violet-blue bells, and *C. garganica* AGM is neat and compact.

COMPANIONS I have seen a paved terrace and flight of steps where *C. porscharskyana* and *Alchemilla mollis* had both run amok. There was hardly a space to put your foot, but it looked wonderful.

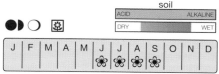

CAMPANULA COCHLEARIIFOLIA

CAMPANULA PERSICIFOLIA

Peach-leaved bellflower, an evergreen hardy perennial (Europe). Mature at 3 years: 90 x 30cm (3 x 1ft).

The peach-leaved campanula has flattish rosettes of narrow pointed leaves. At midsummer each rosette produces a strong slender stem covered with blue, mauve or white bells. It quickly colonizes empty ground by means of runners, with a fresh rosette developing at the end of each, but it is never a nuisance.

USES Like most campanulas, tall as well as prostrate, it makes good ground cover, with the bonus of supplying the vertical line that is so often needed for contrast among roses, and other shrubs without much shape to them.

CULTIVATION Plant from autumn to spring in ordinary garden soil, in sun or shade. It may need some support in the form of short pea sticks or horizontal netting, but if it is grown among shrub roses they will hold it up, and if it flops, it does so gracefully.

PROPAGATION Dig up and replant the offset runners in autumn or spring.

PESTS AND DISEASES Fairly trouble free.

OTHER VARIETIES *C. p.* var. *alba* has white flowers; 'Telham Beauty' has large blue flowers; 'Wortham Belle', double, pale blue.

OTHER SPECIES *C. lactiflora* AGM, 90cm (3ft), flowers a little later, with big trusses of lavender-blue flowers on stout stems; 'Loddon Anna' AGM, 75cm (30in), is pale mauve-pink; 'Pouffe' and 'White Pouffe' make long-flowering mounds just 20cm (8in) high. *C. latiloba* 'Alba', white, 'Hidcote Amethyst', mauve-pink and 'Percy Piper', lavender blue (all AGM), have spires of bell flowers on stems to 90cm (3ft) tall.

GOOD COMPANIONS Tall campanulas are a wonderful foil for old roses, and the later flowering types associate well with lilies.

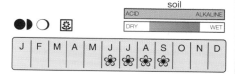

CAMPANULA LATILOBA ALBA

CAMPANULA PERSICIFOLIA

C

CANNA

Canna lily, a tender, rhizomatous perennial (S. America, W. Indies, mid 16th century). Mature at 2 years: to 120 x 60cm (4 x 2ft).

Although frost-tender, cannas are robust plants with huge pointed, broadly lance-shaped leaves, ranging from fresh bright green to dusky bronze-purple. In late summer and autumn, stout upright stems bear lily-like flowers in yellow, orange, apricot, scarlet or deep crimson red.

USES Canna lilies make splendid focal points in formal bedding schemes, and do well in pots or tubs on terraces, balconies and roof gardens. They can be plunged in their pots to fill gaps in beds and borders.

CULTIVATION Plant the rhizomes in very early spring, in pots or boxes, at 16°C (61°F), just covering them with rich compost. Water sparingly at first and set out in early summer in a sunny, sheltered position. In autumn, lift before frosts occur and dry partially before cutting off the leaves and roots. Store in just moist compost or leaf mould in a frost-free place. If too dry they will shrivel, and will rot if too wet.

PROPAGATION Section the rhizomes in early spring, so that each piece has a strong shoot. Presoak seeds in warm water for 24 hours, or nick the seed coat, then sow at 21°C (70°F) in winter.

PESTS AND DISEASES Generally trouble free, but slugs, leatherjackets and cutworms can attack the young shoots and the rhizomes.

VARIETIES There are numerous cultivars. Those with dark leaves and rich red flowers are wonderfully dramatic.

GOOD COMPANIONS For a hot combination, plant cannas with cactus-flowered dahlias or with begonias, or in colour schemes using purple foliage plants.

soil		
ACID		ALKALINE
DRY		WET

J	F	M	A	M	J	J	A	S	O	N	D

CANNA MUSIFOLIA 'ROSEMOND COLES'

CARAGANA ARBORESCENS

Pea tree, a deciduous shrub (Siberia and Mongolia, 1752). Mature at 30 years: 6 x 4m (20 x 12ft).

A fast-growing, sparsely-branched shrub that has small clusters of pea-like yellow flowers in late spring, when the soft green pinnate leaves are almost fully grown.

USES Caragana is a nitrogen-fixing plant, and is extremely tolerant of difficult conditions. This makes it a valuable ground cover plant, as it can be used to establish cover on poor soils, exposed sites or in areas of industrial pollution; it also provides food for bees.

CULTIVATION Plant in autumn, in any light soil in sun or shade. To train a young shrub into a tree, remove side shoots and tie a leading shoot to a tall cane. Caraganas resent heavy pruning, so establish the framework while the plant is young, then let well alone.

PROPAGATION Take softwood cuttings in summer or sow seeds in autumn. If sowing in spring, presoak seeds in warm water.

PESTS AND DISEASES Generally trouble free.

OTHER VARIETIES *C. arborescens* 'Lorbergii' AGM is half the size of the species and has arching branches with very narrow leaflets, giving a feathery effect. There is a pretty cultivar, 'Pendula', that is top-grafted to make a miniature weeping tree. *C. arborescens* 'Walker' also weeps, and has finely-cut leaves.

soil		
ACID		ALKALINE
DRY		WET

J	F	M	A	M	J	J	A	S	O	N	D

CARAGANA ARBORESCENS 'PENDULA'

CARDAMINE PRATENSIS 'FLORE PLENO'

Double lady's smock, cuckoo flower, a hardy perennial (Europe, including Britain, Asia). Mature at 3 years: 45 x 30cm (18 x 12in). AGM

Lady's smock is a native of water meadows and other damp places. Dark green, deeply divided leaves form neat rosettes, and loose clusters of pretty little flowers are held on smooth stems from spring to midsummer. They are white or very pale mauve-pink. The seeds are carried in narrow pods, which burst open explosively, ejecting the seeds some distance from the parent plant, in this way colonizing a wide area for such a small plant.

USES Lady's smock can be naturalized at the margins of ponds or streams, or in damp meadows. It will also do well in borders provided the soil is always moist. As it flowers early it is attractive to a wide range of insects, including the Orange Tip butterfly. Lady's smock is a form of bittercress and the leaves can be used (sparingly) in salads.

CULTIVATION Plant in the autumn in moist soil that is neutral to slightly alkaline, in sun or in light shade.

PROPAGATION In early autumn or early spring, sow seeds thinly in the final flowering position, covering them lightly. Thin out the seedlings to 20cm (8in) apart. Or sow in pots or trays in compost, keep moist, and plant out in autumn. The plants can also be divided.

PESTS AND DISEASES The caterpillars of the Orange Tip butterfly feed on the leaves, but you could hardly describe them as pests. The plants usually survive to flower and provide nectar for the butterflies.

COMPANIONS The snakeshead fritillary, *Fritillaria meleagris*, enjoys the same moist conditions, and the two plants naturalized together make a pretty mini-meadow.

soil		
ACID		ALKALINE
DRY		WET

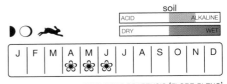

J	F	M	A	M	J	J	A	S	O	N	D

CARDAMINE PRATENSIS 'FLORE PLENO'

CAREX HACHIJOENSIS 'EVERGOLD'

Syn. C. oshimensis 'Evergold', sometimes erroneously offered as C. morrowii 'Variegata', Japanese sedge grass, an evergreen perennial grass. Mature at 3 years: 20 x 20cm (8 x 8in)

Golden yellow, grassy leaves with narrow green borders fan out from the centre of a compact clump. The plant is grown for its leaves, and does not always produce flowering stems.

USES In recent years ornamental grasses have become better appreciated as garden plants. They make splendid ground cover and their narrow leaves provide valuable contrasts with other foliage shapes and textures. Use this one in front of plants with darker foliage, in a position where its sunlit effect will be fully appreciated during the winter months.

CULTIVATION Plant this in early spring in any reasonable soil, preferably quite damp. The yellow form is best in dappled shade, where the leaves will not scorch. In spring, cut the tufts back hard to encourage fresh new leaves to grow.

PROPAGATION Divide the roots of established plants in early spring, and replant. Do not try to do this in autumn.

PESTS AND DISEASES Generally trouble free.

OTHER VARIETIES AND SPECIES *C. pendula*, to 90cm (3ft), has long arching stems rising out of grassy tufts; each stem ends in a foxtail flowering panicle. *C. elata* 'Aurea' Bowles' AGM (golden sedge) has bright yellow grass-like leaves and stiff stems ending in pointed clusters of brown flowers.

COMPANIONS Some gardeners fret about how to use grasses in their planting schemes. The answer is to stop thinking of them as a separate category and start thinking of them as another useful herbaceous plant. Plant them to contrast with shrubs and perennials of more solid form and with more emphatic flower heads.

CAREX COMANS

CAREX HACHIJOENSIS

CARPINUS BETULUS

C

Hornbeam, a deciduous tree (Europe, including Britain, Turkey and Ukraine). Mature at 60 years: height 8m (25ft) after 20 years; 25 x 20m (80 x 70ft) at maturity. AGM

Handsome, round-headed trees with dense canopies of oval, prominently veined, dark green leaves that turn russet in autumn. They bear green catkins from late spring to autumn, when clusters of winged nuts appear. They resemble beech trees, but the leaves are darker and more deeply veined, and a more subdued colour in autumn – buff-brown rather than orange-brown. The trunk is grey and fluted, not smooth like that of beech.

USES Like beech, the hornbeam makes excellent hedges; when clipped it retains its dead leaves until the new ones grow in spring. For the same reason, it can be clipped into geometric shapes to make unusual topiary. It is an excellent alternative to beech on heavy, wet soils, and tolerates industrial pollution. It will grow in both acid and alkaline soils and in cold, exposed inland sites. Because of all these qualities, the fastigiate form is used as a street tree.

CULTIVATION Plant in autumn, in almost any soil that is not waterlogged or very dry, in sun or partial shade. For a hedge, use plants 45-60cm (18-24in) tall, 45cm (18in) apart. Trim hedges in late summer or in winter.

PROPAGATION Sow seeds in autumn.

PESTS AND DISEASES Honey fungus can kill the trees. Otherwise, generally trouble free.

OTHER VARIETIES *C. betulus* 'Fastigiata' AGM, 7m (22ft) high after twenty years, 10 x 5m (30 x 15ft) at maturity. The dense upward-pointing growth makes a neat outline like a toytown tree. The leaves are brighter and more glossy than those of the species, turning gold and orange in autumn.

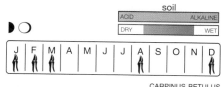

CARPINUS BETULUS

C

CARYOPTERIS X CLANDONENSIS

A deciduous shrub (garden origin). Mature at 5 years: 1 x 1m (3 x 3ft).

The garden plant is a hybrid of *C.incana* and *C.mongolica*. It is a bushy shrub with aromatic narrow, grey-green leaves, some toothed and some entire. Clusters of bright blue tubular flowers appear from late summer into autumn.

USES Late-flowering shrubs are at a premium; so are shrubs with blue flowers, so caryopteris is much in demand for late colour in beds and borders. Aromatic foliage, which looks good from spring onwards, is a bonus. Plant in groups of at least three for impact.

CULTIVATION Caryopteris thrives in any ordinary well-drained soil. Plant it in spring, in groups of three or five, setting the plants 45cm (18in) apart. Caryopteris needs a sunny position and, in cold areas, it will benefit from some shelter. Every spring cut the previous year's growth back to within two leaf buds of the old wood. Weak stems should be cut back to their base.

PROPAGATION Take 8-10cm (3-4in) cuttings of semi-ripe lateral shoots in late summer, and insert in sandy soil in a cold frame.

PESTS AND DISEASES Generally trouble free, but mealy bugs may attack the roots.

OTHER VARIETIES Named cultivars include 'Heavenly Blue' AGM, which has darker blue flowers than 'Arthur Simmonds', with blue or purplish-blue flowers.

COMPANIONS Plant a group of caryopteris in front of *Fremontodendron californicum* or *Eccremocarpus scaber* AGM, which enjoy the same sunny conditions and provide a colour contrast.

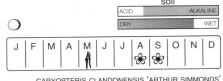

CARYOPTERIS CLANDONENSIS 'ARTHUR SIMMONDS'

CASTANEA SATIVA

Sweet chestnut, Spanish chestnut, a deciduous tree (S. Europe, N. Africa, S.W. Asia. Probably brought to Britain by the Romans and certainly introduced before the Norman Conquest). Mature at 50 years: 12m (38ft) high after 20 years; 30 x 15m (100 x 50ft) at maturity. AGM

A fast-growing, stately tree of strong character, developing a tall domed crown. The trunk eventually grows to a massive girth and the bark develops deep, grooved spiral ridges. The oblong, glossy dark green leaves turn yellow in autumn. Erect, pale green-yellow catkins borne in summer develop into spiny burrs which contain edible red-brown nuts. Unusually for a fast-growing tree, it is also very long-lived.

USES Such fast-growing trees make fine avenues or specimens for parks or large gardens. They provide food for bees and, in warm climates where the nuts can develop and ripen, food for humans, including marrons glacés. The timber is easily cleft, and much used for paling fences.

CULTIVATION Plant in autumn in full sun, preferably in light sandy soil, and not on chalk or lime. Sweet chestnuts are well suited to a warm, dry climate.

PROPAGATION Sow seeds when ripe, usually in autumn. Protect from mice and other rodents.

PESTS AND DISEASES Generally trouble free.

OTHER VARIETIES *C. sativa* 'Albomarginata' has leaves with white margins.

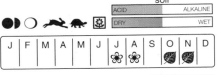

CASTANEA SATIVA

CATALPA BIGNONIOIDES

Indian bean tree, a deciduous tree (Eastern N. America, 1726). Mature at 50 years: 6 x 6m (20 x 20ft) after 20 years, 12 x 10m (40 x 38) at maturity. AGM

A decorative, hardy and vigorous tree with large, heart-shaped, light green leaves that are purplish in bud. They have a pungent smell when crushed. The flowers, borne in clusters at midsummer, are white with yellow and purple markings, rather like foxgloves but slightly frilled. They are followed by long slender seed pods.

USES This is one of the best shade trees, developing quite quickly into a broad dome.

CULTIVATION Plant at any time between autumn and spring in a sunny, fairly sheltered position. Mulch the root area every spring until growth is well established, and keep young trees copiously watered during dry spells. No pruning is necessary.

PROPAGATION In summer, take heeled, semi-ripe cuttings 8-10cm (3-4in) long.

PESTS AND DISEASES Generally trouble free but physiological disorders occur as a result of unsuitable soil conditions.

OTHER VARIETIES *C. bignonioides* 'Aurea' has spectacular bright acid yellow leaves, which are bronze in their early stages and appear in early summer. If left unpruned it will reach 10 x 10m (30 x 30ft). A neon yellow tree of this height is difficult to place: restrict its size by stooling every spring. Cut all the branches back to a couple of buds and the leaves will develop to a magnificent size.

COMPANIONS The green catalpa needs no company: plant as a specimen on a lawn with a seat positioned in its shade. The yellow-leaved form should, if possible, be seen against a sober background such as yew. Don't over-egg the pudding by mixing it with other yellow-leaved plants.

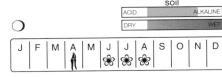

CATALPA BIGNONIODES

C

CEANOTHUS 'GLOIRE DE VERSAILLES'

Syn. **C. x delilianus** *'Gloire de Versailles', Californian lilac, deciduous shrub. Mature at 5 years: 1.8 x 2.5m (6 x 8ft). AGM*

Deciduous ceanothus flower from late summer to autumn, whereas the evergreen kinds are spring- and early summer-flowering. Pointed, veined mid-green leaves are born on a bushy plant. The first panicles of soft powder-blue, fragrant flowers open at midsummer and they continue until the autumn.

USES All ceanothus are quick growing, so they are useful if you need to make a quick screen for privacy or to hide an unattractive view. The deciduous kinds are hardier than the evergreens, and will grow happily in a border or shrubbery. They are nitrogen-fixing and good bee plants.

CULTIVATION Plant in spring in an open position, in any reasonable soil except shallow soil over chalk. Flowering will be more prolific if you cut back all the previous year's shoots to within 8cm (3in) of the old wood in late spring. This will also keep the plant shapely and prevent it becoming leggy.

PROPAGATION Take heeled cuttings of firm lateral shoots, 8-10cm (3-4in) long, during the summer.

PESTS AND DISEASES The leaves may be attacked by scale insects. Chlorosis (yellowing leaves) can occur if the soil is too limy.

OTHER VARIETIES C. 'Topaze' is a stronger brighter blue than 'Gloire de Versailles', but not so hardy. 'Marie Simon' and 'Perle Rose' have similar flowers, but soft pink.

COMPANIONS The powdery blue of 'Gloire de Versailles' makes a cool contrast to the orange scarlet flowers of *Crocosmia* 'Lucifer' or the remarkably clear orange of *Geum* 'Borisii'.

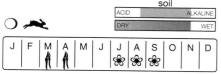

	soil	
	ACID	ALKALINE
	DRY	WET

J	F	M	A	M	J	J	A	S	O	N	D

CEANOTHUS 'GLOIRE DE VERSAILLES'

CEANOTHUS 'ITALIAN SKIES'

Evergreen shrub. Mature at 10 years: 1.5 x 3 m (5 x 10ft). AGM

Evergreen ceanothus are not reliably hardy, but give such a wonderful display and are so quick-growing that they are worth risking. This one makes a spreading bush with densely set, shiny dark green leaves, smothered, in early summer, with brilliant blue flowers in dense, conical trusses.

USES The dense mass of foliage is useful to hide drainpipes against a house wall, or manholes on the ground. They are good host plants for clematis of the Viticella and Texensis groups.

CULTIVATION In sheltered gardens in mild areas, grow as free-standing shrubs; elsewhere they need the protection of a sunny wall. Plant in any reasonable well-drained soil except thin soil over chalk. For the first season, water during dry spells. No regular pruning is necessary but if the plant outgrows its space, cut out flowered branches and shorten new shoots when they have finished flowering.

PROPAGATION In summer, take heeled semi-ripe cuttings, 8-10cm (3-4in.) and root with gentle bottom heat. Overwinter young plants in a cold frame.

PESTS AND DISEASES Generally trouble free, but leaves can be attacked by scale insects and suffer chlorosis (yellowing leaves) in extremely alkaline soil.

OTHER VARIETIES 'Autumnal Blue' AGM is the hardiest, followed by 'Burkwoodii' AGM, both flower from mid- to late summer. The early flowering kinds are less hardy, but of these, *C. impressus* and 'Cascade' AGM, with hanging tips of dark blue flowers, come through most winters against a warm wall. *C. thyrsiflorus* 'Repens' AGM makes excellent ground cover in all but the harshest climates.

COMPANIONS Interweave *C. thyrsiflorus* 'Repens' with Cistus 'Silver Pink'. Blue ceanothus flowers contrast well with *Cytisus praecox*, the Warminster broom.

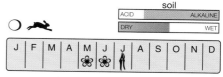

	soil	
	ACID	ALKALINE
	DRY	WET

J	F	M	A	M	J	J	A	S	O	N	D

CEANOTHUS GRISEUM VAR. HORIZONTALIS 'YANKEE POINT'

CEANOTHUS THYRSIFLORUS 'REPENS'

C

CENTAUREA CYANUS

Blue-bottle, cornflower, a hardy annual (Europe, including Britain). Mature at 3 months: 30-90 x 30cm (1-3 x 1ft).

The cornflower is now rarely seen in the wild. By way of compensation it is one of the easiest annuals to raise from seed in the garden. The leaves are narrow and grey-green. The very double flowers are composed of numerous tiny florets. Between 2.5- 5cm (1- 2in) across, they are held facing upwards at the ends of branching stems from midsummer to early autumn. As well as improved forms of the true-blue native, pink, purple and white forms are available of tall or compact habit. Beware of its perennial cousin *Centaurea montana*, a coarse, aggressive plant which quickly becomes a weed.

USES Sow cornflower seed as a quick filler between slower-growing plants, or grow it in a separate cut-flower border.

CULTIVATION Cornflowers need sun and will grow in any soil that is not too wet. In summer, dead-head the plants to keep the flowers coming.

PROPAGATION Sow the seeds in their final position in early autumn or early spring. Thin out the seedlings to 25cm (10in) apart.

PESTS AND DISEASES Petal blight can cause watery spots on the petals. Plants can be attacked by powdery mildew and rust.

OTHER VARIETIES Seeds are available in individual or mixed colours – pink, red, white, purple – as well as the traditional true blue.

COMPANIONS Plant cornflowers with *Calendula officinalis* for a vibrant, sock-it-to-them colour contrast. For a softer effect, use *C. cynanus* with pale yellows such as *Sisyrinchium striatum*, *Achillea* 'Taygetea', or *Potentilla* 'Primrose Beauty'.

soil

ACID		ALKALINE
DRY		WET

J	F	M	A	M	J	J	A	S	O	N	D

CENTAUREA CYANUS

CENTRANTHUS RUBER ATROCOCCINEUS

Red valerian, perennial (Mediterranean, naturalized in Britain). Mature at 1 year: 60-90 x 45cm (2-3ft x 18in).

Its ability to seed itself in the most inhospitable places almost qualifies red valerian as a weed. But it is hardy, easily grown, colourful, handsome and long-flowering. The glaucous leaves and stems are robust and manage to survive high winds when the roots are clinging to a crevice in a vertical cliff. Branching, broadly conical heads of tiny pinky-red, star-shaped flowers are poised on erect stems from early to late summer. They are followed by small seeds, each with a tiny fluffy parachute to aid wind distribution.

USES Given a nudge to start it off, valerian will colonize walls, rocky banks and areas of poor soil, especially on chalk or limestone. It is a good nectar plant for insects.

CULTIVATION Plant in early spring in sun on poor, well-drained soil. If you don't want the plants to seed, be vigilant and cut down the flowering stems as soon as the flowers begin to fade. Otherwise, cut down the dead growth in autumn.

PROPAGATION Sow seeds in spring or early summer, either where plants are to flower or in a seed bed. Thin the seedlings to about 45cm (18in) apart.

PESTS AND DISEASES Generally trouble free.

OTHER VARIETIES *C. ruber albus* has white flowers; *atrococcineus* and *coccineus* are a stronger red than the wild form, which can be rather a dingy pink.

COMPANIONS It is such an informal plant and shows such independence that it is not appropriate to use it in contrived planting schemes. But it does look good with that other independent and prolific self-seeder *Alchemilla mollis*.

soil

ACID		ALKALINE
DRY		WET

J	F	M	A	M	J	J	A	S	O	N	D

CENTRANTHUS RUBER F. ATROCOCCINEUS

CERATOSTIGMA WILLMOTTIANUM

Deciduous shrub (W. China, 1908). Mature at 10 years: 60 x 45cm (24 x 18in) after 5 years; 1 x 1m (3 x 3ft) at maturity.

This plant may lose all its top growth in a severe winter, but it will not be dead: new growth will develop from the base. In cold gardens it needs the warmest, sunniest site if it is to flower well before the frosts. It makes a bushy shrub, with small dark green, diamond-shaped leaves; they turn glowing red in autumn. Clusters of small sky blue flowers appear from late summer to autumn.

USES Plant ceratostigma in schemes planned for autumn effect. It will make effective ground cover in sheltered shrubberies.

CULTIVATION Plant in groups of three or more, in late spring or early summer, in full sun on a sheltered site. Add farmyard manure or garden compost to light soils. When planting, cut back all shoots to within 5cm (2in) of the old wood. In future years cut back the shoots to just above a live bud in spring.

PROPAGATION Take heeled semi-ripe cuttings of lateral shoots 8cm (3in) long during summer.

PESTS AND DISEASES Generally trouble free.

OTHER VARIETIES *C.plumbaginoides* AGM is a shrubby perennial with similar flowers and leaves, growing to 30cm (12in). It makes excellent ground cover, but if well-suited can become a nuisance, spreading too far, too fast. Good in a rock garden, or dry wall, but do not plant where it will crowd choice specimens. Separate rooted suckers in late spring, pot up and grow on until they are large enough to plant out.

COMPANIONS The blue flowers show to advantage against the autumn leaves of berberis and cotoneaster, or the warm red autumn flowers of *Hydrangea* 'Hamburg' or *H.* 'Preziosa' AGM.

soil

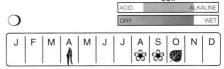

ACID		ALKALINE
DRY		WET

J	F	M	A	M	J	J	A	S	O	N	D

CERATOSTIGMA WILLMOTTIANUM

CERCIDIPHYLLUM JAPONICUM

Katsura tree, deciduous tree (Japan and China, 1881). Mature at 50 years: 7m (25ft) high after 10 years; 20 x 14m (65 x 46ft) at maturity. AGM

A large plant, often multi-stemmed, growing eventually into a large tree with a rounded crown of pendulous branches and spirally ridged bark. The leaves are rounded and heart-shaped like those of the Judas tree (*Cercis siliquastrum*). They are bronze-pink when they open, then rich sea green. In autumn they become multi-coloured, with red, orange, yellow, pink, mauve and green leaves, sometimes all on the same plant, especially on acid soil. The fallen leaves are said to smell of burnt toffee.

USES This is essentially a plant to grow for its autumn colour, so it needs a sheltered position where the leaves will not be blown away as soon as they turn colour. Give it sufficient space to develop to the full. Plant it where it can be seen from indoors.

CULTIVATION Plant in autumn, in any fertile, moisture-retentive soil in a position sheltered from early morning frosts and cold winds; woodland conditions are ideal. Late frosts may damage young shoots, but do not usually cause lasting harm. Although cercidiphyllum tolerates lime, the autumn colours are better on acid soils.

PROPAGATION Sow seeds in spring.

PESTS AND DISEASES Generally trouble free.

CERCIS SILIQUASTRUM

Judas tree, redbud, deciduous tree (China, N. America and S. Europe, 17th century). Mature at 30 years: 3 x 2.5m (10 x 8ft) after 10 years; 10 x 10m (30 x 30ft) at maturity. AGM

A large shrub or small tree with low-branching stems supporting a broad, domed head. Clusters of pea-like, pale to bright pink flowers appear in late spring, just before or at the same time as the smooth, heart-shaped leaves which stay sea green and fresh looking all summer. They are followed by long purplish-red pods, which remain on the tree in winter. The popular name is derived from a legend that this was the tree from which Judas hanged himself.

USES Such a beautiful tree makes a fine specimen on a lawn or paved terrace in even the smallest garden. The flowers are well worked by bees. They have a sweetish, acid taste, and can be used in salads.

CULTIVATION Plant in autumn or spring, in any reasonable soil except really heavy clay. *C. siliquastrum* is a sun-loving plant, and in colder districts needs a site with good shelter from cold, dry winter winds. Choose a position sheltered from late frosts to avoid damage to the flowers. Once they are established, the plants resent any disturbance to their roots.

PROPAGATION Sow seeds as soon as ripe in autumn, or in spring at 13-16°C (55-61°F).

PESTS AND DISEASES Coral spot can cause die-back of shoots: pink to red pustules appear towards the base of the dead wood.

OTHER SPECIES AND VARIETIES
C. siliquastrum f. *albida*, syn. 'Alba', has white flowers. *C. canadensis* 'Forest Pansy' AGM is a similar plant of elegant, spreading habit, with pink flowers on bare branches followed by red-purple leaves.

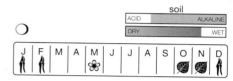

		soil		
		ACID		ALKALINE
○		DRY		WET

J	F	M	A	M	J	J	A	S	O	N	D

CERCIS SILIQUASTRUM

CERCIS SILIQUASTRUM

		soil		
		ACID		ALKALINE
●◐ ○ 🐇 ❋		DRY		WET

J	F	M	A	M	J	J	A	S	O	N	D

CERCIDIPHYLLUM JAPONICUM

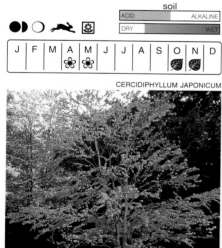

C

CHAENOMELES SPECIOSA

Japonica, Japanese quince, deciduous shrub (China, 1896). Mature at 7 years: 1.5 x 1.5m (5 x 5ft) after 5 years, 2.5 x 3m (8 x 10ft) at maturity.

Without doubt this is one of the top twenty shrubs. It is completely hardy and bears exceptionally beautiful flowers over a long period early in the season. The leaves are dark green, glossy and oblong. Large single flowers appear at the end of the winter and continue throughout spring. They are white, pink, apricot or red and are followed by large, edible, pear-shaped green-yellow fruits with a distinctive scent.

USES Flowering quinces are very adaptable and will tolerate a wide range of situations, including cold exposed sites, free-standing, or against a wall of any aspect. They are among the few plants that will succeed in the shady, draughty passage that runs down the side of a semi-detached house. The fruit can be used for jam or quince cheese but *Cydonia oblonga*, the orchard quince, is more aromatic and strongly flavoured.

CULTIVATION Plant from autumn to spring, in any ordinary soil including clay, in sun or shade. The plants will flower much more prolifically in sun. If you are planting against a wall, position the plant at least 45cm (18in) out from the wall, leaning it towards the wall and its supports. Provide wires, or a trellis framework to tie the

shoots to; it is not self-clinging. Plant from autumn to spring. Pruning encourages more flowers and keeps the plants bushy and tidy. On bushes, cut all shoots back in early spring to where there are flower buds. After flowering thin out crowded branches and remove weak stems. Wall-trained plants should be pruned in summer by cutting back the new season's growths to a few centimetres from the main stem, and by removing or shortening shoots growing out from the wall.

PROPAGATION Take semi-ripe cuttings in early summer. They should root easily in pots covered in a plastic bag. Alternatively, layer long shoots in late summer, separating rooted shoots from the parent plant one or two years later.

PESTS AND DISEASES Birds sometimes peck the buds, and aphids may attack the shoot tips in spring. Pinch out the affected tips. Plants can be attacked by fireblight. Cut off and burn all affected branches.

GOOD CULTIVARS *C. speciosa* cultivars are mostly tall and make good wall plants. They include 'Moerloosei', syn. 'Apple Blossom' AGM; the synonym accurately describes the flowers. 'Jet Trail' AGM is a compact white-flowered variety; 'Simonii' AGM is almost prostrate with deep blood red flowers. *C. x superba* cultivars make wider, bushy plants. Good reds are 'Crimson and Gold' AGM; 'Knap Hill Scarlet' AGM and 'Rowallane' AGM. 'Pink Lady' AGM is a good pink; 'Geisha Girl' has apricot flowers.

COMPANIONS The red colouring of many of the flowering quinces is very welcome at a season when most flowers are yellow or blue. Plant them informally in the shade of trees with bluebells and primroses, and add a summer-flowering clematis to trail through them.

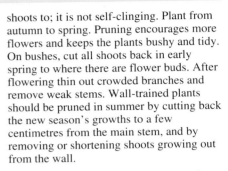
CHAENOMELES JAPONICA

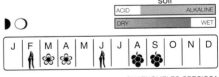

CHAENOMELES SPECIOSA

CHAMAECYPARIS LAWSONIANA 'COLUMNARIS GLAUCA'

Lawson cypress, evergreen coniferous tree.
Mature at 30 years: 3.5m x 60cm
(12 x 2ft) after 10 years; up to 10 x 1m
(33 x 3ft) at maturity.

This useful and elegant conifer is hardy and easy to grow, making a slender, upright column of blue-grey foliage. It produces globular cones after a few years.

USES It can provide the vertical line that makes so much difference to the composition of mixed plantings of shrubs. In formal gardens, plant a pair flanking a path or flight of steps, or a short avenue marching either side of a path.

CULTIVATION Plant in any ordinary, well-drained soil. Plant in early autumn on light soils, in spring on heavy soils, and water during dry spells for the first year or two until well established, especially on poor soils. Large specimen plants are available, but they need care and attention. Small plants of 45cm (18in) or so will establish more easily, grow faster and need no staking. Pruning is not usually necessary, but watch out in spring for forking of the leading shoot, and if this occurs prune to ensure a single strong leader. Trim plants grown for hedging in late spring or early autumn, but trim regularly every year to keep a close dense finish; they do not break from old wood.

PROPAGATION Named cultivars do not come true and must be raised from cuttings of about 10cm (4in) with a heel, in late spring or late summer. Dwarf cultivars are often grafted in late winter or early spring. Seeds of the species can be sown under glass in late winter or outside in spring. When the seedlings are 8cm (3in) high prick them out into nursery rows and grow on for two years before transplanting to permanent sites.

PESTS AND DISEASES Generally trouble free, but susceptible to honey fungus, and to *Phytophthora* root rot.

OTHER VARIETIES 'Fletcheri' AGM has soft grey-green foliage and makes a broad column about 2.5m (8ft) in ten years. 'Kilmacurragh' AGM is dark green, tall and narrow, with billowing sprays of foliage; it closely resembles an Italian cypress, but is much hardier. 'Pembury Blue' AGM has very blue foliage, 2.5 x 1.5m (8 x 5ft) after ten years, eventully 15 x 5m (50 x 15ft). 'Broomhill Gold' is yellow, 1.5m (5ft) tall after ten years. The variety to choose for a quick-growing hedge (60cm/2ft apart) or screen (1.5m/5ft apart) is 'Green Hedger'. 'Fletcheri' also makes an attractive hedge.

COMPANIONS Use these upright conifers singly as exclamation marks among horizontal conifers such as *Juniperus x pfitzeriana* AGM or with other evergreen shrubs of rounded habit. Alternatively, group three of them together in an irregular triangle to dominate a scheme planned for all-year-round interest.

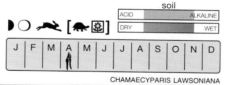

CHAMAECYPARIS LAWSONIANA

CHAMAEMELUM NOBILE

C

*Syn. **Anthemis nobilis**. Chamomile, hardy perennial (Europe, including Britain). Mature at 3 years: 10 x 45cm (4 x 18in)*

A completely hardy, evergreen creeping perennial with small ferny leaves of emerald green and small yellow-centred, white daisy flowers in summer. The leaves are aromatic when crushed. In time, the plant spreads to form a dense mat which can become invasive.

USES Chamomile was once, and sometimes still is, used to make a lawn. It gives off a delicious herbal fragrance when crushed underfoot, and is more drought-resistant than grass. It will not, however, stand up to much regular foot traffic and, in time, the the centre of the plant tends to become bare. To keep it looking good, frequent hand-weeding is needed, especially in the early stages. But a small patch of camomile lawn, perhaps at the centre of a herb garden, is a delight to see, touch and smell. It can also be used to edge a gravel path, to fill gaps in paving or in a raised bed to make a seat; in any situation, in fact, where occasional pressure can release its refreshing scent. Tea made from the flowers is a mild sedative. It can be used as a rinse for blonde hair.

CULTIVATION Plant in spring in well-drained soil in full sun. For a lawn, place rooted shoots 10-15cm (4-6in) apart. Weed carefully and water until established. Once or twice a year, cut with a mower or shears.

PROPAGATION Divide in autumn or spring, or sow seeds in spring.

PESTS AND DISEASES Trouble free.

OTHER VARIETIES *C. n.* 'Flore Pleno' has cream, very double flowers like little pom-poms. *C. n.* 'Treneague' is a compact, non-flowering form; the best for making a lawn.

CHAMAEMELUM NOBILE 'FLORE PLENO'

C

CHIONODOXA LUCILIAE

Syn. C. gigantea. Glory of the snow, hardy bulbous perennial (W. Turkey, late 19th century). Mature at 6 months: 10 x 5cm (4 x 2in). AGM

One of the earliest spring bulbs, chionodoxas produce two glossy spear-shaped leaves, followed by bare stems holding upward-facing, star-shaped flowers. The petals are pale blue with a darker blue stripe down the centre, and each flower has a white centre.

USES Chionodoxas are easy to grow in rock gardens, in short grass under deciduous trees or in the open, in the front of borders or beneath roses and other shrubs.

CULTIVATION Plant in autumn, 5-8cm (2-3in) deep, in any well-drained soil, in full sun or light shade. To make informal groups for naturalizing, scatter bulbs at random and plant them where they fall. The larger the group the better. Allow the leaves to die down before mowing or cutting them back.

PROPAGATION Chionodoxas will increase by seeding and by multiplying underground to produce widening colonies of bulbs. If you want to start a new colony, collect the seed pods in late spring when the seeds are ripe, but before the capsules split. Sow in a cold frame and transplant to their final position in their second summer. Lift and divide overcrowded plants as the leaves die down.

PESTS AND DISEASES Generally trouble free.

OTHER VARIETIES There are pink forms, 'Rosea' and 'Pink Giant', and a white form 'Alba'. *C. sardensis* AGM has slightly pendent flowers which are a wonderful intense cobalt blue.

GOOD COMPANIONS Naturalize with groups of other early bulbs such as yellow or white crocus and dwarf narcissus. The white trunks of *Betula utilis* var. *jacquemontii* look very beautiful rising out of a sea of *C. sardensis*.

soil

ACID	ALKALINE
DRY	WET

J	F	M	A	M	J	J	A	S	O	N	D

CHIONODOXA LUCILIAE

CHOISYA TERNATA

Mexican orange blossom, evergreen shrub (Mexico, early 1800s). Mature at 10 years: slowly reaching 2 x 1.5m (6 x 5ft) after 10 years; 2.5 x 2m (8 x 6ft) at maturity.

A dense rounded bush with glossy mid-green rounded leaves. The leaves are aromatic when crushed. The white star-shaped flowers appear in clusters in spring and intermittently throughout the summer. They are scented but, in spite of the shrub's popular name, the resemblance to orange blossom in both appearance and fragrance is hardly noticeable.

USES Having got its main flush of flowering over early, choisya makes an invaluable solid green background to other plants. It is also useful alone, or as part of a mixed group of shrubs to blot out unwanted views.

CULTIVATION Plant choisyas in late spring in any well-drained soil, including chalk, in sun or light shade. They need shelter from cold winds. No pruning is needed except to remove frost-damaged shoots in spring and tidy straggly branches after flowering.

PROPAGATION Take semi-ripe cuttings in late summer.

PESTS AND DISEASES Generally trouble free, although choisyas are susceptible to honey fungus.

OTHER VARIETIES *Choisya* 'Aztec Pearl' AGM is a smaller compact shrub with slender divided leaves. It is not a robust plant and needs more care and attention than *C. ternata*. There is a popular form of *C. ternata* called 'Sundance' AGM which has leaves of brilliant neon lime yellow.

GOOD COMPANIONS The dense, plain green foliage of *C. ternata* contrasts well with shrubs with variegated leaves such as *Elaeagnus pungens* 'Maculata' AGM or *Cornus alba* 'Elegantissima' AGM.

soil

ACID	ALKALINE
DRY	WET

J	F	M	A	M	J	J	A	S	O	N	D

CHOISYA 'AZTEC PEARL'

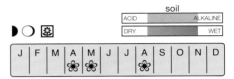

CHOISYA TERNATA

C

CICHORIUM INTYBUS

Chicory, hardy perennial (Europe including Britain). Mature at 2 years: 120 x 45cm (4ft x 18in). AGM

Strong stems of soft mid-green arrow-shaped leaves emerge from a robust tap root in spring and branch at the top to bear many-petalled, daisy flowers of a pure soft blue, held close against the stems. All the flowers open at the same time each day and close again five hours later. The plants are in flower from midsummer until autumn.

USES Besides being a decorative flowering plant, chicory is a vegetable. The roots can be lifted and forced in darkness to produce chicons, leafy white hearts eaten in salads or braised in butter, known as chicory or endive. The dried and roasted roots are sometimes used to flavour coffee.

CULTIVATION Plant in deep light soil, preferably alkaline, and water until established. Cut the stems down in autumn or winter. To force chicons, dig up the roots, trim the stem to 2.5cm (1in) and trim 2.5cm (1in) off the root. Then bury the roots in sandy compost, water and leave in a cellar, garage or shed. The chicons should be big enough to eat in three or four weeks.

PROPAGATION Sow seeds in the open in early summer.

PESTS AND DISEASES Generally trouble free.

OTHER VARIETIES *C. intybus* 'Album' and 'Rosea' have white and rose-pink flowers respectively.

○

soil

ACID									ALKALINE
DRY									WET

J	F	M	A	M	J	J	A	S	O	N	D
						✿	✿	✿	✿	✂	✂

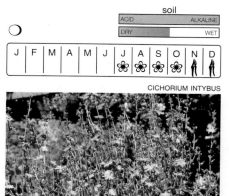
CICHORIUM INTYBUS

CISTUS X CORBARIENSIS

Syn. **C. x hybridus**. *Rock rose, evergreen shrub (S. Europe, mid 16th century). Mature at 5 years: 60 x 90cm (2 x 3ft). AGM*

With their evergreen leaves and prolific flowers cistus are unrivalled for hot, dry sites. Unfortunately they are vulnerable to frost, to winter wet and cold winds. This is one of the hardiest; it has matt, dark green pointed, wrinkled leaves and masses of saucer-shaped white flowers, which emerge from pink buds from late spring to early summer. It sheds its tissue paper petals at the end of each day, but new flowers continue to be produced.

USES If chalkly or sandy soil is your problem, a cistus can solve it, provided you give it a sunny sheltered spot. The smaller forms, including *C. x corbariensis,* are dense enough to make good ground cover. They look appropriate in gravel or paving.

CULTIVATION Plant in late spring, in sharply drained soil in full sun. Prune off any frost-damaged shoots in spring. To keep the plants neat and bushy, clip with shears after flowering, taking off about two-thirds of the new growth. Never cut into old wood; this may kill the plant.

PROPAGATION Take cuttings routinely early every autumn, in case you lose the parent plants to a hard frost. Overwinter the cuttings in a frost-free frame or greenhouse.

PESTS AND DISEASE Generally trouble free.

OTHER VARIETIES *C.* 'Peggy Sammons', 90 x 90cm (3 x 3ft) AGM is a fairly hardy bush with greyish-green leaves and pale pink flowers; 'Silver Pink is similar. *C. x purpureus* AGM is less hardy, but has beautiful large magenta-pink flowers with yellow centres and maroon blotches at the petal base; *C. monspeliensis* is frost hardy, with pure white petals.

soil

ACID									ALKALINE
DRY									WET

○ 🐇 ❄

J	F	M	A	M	J	J	A	S	O	N	D
					✿	✿	⚘				

CISTUS 'SILVER PINK'

CISTUS MONSPELIENSIS

C

CLEMATIS

Old man's beard, traveller's joy, virgin's bower, mostly hardy, evergreen or deciduous woody, twining climbers, or herbaceous perennials. Mature at 7 years: from 75 x 75cm (30 x 30in) to 12 x 3m (40 x 10ft).

This versatile and beautiful genus falls into three main categories, which are described separately in more detail below. All except the herbaceous types share the characteristic method of climbing by means of twining leaf stalks, which hook around whatever support they encounter. The flowers vary enormously. In some species they resemble nodding, graceful bells, while some of the large-flowered cultivars are more like dinner plates. The wide colour range includes all shades of red and blue, violet, black-purple, white and yellow. Some forms have decorative, fluffy seed heads.

USES Depending on which species or cultivar you choose, there is a clematis for almost every situation a climbing plant can fill: on trellises, walls, fences, arches or pergolas; up a tree, or rambling through a shrub; hanging from a retaining wall or covering a bank. The late large-flowered

CLEMATIS 'NELLY MOSER' (GRP 2)

CLEMATIS 'VILLE DE LYON' (GRP 3)

hybrids very considerably flower at that awkward time after midsummer when the roses are past their best and nothing much has come to take their place.

CULTIVATION All clematis need a cool, deep, moist root run. Provide it by digging a hole at least 45cm (18in) deep and wide. Fill it with good soil mixed with compost or leaf mould and bonemeal. Bury the plant with its crown 7cm (3in) below the surface, leaning the stems and their supporting cane towards the support. Don't plant climbers right up against a wall where the soil is invariably poor and dry. Plant at least 45cm (18in) out from the wall. Sink a plastic flower pot or short length of plastic pipe beside the root ball to make watering easy. Protect the fragile shoots with a cylinder of wire netting about 30cm (12in) high. Shade the roots with paving slabs or a layer of pebbles. For good results, mulch with well-rotted manure in autumn, or add some bonemeal. In spring, apply sulphate of potash.

PRUNING AND TRAINING The first spring after planting, cut back all the stems to just above the lowest pair of strong healthy buds. Further pruning depends on the species or type. If in doubt, just tidy straggly stems after flowering. In spring and summer the shoots grow very rapidly. It pays to be vigilant and coax the developing tendrils around their supports, getting a wide horizontal coverage so that the whole plant doesn't end up as a tangle of stems well above eye level.

EARLY FLOWERING SPECIES AND CULTIVARS (Group 1) *Clematis alpina* flowers in spring and *C. macropetala* a little later. Both grow to about 2.5 x 1.5m (8 x 5ft) and have masses of nodding flowers: blue, pink, or white, according to the named cultivar. Pruning is optional; plants can be tidied after flowering or cut back hard to a pair of strong buds to encourage new growth from the base. *C. montana* is the rampant plant that will swarm up a tall tree or smother a garden shed. Where there is space, it is a fine sight in late spring, smothered in vanilla-scented white, cream, or pink

CLEMATIS JACKMANII (GRP 3)

CLEMATIS 'WILLIAM KENNETT' (GRP 2)

CLEMATIS 'HENRYI' (GRP 2)

CLEMATIS MONTANA 'ELIZABETH' (GRP 1)

C

CLEMATIS 'H.F. YOUNG' (GRP 2)

CLEMATIS 'LASURSTERN' (GRP 2)

CLEMATIS 'DUCHESS OF EDINBURGH' (GRP 2)

CLEMATIS 'MRS CHOLMONDELEY' (GRP 2)

CLEMATIS ARMANDII (GRP 1)

four-petalled, open-faced flowers. Prune after flowering only if necessary to keep it within bounds.

LARGE-FLOWERED CULTIVARS (Group 2)
These bloom from early to midsummer. 'Nelly Moser' AGM is a reliable old favourite, climbing to 4 x 2m (12 x 6ft) from the third year after planting. The eight-petalled flowers, 18-23cm (7-9in) across, appear in early summer and intermittently until the end of summer. Each pale mauve petal is strongly marked with a pink central stripe when grown in shade, but the colour fades in strong sun. It is ideal for a north or east aspect, either alone or twining through the bare legs of a climbing rose. 'Nelly Moser' needs a dark background. Prune this, and other clematis that flower in early summer, by lightly trimming back the shoots to strong buds in early spring.

LATE FLOWERING SPECIES, AND SMALL AND LARGE-FLOWERED CULTIVARS (Group 3)
C. viticella and its named cultivars flower after midsummer through early autumn.

The late large-flowered cultivars include 'Gipsy Queen' AGM with velvety, violet-purple flowers, and 'Huldine', with smaller flowers, one of the best white clematis. Prune hard at the end of winter, cutting to a pair of strong buds about 20cm (8in) above soil level, just above the second pair of leaf nodes.

PROPAGATION Softwood or semi-ripe cuttings during summer, or layers in early spring.

PESTS AND DISEASES Slugs can eat young shoots and aphids infest the growing tips. Powdery mildew and a virus causing yellow mottling on leaves are disfiguring. Clematis wilt sometimes affects shoots from the tip down to the base, though it seldom kills the whole plant. Cut off affected branches as soon as you detect the wilt.

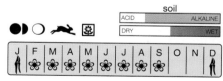

CLEMATIS ORIENTALIS (GRP 3)

CLEMATIS ALPINA (GRP 1)

C

CLERODENDRUM TRICHOTOMUM

Deciduous shrub (China, Japan). Mature at 15 years: 1.5 x 1.5m (5 x 5ft) after 5 years; 3 x 2.5m (10 x 8ft) at maturity.

This upright, round-headed shrub comes into its own from late summer through to autumn. It is vigorous but only moderately hardy, especially when young. The leaves, which are purplish when they emerge, are large, pointed and soft in texture, with an unpleasant smell when crushed. However the flowers have quite a pleasing fragrance. They are like white stars opening from pink buds in late summer and are followed by vivid turquoise-blue berries, each held at the centre of a deep red star formed by the calyx. Later in the season the berries turn blue-black.

USES Make this shrub part of a group planned for autumn display.

CULTIVATION Plant in spring in ordinary garden soil that does not dry out, but is not boggy either. Clerodendrums need plenty of light, but a position providing partial shade in the summer. Fairly open woodland conditions are ideal. In the first summer,

water during dry spells. Pruning is not needed except for the removal of any frost-damaged shoots in spring.

PROPAGATION You will usually find rooted suckers around the plant; these can be detached and planted elsewhere.

PESTS AND DISEASES Plants may suffer attacks from whitefly, red spider mites and mealy bugs.

OTHER VARIETIES *C. trichotomum* var. *fargesii* is an exceptionally free-fruiting form. *C. bungei* AGM is an invasive suckering shrub with large coarse, purple-green leaves and dome-shaped heads of purple-pink flowers at the top of each stem. The plant grows to about 2m (6ft) tall and spreads indefinitely. The whole plant is invariably cut to ground level by frost, but new shoots appear in spring.

CLERODENDRUM TRICHOTOMUM

COLCHICUM SPECIOSUM

Syn. C. bornmuelleri of gardens. Autumn crocus, a hardy corm (Caucasus). Mature at 2 years: 15 x 15cm (6 x 6in). AGM

Lilac-pink goblet-shaped flowers with white throats emerge from bare ground in early autumn before the leaves appear. The flowers are followed in winter or early spring by large, rather coarse erect leaves that die down at the end of summer before the flowers.

USES Autumn crocuses will naturalize if they are suited to the soil and position. In such a case they are almost completely trouble free, providing ground cover with their broad leaves and quite content to look after themselves.

CULTIQUITEVATION Plant the corms, in late summer, in groups of five or more, in light soil, preferably enriched with decayed farmyard manure or with leaf mould. They should be 8cm (3in) deep and about the same distance apart. Suitable positions include shrubberies and short grass in full sun, or under trees with a light canopy. When grown in rock gardens, bear in mind that the large leaves will swamp smaller alpines, so site them at the base of the rockery where they won't be a threat.

PROPAGATION Seedlings take four or five years to grow to flowering size, so the best way to propagate colchicums is to dig up and divide established clumps in late summer as the leaves fade.

OTHER VARIETIES *C. autumnale* is British meadow saffron, now very rare in the wild and worth conserving in our gardens. There are several named cultivars of autumn crocus in shades of purple, pink and white, with single, double and 'waterlily' flowers.

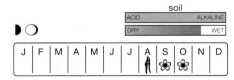

COLCHIUM AUTUMNALE

COLUTEA ARBORESCENS

Bladder senna, hardy shrub (S. Europe, mid 16th century). Mature at 7 years: 1.5 x 1.5m (5 x 5ft) after 5 years, 3 x 3m (10 x 10ft) at maturity.

This shrub is grown mainly for its curious seed pods. They are 8cm (3in) long, pale green suffused with pinkish buff, of a papery texture and inflated so that they pop when squeezed: fun for children but they must be warned that the seeds are poisonous. *C. arborescens* is a much-branched, bushy and vigorous shrub. The soft pale green leaves are divided into many paired leaflets and the pea flowers are yellow. It has a long flowering season from midsummer until early autumn when the bladder-like pods appear and remain for about two months.

USES It is drought tolerant and will grow happily in chalk, in seaside conditions and in areas of industrial pollution. The flowers provide food for bees. Colutea makes an easy and useful space-filler for the wilder parts of the garden.

CULTIVATION Colutea is very easy to grow in any soil that is not waterlogged, and in full sun or light shade, though in shade it will flower and fruit less prolifically. Plant between autumn and spring. In late spring prune by removing one stem in three to ensure a continuing supply of new wood. If it grows too big for its position, all stems can be shortened.

PROPAGATION It grows easily from seed sown in spring.

PESTS AND DISEASES Generally trouble free.

OTHER VARIETIES *C.* x *media* 'Copper Beauty' has prettier, grey-green leaves and pale copper-coloured flowers, but the latter are disappointingly sparse.

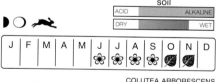

soil

ACID		ALKALINE
DRY		WET

J	F	M	A	M	J	J	A	S	O	N	D

COLUTEA ARBORESCENS

CONVALLARIA MAJALIS

Lily-of-the-valley, rhizomatous perennial (Europe, including Britain). Mature at 3 years: 16cm (6in) high with indefinite spread. AGM

Lily-of-the-valley is much loved for the sweet fragrance of the flowers. They hang like small rounded white bells along arching dark green stems. The flowering stems emerge in late spring between two upright, lance-shaped pointed dark green leaves.

USES Where the plants settle in well they make excellent ground cover. The flowers can be picked to make scented posies and are traditionally included in bridal bouquets.

CULTIVATION Plant the crowns in early autumn, 8cm (3in) apart with their tips just below the surface. Lilies-of-the-valley can be temperamental about where they want to grow, but in theory they prefer a lightly shaded position under trees or below a north-facing wall or hedge. Their preferred soil is a well-drained loam with plenty of organic material in the form of leaf mould or garden compost. Perfectionists would mulch with decayed manure towards the end of the winter and administer a feed of liquid manure weekly throughout the growing season. But if the plants are happy they will thrive in quite poor conditions.

PROPAGATION Lift and divide the rhizomes at four-yearly intervals after flowering, or in the autumn.

PESTS AND DISEASES Generally trouble free.

OTHER VARIETIES 'Fortin's Giant' is, at a height of 45cm (18in), larger in all its parts, and 'Flore Pleno' has double flowers. There is also a desirable form which has white-striped variegation on its leaves, *C. majalis* 'Albostriata'.

soil

ACID		ALKALINE
DRY		WET

J	F	M	A	M	J	J	A	S	O	N	D

CONVALLARIA MAJALIS

C

CONVOLVULUS CNEORUM

Evergreen shrub (S. Europe, before 1640). Mature at 5 years: 60 x 60cm (2 x 2ft). AGM

Not to be confused with the twining convolvulus which, in the form of bindweed, tortures the tidy gardener. This shrub shares with its aggressive relative only the single, funnel-shaped flowers. True, it only just scrapes in here, because it is not entirely hardy. Nevertheless it is included because it is a plant of beauty and distinction. It forms a dense mound covered in narrow, silky tactile leaves. For once the epithet 'silver' is accurate. In early summer terminal clusters of pink buds open into pink-tinged, white trumpet flowers.

USES Its tenderness limits its usefulness in the garden, but it makes excellent ground cover in a sunny sheltered place, or on a rock garden; if container-grown it can be moved to a cool greenhouse for the winter.

CULTIVATION Good drainage is the main requirement if this shrub is to survive winter frosts. It seems to grow best in virtually soil-less stony rubble in full sun. The shelter of a southwest-facing wall is ideal. Plant in spring. Don't prune, except to tidy straggling shoots.

PROPAGATION Cuttings taken in late summer root quite easily in a cold frame.

PESTS AND DISEASES Generally trouble free

OTHER VARIETIES *C. sabatius*, syn. *C. mauritanicus* AGM is also not quite hardy, but comes through mild winters in a sharply drained sheltered position. It is a trailing perennial, 15cm (6in) high, with attractive greyish-green leaves. Draped over the front of a raised bed, it will produce small blue funnel-shaped flowers all summer.

COMPANIONS Grow with other grey-leaved plants that enjoy sunny, well-drained conditions – lavenders, santolinas, *Phlomis italica*.

soil	
ACID	ALKALINE
DRY	WET

J	F	M	A	M	J	J	A	S	O	N	D

CONVOLVULUS CNEORUM

CONVOLVULUS CNEORUM

CORNUS ALBA

Cornel, dogwood, deciduous shrub (Siberia, 1741). Mature at 10 years: 2 x 2m (6 x 6ft) after 10 years; 3 x 3m (10 x 10ft) at maturity.

Dogwoods in this group are grown mainly for their colourful stems. They are very hardy and easy to grow, making vigorous upright bushes; the bark on the previous summer's growth is brightly coloured, darkening towards spring. The elliptic mid-green leaves are variegated in some forms and often turn red or orange in autumn. Rounded clusters of small star-shaped yellow-white flowers in early spring are followed by blue-black berries.

USES These shrubs will grow almost anywhere provided there is some moisture in the soil. They like their roots in water and are useful for stabilizing the banks of rivers and lakes and preventing erosion. The stems provide a fine display of winter colour.

CULTIVATION Plant in spring in sun or shade, in any position that is not hot or dry, including waterlogged ground. Prune by cutting hard back to within a few centimeters of the ground in spring.

PROPAGATION Take semi-ripe cuttings in summer or hardwood cuttings in autumn, or detach and replant suckers between autumn and spring. Layer long shoots in late summer and sever from the parent plant during the following autumn.

PESTS AND DISEASES Generally trouble free.

GOOD CULTIVARS *C. alba* can be an aggressive colonizer, so choose one of the following instead: 'Sibirica' AGM has stems of the brightest red; 'Spaethii' AGM has red stems, yellow-variegated leaves and good autumn colour. 'Elegantissima' has a white variegation. *C. stolonifera* 'Flaviramea' AGM has yellow stems and green leaves.

soil	
ACID	ALKALINE
DRY	WET

J	F	M	A	M	J	J	A	S	O	N	D

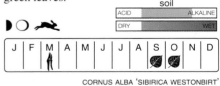

CORNUS ALBA 'SIBIRICA WESTONBIRT'

CORNUS CONTROVERSA 'VARIEGATA'

Wedding cake tree, deciduous tree (China, Himalaya, Japan, 1890). Mature at 30 years: 3 x 3m (10 x 10ft) after 10 years, 8 x 8m (25 x 25ft) or more at maturity. AGM

Its elegant, tiered habit of growth and creamy white variegated leaves make this an exceptionally beautiful tree. In winter the young growth is a warm dark red and, in early summer, flat clusters of small star-shaped cream flowers are carried along the tops of the horizontal branches.

USES It deserves to stand alone on a lawn, against a dark background.

CULTIVATION Plant in spring, in fertile well-drained soil.

PROPAGATION The variegated form is usually propagated by grafting.

PESTS AND DISEASES Generally trouble free

OTHER VARIETIES *C. controversa*, the non-variegated species, is a very handsome tree in its own right, with the same tiered habit and slightly larger green leaves which, on some soils, turn purple in the autumn. *C. alternifolia* 'Argentea' AGM is a multi-stemmed shrub or small tree, with a similar, very graceful tiered habit and white-margined leaves; it reaches 6m (20ft) high by as much across at maturity, and is the one to go for in smaller gardens. *C. florida* and *C. kousa* have a similar but less exaggerated tiered habit, but they are grown mainly for their beautiful white or coloured bracts, which look like the petals of large flowers. On *C. florida* 'Cherokee Chief' AGM they are deep pink. As well as spectacular white bracts, *C. kousa* var. *chinensis* has leaves that turn crimson in autumn. Don't expect the bracts to develop for several years after planting. These cornus all need warmth and shelter from cold drying winds to do well.

soil		
ACID		ALKALINE
DRY		WET

J	F	M	A	M	J	J	A	S	O	N	D
				❀	❀						

CORNUS CONTROVESA 'VARIEGATA'

CORTADERIA SELLOANA 'SUNNINGDALE SILVER'

Pampas grass, evergreen perennial grass (Argentina). Mature at 5 years: 2.1 x 1.2m (7 x 4ft). AGM

This hardy grass forms a big clump of slender arching leaves. Their margins are rough-edged and sharp; it is easy to cut yourself on them if you are not careful. Closely grouped stems rise erect above the clump in late summer, topped with loose silky white plumes which wave in the slightest breeze. In the species, which usually bears male and female plumes on different plants, the female plumes are more silky than those of the males. The plumes of 'Sunningdale Silver' are more weather resistant than most.

USES Victorian and Edwardian traditional style places a pampas grass on the front lawn of every house in suburbia, but they are also splendid plants for large scale beds and borders, among large shrubs and for waterside plantings.

CULTIVATION Plant in spring, in well-drained fertile soil in a reasonably sheltered sunny site. Tidy the plants in spring by removing the dead leaves. Wear gloves to protect your hands from sharp leaf edges.

PROPAGATION Divide and replant in spring.

PESTS AND DISEASES Generally trouble free.

OTHER VARIETIES *C. selloana* 'Pumila' AGM is more compact at 1.5m (5ft) high, with upright, creamy-white plumes.

COMPANIONS Their strong character and distinctive form make the larger grasses quite difficult to place in the garden. They have no place among 'pretty' plants, but need sculptural plants such as bergenias nearby, and a contrasting background of solid dense foliage – yew, perhaps, or conifers such as *cryptomeria* and some of the lawson cypresses.

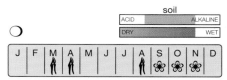

soil		
ACID		ALKALINE
DRY		WET

J	F	M	A	M	J	J	A	S	O	N	D
		♟	♟					♟	❀	❀	❀

CORTADERIA SELLOANA 'SUNNINGDALE SILVER'

C

CORYDALIS LUTEA

Syn. **Pseudofumaria lutea,** *evergreen hardy perennial (Europe). Mature at 2 years: 30 x 30cm (1 x 1ft).*

This is one of those plants that would be more highly valued if it were not so easy to grow. In many gardens it arrives uninvited and makes itself at home. It produces mounds of soft fern-like, pale green leaves on brittle translucent stalks. From spring until autumn they are scattered over with tiny yellow, snapdragon-shaped flowers.

USES This corydalis will quickly make ground cover in any out-of-the-way part of the garden, or may position itself in walls and paving. Both leaves and flowers are pretty for small scale flower arrangements.

CULTIVATION Plant in early spring, in any fertile, well-drained garden soil and in sun or shade. It seeds itself promiscuously, so keep watch for unwanted seedlings and pull them up while they are still small.

PROPAGATION Sow the seeds *in situ,* or in a cold frame in late winter or early autumn, directly into small pots so they can be planted out with minimum disturbance, as the stems and roots are very brittle.

PESTS AND DISEASES Generally trouble free.

OTHER VARIETIES There are some very pretty corydalis that need more care to satisfy their needs. *C. cashmeriana* is a good rock garden plant with dense spikes of bright blue flowers. It needs cool, humus-rich neutral to acid soil in partial shade. It dies down in winter.

soil		
ACID		ALKALINE
DRY		WET

J	F	M	A	M	J	J	A	S	O	N	D
				✽	✽	✽	✽	✽	✽		

CORYDALIS LUTEA

CORYLUS AVELLANA

Hazel or cobnut, deciduous shrub or small tree (Europe). Mature at 15 years: 2.5 x 2.5m (8 x 8ft) after 10 years; 6 x 4.5m (20ft x 15ft) at maturity.

In Britain's winter hedgerows hazel catkins hanging from the branches are one of the first indications that spring is on the way. The catkins are a soft shade of yellow with the tight woolly texture of miniature lambs' tails, and are followed by broad, serrated mid-green leaves which turn yellow in autumn. In early autumn the nuts appear in clusters of two to four. Their smooth pale green shells are enclosed in a leafy cup and both shell and cup ripen to pale buff brown.

USES Hazel bushes are grown for their nuts, as components in rural hedges and, in ornamental cultivars, for their coloured leaves or contorted stems. Very hardy, they thrive in exposed sites, on consolidated soils and in areas of industrial pollution.

CULTIVATION Plant between autumn and spring in any reasonable soil, including clay or sandy soil, in sun or in partial shade. In a nuttery, plant 3m (10ft) apart. Hazel produces a lot of twiggy growth and tends to sucker. Remove suckers annually and thin to five or six main branches; shorten all branches by up to one-third if needed. Gather the nuts when the husks begin to turn brown.

PROPAGATION Dig up and replant rooted suckers. Peg down layers in autumn, severing them when well rooted.

PESTS AND DISEASES Trouble free, except that squirrels usually take most of the nuts.

OTHER VARIETIES The most garden worthy is *C. maxima* 'Purpurea' AGM with leaves of dark maroon-purple and purplish-pink catkins. *C. avellana* 'Contorta' AGM, the corkscrew hazel, has twisted and contorted stems. It is slow growing.

soil		
ACID		ALKALINE
DRY		WET

J	F	M	A	M	J	J	A	S	O	N	D
	✽	✽							🍃	🍃	

CORYLUS MAXIMA 'PURPUREA'

CORYLUS AVELLANA

COSMOS BIPINNATUS

Half-hardy annual (Mexico, 1835). Mature at 6 months: 30-120 x 45-60cm (12-48 x 18-24in).

This reliable easily-grown annual has sturdy stems with feathery thread-like leaves. From summer to early autumn, large open flowers bloom at the end of each stem. In shape and texture they are somewhere between a daisy and a single dahlia. Seed strains are usually sold in a colour range of crimson, pink, red and white.

USES Annual cosmos seeds are usually only available in mixed colours, which look best planted in informal drifts. They are ideal as fillers in a mixed or herbaceous border. In the·southern states of the United States they are often used to brighten highway verges.

CULTIVATION Cosmos need sun and prefer a light rather poor soil, performing best in hot, dry seasons. Rich soils produce excess foliage and delayed flowering. The flower stems need staking if they are grown in exposed positions. Dead-head to ensure a succession of large flowers.

PROPAGATION Sow seeds under glass in late winter. Prick out the seedlings and harden off in a cold frame before planting them in their flowering positions in early summer.

PESTS AND DISEASES Generally trouble free.

GOOD CULTIVARS Sensation Series cultivars have large red, pink and white flowers. Cultivars of *C. sulphureus,* such as the Bright Lights Series, have yellow, orange and red flowers. There is a much sought-after tuberous perennial, *C. atrosanguineus* (*syn. Bidens atrosanguinea*), with very dark maroon, velvet flowers that smell of chocolate. It is liable to succumb to winter frosts but will usually survive if well protected with a deep dry mulch.

soil

ACID			ALKALINE
DRY			WET

J	F	M	A	M	J	J	A	S	O	N	D

COSMOS

COTINUS COGGYGRIA

Syn. Rhus cotinus Smoke tree, Venetian sumach, deciduous shrub (S. Europe, eastwards to central China). Mature at 15 years: 2 x 2m (7 x 7ft) after 10 years; 5 x 5m (15 x 15ft) at maturity. AGM

Grown for their beautifully shaped and colourful leaves and their unique flowers, these plants form dense rounded bushes. Some cultivars have purple leaves. In the species, the rounded leaves are light green and smooth with a light sheen. They turn brilliant orange-red in autumn. In summer feathery panicles of tiny pale pinky-buff flowers seem to hover like smoke above the shrub, becoming grey as autumn advances.

USES The purple-leaved forms make a dark matt background for other flowering plants. All forms have good autumn colour and tolerate air pollution.

CULTIVATION Plant between autumn and spring in well-drained soil. The autumn colour will be less brilliant in fertile, manured soil, but the plants will grow quicker and stronger. These shrubs will tolerate light shade, but purple-leaved forms colour best in sun. To make a shapely bush, cut back all shoots by one-third in the first spring. Where space is limited this can be repeated annually, but the dense leafy growth will be at the expense of flowers.

PROPAGATION Layer long shoots in early autumn, or take cuttings in late summer.

PESTS AND DISEASES Generally trouble free.

OTHER VARIETIES *Cotinus* 'Flame' AGM has green leaves and exceptionally brilliant red-orange autumn colour. 'Notcutt's Variety', 'Royal Purple' AGM and 'Grace' AGM, all have purple leaves. *C. obovatus,* syn. *C. americanus, Rhus cotinoides* AGM is larger at 10 x 8m, (30 x 25ft) with glaucous green leaves, turning brilliant crimson and orange in autumn. The flower plumes are pinkish.

soil

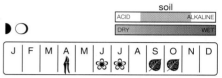

ACID			ALKALINE
DRY			WET

J	F	M	A	M	J	J	A	S	O	N	D

COTINUS COGGYGRIA

COTINUS COGGYGRIA

C

COTONEASTER

Evergreen, semi-evergreen and deciduous shrubs and trees (northern temperate regions from Europe to the Himalayas and China, and N. Africa). Mature at 15 years: from 7cm x 2m (3in x 6ft) to 10 x 10m (30 x 30ft).

Cotoneasters are a wonderfully varied and versatile group of shrubs, ranging from prostrate ground cover plants to small trees. The leaves and flowers are attractive and most forms produce spectacular berries in the autumn. Some species are particularly graceful in form.

USES Depending on the species and cultivar, cotoneasters can make excellent ground cover, especially on dry, stony banks. Alternatively they may be grown in shrub borders or as specimens. The species *C. lacteus* and *C. simonsii* are recommended for hedges. Cotoneasters tolerate a wide range of soils, including the extremes of acidity and alkalinity, and are very hardy and wind resistant. The flowers attract bees.

CULTIVATION Plant between autumn and spring in any soil that is not waterlogged. Evergreens will grow in sun or light shade; deciduous species prefer full sun. No regular pruning is necessary, but plants that have outgrown their space can be given a fresh start by cutting hard back in late winter or early spring.

PROPAGATION Cotoneasters seed themselves quite freely, but they mix promiscuously and the results will be variable. Nevertheless, self-sown seedlings may be worth potting up and growing on for background planting or shelter belts. To propagate named evergreen cultivars take cuttings of semi-ripened shoots in late summer. Take cuttings of deciduous species in early summer, just as the first flush of growth begins to ripen. Prostrate cultivars often layer themselves, and the rooted shoots can be detached and replanted.

PESTS AND DISEASES Generally trouble free, but fireblight is a risk, especially on cultivars of *C. salicifolius*. Remove and burn affected branches and, if necessary, the whole plant.

SPECIES AND VARIETIES There is only space to list a few of the many excellent forms available. They are given below.

PROSTRATE EVERGREENS *C. conspicuus* syn. *C. conspicuus* var. *decorus* AGM, 30cm x 2-3m (1 x 6-10ft), has low arching branches of small dark green glossy leaves, small white flowers and large orange-red berries, which are left alone by the birds. *C. dammeri* AGM, 7cm x 1.5-2.1m (2-3in x 5-7ft), is completely prostrate with creeping stems that hug the ground, and dark green glossy, ovate leaves. The white flowers, which are produced at midsummer, are followed by sealing-wax red berries.

COTONEASTER WATERERI

PROSTRATE DECIDUOUS *C. adpressus* AGM, 30cm x 2m (1 x 6ft), has tiny leaves neatly arranged on stiff little branches. The leaves turn red in autumn. The plant creeps over the ground, rooting as it goes. The small flowers are pink, the berries red. *C. horizontalis*, the herringbone cotoneaster, will hug the ground or press up against a wall. Its autumn leaves and berries are brilliant red.

LARGE SEMI-EVERGREENS *C.* 'Cornubia' AGM, 3 x 3m (10 x 10ft) after ten years, 5 x 5m (16 x 16ft) at maturity; a shapely, wide-spreading shrub or small tree, with prolific cream flowers followed by huge clusters of red berries. *C.* 'Rothschildianus' AGM, has wide arching branches and reaches 5 x 5m (16 x 16ft). Its exciting feature is its golden yellow berries, remaining all winter. It is more robust than the cultivar 'Exburiensis', which has cream-yellow berries and usually fewer of them, but nurseries and garden centres often confuse these two plants.

soil

ACID		ALKALINE
DRY		WET

J	F	M	A	M	J	J	A	S	O	N	D

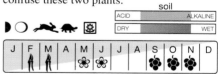
COTONEASTER DAMMERI

COTONEASTER 'CORNUBIA'

COURGETTES 'DEFENDER', 'SUPREMO'

Cucurbita pepo. *Zucchini, half-hardy annual. Mature at 6 months: 45 x 90cm (18 x 36in).*

The leaves of this vegetable are large, coarse and hairy. Prostrate thick green stems spread from the centre and, in midsummer, large golden yellow, urn-shaped flowers appear, followed by long shiny, dark green striped fruits. Yellow-skinned cultivars are also available. Courgettes are marrows that are bred to be picked and eaten when small.

USES Both flowers and fruit are edible. The flowers can be picked as they open, stuffed, battered and deep fried. Harvest courgettes at 10-15cm (4-6in) long. If a few escape you at this stage of their growth, leave them growing and get children to carve their initials into the skin of the marrows. As the fruit proceeds to grow to giant proportions, so too will the letters.

CULTIVATION Courgettes can be grown on any fertile and well-drained soil, preferably rich in organic material and in a sheltered, sunny position. Set the plants out in early summer and pinch out the points of the main shoots when they are 45cm (18in) long. If the fruit appears not to set well the plants can be pollinated by hand. Pull off a male flower and rub the pollen on to the stigma of the female. The male flowers have long stalks and the females have a swelling just behind the bloom. Water freely in dry weather.

PROPAGATION Sow the seeds in spring under glass.

PESTS AND DISEASES Generally trouble free but cucumber mosaic virus often affects the leaves. It does not seem to harm the fruit. The cultivars 'Defender' and 'Supremo' have some resistance to the virus.

COURGETTE

CRAMBE CORDIFOLIA

C

Hardy perennial (Caucasus, 1822). Mature at 2 years: 1.8 x 1.2m (6 x 4ft).

A spectacular plant with clumps of massive, broad dark green, veined and crinkled leaves. They are carried on stout pale green stalks and at midsummer stout smooth stems rise up and branch into a huge cloud of small white, star-like flowers with a strong honey scent.

USES Few gardens have space for more than one crambe to introduce a touch of drama to beds and borders, or to form a small colony at the edge of a lawn.

CULTIVATION Give the plant enough space in the right place. If you find you made a mistake and want to dig it up, it will not be easy: a fragment of root always seems to remain to grow into yet another giant. Crambes are easily pleased in rough well-drained soil, preferably in full sun, but they will tolerate some shade. The huge flower stalks are heavy and it is as well to stake them before they fall over.

PROPAGATION Divide the roots in autumn or spring.

PESTS AND DISEASES Slugs eat the leaves.

OTHER VARIETIES *Crambe maritima*, sea kale, 60 x 60cm (2 x 2ft), is more compact with blue-grey cabbage-like leaves. The cream-white flower clusters are on squat stems. The leaves mix well with other, more delicate greys and blues and, as a bonus, the leaf stems can be picked, blanched and eaten as a vegetable.

GOOD COMPANIONS *C. cordifolia* grows so big that while it is dormant there is an empty circle of 1.2m (4ft) diameter, best filled with spring-flowering bulbs; their dying leaves will be hidden by the emerging leaves of the crambe.

CRAMBE CORDIFOLIA

C

CRATAEGUS LAEVIGATA

Syn. C. oxyacantha. Midland hawthorn, may, deciduous tree (Europe, including Britain). Mature at 30 years: 3 x 4m (10 x 13ft) after 10 years; 6 x 6m (20 x 20ft) at maturity.

This familiar hedgerow tree forms a broad dense dome of glossy toothed leaves. In late spring and early summer the branches are laden with clusters of scented cream-white flowers. Small round crimson haws ripen in early autumn.

USES Grow as a lawn specimen in a small garden, or in a container. It can be clipped to make hedges or topiary. It provides food and shelter for wildlife.

CULTIVATION Very hardy, and thrives in virtually any soil. It is shade tolerant but flowers and fruits better in sun. For hedges, plant 60-100cm (2-3ft) tall plants 30cm (12in) apart. Trim to shape as they develop at any time from late summer through winter. Cut neglected hedges hard back in late summer.

PROPAGATION Seeds of the species will take 18 months or more to germinate. Named cultivars are budded or grafted.

PESTS AND DISEASES Caterpillars, fireblight, honey fungus, powdery mildew, rust.

OTHER VARIETIES *C. laevigata* 'Rosea Flore Pleno' AGM has double pink flowers. 'Paul's Scarlet' AGM, not scarlet, but light crimson. *C. persimilis* 'Prunifolia' to 6 x 6m (20 x 20ft) AGM has a compact head of spiny branches and toothed, glossy green leaves turning orange and scarlet in autumn. The white flowers of midsummer are followed by large, winter-persistent, red haws.

COMPANIONS Use as the basis for a country hedge mixed with blackthorn, field maple, hazel, dog rose.

soil	
ACID	ALKALINE
DRY	WET

J	F	M	A	M	J	J	A	S	O	N	D

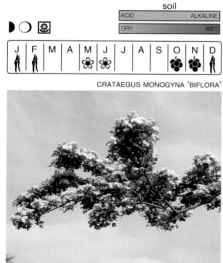
CRATAEGUS MONOGYNA 'BIFLORA'

CRATAEGUS PERSIMILIS 'PRUNIFOLIA'

CRATAEGUS MEYERI

CRINUM X POWELLII

Bulbous perennial (hybrid of two S. African species, C. bulbispermum and C. moorei). Mature at 3 years: 1m x 60cm (3 x 2ft). AGM

These lily-like plants look tropical, but are hardy in all but the coldest gardens. Strap-shaped, glossy mid-green leaves arch out from a very large long-necked bulb. Towards the end of the summer long, smooth juicy stems appear, and a cluster of buds at the top opens into several well poised, outward-facing trumpet-shaped flowers. They come in various shades of pink. The flowers are scented.

USES Crinums do well in large pots, and in very cold areas can be moved under glass in winter. They provide interest well into autumn in a warm sheltered border, and are excellent for seaside gardens.

CULTIVATION Plant the bulbs in spring in rich deep soil, digging in well-rotted manure before planting. They seem to be hardy in the open, but will flower better if positioned at the foot of a warm sunny wall. If planted too deep they may not flower at all; make sure the necks of the bulbs are above the ground. Water them thoroughly in dry spells during the summer and, in cold areas, protect the emerging shoots against frost. Mulch with manure every few years.

PROPAGATION Sow the large seeds singly as soon as they are ripe, or dig up established clumps in early spring, detach offsets and pot them up. They will take several years to reach flowering size.

PESTS AND DISEASES Generally trouble free, but they may be attacked by bulb mites.

OTHER VARIETIES *C. x powellii* 'Album' is a handsome white form.

CROCOSMIA MASONIORUM

Deciduous perennial corm (S. Africa). Mature at 3 years: up to 1.5m x 45cm (5ft x 18in).

This is a grand relation of montbretia (see Other Varieties, below). It forms a robust clump of strong, erect sword-shaped leaves, prominently ridged. From late summer to early autumn, smooth flower stems arch above the leaves. The top few centimeters of each stem are bent horizontal to display a row of upright, orange-red trumpets.

USES The leaves provide the vertical line that is always much in demand to contrast with the indeterminate or rounded shapes of other plants. Ordinary montbretia is a useful colonizer of empty ground in sun or shade, almost to the point where it has itself become a weed. All forms are good for cutting.

CULTIVATION Bury the corms in close groups in early spring, choosing a sunny sheltered site with well-drained soil.

PROPAGATION Collect seeds in autumn and sow in a cool greenhouse or frame. The seeds should germinate by spring to flower one or two years later. Lift and divide the corms every three or four years, either just after flowering or before growth starts again.

PESTS AND DISEASES Generally trouble free.

OTHER VARIETIES There are many of named varieties, mostly *C. x crocosmiiflora*. Not all are completely hardy, particularly those with yellow or apricot flowers, so in cold districts stick to *C. masoniorum* or the robust 'Lucifer', which has flame-red flowers at midsummer.

GOOD COMPANIONS The soft powder blue of *Ceanothus* 'Gloire de Versailles' cools the fiery scarlets and oranges of crocosmia. Dark red-purple foliage also softens their impact by absorbing the strength of their colouring.

CROCUS TOMMASINIANUS

Perennial corm (East coast of the Adriatic). Mature at 6 months: flowers 8cm (3in) high. AGM

Shaped like small elongated urns, the delicate flowers, in shades of mauve with golden yellow stamens, appear in late winter or early spring. Initially the sparse flowers are vulnerable to harsh weather, but their fragile appearance is deceptive and the bulbs soon increase and clump up, protecting one another. The cultivar 'Whitewell Purple' has a stronger colour.

USES Plant pools of crocus in short grass under deciduous trees, or plant in clumps among alpines and other low plants.

CULTIVATION Plant the bulbs in early autumn, 8cm (3in) deep and about 8cm (3in) apart, either in turf or in beds among other, later-flowering plants. After flowering let the leaves die before cutting them. Crocuses thrive in well-drained poor or fertile soil, in sun.

PROPAGATION Dig up established clumps and separate the corms. *C. tommasinianus* will self-seed freely

PESTS AND DISEASES Mice eat the corms and birds peck at the flowers, especially yellow ones. The corms can be attacked by various types of rot, but this is seldom a problem.

GOOD VARIETIES Crocuses that have a natural look when planted in grass include *C. speciosus*, *C. chrysanthus* 'Blue Pearl', 'Cream Beauty', 'E.A. Bowles' (yellow) and 'Snow Bunting' (white), all AGM. If a stronger impact is wanted choose the more showy Dutch hybrids (*C. vernus*).

COMPANIONS Mix crocus bulbs with others that flower later, such as grape hyacinths and narcissus, or plant among ground-hugging *Ajuga, Lamium,* or *Viola.*

soil

| ACID | ALKALINE |
| DRY | WET |

| J | F | M | A | M | J | J | A | S | O | N | D |

CRINUM X POWELLII 'ALBUM'

CROCOSMIA

CROCUS CHRYSANTHUS 'E.A. BOWLES'

C

CRYPTOMERIA JAPONICA 'ELEGANS'

Evergreen conifer (Japan). Mature at 20 years: 3 x 1.5m (10 x 5ft) after 10 years; up to 5 x 2m (15 x 6ft) at maturity.

This evergreen conifer has the unusual quality of changing colour in autumn and winter. Its shape is that of a broad blunt cone clothed to the ground with foliage, which is blue-green in summer and purplish or reddish-bronze in winter. The fine needles of juvenile foliage are retained throughout the tree's life, making it soft to touch and giving it a fluffy appearance when it is seen from a distance. The true species, *C. japonica*, the Japanese cedar, makes a tall forest tree to 25m (80ft) or more in height.

USES It is beautiful and interesting enough to be planted as a solitary specimen, but it is also almost indispensable in groups of conifers for its unusual texture and colouring, and its moderate height.

CULTIVATION Cryptomerias tolerate most soils, but do best in slightly acid, damp but well-drained soil. The cultivars, most of which are relatively dwarf conifers, grow slowly in shade, preferring a sunny position with shelter from cold dry winds. Plant in autumn on light soils, and in spring in heavier soils. Small 60cm (24in) plants are easiest to establish. An annual dressing of general fertilizer in early summer stimulates growth and improves colour.

PROPAGATION Take ripewood cuttings in late summer or early autumn.

PESTS AND DISEASES Generally trouble free.

OTHER VARIETIES *C. japonica* 'Bandai-sugi' AGM to 2m (6ft), is an irregularly rounded shrub with foliage that turns bronze in winter.

CRYPTOMERA JAPONICA 'ELEGANS'

x CUPRESSOCYPARIS LEYLANDII

Leyland cypress, evergreen conifer. Mature at 20 years: to 10m (33ft) high in 10 years; 15 x 4.5m (50ft x 15ft) in 25 years.

Almost too familiar to need describing, the Leyland cypress is a cross between *Cupressus macrocarpa* and *Chamaecyparis nootkatensis,* which occurred accidentally on an estate near Welshpool in 1888. Leyland cypress is famous for its rapid growth, vigour and hardiness. The triangular, scale-like leaves are grey-green, the shape columnar.

USES Probably no plant has had a greater effect on the British landscape in this century. They have been – and are still – much used for windbreaks and screens. They are almost invariably planted in a straight row, which is a pity as, when informally grouped, alone or with other conifers, they can be a noble sight. For a quick-growing hedge there is nothing to touch them, and when carefully maintained will make a fine-textured background of sober colouring.

CULTIVATION Plant in spring in well-drained soil in sun or light shade. On shallow soils, rapid growth may make the plants unstable. If they start to lean, pull each tree back to the vertical and stake it. Plants 45-60cm (18-24in) tall establish quickly. For hedges, space 45-60cm (18-24in) apart. Let the leading shoots grow 30cm (12in) above the desired height, then cut to 30cm (12in) below the desired height. Side-shoots then grow to form a solid top. Clip established hedges in late summer. In poor soil, keep the root area weed-free and feed annually with a general fertilizer.

PROPAGATION Take semi-ripe cuttings in early autumn.

PESTS AND DISEASES Generally trouble free.

OTHER VARIETIES There are several yellow-leaved forms, the most planted and most easily obtainable being 'Castlewellan', syn. 'Galway Gold'.

X CUPPRESSOCYPARIS LEYLANDII

CURRANT

Ribes *species, hardy, deciduous shrub (Europe, Asia). Mature at 5 years: 1.5 x 1.2m (5 x 4ft).*

Black, red and white currants are of the same genus as the flowering currant. The wide, three-pointed leaves are mid-green and, in the case of blackcurrants, aromatic.

USES All three are cultivated for their edible fruit. Red and white currants can be grown as cordons or espaliers to make an attractive barrier. Currants can also be successfully grown in pots.

CULTIVATION Currants grow in almost any reasonably moisture-retentive soil, but will not tolerate bad drainage. Grow in an open position in sun or partial shade, sheltered from late frosts. Plant when dormant, preferably in autumn. Currants are shallow rooting so control weeds with a mulch, not a hoe. Net red and white currants to protect them against birds. When planting blackcurrants, cut all stems to one bud above ground level. In later years cut out one in three branches at the base, in winter. Do not shorten the tips. For red and white currants, shorten stems by half in the first year and remove the lowest shoots to leave a 'leg' of 10cm (4in). The next winter, shorten new main stems by half and cut back side shoots to one bud. In subsequent years, cut the side shoots and back to one bud and shorten the main branches as required.

PROPAGATION Take hardwood cuttings during the autumn.

PESTS AND DISEASES Blackcurrant gall mites, birds and aphids. *Botrytis*, powdery mildew and leaf spot can also be a problem.

GOOD VARIETIES 'Ben Lomond' and 'Ben Sarak' are reliable, disease-resistant blackcurrants with good flavour. The same applies to the redcurrant 'Red Lake' and the white currant 'White Grape'.

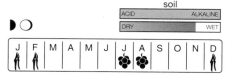

BLACKCURRANT

WHITE CURRANT

CYCLAMEN COUM

C

Syn. C. orbiculatum, C. vernale, *tuberous perennial (S.E. Europe, Bulgaria, Caucasus, Turkey, late 16th century). Mature at 5 years: to 10 x 10cm (4 x 4in). AGM*

These small hardy cyclamen are not to be confused with the showy, tender house plants available around Christmas time. Hardy cyclamens are delicate miniatures with smooth, heart-shaped leaves, dark greenish-grey above and dark red beneath, patterned with symmetrical silver-white marbling. In winter, before any leaves appear, slender ringlet stems uncurl to produce flowers with broad, swept back petals in shades of pink or carmine and occasionally white. The corms grow until they are as wide as large saucers.

USES Hardy cyclamen are a boon for creating beautiful cover in that most inhospitable situation, dry shade. They will even grow under the dense canopy of beech trees and will colonize hedge bottoms.

CULTIVATION Plant in late summer and early autumn, in a shady sheltered position in well-drained soil with leaf mould or other organic material dug in. Plant shallowly with the top of the tuber at soil level. Plant them the right way up: if you look closely you can see which side has the remnants of dried roots. Weed around them for a few seasons, then let well alone.

PROPAGATION Sow seeds in autumn in a cold frame, or wait for the plants to seed themselves in the open. They take a few years to reach flowering size.

PESTS AND DISEASES Generally trouble free.

OTHER VARIETIES *C. hederifolium*, syn. *C. neapolitanum* AGM has ivy-shaped leaves and flowers in autumn, as does the slightly less hardy *C. cilicium*, AGM.

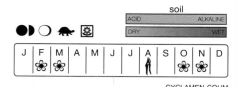

CYCLAMEN COUM

C

CYDONIA OBLONGA

Quince, deciduous tree (S. Europe and Asia). Mature at 30 years: 4.5 x 3m (15 x 10ft).

For the flowering quince or japonica, see under *Chaenomeles*. The true quince is grown for its fruit. Nevertheless, the blossom is very beautiful in late spring; the flowers are large, single and open, the palest possible pink. The tree has an attractive low-branching habit. The large leaves are white felted on their undersides and sometimes turn bright yellow in autumn. The trees are self-fertile, producing very aromatic golden-yellow pear-shaped fruits.

USES The fruit is far too sharp and astringent to eat uncooked but it makes good jelly or jam and is used to add its flavour to apple and pear dishes. The raw fruit looks and smells good piled in a dish on its own. Keep quinces away from other fruit if you do not wish them to absorb the scent of the quince.

CULTIVATION Plant in autumn in a sunny open but sheltered position, or against a wall in any reasonable soil. Crowded branches can be thinned out in winter and branches of wall-trained trees cut back to within two or three buds of a framework.

PROPAGATION Take hardwood cuttings in autumn. Long branches may be layered in early autumn and should be ready for severing one year later.

PESTS AND DISEASES Mildew, brown rot and fireblight can attack quinces. Remove and burn the infected branches.

OTHER VARIETIES *C. oblonga* 'Vranja' AGM is considered the best for fruit.

CYDONIA OBLONGA 'VRANJA'

CYNARA SCOLYMUS

Globe artichoke, hardy perennial (origin uncertain). Mature at 2 years: 1.2 x 1.2m (4 x 4ft).

Massive, handsome leaves arch out from a central crown with a sturdy taproot. The leaves are grey-green with a pale central rib and are deeply cut. The flowers are carried on sturdy stems. If they are not cut in bud, they open into blue-purple thistles.

Uses The flowers, known as globe artichokes, are edible while still in bud. The plant's sculptural shape is too handsome to be relegated to the vegetable garden, and it makes a fine foliage plant in the border. The huge thistle flowers of the cardoon open in water if picked in bud and dry well.

Cultivation Plant offshoots in spring, in triangles with 23cm (9in) between them and at least 60cm (2ft) between groups. They will grow in any ordinary garden soil but do best in deeply dug soil with manure added. Ideally, mulch with manure every spring and divide and replant every four years. In cold areas, protect the crowns from frost.

Propagation Dig up established plants and separate the suckers.

Pests and diseases Generally trouble free.

Other varieties *C. cardunculus*, the cardoon, is an even more handsome foliage plant, to 1.8m (6ft) or more, with even larger, more silvery leaves. It is the ribs of the cardoon's leaves, not the flower heads, that are treated as a vegetable. They need to be blanched to make them edible: the easiest way is to tie the leaves loosely together when they are about 30cm (12in) long and cover the plant with a terracotta rhubarb forcer.

CYNARA CARDUNCULUS

CYTISUS BATTANDIERI

Syn. **Argyrocytisus battandieri.** *Pineapple broom, deciduous shrub (Morocco, 1922). Mature at 15 years: 3 x 2m (10 x 6ft) after 10 years; to 4.5 x 3.5m (15 x 12ft) at maturity. AGM*

This is so different from other brooms that it gets a separate listing. It has long, flexible stems and, although hardy enough to grow in the open in sheltered areas, its habit makes it ideal for wall-training. The leaves are larger than those of any other broom, trifoliate, with a silvery, silky covering of fine hairs. At midsummer conical flower heads are held erect, densely packed with golden-yellow pea flowers smelling distinctly of pineapple.

USES Its colouring is particularly attractive against a red brick wall. Its distinctive scent makes it a prime candidate for gardens planned for blind or partially sighted people.

CULTIVATION This broom is not difficult to grow, but it resents root disturbance. In early spring, plant pot grown specimens carefully, in sun, in ordinary well-drained soil, but avoid excessively alkaline soil. It is better suited to poor soil than soil that is too rich. Tie in the shoots of wall-trained plants as they grow. In the open, three or more plants together are more effective than one solitary specimen. Pruning is a matter of ensuring a continuing supply of young wood. After flowering remove old straggly growth at the base and trim wayward shoots. Neglected plants can be renewed by drastic pruning.

PROPAGATION Seeds germinate easily but this broom will only set seed in a warm summer. Cuttings can be taken in summer.

PESTS AND DISEASES Generally trouble free.

GOOD COMPANIONS *Solanum crispum* 'Glasnevin' AGM, with mauve-blue flowers, makes a good contrast, but don't let its vigour swamp the broom.

soil		
ACID		ALKALINE
DRY		WET

J	F	M	A	M	J	J	A	S	O	N	D
					✿	✿					

CYTISUS BATTANDIERI

CYTISUS X PRAECOX 'WARMINSTER'

Warminster broom. A hybrid of C. purgans (southern France) and C. multiflorus (Spain and Portugal), deciduous shrub (Britain, 1867). Mature at 5 years: 1.2 x 1.2m (4 x 4ft). AGM

Although they are deciduous, these brooms look like evergreens because their slender stems remain green all the year round. In late spring masses of small winged pea flowers smother the whole length of the stems, causing them to arch gracefully. The flowers of 'Warminster' are bright cream-yellow. They are followed by narrow grey-green seed pods. Brooms are not long-lived; the plants will deteriorate and need replacing after about ten years.

USES Brooms withstand industrial pollution and flourish in light, droughty soils. The flowers attract bees.

CULTIVATION Plant pot grown specimens with minimum disturbance to the roots, in an open sunny position in free-draining soil. Most brooms are short-lived on alkaline soil; for lime-tolerant kinds see 'Good Varieties' below. To prevent plants becoming leggy cut all stems back by half, after flowering. Do not cut into the old wood.

PROPAGATION Brooms grow easily from seed but varieties do not come true. To reproduce named varieties take semi-ripe cuttings in summer.

PESTS AND DISEASES Generally trouble free.

GOOD VARIETIES *C. x praecox* 'Albus' has white flowers and 'Allgold' AGM bright yellow. Hybrids flowering a little later in early summer include the following: 'Hollandia' AGM with bicoloured flowers purple-red and cream; 'Killiney Red', 'Killiney Salmon' and 'Zeelandia' AGM cream and lilac. *C. x beanii* AGM is a yellow-flowered, low-growing hybrid that is lime tolerant. It makes a mound 30 x 50cm (12 x 20in). *C. decumbens*, syn. *Genista procumbens*, 20cm x 1.5m, (8in x 5ft) is also lime tolerant and makes a ground-hugging carpet.

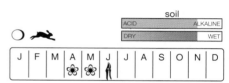

soil		
ACID		ALKALINE
DRY		WET

J	F	M	A	M	J	J	A	S	O	N	D
				✿	✿		🔧				

CYTISUS X PRAECOX 'WARMINSTER'

D

DAHLIA

*Half-hardy, tuberous perennial (Mexico).
Mature at 3 years: varying in size from
dwarfs at 30 x 30cm (12 x 12in) to giants
at 1.8 x 1.8m (6 x 6ft)*

Dahlias are back in fashion after a long spell
in the wilderness of plant snobbery where
the huge shaggy flowers and bright colours
of some varieties were written off as vulgar.
Quite large, deeply divided leaves are mid-
green, bronze or dark greenish-purple. The
flowers are prolific from midsummer until
the first severe frost, in almost any colour
except blue. Hybridizing has led to a number
of very distinctive flower shapes: single,
waterlily, collerette, anemone, pompon, ball,
semi-cactus, cactus and decorative, along
with a miscellaneous group with flowers that
don't fit into these divisions.

USES Dahlias come to the rescue just when
roses and other midsummer flowers have
faded. Either plant them in borders in gap-
filling positions, or grow them in pots and
plunge the pots into the ground as gaps
appear. Some seed-raised dahlias have been
bred especially for bedding. They all make
excellent cut flowers and are traditional
exhibits at horticultural shows.

CULTIVATION Plant the tubers in spring, in a
sunny position in well-drained soil enriched
with farmyard manure or garden compost,
setting them 8cm (3in) deep. They can also
be started in pots in the greenhouse and
planted out in late spring or early summer,
when danger of frost has passed. Water the
plants during dry spells. Pinch out the tips
of the shoots to encourage bushy growth.
The flowers are heavy, so, except for dwarf
varieties, support each

flower stem separately with a thin cane. In
frost-free areas the tubers can be left in the
ground all winter, but elsewhere, as soon as
the first frost blackens the leaves, they
should be lifted, dried, dusted with
fungicide and stored in a dry well-
ventilated, frost-free place.

PROPAGATION Seed of bedding dahlias can
be sown under glass, at 16°C (61°F) in early
spring. For other types, take 8cm (3in) long
basal cuttings taken from the new shoots
issuing from the tubers. Sprouted tubers can
be divided in spring, each section with one
growing shoot.

PESTS AND DISEASES Aphids, red spider
mites and thrips all attack dahlias,
sometimes with devastating results. They
are also prone to virus infections.

GOOD VARIETIES The named hybrids are
legion, and the flower shapes and colours
you choose are a matter of personal
preference. 'Bishop of Llandaff' AGM
1 x 1m (3 x 3ft) seems to be everyone's
favourite with finely-cut bronze leaves and
large, semi-double flowers of dark, rich red.
'David Howard' AGM has darker bronze
leaves and orange decorative flowers.
Dahlias with pink flowers include 'Athalie'
(cactus), 'Vicky Crutchfield' (waterlily) and
'Rhonda' (pompon); good yellows are
'Yellow Hammer' AGM (dwarf single),
'Clair de Lune' AGM (collerette) and
'Butterball' (decorative). Among the
dahlias with white flowers are 'Easter
Sunday' (collerette), 'White Klankstad'
(cactus) and 'Small World' (pompons).

COMPANIONS Plant dahlias as solid, bright
accents among airy pale blue and mauve
Michaelmas daisies. Use the reds and
oranges to contribute to an autumn blaze
with cotinus and berberis foliage.

MIXED DAHLIAS

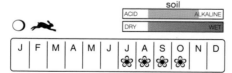

DAHLIA 'DAVID HOWARD'

DAPHNE MEZEREUM

*Mezereon, deciduous shrub (Europe,
Caucasus, Turkey to Siberia). Mature at
7 years: 120 x 90cm (4 x 3ft).*

Daphnes are grown for the wonderful scent
of their flowers, and that of *D. mezereum*,
flowering as it does in winter, is especially
welcome. It is a compact woodland shrub
with light, slightly greyish-green oval
pointed leaves. Before the leaves appear the
bare branches are covered with small
purplish-pink star-shaped flowers. They are
followed by poisonous red berries.

USES Plant scented daphnes beside a path or
a door, so you can get a whiff of the scent
whenever you pass. Their compact habit
makes them ideal plants for small gardens.

CULTIVATION Plant in the autumn or spring
in light shade, in any soil that does not dry
out. Most will grow in sun provided the
roots are kept moist, so mulch annually in
spring. They tolerate chalk soil if copious
organic material is added. Pruning is best
kept to a minimum.

PROPAGATION Grow from seed or take
cuttings in summer. Cuttings are difficult to
root, so take plenty. Layers taken in spring
take up to 18 months to root.

PESTS AND DISEASES Prone to viruses,
which cause unsightly distortim and
yellowing,, but the plants usually survive.

OTHER VARIETIES *D. mezereum* f. *alba* is a
white-flowered form. *D. odora*
'Aureomarginata' is another easy winter-
flowering shrub. This hardy evergreen, to
1.5m (5ft), has rosettes of smooth, pointed
leaves, each with a narrow thread of gold at
the margin. The buds are red-purple and the
flowers pale mauve-pink with a strong,
sweet scent. *D.* x *burkwoodii* 'Somerset' is
similar, but flowers in early summer and
sometimes again in late summer.

DAPHNE MEZEREUM

DELPHINIUM

Hardy perennial (northern hemisphere). Mature at 2 years: 180 x 60cm (6 x 2ft).

At midsummer the magnificent spires of delphiniums are reminiscent of the glories of Edwardian herbaceous borders. Stout stems rise from a base of broad, finely-cut leaves, each closely studded with cup-shaped flowers with spurs and often with a contrasting eye at the centre. The colour ranges from intense, vibrant blues and violets to pale mauve-pink and white.

USES Delphiniums are an almost compulsory component of herbaceous borders. Their shape and colour range make a good contrast with shrub roses. Excellent as cut flowers.

CULTIVATION Unless you aspire to producing giant spikes of flower show proportions, delphiniums are not difficult, but success does involve taking some trouble. Plant them in spring in an open, sunny position, in ground that has been dug deeply with a generous amount of manure added. Protect the young shoots from slugs and snails. The flower spikes need support either from a grow-through support, or from individual canes. Cut down stems as the flowers fade; you may get a small second crop. Mulch with manure every spring.

PROPAGATION You can grow from seeds or basal cuttings, but the easiest way is to divide in autumn.

PESTS AND DISEASES Slugs and snails will eat the young shoots.

GOOD VARIETIES Pacific Giant hybrids are tried and tested favourites. They include 'Black Knight' dark bright blue, 'Galahad' white, 'Astolat' lilac pink, 'King Arthur' violet. It is worth ordering from a specialist after making your choice at a flower show. Belladonna hybrids are shorter, 1.2m (4ft), more branched with looser flower spikes.

soil	
ACID	ALKALINE
DRY	WET

J	F	M	A	M	J	J	A	S	O	N	D

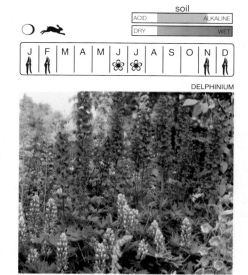

DELPHINIUM

DEUTZIA

Hardy, deciduous shrubs (China and Japan, 18th and 19th centuries). Mature at 10 years: from 80 x 60cm (2ft 6in x 2ft) to 2.5 x 2m (8 x 6ft).

Deutzias flower profusely in late spring or early summer. Long stems arch over with the weight of numerous clusters of pink or white flowers. The leaves are mid-green, pointed and medium sized.

USES Deutzias are among those useful shrubs which, having flowered relatively early, settle down to provide a sober background to other plants. They tolerate chalky soil and will grow in cold exposed sites and in areas of industrial pollution.

CULTIVATION Plant between autumn and spring, in sun or light shade in any reasonable soil. The flower buds may be damaged by late frosts, so avoid known frost pockets in your garden. Prune by removing some of the oldest flowering branches, if not every year, every few years. Do not remove new shoots as they will bear the following season's flowers.

PROPAGATION Take semi-ripe cuttings in summer, or hardwood cuttings in winter.

PESTS AND DISEASES Generally trouble free.

GOOD VARIETIES *D*. x *elegantissima* 'Rosealind' AGM, 1.2 x 1.2m (4 x 4ft) has deep carmine-pink flowers. *D*. 'Mont Rose' AGM, 1.8 x 1.2m (6 x 4ft), has large, pale mauve-pink flowers, and *D*. x *rosea* is early to flower, only 80 x 60cm (2ft 6in x 2ft) and of graceful habit. The double white-flowered *D. scabra* 'Pride of Rochester' has erect branches covered with cinnamon-coloured peeling bark. It grows to 2 x 1.5m (6 x 5ft) or more.

soil	
ACID	ALKALINE
DRY	WET

J	F	M	A	M	J	J	A	S	O	N	D

DEUTZIA SCABRA 'CANDIDISSIMA'

DEUTZIA 'ROSEALIND'

D

DIANTHUS

Carnations, pinks, sweet williams, evergreen perennials and biennials, and annuals (Europe, including Britain, Asia, Southern Africa). Mature at 2 years: from 10 x 10cm (4 x 4in) to 45 x 30cm (18 x 12in).

The genus *Dianthus* also includes perpetual and Malmaison carnations, but although fascinating, growing them is a specialized interest. Garden pinks have mats of characteristic narrow blue-grey, grey or grey-green leaves. Smooth branching stems carry smooth pointed buds at their tips, which open into flowers that may be single, semi-double, or fully double with rounded, fringed or frilled petals. They are white, or any conceivable shade of red or pink, often prettily marked, streaked or picotee-margined, and have a strong but soft spicy scent. Those described as 'clove pinks' have a pronounced clove fragrance. The biennial sweet williams, *D. barbatus*, has taller, stouter stems clothed in outward-curving, narrow green leaves. The individual flowers are smaller but they are massed in multiple flat heads giving the effect of a solid block of colour.

USES Pinks can be planted as edging or as an informal front row ground cover; the leaves make an attractive dense carpet when the plants are not in flower. The alpine species are suitable for rock gardens, walls and raised beds. Use sweet williams in groups in herbaceous and mixed borders, massed for bedding, or in a cutting border if you have one. Both pinks and sweet williams last well as cut flowers.

CULTIVATION Pinks do best in free-draining, slightly alkaline soil in full sun. Plant them about 23cm (9in) apart in spring. If they are planted alongside a gravel path or terrace, mulch by extending the gravel up to the necks of the young plants. After the first flush of flowers, clip over the plants to remove the flower stems.

PROPAGATION Sow seeds of pinks in spring. With luck a packet of seed will provide a variety of flower colours and shapes for you to select from. Then you can take cuttings or pipings the following summer. Pipings are new shoots pulled from the plant and treated in the same way as cuttings. Plants are not long-lived, so renew them in this

MIXED DIANTHUS

DIANTHUS 'DORIS'

way every three or four years. Seeds of sweet williams are sown in the open in spring and moved to their flowering site in the late summer.

PESTS AND DISEASES Plants may suffer from red spider mites, rust or virus infection, but it is possible to purchase plants that come from virus-free stock.

GOOD VARIETIES The Monarch Series of sweet williams gives a good mix of colours and flower patterns. As far as the pinks are concerned, modern varieties are repeat-flowering, whereas the old-fashioned pinks flower just once at midsummer. Some old varieties, once seen, are irresistible. Of the strongly scented moderns, 'Doris' AGM is an excellent, prolific flowerer, with pale pink blooms with darker centres. 'Fair Folly' and 'Alice' are intriguingly patterned with crimson on a white ground. 'Haytor White' AGM and 'Devon Dove' AGM are pure white. 'Valda Wyatt' AGM, 'Pink Jewel', 'Joy' AGM and 'Diane' are various shades of pink. *D. deltoides*, the maiden pink AGM and *D. gratianopolitanus* AGM Cheddar pink, are pretty little plants for the rockery or the top of a wall.

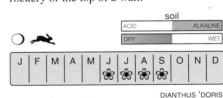

soil	
ACID	ALKALINE
DRY	WET

J	F	M	A	M	J	J	A	S	O	N	D

DIANTHUS 'DORIS'

DIASCIA BARBRAE

Hardy, semi-evergreen perennial (S. Africa, mid 18th century). 15 x 30cm (6 x 12in).

An extremely valuable and comparatively recent introduction to our gardens, diascias were formerly thought to be too tender to survive winter in the open. It is now known that, provided they have sun, shelter and good drainage, most diascia species are quite hardy, to about -8°C (18°F), possibly more. Diascias are low, mat-forming or sprawling plants with small pointed pale green leaves and lots of flowers. The flowers, like miniature pink larkspurs, are held along slender wiry stems. They flower nonstop from late spring until the first severe frost.

USES Plant diascias as informal edging, in paving cracks on terraces and patios, in gravel at the edge of a path, or at the top of a retaining wall to trail down.

CULTIVATION Plant in spring in ordinary well-drained soil in full sun. Every spring cut back the old stems to the base.

PROPAGATION Sow seeds in autumn or take semi-ripe cuttings in late summer.

PESTS AND DISEASES Generally trouble free.

GOOD VARIETIES *D.* 'Ruby Field' AGM has flowers that are salmon pink, not ruby red. The flowers of 'Blackthorn Apricot' AGM are a soft shade of apricot. *D. rigescens* AGM has a more upright habit and deep pink flowers. Every year a few more named cultivars are launched and forms are now available with lilac-pink flowers, such as 'Lilac Belle', as well as the salmon shades.

COMPANIONS *Convolvulus sabatius* enjoys the same conditions and would provide a pretty contrast of colour and flower shape.

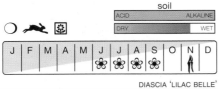

soil
| ACID | | | | | | | | | ALKALINE |
| DRY | | | | | | | | | WET |

| J | F | M | A | M | J | J | A | S | O | N | D |

DIASCIA 'LILAC BELLE'

DICENTRA FORMOSA

Hardy perennial (N. America, early 18th century). Mature at 3 years: 45 x 30cm (18 x 12in).

One of my top twenty perennials, this dicentra and its named cultivars make low mounds of soft, very finely-cut leaves. From late spring right through summer, small pinkish white flowers hang like lockets from almost translucent, dusky pink stems.

USES Plant in bold groups at the front of shrub, mixed or herbaceous borders. They deserve a prime position on a corner or curve where you will pause to look closer. The leaves are good for flower arranging.

CULTIVATION Plant in autumn or spring, preferably in semi-shade, but they also seem to thrive in full sun. They need soil that does not dry out, so when you plant them add humus in the form of manure, leaf mould or garden compost. In autumn, cut down the old leaves and flower stems.

PROPAGATION Divide the crowns in late winter, handling with great care, as the brittle roots break very easily. The species may well seed themselves.

DICENTRA SPECTABILIS

PESTS AND DISEASES Generally trouble free.

GOOD VARIETIES 'Bacchanal' has dark red flowers over grey-green leaves; 'Langtrees' AGM has cream-pink flowers with steel blue leaves, 'Stuart Boothman' AGM is a little taller, with dusky pink flowers and grey leaves that are suffused with bronze. *D. spectabilis* AGM bleeding hearts or Dutchman's breeches, and its white form 'Alba', are favourite cottage garden plants, airily elegant in leaf and flower. *D.* 'Bountiful' is another good plant.

COMPANIONS Group those with grey-blue leaves with plants of similar colouring: hostas, rue, *Rosa glauca*. *D.* 'Stuart Boothman' looks terrific with red-purple tulips and, a little later in the season, with *Allium christophii*.

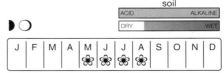

soil
| ACID | | | | | | | | | ALKALINE |
| DRY | | | | | | | | | WET |

| J | F | M | A | M | J | J | A | S | O | N | D |

DICENTRA

DICENTRA 'BOUNTIFUL'

D

DICTAMNUS ALBUS

Syn. D. fraxinella, **burning bush, hardy perennial (Europe to N. China and Korea, late 16th century). Mature at 3 years: 60 x 45cm (24 x 18in). AGM**

This plant has clumps of light green, citrus-scented divided leaves, and at midsummer produces spikes of white star-shaped flowers with long stamens, followed by star-shaped seed pods. It has a strange characteristic: in warm, dry, still weather, in a sheltered site, it gives off an inflammable vapour and sometimes, if you put a match to it, the plant will flare up, hence the name burning bush.

USES A plant with white flower spikes is always useful in planting schemes. Herbalists use the leaves in potpourri and as a herbal tea. A tincture of the flowers and leaves is said to relieve rheumatic pain, but self-medication is not recommended, as it can cause stomach upsets. Contact with the sap can cause the skin to become super-sensitive to light.

CULTIVATION Plant in autumn or spring in ordinary well-drained garden soil in sun or light shade. A free-draining alkaline soil is ideal. After flowering, or in autumn, cut the dead flower spikes down to the ground. This plant resents disturbance to its roots, so let well alone until a clump becomes seriously overcrowded.

PROPAGATION Sow seeds outdoors in late summer, or divide the roots in autumn or spring. They will be slow to re-establish.

PESTS AND DISEASES Generally trouble free.

OTHER VARIETIES *D. albus* var. *purpureus* AGM has soft mauve-pink flowers, with darker pink veins.

soil

ACID	ALKALINE
DRY	WET

J	F	M	A	M	J	J	A	S	O	N	D

DICTAMNUS ALBUS VAR. PURPUREUS

DIGITALIS PURPUREA

Foxglove, biennial (Europe, including Britain). Mature at 1 year: up to 1.5 x 60cm (5 x 2ft).

One of the most garden worthy of all native plants, the foxglove forms a rosette of large, velvety grey-green leaves in its first summer. The second year, a tall spike rises up, its top half closely set with round, grey-green buds that open into purplish-pink tubular flowers. Flowering begins with the lowest buds, and by the time the topmost buds are open, the lowest flowers have fallen. The inside of each flower is spotted and freckled, purple on white.

USES The spires provide a desirable vertical line among old-fashioned roses and other informal shrub groups, and are essential in the wild or woodland garden. By allowing foxgloves to seed themselves and removing only those seedlings that are in the way, you can achieve just the right degree of inconsequential informality in the garden.

CULTIVATION Set out young plants in autumn 45cm (18in) apart. They will tolerate a dry exposed site, but prefer light shade on soil that does not dry out. If you cut down the flowering stems, secondary flowering spikes may appear.

PROPAGATION Sow seeds outdoors in shade, thinning or transplanting as necessary. Transplant self-sown plants in autumn.

PESTS AND DISEASES Generally trouble free.

GOOD VARIETIES The white variety *D. albiflora* AGM is very elegant. To maintain a pure stock of white foxgloves, pull out any seedlings with purplish leaf stalks – this colouring is a sign that the flowers will be pink. *D. grandiflora* AGM is perennial, 75 x 30cm (30 x 12in) with yellow flowers and smooth dark green leaves.

COMPANIONS *D. grandiflora* looks good with the dark purple-reds of old roses.

soil

ACID	ALKALINE
DRY	WET

J	F	M	A	M	J	J	A	S	O	N	D

DIGITALIS PURPUREA ALBA

DORONICUM 'MISS MASON'

Leopard's bane, hardy perennial. Mature at 3 years: 45 x 30cm (18 x 12in). AGM

Rather out of fashion at the moment, but *Doronicum* is one of the earliest perennials to flower, at a time when its large yellow daisies are very welcome. The leaves, too, provide attractive cover, making low mounds early in the year when there is rather a lot of bare earth. They are heart-shaped and a fresh light shade of green.

USES The flowers last well in water, and the plants can be grown in pots and brought on in a cold greenhouse to flower early. *D.* x *excelsum* 'Harpur Crewe' is tolerant of dry shade.

CULTIVATION Plant doronicums in autumn or spring in groups of five or more, depending on the space available. They will grow in any reasonable garden soil in sun or in the dappled shade under trees.

PROPAGATION Divide the roots of established clumps during the autumn.

PESTS AND DISEASES Generally trouble free.

GOOD VARIETIES *D.* x *excelsum* 'Harpur Crewe', syn. *D. plantagineum* 'Excelsum', is an improved form of a plant native to Britain. It is larger than 'Miss Mason', reaching 90cm (3ft) high and 60cm (2ft) wide when in flower. It makes a handsome clump and carries three or four large yellow daisies on each stem.

soil

ACID	ALKALINE
DRY	WET

J	F	M	A	M	J	J	A	S	O	N	D

DORONICUM X EXCELSUM 'HARPUR CREWE'

DRYOPTERIS FILIX-MAS

Male fern, partially deciduous fern (temperate zones, N. America and Europe, including Britain). Mature at 3 years: up to 1.2 x 1m (4 x 3ft). AGM

This is a dramatic and graceful plant with well-poised, feathery light green fronds arching out from a central crown above an upright rhizome covered in brown scales. The leaves do not die back in the autumn, but lie prostrate in the winter, protecting the crown until the new season's fronds sprout up and start to unfurl.

USES The male fern is a plant of distinction for a woodland garden, or any situation that mirrors woodland conditions. Like other ferns it is particularly well-suited to a shaded position beside a rocky watercourse, but it will also grow in inhospitable places.

CULTIVATION Plant in spring in any shaded site where the soil is reasonably moisture-retentive but not boggy. Water copiously in dry spells. Leave the dead fronds on the plant until spring, and then, after clearing away any debris, mulch well with leaf mould or garden compost. In the right position, once established, ferns will look after themselves.

PROPAGATION Lift and divide established plants as growth begins in spring, separating entire side-crowns from the parent clump.

PESTS AND DISEASES Generally trouble free.

OTHER VARIETIES As with most ferns, sports have arisen to produce various strange, contorted forms, some of them of little interest except as freaks. *D. filix-mas* 'Crispa' is an attractive dwarf form with crimped fronds.

COMPANIONS Plant the male fern with other woodland plants: foxgloves, *Tiarella*, *Polygonatum* (Solomon's Seal) and ivies.

soil

ACID	ALKALINE
DRY	WET

J	F	M	A	M	J	J	A	S	O	N	D

DRYOPTERIS FILIX-MAS

E

ECHINOPS BANNATICUS 'TAPLOW BLUE'

Globe thistle, hardy perennial (S.E. Europe, mid 19th century). Mature at 3 years: to 1.2 x 1m (4 x 3ft). AGM

A thistle-like plant in all its parts, this *Echinops* makes a handsome clump of large, much divided, slightly prickly grey-green leaves. Several stout grey stems arise in late summer carrying at their tips globular heads of tiny powder-blue flowers emerging from metallic buds.

USES This is a plant for poor, stony soil in full sun. Don't waste a prime position on it. The flowers are much visited by bees. They last well as cut flowers.

CULTIVATION Plant groups of three or more in autumn or spring, in ordinary or poor well-drained soil in full sun. In autumn, cut down the flower and leaf stems to the base.

PROPAGATION Divide in autumn or early spring, or sow seeds outdoors in spring.

PESTS AND DISEASES Generally trouble free.

OTHER VARIETIES *E. ritro* AGM, 60 x 45cm (24 x 18in), is similar with greyish blue flowerheads. *E. ritro* 'Veitch's Blue' is a little taller, to 90cm (36in), and has the same globular flower heads, but of a stronger shade of violet-blue.

COMPANIONS These soft greyish-blues have a cooling effect on hot scarlets, oranges and golden yellow. Plant them with crocosmias, dahlias, hemerocallis or *Hypericum* 'Hidcote' AGM.

	soil	
	ACID	ALKALINE
○	DRY	WET

J	F	M	A	M	J	J	A	S	O	N	D

ECHINOPS BANATICUS

ECHIUM VULGARE

Viper's bugloss, hardy biennial (Europe, including Britain). Mature at 1 year: 30 x 20cm (12 x 8in).

In the wild this borage-like plant can grow to 90cm (3ft) tall, and it is worth bringing into the garden. In its first year it forms a rosette of dark green, hairy lance-shaped leaves. The following summer it produces long spikes of tubular flowers; they open reddish-purple and change to intense blue. The form usually sold for ornamental use is smaller and less sprawling with flowers in shades of blue, purple, pink and white. Both wild and cultivated forms flower from early summer to early autumn.

USES The nectar of echium attracts numerous insects, including butterflies. The seeds are said to resemble snakes' heads and there is a tradition, without scientific foundation, that the plant is a remedy for snake bite. Herbalists use an infusion of the leaves to relieve colds and headaches.

CULTIVATION Viper's bugloss is a native of chalk and seaside cliffs. Sow the seeds in summer in pots or directly in their intended position, in the sun and in ordinary well-drained soil. Thin to 30-45cm (12-18in) apart, or set out pot grown plants at this distance in autumn. Water until well-established. Treat the garden form in the same way.

PROPAGATION Sow seeds during summer. Once you have established plants they will self-seed freely.

PESTS AND DISEASES Generally trouble free.

	soil	
	ACID	ALKALINE
○	DRY	WET

J	F	M	A	M	J	J	A	S	O	N	D

ECHIUM VULGARE

ELAEAGNUS X EBBINGEI

A hybrid of E. macrophylla *and* E. pungens*. Oleaster, an evergreen shrub (Holland, 1929). Mature at 10 years: 3 x 2m (10 x 6ft) after 10 years; to 5 x 5m (15 x 15ft) at maturity.*

This fast-growing, dense bushy shrub has broad pointed leathery, grey-green leaves with silver-white undersides and an overall silvery sheen on new shoots. The flowers appear in autumn. They are insignificant but have a wonderful vanilla scent at a time of year when there are few other fragrant plants in the garden.

USES Being fast-growing and tolerant of wind, including salt-laden seaside winds, it makes an excellent informal hedge or shelter belt. It succeeds in areas of industrial or traffic pollution. The foliage is dense enough to make good ground cover and the flowers attract bees. The variegated forms provide winter colour: plant them where the low sun will light them up.

CULTIVATION Plant in autumn or spring, in any soil that is not waterlogged, including sandy and chalky soils, in sun or shade. Prune in spring if the plants outgrow their position or become straggly.

PROPAGATION Take cuttings between late winter and early spring.

PESTS AND DISEASES Generally trouble free, but may be attacked by coral spot. If so, cut out and burn infected branches.

OTHER VARIETIES There are two variegated forms, *E.* x *ebbingei* 'Gilt Edge' AGM has bright yellow leaf margins, and 'Limelight' has central yellow splashes on the leaves. In both the variegation is a rather harsh shade; for a softer, more buttery yellow choose the old favourite *E. pungens* 'Maculata' AGM. *E. angustifolia* AGM makes a handsome deciduous shrub or small tree with narrow silvery leaves, fragrant flowers at midsummer followed by silvered yellow berries. It does best in an open position with side shelter.

	soil	
	ACID	ALKALINE
	DRY	WET

J	F	M	A	M	J	J	A	S	O	N	D

ELAEAGNUS PUNGENS 'MACULATA'

ELAEAGNUS X EBBINGEI 'GILT EDGE'

ENKIANTHUS CAMPANULATUS

E

Deciduous shrub (Japan, 1880). Mature at 15 years: 1.8 x 1.2m (6 x 4ft) after 10 years; 3 x 3m (10 x 10ft) at maturity. AGM

This slow-growing, lime-hating shrub is grown mainly for its spectacular autumn colour. The branches are held in whorls, giving the whole shrub an attractively layered shape. The young shoots are red and the leaves grow in clusters at their tips. The leaves are oval, finely toothed and a quiet, soft shade of green until they burst into fiery red in autumn. The flowers, produced in late spring or early summer, are clusters of hanging bells, cream-yellow with red veining.

USES This is a plant for the woodland garden, enjoying the same type of soil and sheltered, lightly shaded site as rhododendrons and azaleas. It can also be grown in beds and borders provided these requirements are satisfied.

CULTIVATION Plant between autumn and spring in neutral or acid soil. The ideal position is in semi-shade in open woodland. Make sure the soil does not dry out; mulch annually with leaf mould or garden compost and water in dry spells with rainwater until the shrub is established. No pruning is necessary except to remove any frost-damaged shoots. Overgrown plants can be given a new lease of life by cutting them hard back in spring.

PROPAGATION As the lower branches tend to sweep the ground, it often layers itself, and can also be layered artificially in autumn. Alternatively you can collect the seed in winter and sow in warmth.

PESTS AND DISEASES Generally trouble free.

COMPANIONS The shape, texture and colouring of enkianthus make it an ideal contrast to rhododendrons and hydrangeas, which both enjoy the same conditions.

	soil	
	ACID	ALKALINE
	DRY	WET

J	F	M	A	M	J	J	A	S	O	N	D

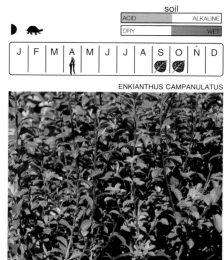
ENKIANTHUS CAMPANULATUS

E

EPILOBIUM GLABELLUM

Willow herb, hardy perennial. Mature at 3 years: 20 x 15cm (8 x 6in).

A delicate-looking and pretty ground cover plant, this dwarf willow herb makes clumps of small, oval, mid-green leaves, which persist throughout mild winters. Cream-white, funnel-shaped flowers are born on slender wiry stems throughout the summer and into autumn.

USES This epilobium makes good ground cover under shrubs and can also be used effectively as formal or informal edging at the front of a border. The tall variety *E. angustifolium* f. *album* is a useful plant for quick effect in sun or shade and looks appropriate beside water.

CULTIVATION Plant 15cm (6in) apart, in autumn or spring in any reasonable soil in sun or light shade. In autumn, when the flowers have faded, clip the plants over with shears to keep them neat and bushy, and to prevent *E. angustifolium* f. *album* from self-seeding.

PROPAGATION Sow seeds in autumn, or take cuttings from the side shoots in spring.

PESTS AND DISEASES Generally trouble free.

OTHER VARIETIES *E. angustifolium album* is the white version of rose bay willow herb which, in its pink form, although handsome is an aggressive weed that spreads by seed and stolon. This one's tall green and white spires, flowering towards the end of the summer, bring cool elegance to tired borders. They grow to 1.2 x 0.5m (4ft x 20in) above narrow lance-shaped leaves. Like the pink version it is liable to spread rapidly, so plant it where that is a virtue and not a vice.

soil

				ACID						ALKALINE
				DRY						WET

J	F	M	A	M	J	J	A	S	O	N	D

EPILOBIUM GLABELLUM

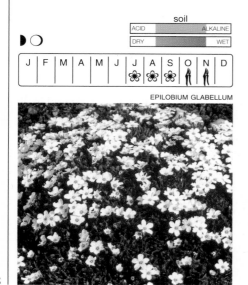

EPIMEDIUM

Hardy perennials (S. Europe, Turkey, Caucasus, Japan, late 16th century). Mature at 3 years: 23-45 x 30-45cm (9-18 x 12-18in)

Among the very best plants to grow in shade, epimediums make dense, level clumps of fresh-looking leaves, slowly spreading by means of creeping rootstocks. The newly emerging leaves are pinky-beige, or reddish bronze, varying in colour according to the species or cultivar. They mature to a light green, which always looks fresh. In spring delicate flowers hang from thin wiry stems in widely spaced clusters, crimson, pink, pale yellow or white. In some species there is the bonus of vivid autumn colour.

USES Plant epimediums in bold drifts to form a weed-smothering carpet under trees in woodland, or in other shady situations.

CULTIVATION Although they will tolerate that most difficult of situations, dry shade, epimediums are happiest of all in damp leaf-mould. Plant between autumn and spring in big groups, setting the plants 23cm (9in) apart. Clip over in spring just before new growth starts, using shears or, in extensive plantings, a strimmer.

PROPAGATION Divide in autumn or spring.

PESTS AND DISEASES Generally trouble free.

GOOD VARIETIES There are plenty of excellent species and varieties to choose from, among them: *E. grandiflorum* 'Rose Queen' AGM, 30 x 30cm (12 x 12in) with comparatively large deep pink flowers, and 'White Queen' AGM. *E.* x *perralchicum* is a little taller, at 45cm (18in), and has sprays of yellow flowers above dark evergreen leaves. The heart-shaped leaves of *E.* x *rubrum* AGM, go from red-bronze to light green and in autumn flare into red. *E.* x *versicolor* 'Neosulphureum' is another evergreen with yellow flowers. *E. perralderianum* is another good plant.

soil

				ACID						ALKALINE
				DRY						WET

J	F	M	A	M	J	J	A	S	O	N	D

EPIMEDIUM X VERSICOLOR 'NEOSULPHUREUM'

EPIMEDIUM PERRALDERIANUM

ERANTHIS HYEMALIS

Winter aconite, hardy, tuberous perennial (Europe, including Britain). Mature at 1 year: 5-10 x 8-10cm (2-4 x 3-4in). AGM

Winter aconites are, with snowdrops, the welcome first sign in the garden that winter has not much longer to run. They are quite likely to push up through a light blanket of snow and the yellow, cup-shaped flowers, surrounded by a ruff of dark green bracts, are a heartening sight. By the end of spring, the leaves have died away leaving no trace.

USES All winter-flowering plants are best positioned where you can see them from indoors. Winter aconites will thrive under trees or shrubs where they can make their seasonal display and be ignored for the rest of the year.

CULTIVATION Plant in partial or total shade in any reasonable soil. The results from dry tubers planted in the autumn are usually very disappointing: few, if any, flowers appear. It is better to plant eranthis 'in-the-green', dug up in spring with the leaves still on the plants. Plants bought at this stage of their annual cycle are more expensive, but in the long run will prove more cost effective. Plant them 5cm (2in) apart, with the tubers 5cm (2in) deep.

PROPAGATION Dig up established clumps in the spring, divide the tubers and replant immediately. Or sow seeds in the autumn. Established colonies will gradually increase their area by self-seeding.

PESTS AND DISEASES Generally trouble free.

OTHER VARIETIES *E.* x *tubergenii* 'Guinea Gold' AGM has darker, golden-yellow flowers; the ruff is bronzy green.

COMPANIONS Plant interlocking drifts of snowdrops and winter aconites, or plant them among herbaceous perennials that will follow on after they have flowered.

soil

| ACID | | | | | | | | | ALKALINE |
| DRY | | | | | | | | | WET |

J	F	M	A	M	J	J	A	S	O	N	D
	✿	✿									

ERANTHIS HYEMALIS

ERICA CARNEA

Syn. E. herbacea. Heather, ling, hardy shrub (Europe, including Britain). Mature at 3 years: to 30 x 45cm (12 x 18in) or more.

There is an enormously wide range of heathers available, including tree heaths (not dealt with here). All share the same semi-prostrate habit of growth with dense, bushy, wiry stems and stubby scale-like leaves. The leaves are dark grey-green and, in some varieties, golden, orange-brown, or bronze. Small, single or double flowers, papery in texture, are borne alongside the new shoots, usually for at least two months. Winter and summer-flowering kinds (e.g. cultivars of *E. tetralix*, *E. vagans*) are available, in shades of white, pink, or purple.

USES Heathers make excellent ground cover in sun or partial shade, particularly when winter colour is wanted. They will grow in areas of industrial pollution and they provide food for bees.

CULTIVATION Many heathers are not lime tolerant and will only grow in peaty, acid soils. However the winter-flowering varieties of *Erica carnea* and cultivars of *E. vagans* can be grown in slightly alkaline soils provided they are humus-rich and moisture-retentive. Plant from late winter to early summer, or in autumn. They flower best in an open position in full sun, but tolerate light shade. Plant deeply, burying the whole stem. In dry soil add moist leaf mould around roots and mulch annually with leaf mould or granulated, composted bark. Water thoroughly in spring and during dry spells until well-established. In spring, clip over the plants with shears to remove the dead flower stems and prevent growth becoming leggy. In autumn, don't allow dead leaves from neighbouring trees and shrubs to lie on the heather.

PROPAGATION Layering is by far the easiest way and can be done at any time. Alternatively, take semi-ripe cuttings in mid- to late summer.

PESTS AND DISEASES Generally trouble free. Any problems are likely to be caused by the fine roots drying out.

GOOD VARIETIES Of the enormous number that is available, the following varieties of *E. carnea*, the lime-tolerant, winter-flowering heather, are recommended: 'Springwood White' AGM has bright green leaves and long spikes of white flowers throughout winter and spring; 'Myretoun Ruby' AGM has ruby-red flowers; 'R.B. Cooke' AGM has shell-pink flowers. 'Vivelli', syn. 'Urville' AGM has dark bronze leaves and red flowers, a more successful colour combination than that of gold leaves with lilac- or magenta-pink flowers, only too common among heathers.

GOOD COMPANIONS Despite their many admirable qualities, heathers are difficult to place in the garden. They really only look right in very informal plantings, preferably in gardens where the local landscape is similar to their native peat moorland. For addicts, a separate heather bed can be made to house their collection. For others, a tapestry of mixed heathers under trees or in front of shrubs can cheer winter's gloom.

soil

| ACID | | | | | | | | | ALKALINE |
| DRY | | | | | | | | | WET |

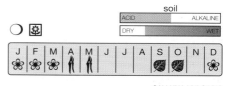

J	F	M	A	M	J	J	A	S	O	N	D
✿	✿	✿	🌿	🌿					🍃	🍃	✿

CALLUNA VULGARIS

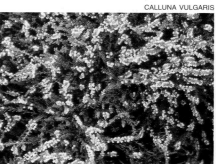

ERICA CARNEA

E

ERUCA VESICARIA SSP. SATIVA

Salad rocket, hardy annual (Europe, including Britain). Mature at 6 weeks: 60cm tall.

Rocket grows fast, providing the first crop of leaves after about six weeks. They are mid-green, long and pointed, and those growing near the base of the plant are deeply indented. The flowers are produced on stems that branch near the top. They are small with four rather sparse cream petals. The flowers are not unattractive, but they are not showy enough to make much of an impact in the garden.

USES The leaves have an unusual spicy taste, which makes them a good ingredient of green salads, especially in winter. They are easy to harvest on a cut-and-come-again basis; there is no need to dig up the whole plant. Use the leaves before the plant flowers; once it reaches the flowering stage the leaves become coarse and so does their flavour.

CULTIVATION Sow the seeds in rows in any reasonable soil that does not dry out. A position in light shade is best, and several sowings, at four week intervals from early spring to late summer, will provide a succession of young salad leaves from late spring until winter. Water in dry spells and keep weeded by hoe or by hand.

PROPAGATION Sow seeds (see above).

PESTS AND DISEASES Generally trouble free, but sometimes the leaves become pitted with tiny spots. They are made by flea beetles, insects that overwinter among plant debris, so maintaining a tidy garden helps to thwart them.

soil		
ACID		ALKALINE
DRY		WET

J	F	M	A	M	J	J	A	S	O	N	D

ERUCA SATIVA

ERYNGIUM

Sea holly, hardy perennial (Europe, 1597). Mature at 3 years: 30 x 30cm (12 x 12in) to 1 x 0.5m (36 x 20in).

Eryngiums flower after midsummer and remain in flower for a long time. The leaves, green and rounded in some species, grey-green, deeply cut and prominently veined in others, form ground-hugging rosettes. Stout blue-grey stems branch at their tops to display several thistly flowers. Each head is a round-topped, blue or blue-grey cone, with a spiky or feathery ruff of metallic bracts beneath.

Uses They make good ground cover and are excellent for flower arranging and drying.

Cultivation Plant in autumn or spring in sun, in any well-drained soil in groups of three or more. Eryngiums tolerate poor and very alkaline soils and stony sites.

Propagation Divide established clumps in autumn or spring, or sow seeds in spring; the seedlings may not come true as the species hybridize freely.

Pests and diseases Generally trouble free.

Good varieties *E. alpinum* AGM, 75 x 45cm (30 x 18in) produces the largest flowers – mauve-blue with feathery collars. *E. bourgatii* is blue-green and more compact at 60 x 30cm (2 x 1ft). *E. maritimum* has blue flowers with grey collars and grey-blue leaves. It needs a hot sandy soil to do well. *E. giganteum* AGM is biennial; it is known as Miss Willmott's ghost because the famous gardener carried its seeds in her pocket and scattered a few wherever she went. It is tall, to 1.2m (4ft), with very silvery bracts. *E.* x *oliverianum* AGM and *E.* x *tripartitum* AGM are both bright steel blue.

Companions The soft blue-grey has a cooling effect on the terracotta and mahogany of some hemerocallis, gaillardias and *Helenium* 'Moerheim Beauty'.

soil		
ACID		ALKALINE
DRY		WET

J	F	M	A	M	J	J	A	S	O	N	D

ERYNGIUM APLINUM

ERYSIMUM

Syn. Cheiranthus. Wallflower, gilliflower, hardy, shrubby perennials, usually grown as biennials (Europe, including Britain). Mature at 1 year: from 5 x 20cm (2 x 8in) to 60 x 38cm (24 x 15in).

Erysimum is not botanically separate from *Cheiranthus*, but is often treated so in catalogues. These plants divide neatly into two categories: taller kinds grown as biennials, and prostrate perennials. Both develop woody stems covered in lance-shaped, dark green leaves. In spring the stem tops are smothered in velvety flowers in dark maroon-purple, red, orange, yellow, or cream. Tall forms are mostly strongly scented, prostrate forms hardly at all.

CULTIVATION Plant low-growing perennials in spring, in a sheltered sunny place, in gravel or limestone or any free-draining soil. Plant out biennials 30cm (12in) apart from late summer to early autumn. They thrive in poor soil but need good drainage and shelter from wind. Clip over perennials after flowering to keep neat and bushy.

PROPAGATION Sow seeds of biennials in early summer in well-drained soil. On acid soils add lime. Thin to 15cm (6in) apart and, when seedlings are 15cm (6in) tall, pinch out the tips to encourage bushiness. Take cuttings of perennials in late summer as a precaution against losses during a hard winter.

PESTS AND DISEASES Flea beetles can attack and disfigure the seedlings' leaves, but seldom kill the plants.

GOOD VARIETIES Among the prostrate perennials 'Moonlight' is an excellent yellow variety; 'Constant Cheer' AGM and 'Jacob's Jacket' mix orange, mauve and cream in each individual flower. 'Bowles Mauve' AGM is a shrubby perennial with mauve flowers produced non stop from spring to autumn.

COMPANIONS Groups of mixed colours of wall flowers are best left to themselves. Tulips are the traditional flower to grow with single colours. The plants are equally good in formal bedding or informal groups.

soil

| | | | | | | ACID | | | ALKALINE |
| | | | | | | DRY | | | WET |

J	F	M	A	M	J	J	A	S	O	N	D

ERYSIMUM

ERYSIMUM 'MOONLIGHT'

ERYTHRONIUM DENS-CANIS

Dog's tooth violet, hardy bulbous perennial (Europe, Asia). Mature at 2 years: 15-25 x 8-10cm (6-10 x 3-4in). AGM

This is a spring flowering woodland plant. First two broad, smooth leaves appear, with a mottled and marbled surface. They are followed by pink, mauve or occasionally white flowers with their petals swept back like cyclamen around a central brush of prominent anthers. In summer the leaves and flowers die down.

USES A good plant to naturalize under trees.

CULTIVATION Plant the bulbs 8cm (3in) deep and about 5cm (2in) apart in late summer, grouping them at random. They will grow in any reasonable garden soil but are best suited to a retentive soil with leaf mould or garden compost added. Once planted let well alone except for (ideally) an annual mulch of leaf mould or compost.

PROPAGATION Dig up established clumps and detach and replant offsets.

PESTS AND DISEASES Generally trouble free.

GOOD VARIETIES A little harder to please, but not difficult to succeed with are *E. californicum* 'White Beauty' AGM, 20 x 10cm (8 x 4in) and 'Pagoda' AGM, 30 x 15cm (12 x 6in) with pale yellow flowers held well above the shiny, faintly mottled leaves. They prefer partial shade and a moist cool climate.

COMPANIONS Plant erythroniums in front of bluebells or among plants that enjoy the same cool conditions, and which emerge just as the erythroniums are dying down, such as ferns and the smaller hostas *H. fortunei* 'Albopicta' AGM or 'Midas Touch'.

soil

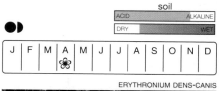

| | | | | | | ACID | | | ALKALINE |
| | | | | | | DRY | | | WET |

J	F	M	A	M	J	J	A	S	O	N	D

ERYTHRONIUM DENS-CANIS

E

ESCALLONIA

Evergreen, or semi-evergreen shrubs (S. America, early 19th century). Mature at 7 years: from 1.5 x 1.5m (5 x 5ft) to 4 x 5m (13 x 17ft).

Few escallonias are reliably hardy inland, but most are excellent seaside plants. The dark green shiny leaves vary from very small to medium sized. At midsummer arching stems are covered in small red, pink or white flowers for at least six weeks.

USES In seaside areas plant as hedges or as part of a shelter belt. When not in flower they make good background plants. They tolerate industrial pollution and provide nectar for bees.

CULTIVATION Plant in late spring or early summer in any reasonable, well-drained soil including chalk. Even for hardy species it is wise to choose a sunny site protected from north and east winds. Prune young plants in spring to encourage a bushy shape. Established plants only need pruning to keep them within bounds.

PROPAGATION Take semi-ripe cuttings in late summer.

PESTS AND DISEASES Generally trouble free.

GOOD VARIETIES For hardiness, choose: 'Donard Seedling', 2.5 x 2.5m (8 x 8ft), with pink flushed white flowers opening from pink buds; 'Red Elf', a compact 1.5 x 1.5m (5 x 5ft) with dark crimson flowers; 'Edinensis' AGM, 2 x 3m (6 x 10ft), with bright green leaves and pink flowers. The rest are only for mild coastal or sheltered gardens: 'Apple Blossom' AGM, 1.5 x 1.8m (5 x 6ft); 'Iveyi' AGM, to 4 x 5m (13 x 17ft), very handsome with dark green leaves and white flowers. *E. rubra* 'Crimson Spire' AGM, makes a 1.8m (6ft) hedge in four years. 'Silver Anniversary', 1.5 x 1.5 (5 x 5ft) has silver-edged leaves and deep pink flowers.

soil		
ACID		ALKALINE
DRY		WET

J	F	M	A	M	J	J	A	S	O	N	D

ESCALLONIA X IVEYI

EUCALYPTUS GUNNII

Cider gum, evergreen tree (Australia, 1840s). Mature at 20 years: 20 x 6m (65 x 20ft). AGM

This is one of the few eucalypts that can really be trusted for hardiness, but it still needs a reasonably sheltered position. It grows very fast, by as much as 2m (6ft) a year. The bark on young stems is a very pale bluish-grey, and brown when mature, peeling to show cream and warm pink underneath. The trees carry two kinds of foliage: the juvenile leaves are very decorative blue-grey discs. The adult leaves are long and pointed and not quite as blue.

USES Although it is fairly openly branched, in mild areas this eucalypt makes an effective, very quick screen to hide ugly features in the landscape, and is tolerant of industrial pollution. Flower arrangers love the juvenile foliage.

CULTIVATION Plant pot-grown trees of the smallest size obtainable in late spring. The ideal site is sunny, sheltered from cold winds and on well-drained soil, although clay soil is tolerated. Water in dry spells for the first year or two. If you want to keep the foliage in its juvenile state, cut hard back every spring, treating the plant as a shrub rather than a tree.

PROPAGATION Eucalypts can only be grown from seed sown in spring or autumn.

PESTS AND DISEASES Generally trouble free.

OTHER VARIETIES *E. pauciflora* AGM and *E. pauciflora* ssp. *niphophila*, the snow gum AGM may turn out to be equally hardy. They are slow growing for the first two years, but then put on 1m (3ft) annually. The bark flakes and the grey-green juvenile leaves open from red buds.

soil		
ACID		ALKALINE
DRY		WET

J	F	M	A	M	J	J	A	S	O	N	D

EUCALYPTUS GUNNII

EUONYMUS GUNNII JUVENILE FORM

EUONYMUS EUROPAEUS 'RED CASCADE'

Spindle bush, hardy, deciduous shrub (Europe). Mature at 15 years: 2 x 1.5m (6 x 5ft) after 10 years, 2.5 x 2m (8 x 6ft) at maturity. Poisonous. AGM

This and other deciduous *Euonymus* species are grown for their brilliant red autumn colour and their startling berries, which are shocking pink opening to reveal orange seeds. Earlier in the year, the leaves are a discreet, darkish green.

USES The wood is very hard and was once used to make spindles. The shrub will grow almost anywhere and is quite happy on chalk. As so many plants with good autumn colour perform badly or not at all on chalk, spindle bushes go a long way to redress the balance. They have been planted along motorway verges in chalk areas where they make a fine show in autumn.

CULTIVATION Plant between autumn and spring in any reasonable soil, in sun or light shade. No pruning is necessary unless the shrub grows too big for its position, in which case it can be cut back in winter.

PROPAGATION Take greenwood cuttings in summer, or sow fresh seeds in autumn.

PESTS AND DISEASES Caterpillars sometimes infest the bushes, eating the young shoots and preventing fruit from forming. Otherwise, generally trouble free.

OTHER VARIETIES *E. alatus* AGM has very good red autumn colour and corky, winged bark. *E. alatus* 'Compactus' is a particularly good, small, dense-growing variety. *E. planipes* has red leaves in autumn and red fruit with orange seeds.

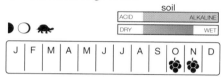

EUONYMUS EUROPAEUS 'RED CASCADE'

EUONYMUS PLANIPES

EUONYMUS ALATUS 'COMPACTUS'

EUONYMUS FORTUNEI

Hardy evergreen shrub of variable size (Japan). Mature at 12 years.

These shrubs are dense and compact, shade tolerant and quick growing. They are low spreading plants but they will, if planted against a wall or fence, put out long climbing shoots with aerial roots. The leaves are shiny and ovate, plain green or variegated almost white in some cultivars, bright yellow in others.

USES The variegated forms are among the best of all ground cover plants for a shady situation. They are also extremely useful climbers for a north-facing wall or fence. They are hardy and grow in most adverse situations including chalk soil, cold winds, salt-laden winds and industrial pollution.

CULTIVATION Plant between autumn and spring in any well-drained soil, in sun or shade. No pruning is needed, except to thicken up straggly plants or to prevent spreading by clipping in spring.

PROPAGATION Take semi-ripe cuttings in summer, or hardwood cuttings in winter.

PESTS AND DISEASES Generally trouble free.

GOOD VARIETIES 'Silver Queen' AGM has very white variegation. It grows no higher than 90cm (3ft) but will spread to 1.8m (6ft). Against a wall or fence it will reach 3 x 1.8m (10 x 6ft). Mature plants sometimes produce poisonous, orange-pink berries. 'Emerald Gaiety' AGM also has white margins; it is more compact and tolerates quite deep shade. 'Emerald and Gold' AGM has startlingly bright yellow variegations.

COMPANIONS Even in shade, strongly variegated foliage can be rather overwhelming. These splendid plants are best used quite sparingly, with plenty of plain green around them to rest the eye.

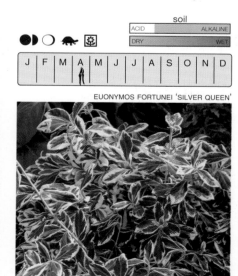

EUONYMOS FORTUNEI 'SILVER QUEEN'

E

E

EUPHORBIA

Spurge, milkweed, hardy deciduous or evergreen perennials (Europe and Asia). Mature at 3 years: from 8 x 30cm (4 x 12in) to 1 x 1m (3 x 3ft). This genus also includes tropical and subtropical succulents.

Euphorbias have unbranching stems closely covered in narrow leathery or succulent leaves growing around the stem, bottle-brush fashion. Cut stems exude milky juice, which can irritate the skin. The flower heads are studded with conspicuous bracts, usually lime green or bright greenish-yellow.

USES Most make good ground cover, either in sun or in shade.

CULTIVATION Plant in autumn or spring, in any ordinary soil in sun or light shade. *E. amygdaloides* var. *robbiae* will grow in dense shade.

PROPAGATION Divide established clumps in autumn or spring. *E. amygdaloides* var. *robbiae* and *E. cyparissias* will spread by underground runners. *E. charbacias* self-seeds freely.

PESTS AND DISEASES Generally trouble free.

GOOD VARIETIES Starting with the largest, *E. charbacias* ssp. *wulfenii* AGM, 90 x 90cm (3 x 3ft) is a sculptural plant with

biennial stems of grey-green leaves. The following spring, flower heads appear with masses of green-yellow bracts with black centres looking rather like frogspawn. *E. griffithii* 'Fireglow' and 'Dixter' AGM, 75 x 60cm (2ft 6in x 2ft), is upright with leaves and flowerheads suffused with brick-orange from late spring to midsummer. *E. polychroma* AGM, 45 x 45cm (18 x 18in), makes a tidy dome covered with rosettes of large neon-yellow bracts. *E. amygdaloides* var. *robbiae* is valued because it will grow where virtually nothing else will, in dry shade.

COMPANIONS In shade, the magenta flowers of honesty, *Lunaria annua*, make startling contrasts with the lime green of *E. amygdaloides* var. *robbiae*. *E. griffithii* contrasts well with blue or purple forms of *Iris siberica*.

EUPHORBIA CHARACIAS SSP. WULFENII 'JOHN TOMLINSON'

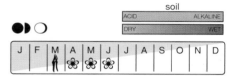

soil

ACID		ALKALINE
DRY		WET

J	F	M	A	M	J	J	A	S	O	N	D

EUPHORBIA POLYCHROMA

EUPHORBIA GRIFFITHII 'FIREGLOW'

FAGUS SYLVATICA

Beech, a deciduous tree (Europe, including Britain). Mature at 50 years: 8m (25ft) tall after 20 years; up to 25 x 25m (80 x 80ft) at maturity.

A very hardy majestic tree of chalk and limestone hills, beech has smooth, elephant grey bark and a dense canopy of smooth, ribbed pointed leaves of fresh light green or dark coppery-purple. The leaves turn bright russet in autumn and, on young trees and hedges, remain all winter.

USES Beech trees grow too big for most gardens but where there is space a single specimen on a lawn is very handsome. Beech is a classic hedging plant and can also be pleached to make a hedge on stilts.

CULTIVATION Plant in autumn or early winter, in any well-drained soil, alkaline or acid, in sun or semi-shade. Small sizes, up to 1m (3ft) tall, establish best. For the first two seasons water well during dry spells. For hedges, plant 45cm (18in) apart and, for quick results, keep weeded and feed with a general fertilizer every spring. Cut hedges once a year in late summer.

PROPAGATION Sow seeds in autumn. Ornamental forms should be budded during late summer.

PESTS AND DISEASES Beech can be attacked by various fungi, by aphids and by soft scale.

OTHER VARIETIES *F. sylvatica* 'Dawyck' AGM is a slender, upright form with good autumn colour. *F. sylvatica* 'pendula' AGM, the weeping beech, is sometimes temperamental and difficult to persuade to grow upwards, but when it behaves it is very attractive. *F. sylvatica* 'Purpurea Pendula' is a weeping tree with black-purple leaves. *F. sylvatica* 'Riversii' AGM, is the darkest form of copper beech.

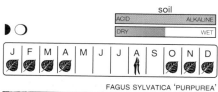

FAGUS SYLVATICA 'PURPUREA'

FAGUS SYLVATICA 'PURPUREA'

X FATSHEDERA LIZEI

F

Evergreen shrub. Mature at 12 years: 2.5 x 3m (8 x 10ft). AGM

This is a cross between *Hedera hibernica*, the large-leaved Irish ivy and *Fatsia japonica* 'Moseri', a Japanese shrub with very large, glossy fig-like leaves that was fashionable as a house plant in the last century. The hybrid has elegant dark green, glossy fingered leaves. It has loose flexible branches that can be trained to a wall or pillar, or left to build up a mound of greenery. In autumn small white flowers are carried in clusters.

USES Like both its parents, x *Fatshedera* has the virtue of being shade tolerant and able to withstand air pollution. It is a good container plant for such unpromising sites as the basement area of a terraced town house.

CULTIVATION Plant in early summer in any well-drained soil, in partial or full shade and in a sheltered position. Water in dry spells until established and, in cold areas, cover the whole plant as a precaution against severe frosts. In spring, cut out dead or weak branches.

PROPAGATION Take semi-ripe cuttings during the summer.

PESTS AND DISEASES Generally trouble free.

OTHER VARIETIES The leaves of x *F. lizei* 'Variegata' have narrow cream-white margins. *Fatsia japonica* AGM, 3 x 3m (10 x 10ft), is larger in all its parts. In late autumn the flowers develop into pale green berries held upright in clusters, later turning black. *F. japonica* also has several variegated forms, but they are tender and better used as house or conservatory plants in cold areas.

COMPANIONS x *Fatshedera* and *Fatsia* make a strong contribution to groups of foliage plants including bamboos, hostas, ivies and ferns.

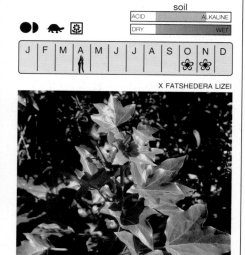

X FATSHEDERA LIZEI

F

FELICIA AMELLOIDES

Syn. **Aster amelloides, F. capensis, F. coelestis. Blue marguerite, blue daisy, a tender evergreen subshrub, usually treated as an annual (S. Africa). Mature at 16 months: 30 x 30cm (12 x 12in).**

The delicate, sky-blue daisy flowers with yellow centres are carried over a long season, from late spring until autumn. They are held on slender stems above bright green oval leaves.

USES Felicias are good as part of a mixed summer display in pots or urns, or planted out in beds and borders for the summer.

CULTIVATION Plant out in late spring in well-drained soil in a sunny position. Dead-head regularly to keep a constant supply of new flowers. In very well-drained soil and a very sheltered site, the plants may survive the winter, but it is a wise precaution to pot them up and bring them into a frost-free greenhouse or a cool room indoors. Keep the soil or compost in the pots barely moist during the winter.

PROPAGATION Sow seeds under glass in early spring, or take stem tip cuttings in late summer and overwinter in a frost-free greenhouse.

PESTS AND DISEASES Generally trouble free.

GOOD VARIETIES *F. amelloides* 'Santa Anita' AGM is a good reliable variety. 'Santa Anita Variegated' AGM has cream-variegated leaves. The true annual, *F. bergeriana*, kingfisher daisy, has similar flowers and is mat-forming; it is noted for its wind resistance and is ideal for window boxes and containers on high balconies.

COMPANIONS In containers, *Felicia* mixes well with the soft, yellow-green leaves of *Helichrysum petiolare* 'Limelight' and the yellow flowers of *Bidens ferulifolia* AGM. In the border, it could be planted next to the silver-grey foliage and cream button flowers of *Santolina neapolitana* 'Edward Bowles'.

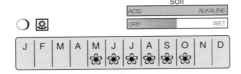

FELICIA AMELLOIDES

FESTUCA GLAUCA

Blue fescue, an evergreen perennial grass (temperate zones of northern and southern hemispheres, including Britain). Mature at 3 years: 30 x 30cm (12 x 12in).

This grass forms neat, noninvasive tufts of very narrow, steely blue-grey leaves about 15cm (6in) high. The unobtrusive flower stalks are the same colour.

USES It makes a neat edging to beds and borders and a well-behaved ground cover at the front of a border, and will colonize gravel on terraces and paths.

CULTIVATION Plant between autumn and spring, in any reasonable soil provided it is well-drained. The leaves will colour best when grown in full sun.

PROPAGATION Divide and replant established clumps every few years during the spring.

PESTS AND DISEASES Generally trouble free.

OTHER VARIETIES *F. glauca* 'Blaufuchs', syn. 'Blue Fox' AGM, has exceptionally blue leaves. Other blue grasses include *Koeleria glauca*, with tussocks of very blue-grey leaves and upright blue-grey flower heads.

COMPANIONS Use a small group to link other blue- and glaucous-leaved plants, such as *Ruta graveolens* to *Hebe pinguifolia* 'Pagei'. Or contrast the texture with blue-grey and blue-purple leaves of sedum.

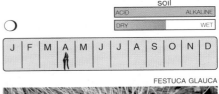

FESTUCA GLAUCA

FICUS CARICA

Fig, a hardy deciduous shrub or tree (Mediterranean mid 16th century). Mature at 15 years: 2.5 x 3.5m (8 x 11ft) or more.

Widely branching stems with smooth grey bark carry large, coarse-textured, mid-green leaves with divided, rounded lobes. Insignificant flowers are followed by large, tear-drop-shaped fruit with smooth soft green or purple skin and juicy flesh. They ripen in late summer.

USES Figs are grown for their edible fruit. In the open they make good shade trees. They make good pot plants for sunny terraces.

CULTIVATION For the fruit to ripen, figs must have a warm wall, preferably facing south or southwest. They also like a dry atmosphere; in cool, damp climates, your fig tree is likely to be biblically barren. To restrict growth and induce good fruiting, plant in brick- or concrete-lined bottomless pits 60cm (2ft) square, and fill the bottom with broken brick. Provide strong wires to support wall-trained plants. Plant in winter. Mulch with well-rotted manure every spring and water during dry spells. In early spring cut back frost-damaged shoots and thin overcrowded branches. Tie in branches to achieve an approximate fan shape against the wall. At midsummer pinch back new shoots to five leaves to encourage the development of embryo figs, which will provide next season's crop.

PROPAGATION Take hardwood cuttings from one-year-old wood or, if your fig tree has produced suckers, dig one up with its roots and transplant it.

PESTS AND DISEASES Generally trouble free, but birds and wasps may get to the ripe fruit before you do. You can net the tree against birds, but the only protection against wasps is to encase individual figs in muslin bags.

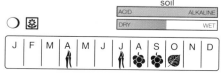

FICUS CARICA

FICUS CARICA

FILIPENDULA

F

Meadowsweet, queen of the meadows, a hardy perennial (Asia, N. America and Europe, including Britain). Mature at 3 years: from 30 x 30cm (12 x 12in) to 1.2m x 60cm (4 x 2ft).

The tall Japanese *F. purpurea* and the British native *F. ulmaria* share the same finely-cut leaves with pointed fingers, making a good, bold clump. At midsummer thin, wiry stems hold up feathery plumes of fluffy little flowers.

USES These are, by nature, waterside or ditch plants and look their best in the wild garden or – at any rate – in informal planting schemes.

CULTIVATION Filipendulas will grow in almost any soil provided it remains damp. In really boggy conditions, or with their roots in the water at the margin of a pond, they will thrive in full sun, but in sites that are not so wet they prefer some shade. Plant in autumn or spring, in groups about 60cm (2ft) apart.

PROPAGATION Divide in autumn or winter.

PESTS AND DISEASES Generally trouble free.

GOOD VARIETIES *F. purpurea* AGM, 1.2m x 60cm (4 x 2ft), is worth tracking down; its flowers are bright crimson. *F. rubra* 'Venusta', syn. 'Magnifica' AGM is a bit aggressive in a small garden, but fine if you have boggy areas to colonize. It reaches 1.8 x 1.2m (6 x 4ft) and produces soft pink flowers. *F. ulmaria* 'Aurea', 30 x 30cm (12 x 12in), is more manageable than either. It is a yellow-leaved form of the native meadowsweet with fluffy white flowers. It needs a shady position as the leaves scorch in strong sunlight.

COMPANIONS The tall pink and crimson forms look good behind the smaller cultivars of blue-leaved hostas. *Iris laevigata* makes a good companion for *F. ulmaria* 'Aurea'.

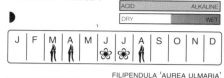

FILIPENDULA 'AUREA ULMARIA'

F

FOENICULUM VULGARE 'PURPUREUM'

Bronze fennel, a hardy perennial (the species grows wild in S. Europe and Britain; the purple-leaved form has naturalized). Mature at 2 years: 1.8m x 45cm.

Thread-like, soft feathery leaves emerge in spring to form smoky, dark reddish-bronze mounds. As the stems grow taller the colouring becomes less intense, fading to dark purplish-green. Branching stems rise above the foliage, carrying flat yellow flower heads, which resemble those of cow parsley from mid- to late summer.

USES Fennel is grown as a culinary herb, the leaves, seeds and stems all being used, particularly to flavour fish dishes. It is also said to reduce the toxic effects of alcohol.

CULTIVATION Set out pot grown plants 45cm (18in) apart, in a sunny position in well-drained soil. They will not do well in clay. If you want to maintain a fairly low dense clump of foliage, cut it down to a few centimeters from the ground once or twice in summer. This will also delay flowering for a week or so. For kitchen use, just cut off a few leaves when you need them.

PROPAGATION Sow seeds in late spring or early summer, or divide established plants in autumn. Dig up and replant self-sown seedlings in autumn or spring; the purple-leaved form comes true from seed.

PESTS AND DISEASES Generally trouble free.

OTHER VARIETIES Although its colouring is not as unusual, the ordinary, plain green form of *F. vulgare* is just as attractive.

COMPANIONS The bronze fennel is a good foil to reds and oranges and a textural contrast to other bronze, red and purple-leaved plants. Hit both targets with *Lychnis* x *arkwrightii* 'Vesuvius' and *Lobelia* 'Queen Victoria' AGM.

FOENICULUM VULGARE 'PURPUREUM'

FORSYTHIA X INTERMEDIA 'LYNWOOD'

F. suspensa x F. viridissima, a hybrid of garden origin. Deciduous shrub. Mature at 15 years: 1.8 x 1.8m (6 x 6ft) after 10 years, 3 x 3m (10 x 10ft) at maturity. AGM

The eponymous William Forsyth, the superintendent of the Royal Gardens at Kensington, would probably be surprised to find his namesake growing in almost every garden in the land. The familiar yellow flowers hang all along the bare grey-brown stems in early spring, and are followed by toothed, light green leaves.

USES If branches are cut while in bud, the flowers will come out in water indoors. The upright habit of *F.* x *intermedia* cultivars make them suitable for a quick-growing hedge; plant 45cm (18in) apart. They can be trained as standards, and tolerate chalk soils and industrial pollution.

CULTIVATION Plant when dormant in any ordinary soil, preferably in sun. Forsythias tolerate shade but flower most prolifically in sun. They keep their shape and flower best if, after flowering, you prune out one-third of the oldest branches. Trim hedges after flowering and renovate neglected plants by cutting them right down.

They will flower again the second year after a hard pruning.

PROPAGATION Hardwood cuttings taken in autumn will root in open ground. Self-layered shoots can be separated when they are dormant.

PESTS AND DISEASES Birds may eat the flower buds and forsythia gall produces harmless, but unsightly, scabby growths on the branches.

GOOD VARIETIES 'Spring Glory', 2 x 1.5m (6 x 5ft), has large paler yellow flowers. *F. suspensa* has an untidy habit with very long, straggling shoots; I might grow it tumbling down a steep bank or hanging from a high retaining wall.

COMPANIONS The spring overdose of yellow from forsythia and daffodils calls for an antidote of blue flowers – swathes of *Anemone blanda*, scillas, or *Muscari*.

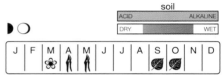

FORSYTHIA SUSPENSA

FRAXINUS EXCELSIOR 'PENDULA'

Weeping ash, a deciduous tree (Britain, mid 18th century). Mature at 30 years: to 15 x 10m (50 x 30ft). AGM

Today's weeping ash trees are thought to be descendants of one found at Gamlingay in Cambridgeshire, and perpetuated by grafting. The branches arch and weep in an attractive, irregular fashion to form a broad umbrella with skirts reaching to the ground. The leaves are late to appear and form a dense curtain encircling the hollow centre around the tree's trunk; a place where a number of children can hide or several adults could shelter from the rain.

USES It should be given pride of place as a specimen tree in the open.

CULTIVATION Like other ashes the weeping ash prefers neutral to alkaline soil, thriving best in an open sunlit position on chalk or limestone. The tree you buy should have been trained with a well-spaced weeping crown, but any crossing branches that develop should be removed; they can provide niches for rot in later years. Once the tree is established, prune only to shorten the tips of the branches when they begin to sweep the ground.

PROPAGATION A job for specialists; it is top-grafted on to a straight-stemmed seedling of the species.

PESTS AND DISEASES Generally trouble free.

OTHER VARIETIES The ordinary *F. excelsior* is handsome in the landscape, but grows too large to plant in most gardens. However, in a large garden a place might be found for *F. ornus* AGM, the manna ash. It is a round-headed tree, reaching 15 x 10m (50 x 30ft). In late spring it bears hanging clusters of white flowers followed by small black berries. The flowers have a scent some people dislike.

FRAXINUS ORNUS

FRITILLARIA IMPERIALIS

Crown imperial, a perennial bulb (S. Turkey to W. Himalaya, before 1590). Mature at 2 years: up to 1.2m x 45cm (4ft x 18in).

In early spring stout, smooth green stems rush out of the ground and stand to attention, their lower half encircled with curved strappy leaves. At each stem top a circle of large, bell-shaped yellow, red, or orange flowers hangs down. At the top of the flower cluster is an upright crest of fresh light green leaves. The whole plant looks strangely exotic, as if it is about to give birth to pineapples.

USES In spite of their strangeness, crown imperials are equally at home in formal or quite wild parts of the garden; they are suitable for a centrepiece in knot gardens, or filling in between shrubs.

CULTIVATION If you can get them, buy fresh bulbs as soon as the flowers have faded in summer. Plant in sun or light shade in deep, rich well-drained soil, 15-20cm (6- 8in) deep. After flowering, cut down the stems but allow the leaves to fade naturally. If they fail to flower, try a mulch of well-rotted manure.

PROPAGATION Detach offsets from crowded clumps in summer, after flowering.

PESTS AND DISEASES Generally trouble free.

OTHER VARIETIES Other fritillaries are much smaller, but all have a strange fascination. *F. meleagris* AGM, snake's head fritillary, is a British native of sunny water meadows and will naturalize where conditions are right. *F. persica* has black-maroon bells with a grapey bloom, but it flowers early and may be hit by frost. Most are not difficult if provided with sun and a rich soil that doesn't dry out. Other hardy species are variations on a theme of purple-brown, yellow and green. Experiment, but beware of addiction.

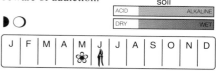

FRITILLARIA IMPERIALIS

FRITILLARIA IMPERIALIS

F

FUCHSIA MAGELLANICA

FUCHSIA SNOWCAP

Deciduous shrub (Chile and Argentina, 1820s). Mature at 5 years: 3 x 2m (10 x 6ft) in warm sheltered areas where the plants are not cut down by frost, otherwise about 90 x 90cm (3 x 3ft).

The Plant Finder lists over two thousand cultivars of fuchsia, most of them tender. The hardy ones are derived mainly from *F. magellanica.* In all but the mildest areas the top growth is killed by frost, but new growth shoots from below ground in late spring and flowers from midsummer well into autumn. Pointed leaves are borne in pairs or threes and the flowers hang from the leaf joints on slender stalks. The flowers, skirted like tiny ballerinas, are usually in two colours, red outer petals partly concealing inner ones of violet. The stamens are usually the same colour as the outer petals.

USES In mild coastal districts fuchsias make excellent hedges. Elsewhere they are perfect for mixed and herbaceous borders, and may be grown in pots for patios or courtyards.

CULTIVATION Grow in any well-drained soil, in sun or light shade. Plant in late spring and, in cold districts, protect the root zone with a 15cm (6in) layer of bark or bracken. Cut the dead wood down to the ground in late spring.

PROPAGATION Take cuttings between spring and autumn. Overwinter rooted cuttings in a frost-free greenhouse.

PESTS AND DISEASES Remove and burn leaves affected by rust and spray the plant with a systemic fungicide.

OTHER VARIETIES *F. magellanica.* var. *gracilis* AGM has red and violet flowers. 'Versicolor' AGM is grown for its pinkish grey, variegated leaves and crimson and violet flowers. *Fuschia* 'Rufus' has slender flowers; the inner and outer petals are red.

FUCHSIA 'RUFUS'

COMPANIONS For harmony of foliage, plant *F. magellanica* 'Versicolor' with *Rosa glauca* and *Dicentra* 'Bountiful', or 'Adrian Bloom'.

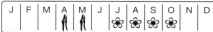

J	F	M	A	M	J	J	A	S	O	N	D

FUCHSIA MAGELLANICA

FUCHSIA MAGELLANICA 'VERISCOLOR'

GAILLARDIA

Blanket flower, a hardy perennial (N. America, late 18th century). Mature at 3 years: 60 x 45cm (24 x 18in).

These short-lived perennials flower late in the summer and contribute to the rusty red and orange colour range that seems to dominate that time of year. They have large daisy flowers with close-set rays around a large reddish-brown centre. The petals are typically deep orange-red with yellow tips, but some varieties are all orange, or all yellow. The leaves and stems are soft green, slightly sticky all over and aromatic.

USES Traditionally gaillardias are plants for growing in herbaceous borders. They are also excellent as cut flowers.

CULTIVATION Gaillardias need a warm, relatively dry site. Plant them during the spring in light soil and mulch with manure or garden compost every following spring. Even in ideal conditions they will need renewing after a few years. The flower stems need the support of pea sticks or grow-through plant supports.

PROPAGATION Divide and replant in autumn or spring. Or sow seeds in gentle heat in spring; most flower in their first year. Take root cuttings in winter.

PESTS AND DISEASES Generally trouble free.

GOOD VARIETIES 'Burgunder', syn. 'Burgundy', has flowers of a uniform deep, warm burgundy-red, 'Dazzler' AGM is two-tone with an outer circle of yellow tips to the red petals, and 'Kobold', syn. 'Goblin', is similar but smaller – just 35cm (14in) high.

COMPANIONS Use as part of a hot colour scheme with red and orange crocosmias, cannas and kniphofias, or provide a cool contrast with eryngiums or *Ceanothus* 'Gloire de Versailles'.

GAILLARDIA 'BURGUNDER'

GALANTHUS NIVALIS

G

Snowdrop, a bulbous perennial (Europe, naturalized in Britain). Mature at 3 years: to 15 x 8cm (6 x 3in). AGM

In some parts of Britain snowdrops have colonized large areas of woodland and in late winter are a beautiful sight. The leaves are narrow and strap-shaped, smooth grey-green with a faint whitish bloom. They form grassy clumps out of which leafless flower stems appear. The white flowers have a three-petalled outer skirt over a shorter inner cup of three green-tipped petals.

USES Snowdrops are best left to naturalize in woodland under trees and shrubs, or at the base of a hedge.

CULTIVATION The best position for snowdrops is in partial shade in humus-rich, moisture-retentive soil. They will also succeed in quite dense shade in rather dry conditions close to a tree trunk. Failure to establish is most often caused by planting dry bulbs. If possible, buy bulbs 'in-the-green'– that is, in leaf, immediately after flowering. Plant bulbs 5cm (2in) deep at random distances apart for a natural look.

PROPAGATION Immediately after flowering, dig up congested clumps and separate and replant the bulbs. Alternatively, transplant self-sown plants.

PESTS AND DISEASES Generally trouble free.

OTHER VARIETIES *G. nivalis* 'Flore Pleno' AGM has double flowers. *G. elwesii* AGM grows to 30cm (12in) and has broader, arching grey-green leaves.

COMPANIONS Snowdrops are often planted with *Eranthis hyemalis* (winter aconites) which produce their yellow flowers at the same time. Make a winter-flowering corner by planting snowdrops under plain or purple-leaved corylus, or *Hamamelis mollis*.

GALANTHUS 'JOHN GRAY'

G

GALTONIA CANDICANS

Cape hyacinth, a bulbous perennial (S. Africa, c.1860). Mature at 2 years: to 120 x 23cm (4ft x 9in).

Large bulbs produce wide strap-shaped leaves, greyish-green and slightly fleshy. In late summer, stout smooth stems up to 1.2m (4ft) high each carry a spire of grey-green buds, which open into large waxy white bells. The flowers are heavily scented. The plants are hardy in all but the most severe of winters.

USES Interplant galtonias with early flowering plants such as peonies, to extend the period of interest.

CULTIVATION Galtonias need rich well-drained soil in an open sunny position. A well-dug and manured herbaceous border is ideal. Plant the bulbs 23cm (9in) deep in early spring. A mulch of manure each or every other year will help the plants keep up a good display.

PROPAGATION Dig up congested clumps and detach and plant offsets of the bulbs, or allow the plants to seed themselves (they do so readily) and wait four or five years for the seedlings to reach flowering size.

PEST AND DISEASES Generally trouble free.

OTHER VARIETIES *G. viridiflora* AGM flowers later than *G. candicans*, in early autumn. *G. viridiflora* is a little less sturdy in appearance, but it has an equally robust constitution. Its flowers are pale green.

COMPANIONS Galtonias associate well with plants of more delicate form, such as *Fuchsia magellanica* or *Caryopteris*.

	soil	
	ACID	ALKALINE
○	DRY	WET

J	F	M	A	M	J	J	A	S	O	N	D
						✿	✿				

GALTONIA CANDICANS

GARRYA ELLIPTICA

Silk tassel bush, an evergreen shrub (California, early 19th century). Mature at 12 years: 3 x 2.5m (10x 8ft) after 10 years; 4 x 3m (13 x 10ft) at maturity.

G. elliptica has long tassel-like catkins, which appear in winter. They grow much longer on the male plants, and only male plants are sold by garden centres and nurseries. It is fast-growing, dense and bushy with leathery, mid- to dark green leaves.

USES *Garrya* can be grown as a wall shrub, tied in to trellis or wires, facing any direction including north. Trained in this way the winter catkins are seen to advantage. As a free-standing shrub in sheltered areas it makes a substantial background to other plants in summer. It is resistant to pollution and salt-laden winds and tolerant of both acid and alkaline soils.

CULTIVATION Plant in any reasonable soil in late spring or early autumn, in a position sheltered from cold winds: plants exposed to frosty winds may not survive, and wind tangles the catkins, spoiling their decorative effect. If the plant is to be trained against a wall or fence, make sure it is planted with its main stem at least 45cm (18in) out from the wall, so that rain can reach its roots. If necessary, cut out one stem in three, in spring, to prevent over-crowding. On wall-trained plants, cut off outward-facing shoots and any others that interfere with the framework of the shrub.

PROPAGATION Take semi-ripe cuttings in summer or early autumn.

PESTS AND DISEASES Generally trouble free.

GOOD VARIETIES *G. elliptica* 'James Roof' has longer, more dramatic catkins than the species. They are up to 35cm (14in) long.

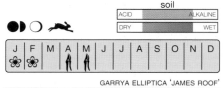

		soil	
		ACID	ALKALINE
◐ ○ 🐇		DRY	WET

J	F	M	A	M	J	J	A	S	O	N	D
✿	✿		♟	♟							

GARRYA ELLIPTICA 'JAMES ROOF'

GAULTHERIA PROCUMBENS

Creeping wintergreen, partridge berry, an evergreen shrub (Eastern N. America, 1762). Mature at 15 years: 5-15cm (2-6in) tall, with indefinite spread. AGM

On acid, peaty soil, gaultheria colonizes ground at a steady pace, creeping along with branching stems that root as they go. The small, glossy rounded leaves are very aromatic when crushed. They take on reddish-purple colouring in winter. The flowers appear in late summer; small, white and urn-shaped like those of lily-of-the-valley, followed by small red berries. Both the flowers and the berries are partly hidden by the leaves.

USES On acid soils only, *Gaultheria* makes ground-hugging evergreen cover in light shade. In more formal gardens it makes a tidy edging. The berries provide winter food for partridges and other birds. Oil containing magnesium, potassium and pain-killing ingredients, can be extracted from the leaves. It is used by herbalists to treat rheumatism and skin complaints.

CULTIVATION Gaultherias must have acid or neutral soil. *G. procumbens* is fairly drought tolerant, but prefers a peaty, moisture-retentive soil. Plant in autumn or spring, adding leaf mould or garden compost to light soils. For ground cover set 45cm (18in) apart. No pruning is necessary except to tidy up straggly branches, or trim edging plants in early spring.

PROPAGATION Sever rooted shoots, then lift and replant with a ball of the original soil clinging to the roots.

PESTS AND DISEASES Generally trouble free.

OTHER VARIETIES *G. cuneata* has narrow leaves, and the white flowers and large white berries are much more prominent. It makes a noninvasive hummock, 30 x 30cm (12 x 12in). *G. shallon* is very invasive, to 1.2m (4ft) high, with pink flowers and dark purple berries.

COMPANIONS *G. procumbens* is ideal as ground cover especially around rhododendrons and azaleas.

GAULTHERIA PROCUMBENS

GAURA LINDHEIMERI

G

Short-lived hardy perennial, sometimes treated as an annual (Louisiana, Texas, 1850). Mature at 2 years: 90 x 60cm (3 x 2ft). AGM

This is a plant that has become very sought after in recent years. Suddenly it is in almost every garden, thanks mainly to Beth Chatto who used it in her own garden to good effect and made it commercially available. It forms an open airy clump, with willow-like leaves on graceful stems. In late summer and on through autumn the slender branches are covered with small, very pale pink tubular flowers.

USES Try planting it, as Beth Chatto does, rising out of gravel, where its graceful shape can be fully appreciated. It is tolerant of drought conditions.

CULTIVATION Plant in spring in a sunny position, in well-drained soil.

PROPAGATION Sow seeds outdoors in spring or autumn.

PESTS AND DISEASES Generally trouble free.

OTHER VARIETIES *G. lindheimeri* 'Jo Adella' is more compact – 50 x 45cm (20 x 18in) – and has dark green leaves with lighter marbling. It will flower prolifically.

COMPANIONS Gaura mixes well with other drought-lovers, especially blue grasses such as *Festuca glauca* and *Helictotrichon sempervirens* AGM.

GAURA LINDHEIMERI

G

GENISTA

Broom, deciduous shrub (Europe). Mature at 15 years: from 30 cm x 1m (1 x 3ft) for G. pilosa, to 4.5 x 4.5m (14 x 14ft) for G. aetnensis.

With *Cytisus*, genistas make up the broom family. They have very small leaves, and sometimes almost none, but their numerous narrow branches, straight in some species, arching in others, give them an evergreen appearance. They have small yellow pea flowers in early or late summer.

USES These are plants for hot dry sites, and they can tolerate industrial pollution. They will grow happily on stony banks.

CULTIVATION Plant between autumn and spring in any well-drained soil in full sun. Prune after flowering, cutting back all new shoots by a third to a half. Never cut into old wood. Brooms are short-lived, so do not be surprised if the plants deteriorate, or even die after ten years or so, for no apparent reason.

PROPAGATION It is easiest to increase genistas from seed, which germinates freely if sown outdoors in spring.

PESTS AND DISEASES Generally trouble free.

GOOD VARIETIES *G. aetnensis* AGM is a tree-like shrub, completely hardy, with its branches arched over with the weight of the yellow flowers in late summer. The flowers have a strong honey scent. Even a small garden can accommodate it, as it does not cast much shade and leaves space for underplanting. *G. tinctoria* 'Royal Gold' AGM, 80cm x 1.5m (32in x 5ft), is an improved form of Dyer's greenweed, a British native, in flower from midsummer until autumn. For flowers in early summer plant *G. lydia* AGM, 90cm x 1.5m (3 x 5ft) tall, or *G. pilosa* 'Vancouver Gold', 30 x 90cm (1 x 3ft).

soil		
ACID		ALKALINE
DRY		WET

J	F	M	A	M	J	J	A	S	O	N	D
				❀		❀	⚚	⚚			

GENISTA TINCTORIA

GENTIANA ASCLEPIADEA

Willow gentian, a hardy perennial (Europe, 1629). Mature at 3 years: to 90 x 60cm (3 x 2ft). AGM

This gentian is very different from the prostrate rock garden plants that fascinate alpine enthusiasts. But it does share with some of them the vibrant, pure blue colour of its flowers. They are trumpet-shaped and appear in early autumn along the top of the arching stems. Elegant, pointed, ribbed leaves grow all the way up the stems. They are not very like willow leaves, but are supposed to be the reason for the plant's English name.

USES Willow gentians look their best in informal or even wild situations, planted in large drifts among shrubs or along the bank of a pond.

CULTIVATION Plant in autumn or spring in partial or full shade, in groups or drifts, planting 40cm (16in) apart. They will grow in almost any soil, including deep soils over chalk, but do best in moist, humus-rich neutral to acid soil. An annual spring mulch of leaf mould or compost helps to maintain optimum conditions.

PROPAGATION Divide established clumps in autumn or spring.

PESTS AND DISEASES Generally trouble free.

OTHER VARIETIES Among alpine gentians, species that are easy to succeed with in a raised bed or trough, or at the top of a retaining wall, include *G. acaulis,* which flowers in late spring, and the autumn-flowering *G. septemfida.* They need to be kept fairly dry in winter and moist in summer, and appreciate humus in the soil. Nearly all the autumn flowering gentians need a neutral or acid soil.

COMPANIONS Ligularias enjoy the same conditions, and their strong yellow and orange-yellow colouring would make a striking contrast.

soil		
ACID		ALKALINE
DRY		WET

J	F	M	A	M	J	J	A	S	O	N	D
⚚	⚚							❀	❀		⚚

GENTIANA ASCLEPIADEA

GERANIUM

GERANIUM RENARDII

Cranesbill, hardy perennials (temperate regions). Mature at 3 years: from 15 x 30cm (6 x 12in) to 90 x 60cm (3 x 2ft).

The hardy geraniums, or cranesbills, are a quite different genus from the tender bedding plants known as geraniums, but which are correctly known as *Pelargonium*. Cranesbills make an enormous contribution to the garden, being very easy to grow and having a wide range of flower colours and flowering seasons. The various species available all make good clumps of more or less rounded leaves, some deeply divided, some evergreen, others colouring in autumn. Saucer-shaped flowers are borne very profusely in clusters held well above the leaves. Flower colours include white, blue, mauve, purple and many shades of pink and magenta.

USES Many cranesbills make excellent ground cover. Others associate particularly well with roses. They look at home in formal borders and in wild areas.

CULTIVATION Grow in any reasonable soil that is not boggy. Most thrive in sun or partial shade and a few prefer a shady site. Any special requirements are noted in the descriptions that follow. Geraniums can be planted in autumn or spring. They look best in groups of three or more. If, after flowering, the whole plant is cut to the ground, a mound of fresh leaves will grow in a few weeks and you may also get a second crop of flowers.

PROPAGATION Divide established clumps in autumn or spring. Most will self-seed, but seedlings will be variable.

PESTS AND DISEASES Generally trouble free.

GOOD VARIETIES G. x *cantabrigiense* 'Biokovo', 30 x 45cm (12 x 18in): low mounds of smooth, divided leaves; pink-veined, white flowers appear at midsummer. Good autumn colour. 'Cambridge' has soft mauve flowers.

G. cinereum 'Ballerina' AGM, 10 x 30cm (4 x 12in): pink, purple-veined flowers in late spring, early summer.

G. clarkei 'Kashmir Purple' syn. *G. pratense* 'Kashmir Purple', 45 x 60cm (18 x 24in): deeply lobed leaves, deep purple flowers in summer.

G. endressii AGM, 45 x 60cm (18 x 24in): sugar-pink flowers all summer and autumn above pretty, pale green leaves.

G. himalayense, syn. *G. grandiflorum*, 30 x 60cm (12 x 24in): flowers of luminous blue in early summer above finely-cut leaves which turn red in autumn.

G. macrorrhizum 'Album' AGM, 30 x 60cm (12 x 24in): very pale pink flowers in late spring over large, smooth, aromatic grey-green leaves that spread slowly to give total ground cover.

G. magnificum, 45 x 60cm (18 x 24in): small clusters of veined, violet-purple cup-shaped flowers appear in summer above hairy leaves.

G. phaeum, Mourning Widow, 60 x 45cm (24 x 18in): tolerant of deep shade; the

black-maroon flowers appear in late spring. f. *album* is a desirable white form.

G. pratense 'Mrs Kendall Clark' AGM, 60 x 60cm (2 x 2ft): a form of the native meadow cranesbill with pearly, grey-blue flowers in midsummer. Needs support.

G. psilostemon AGM, 1.2 x 1.2m (4 x 4ft): a big clump of handsome leaves and, at midsummer, dramatic brilliant magenta flowers with black eyes. Needs support.

G. renardii, 30 x 30cm (12 x 12in): the one with the prettiest leaves – deeply veined, sage-green, round with scalloped edges, forming dense mounds. The flowers are palest mauve-white and are threaded with purple veins.

And many more – if only there was enough space to describe them.

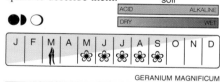

GERANIUM 'KASHMIR PURPLE'

GERANIUM 'MOURNING WIDOW'

GERANIUM MAGNIFICUM

G

GEUM CHILOENSE

Hardy perennial (Chile, 1826). Mature at 3 years: 60 x 45cm (24 x 18in).

Geums make solid clumps of broad, bright green leaves. They are in flower from early summer until autumn if planted in good soil: slender, hairy branching stems carry well-poised, single or double open-faced flowers in yellow, orange, or red.

USES For a long time geums were stalwarts for the front of the herbaceous border, and they can still give a lift to colour schemes in herbaceous or mixed beds. The leaves make good ground cover and the flowers are good for cutting.

CULTIVATION Plant geums in a sunny position in autumn or spring in good garden soil that doesn't dry out. Dead-head to prolong the flowering season. Plants should be divided and replanted every few years to maintain vigour and produce a good display of flowers.

PROPAGATION Divide and then replant established clumps to increase stock.

PESTS AND DISEASES Generally trouble free.

GOOD VARIETIES *G.* 'Georgenberg' is a compact plant with pale coppery-orange flowers on red stems; 'Lady Stratheden' AGM is an old favourite with double, warm yellow flowers. The flowers of 'Mrs J. Bradshaw' AGM are bright brick red. *G. coccineum* syn. *G.* x *borisii*, 30 x 30cm (12 x 12in) has flowers of pure, clear orange.

soil

	ACID		ALKALINE
	DRY		WET

J	F	M	A	M	J	J	A	S	O	N	D
				❀	❀	❀	❀	❀			

GEUM 'LADY STRATHEDEN'

GINKGO BILOBA

Maidenhair tree, a deciduous tree (China, 1754). Mature at 50 years: 6m (20ft) high after 20 years; 25 x 10m (80 x 30ft) at maturity. AGM

The ginkgo is a tree literally in a class of its own: neither a broad-leaved tree nor a true conifer, but a completely separate group dating back to the Jurassic Period when it was a widespread and significant part of the landscape. In the 18th century, European plant hunters encountered it as a cultivated tree in the temple gardens of China and Japan; it is extinct in the wild. The growth is slow at first and the shape can be ungainly and even stunted. In time it develops a distinctive and graceful branching habit. The leaves are like no others; they are fan-shaped, coloured soft bright green, which turns clear yellow in autumn.

USES The fruit, which only develop in climates with a long, warm summer, have edible nuts encased in a putrid fleshy outer shell. Ginkgo trees are much used for avenues and as shade trees in the southern parts of Europe. Although as tall as most forest trees, they are not too broad to make good garden specimens.

CULTIVATION Although they are very hardy against frost, ginkgos need shelter from the wind and plenty of summer sunshine to develop well. Plant them while still small, 90cm-1.2m (3-4ft), in deep well-drained neutral or alkaline soil, between the autumn and the spring.

PROPAGATION Seed is the best method; sow as soon as it is ripe in a cold frame or in containers outdoors. The tree can also be increased by semi-ripe cuttings in summer.

PESTS AND DISEASES Generally trouble free.

soil

	ACID		ALKALINE
	DRY		WET

J	F	M	A	M	J	J	A	S	O	N	D
				🍂	🍂	🍂	🍂	🍂	🍂		

GINGKO BILOBA

GINGKO BILOBA

GLEDITSIA TRIACANTHOS

Honey locust, a deciduous tree (N. America, 1700). Mature at 30 years: 8m (25ft) tall after 20 years; 20 x 15m (70 x 50ft) at maturity.

These graceful trees are open-branched and grown mainly for the sake of their pretty finely-cut ferny leaves. They appear late in the season and are fresh pale green, turning yellow in autumn. In autumn and winter the branches are hung with long twisted pods. When grown in a sunny position the trunks are armed with long sharp thorns, but they do not develop in shade.

USES Gleditsias grow fast, stand up well to drought and to atmospheric pollution and cast only a light shade – qualities that make them much in demand as street trees in spite of their dangerous thorns. They make excellent specimen trees for medium-sized, enclosed town gardens.

CULTIVATION Plant between autumn and spring in sun or shade, in free-draining soil, preferably neutral or acid, although they will tolerate chalk. In the early stages gleditsias are slightly tender, so choose a sheltered position.

PROPAGATION The species can be increased by seed, the selected forms by bud-grafting.

PESTS AND DISEASES Generally trouble free.

OTHER VARIETIES *G. triacanthos* 'Sunburst' AGM is slightly smaller than the species and has leaves that are spectacularly yellow in spring and early summer, then turn green. It has no thorns. On 'Rubylace', a more recent introduction, the young leaves are red at first, then mature to bronze green.

GLEDITSIA TRIACANTHOS

GOOSEBERRY

Ribes uva-crispa, a hardy fruiting shrub. Mature at 5 years: 1.2 x 1.2m (4 x 4ft).

Gooseberries are densely-branched, usually thorny bushes, grown for their juicy, aromatic fruit, which is sharp or sweet according to the cultivar. The fruits are globular and covered in short hairs. Their thin green skins are sometimes suffused with yellow, or with red-purple.

USES The fruit is used for puddings, preserves and sauces. Gooseberries freeze well. The plants can be trained on wires as fans or cordons to divide up the garden, or grafted as standards which are more ornamental and far more accessible for harvesting the fruit.

CULTIVATION Plant between autumn and spring in any reasonable soil. Before planting dig in manure if the soil is very light or very heavy. Plant 1.5-1.8m (5-6ft) apart. Keep the root area weed-free by mulching. Prune in winter; remove old shoots at the base to keep an open centre with young shoots evenly spaced, pointing upwards and outwards.

PROPAGATION Take hardwood cuttings in early autumn, but don't expect a high success rate.

PESTS AND DISEASES Bullfinches may eat the buds in winter, so net the bushes from autumn to spring. Caterpillars eat the leaves in summer. Gooseberries are susceptible to mildew and grey mould; at the first sign, spray with an appropriate fungicide.

GOOD VARIETIES There are cultivars that are mildew-resistant, nearly thornless, or well-flavoured, but none that combine all three qualities. 'Captivator' is nearly thornless (red, late); 'Invicta' AGM (green, mid-season) and 'Lancashire Lad' (red, late) are resistant to mildew; 'Green Gem' (green, mid-season), 'Leveller' AGM (yellow, mid-season) and 'Lord Derby' (red, mid-season) all have good flavour; 'Careless' AGM, 'Greenfinch' AGM and 'Whinham's Industry' AGM are also recommended.

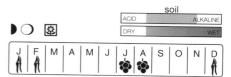

GOOSEBERRY

G

GREENS, ORIENTAL

Mixed hardy annuals grown as salad and vegetable crops (E. Asia). Mature at 1½-3 months.

The more unusual culinary greens are beginning to appear in the seed catalogues. If you follow a traditional crop rotation in the brassica section, pak choi, komatsuna (spinach mustard), mizuna greens and Chinese broccoli are more fun to grow than cabbages and sprouts. Those recommended are mainly vigorous, fast-growing annuals.

USES Oriental greens can be harvested on a cut-and-come-again basis from late summer to spring. Mizuna greens are pretty enough to use as edging in the ornamental garden.

CULTIVATION Sow seeds at any time from spring onwards. Chinese cabbage and some of the others tend to bolt, but are less likely to do so if sown after the longest day to produce autumn and winter crops. Sow in succession every three weeks, in ordinary, preferably slightly acid, garden soil. When seedlings are big enough to thin out, use the thinnings in salads. Begin harvesting cut-and-come-again crops after about five weeks.

PESTS AND DISEASES Flea beetle, cabbage root fly, white mealy aphids, slugs, snails and various caterpillars can all be a nuisance.

GOOD VARIETIES Loose-headed Chinese cabbage forms open heads of light green, mild-flavoured leaves that can be harvested by cut-and-come again or left to develop a mature head. Pak choi are similar but stronger flavoured. Komatsuna has leaves like turnip tops, and are good shredded in salads when young and cooked as greens when mature. Mizuna greens form rosettes of dark green, glossy, finely-cut leaves. Eat the young leaves raw and cook older leaves. Mustard greens, Chinese broccoli (eat the flowering shoots before the flowers open) and Texsel greens are also worth growing.

soil	
ACID	ALKALINE
DRY	WET

J	F	M	A	M	J	J	A	S	O	N	D

GREENS

GUNNERA MANICATA

Hardy perennial (Colombia to Brazil, mid 19th century). Mature at 5 years: 1.8 x 2.5m (6 x 8ft). AGM

This giant should not really be in this book as it is not easy to grow and is too big for the average garden. But it is worth taking some trouble to please and worth sacrificing a few ordinary plants to give it space. In spring thick, brown hairy shoots unfold from the crown like giants' fists, opening and expanding into huge deeply lobed, rhubarb-like leaves. The stalks are prickly and the leaves, measuring over 1.8m (6ft) across, are dull green, coarse and bristly. In early summer olive green flowers are carried on untidy, upright conical spikes.

USES Gunnera is a waterside plant, and needs a large pond to set it off. But it could also be the one magnificent focal point in quite a small garden.

CULTIVATION Plant in spring in deep damp soil, or in waterlogged ground that never dries out. Gunneras need full sun and shelter from the wind. In winter, you should protect the plants from frost by covering their crowns with their own leaves, or with bracken or leaf litter.

PROPAGATION Divide established plants in spring: a job for two or more strong people.

PESTS AND DISEASES Generally trouble free.

OTHER VARIETIES *G. magellanica* is so different from *G. manicata* that it is interesting to grow them side by side. The former is a creeping plant densely set with crinkled leaves just 7cm (3in) across.

COMPANIONS Where space permits, add to the 'Lost World' effect with that other great thug, *Lysichiton americanus* AGM, the skunk cabbage.

soil	
ACID	ALKALINE
DRY	WET

J	F	M	A	M	J	J	A	S	O	N	D

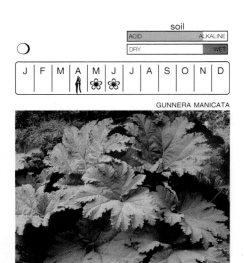

GUNNERA MANICATA

GYPSOPHILA PANICULATA

Baby's breath, a hardy perennial (Central and E. Europe, 1759). Mature at 3 years: 60cm x 1m (2 x 3ft).

The leaves are small, narrow, smooth and of no special interest. The point of the plant is the frothy cloud of tiny white flowers on almost invisible wiry stems. Starting in midsummer, the display continues for about six weeks. There is nothing else like it in the garden. Sadly, although perennial, it tends to be short-lived.

USES Flower arrangers love it. In the garden Gertrude Jekyll liked to use it to grow up and fill gaps left by earlier flowering plants such as the oriental poppies.

CULTIVATION The name *Gypsophila* means 'lover of chalk', and either chalk or a limestone soil in full sun is the ideal. Plant in autumn or spring and, once planted, do not disturb. Cut down the flower stems when they have finished flowering.

PROPAGATION Not easy for *G. paniculata*: try taking cuttings of secondary lateral shoots in summer and placing them in silver sand with gentle bottom heat. The cultivars of *G. paniculata* are usually grafted.

PESTS AND DISEASES Generally trouble free.

GOOD VARIETIES *G. paniculata* 'Bristol Fairy' AGM is the classic plant with double white flowers. *G.* 'Rosenschleier' AGM syn. 'Rosy Veil', is more compact, at 30 x 30cm (12 x 12in). There are also very pretty prostrate forms for the front of a border, or the top of a retaining wall: *G. repens* has white or pale pink flowers; 'Dorothy Teacher' has masses of flowers, which start white and fade to pink. The leaves are bluish like those of a dianthus.

soil	
ACID	ALKALINE
DRY	WET

J	F	M	A	M	J	J	A	S	O	N	D

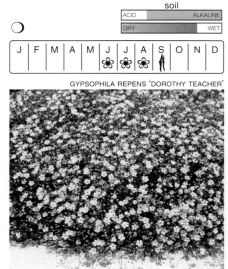

GYPSOPHILA REPENS 'DOROTHY TEACHER'

H

HAMAMELIS X INTERMEDIA 'PALLIDA'

Witch hazel, a deciduous shrub or small tree. Mature at 20 years: 2 x 2m (6 x 6ft) after 10 years; 4 x 3m (13 x 10ft) at maturity.

Of the few shrubs and trees that flower in winter, the witch hazel is perhaps the most beautiful. It is slow-growing, but worth waiting for. Its habit is attractive and spreading, with horizontal zigzag branches; at midwinter, clusters of fragrant pale yellow flowers appear all along the branches. The long narrow petals curve this way and that to give a spidery effect. In spring broadly heart-shaped, mid-green leaves appear, turning soft yellow in autumn.

USES The twigs are said to be effective for water divining in the same way as those of the ordinary hazel. Witch hazel's main use is to cheer one up on a cold winter day.

CULTIVATION Deep rich soil is needed for the plants to thrive, preferably acid and peaty, although *Hamamelis* will grow on deep soils over chalk. Make sure the graft union is above ground, otherwise suckers may become a problem. Prune only to remove dead or diseased branches. Keep the root area weeded and mulched until the plant is well established.

PROPAGATION Difficult. Increase by grafting or by budding.

PESTS AND DISEASES Generally trouble free.

OTHER VARIETIES 'Moonlight' and 'Sunburst' are more recent introductions, said to be as good as 'Pallida'. 'Diane' AGM is a good red-flowered form with exceptional autumn colour.

COMPANIONS As *Hamamelis* is lacking in colour through most of the spring and all summer, underplant it with ground cover that will provide interest at these times.

		soil	
ACID			ALKALINE
DRY			WET

J	F	M	A	M	J	J	A	S	O	N	D

HAMAMELIS 'PALLIDA'

HEBE

Hardy and tender evergreen shrubs (New Zealand). Mature at 7 years: from 30 x 80cm (12 x 32in) to 1.5 x 1.5m (5 x 5ft) or more.

Hebes are easy to recognize by their straight, branching stems closely covered with opposite pairs of smooth leaves; they are borne at regular intervals in two or four ranks. The shape of the leaves varies from tiny, almost scale-like leaves, pressed closely to the stem – as in the 'whipcord' hebes – to larger almost fleshy, ovate or lance-shaped ones. Their colour ranges from bright emerald green, olive green, or reddish-bronze to greys and blue-greens. In most hebes the overall effect is of a more or less dense mound, from miniature buns to those that become almost tree-like at maturity, at least in climates that approximate to those in their native habitats. As a general rule to bear in mind, the larger the leaves the more tender the species. Short spires of small tubular flowers with spreading lobes are borne at the end of every stem so that, at flowering time, the leaves can be rendered almost invisible beneath the mass of flowers. Flower colours range from white through mauve-pink and lavender blue to purple-crimson.

USES Low-growing hebes are grown as much for their leaves as for their flowers: their cushions of dense foliage make excellent ground cover. They are good seaside plants and do well in containers. The smallest are suitable for rock gardens and even, with *H. cupressoides* 'Boughton Dome', in troughs.

CULTIVATION Plant hebes in spring, in ordinary well-drained soil in sun or light shade. Provide a position sheltered from cold winds for the taller, less hardy species. For the first few seasons, until well-established, water during dry spells in spring and summer. The low-growing species do not need regular pruning, but if they get straggly or outgrow their space, cut them back in spring. Taller later-flowering species can be renovated every other year by cutting to the ground in spring. Vigorous new shoots will

HEBE 'MIDSUMMER BEAUTY'

come from the base. This also applies when renovating old, neglected plants.

PROPAGATION Take semi-ripe cuttings in late summer or autumn.

PESTS AND DISEASES Generally trouble free.

GOOD VARIETIES Good low-growing hebes include *H. rakaiensis* AGM, 60 x 90cm (2 x 3ft), with leaves of fresh light green and white flowers in summer; *H. salicifolia* 2.5 x 2.5m (8 x8ft) is a large evergreen shrub with small white or pale lilac flower spikes in summer. *H. pinguifolia* 'Pagei' AGM, 15 x 60cm (6 x 24in) is almost prostrate with small, blue-grey leaves and white flowers, and is best given very good drainage. 'Mrs. Winder' AGM, is larger, up to 90 x 90cm (3 x 3ft), and reasonably hardy, with mauve flowers and leaves suffused with red-bronze. The hardiest of the taller, large-leaved hebes are 'Great Orme' AGM, 1.2 x 1.2m (4 x 4ft) with dark green leaves and pink flowers from midsummer to autumn, and 'Midsummer Beauty' AGM, 1.5 x 1.5m (5 x 5ft) with glossy green, purple-veined leaves and long spikes of mauve flowers. The rest are at risk from hard frosts but do well in seaside or sheltered town gardens.

COMPANIONS The later-flowering blue and mauve hebes are good with hardy fuchsias. Use *H. albicans* and *H. pinguifolia* 'Pagei' in groups with grey foliage.

		soil	
ACID			ALKALINE
DRY			WET

J	F	M	A	M	J	J	A	S	O	N	D

HEBE SALICIFOLIA

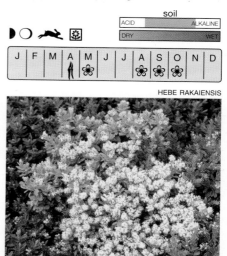
HEBE RAKAIENSIS

H

HEDERA

Ivy, evergreen woody climbers (Asia, N. Africa, Canary Islands and Europe, including Britain). Mature at 10 years: to 10 x 5m (30 x 15ft) or more.

Ivy will cling to any vertical support by means of adventitious rootlets, branching as it ascends, or will creep along the ground, rooting as it goes. Most forms are hardy, but a few need a sheltered site, or are grown indoors. The leaves of most forms are triangular and lobed. Ivies flower only as they reach their adult phase, when the shape of the leaves changes and the plant takes on a shrubby habit. This phase usually develops when the plant has climbed to the top of its support. The flowers are small and green, in globular clusters. The berries, usually black with a grapey bloom, ripen in late winter.

USES As a climber on buildings, ivies can conceal ugliness or enhance beauty. Ivy does not harm sound buildings, but its shoots will discover weak mortar in the joints of brick or stonework, and if allowed to reach roof height will prise away guttering and dislodge tiles. On the plus side, it helps to insulate buildings and protects them from harsh weather. The large-leaved ivies can also be used to trail from the tops of retaining walls, or to make extensive ground cover, especially on rocky and uneven terrain. Ivy trained on chain-link fencing makes a quick 'fedge', or narrow hedge. It can be used to dress urns and pots for the winter, and to make quick-growing topiary. Ivies provide winter food and cover for birds and beneficial insects such as ladybirds.

CULTIVATION Green ivies and those with grey and white variegation will grow in shade, but yellow-variegated forms need sun. Plant in well-drained, alkaline soil, adding lime or old lime mortar to neutral or acid soils. Site at least 45cm (18in) out from the base of a wall or fence, leaning the plant towards the wall on one or more small canes. Bury the bottom inch or so of the ivy's stem below ground level. Don't be seduced into buying large specimens; only new shoots can cling, so you will have trouble introducing a large plant to a wall. A young plant will establish quite quickly: 'The first year it sleeps, the second year it creeps and the third year it leaps.' If you are planting for ground cover, make absolutely sure the ground is weed-free and plant large ivies at 90cm (3ft) apart. In spring, trim hedges and topiary and, if necessary, clip over ground cover or wall-trained ivies to keep them close and dense.

PROPAGATION Take semi-ripe cuttings in summer, or dig up and replant rooted layers in autumn or spring.

PESTS AND DISEASES Generally trouble free.

SPECIES AND CULTIVARS *H. colchica* 'Dentata' is the largest-leaved. The heart-shaped, dark green leaves hang downwards so that a background wall or fence is completely covered. Although the plants are hardy, the leaves droop in a dispirited way during frosty weather. *H. colchica* 'Dentata Variegata' has creamy yellow margins; 'Sulphur Heart' has a central yellow splash. *H. canariensis* 'Gloire de Marengo' has large, handsome leaves with cream and silver-grey variegation; it needs a sheltered site. *H. helix* has hundreds of cultivars, some differing from each other only in minute detail. Those shown here can all be trusted to perform well as ground cover as well as climbers.

HEDERA CANARIENSIS 'GLOIRE DE MARENGO'

HEDERA HELIX 'BUTTERCUP'

HEDERA COLCHICA 'DENTATA VARIEGATA'

soil

| ACID | | ALKALINE |
| DRY | | WET |

| J | F | M | A | M | J | J | A | S | O | N | D |

HEDERA HELIX 'LITTLE DIAMOND'

HELENIUM

*Sneezeweed, a hardy perennial
(N. America, 1729). Mature at 3 years:
1m x 60cm (3 x 2ft).*

The autumnal colouring of these rusty
yellow and orange-brown daisy flowers
signals the end of summer. They are in
flower from late summer to late autumn,
each stout stem branching into a spray of
daisy-like flower heads with a raised brown
or yellow disc at the centre.

USES Heleniums are a traditional component
of herbaceous borders. They are attractive to
butterflies and make good cut flowers.

CULTIVATION Plant in autumn or spring, in
any reasonable well-drained soil, in a sunny
position. Although the stems are strong, the
flower heads weigh them down and they
usually need support of pea sticks or grow-
through supports. After flowering, cut the
flowered stems down to the ground. The
plants need to be divided frequently to keep
a strong, healthy, free-flowering stock.

PROPAGATION Divide established clumps in
autumn or spring.

PESTS AND DISEASES Generally trouble free.

GOOD CULTIVARS Named cultivars include
'Butterpat', 80cm (32in) tall, with warm
yellow flowers; 'Moerheim Beauty', 90cm
(3ft), with a profusion of red-brown flowers.
'Chipperfield Orange' is taller at 1.5m (5ft)
and has orange-yellow flowers. None of
them, strictly speaking, has red flowers,
although catalogues often describe them as
red. In reality they are a warm red-brown,
more accurately referred to as mahogany.

COMPANIONS Too often heleniums are part
of strident colour schemes . They look best
with white *Anemone* x *hybrida* cultivars,
such as 'Honorine Jobert' AGM cream,
Scabiosa caucasica 'Miss Willmott' AGM
or the pale clouds of *Aster divaricatus*.

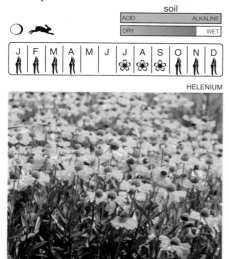

HELENIUM

HELIANTHEMUM

*Rock rose, an evergreen subshrub
(Europe, N. Africa, west and central Asia,
N. and S. America). Mature at 3 years:
10-20 x 40-45cm (4-8 x 12-18in).*

The much branched, woody stems are
covered with small narrow dark green to
silver-grey leaves. They form a compact
mound when young, becoming more open
and straggly with age. In early summer
they bear round, open, single or double
flowers, in white, yellow and a range of
sunset colours, all with small yellow
centres. Each flower lasts only a day, but
the flowers are produced in succession over
about eight weeks.

USES Helianthemums are excellent for
colonizing poor stony soil, for planting in
paving cracks, in gravel at the edges of
paths and beds, and for draping from the
tops of retaining walls.

CULTIVATION Full sun and good drainage
are the two essentials. The soil can be acid
and sandy, or chalk or limestone. Plant in
autumn or spring, 23cm (9in) apart for
ground cover, giving a tapestry carpet effect.
Clip back after flowering to encourage a
modest second flowering and, above all, to
keep the plants dense and shapely.

PROPAGATION Take cuttings during late
summer, or separate rooted pieces in
autumn or spring. They also grow easily
from seed and often self-sow.

PESTS AND DISEASES Generally trouble free.

GOOD CULTIVARS The following AGM
selections give a good range of colours:
'Amy Baring', ground-hugging with apricot
yellow flowers; 'Fire Dragon', flame
orange; 'Henfield Brilliant', terracotta red
flowers and grey-green leaves; 'Jubilee',
double yellow; 'Mrs C.W. Earle', double
red; 'The Bride', white; 'Wisley Primrose',
large, pale yellow flowers with grey leaves;
'Rhodanthe Carneum', syn. 'Wisley Pink',
light rose-pink flowers, grey leaves.

COMPANIONS Plant helianthemums in front
of other plants that enjoy hot, dry
conditions: cistus, lavenders and santolinas.

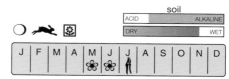

HELIANTHEMUM

H

HELICHRYSUM 'SCHWEFFELLICHT'

Syn. H. 'Sulphur Light', hardy perennial.
Mature at 3 years: 45 x 30cm.

This plant spreads slowly to make clumps of upright stems with narrow, pointed, silver-grey leaves. In late summer, bobbly clusters of small, round flower heads are carried at the top of the stems. The flowers are the papery, unfading kind known as 'everlastings' or 'immortelles'. The colour is soft pale yellow and the stems and flower heads are covered in white felt, giving the whole plant a very light appearance.

USES This is one of those plants that will gradually fill up space at the front of a border without ever becoming a nuisance. The flowers are good for cutting and for dried flower arrangements.

CULTIVATION A place in the sun and well-drained soil are the only requirements. Given these conditions, this helichrysum should be perfectly hardy, but young plants may be susceptible to a cold wet winter, so plant in spring rather than autumn.

PROPAGATION Divide established clumps during the spring.

PESTS AND DISEASES Generally trouble free.

OTHER VARIETIES *H. petiolare* AGM to 30cm x 1.2m (1 x 4ft), is not hardy but it is indispensable for anyone who enjoys devising planting schemes for containers. Long stems of small, softly felted heart-shaped leaves spread horizontally or trail downwards, turning up again at the tips.

H. italicum AGM, 60 x 90cm (2 x 3ft), known as the curry plant because of the intense spicy smell of the leaves, and *H. splendidum* AGM, 1.2 x 1.2m (4 x 4ft), are hardy evergreen, grey-leaved plants.

COMPANIONS Plant *H.* 'Schweffellicht' where its yellow flowers can contrast with magenta border phlox, or purple-red penstemons.

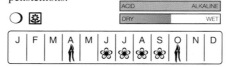

soil

ACID		ALKALINE
DRY		WET

J	F	M	A	M	J	J	A	S	O	N	D

HELICHRYSUM PETIOLARE 'LIMELIGHT'

HELICHRYSUM 'SCHWEFFELLICHT'

HELICTOTRICHON SEMPERVIRENS

Syn. Avena candida, Avena sempervirens, blue oat grass, an evergreen perennial grass (Central and S.W. Europe, 1820). Mature at 3 years: 90 x 60cm (3 x 2ft). AGM.

This grass is noninvasive, forming mounds of stiff needle-thin leaves. They are bright grey-blue. Tall grey stems carry panicles of oat-like inflorescences in summer.

USES This splendid grass looks right in gravel areas and mixed with other grey- and blue-leaved plants to provide a contrasting shape and texture.

CULTIVATION Plant in the spring in a sunny position, in any well-drained soil. Leave the flower heads on through the winter and cut stems and leaves to the ground in spring to ensure fresh new growth.

PROPAGATION Increase by dividing and replanting established clumps in spring.

PESTS AND DISEASES Generally trouble free.

OTHER VARIETIES *H. sempervirens* var. *pendulum* arches its leaves in a particularly elegant fashion.

COMPANIONS It makes an effective contrast, in early summer, with the dark, feathery foliage of bronze fennel. For a strong grouping of spiky, grassy foliage, plant it in front of *Phormium tenax* Purpureum Group AGM and behind *Ophiopogon planiscapus* 'Nigrescens' AGM.

soil

ACID		ALKALINE
DRY		WET

J	F	M	A	M	J	J	A	S	O	N	D

HELICTOTRICHON

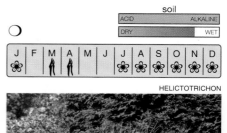

HELIOTROPIUM ARBORESCENS

Syn **H. peruvianum**, *cherry pie, heliotrope, a tender evergreen shrub (Peru, mid 18th century). Mature at 5 years: 60 x 75cm (2ft x 2ft6in).*

Heliotrope makes a small, bushy shrub with dark green deeply veined leaves. Their shape is oval and pointed, their texture wrinkled, matt and crepey. In bad weather they are liable to turn black from the edges inwards. The plants flower from late spring through autumn until the first frosts, with flattish clusters densely packed, composed of small flowers varying in colour from mauve to intense violet. The flowers have a warm, fruity scent like hot cherry jam.

USES Heliotrope's long flowering season, colour and scent make it an ideal pot plant.

CULTIVATION Young plants can be potted up in the greenhouse or on a sunny windowsill from late winter onwards, to be replanted outside in early summer. Water the plants from early spring until autumn, adding a weekly or fortnightly liquid feed while they are in flower, and dead-head regularly. Bring them into the greenhouse in autumn and keep the compost just moist until late winter or early spring. Then prune hard to encourage new growth, and start watering again.

PROPAGATION Sow seeds in spring or take semi-ripe cuttings in early autumn.

PESTS AND DISEASES Generally trouble free outdoors. Whitefly and other greenhouse pests may be a nuisance.

GOOD VARIETIES The species grown from seed may give results of variable colour depth. 'Princess Marina' AGM has flowers of uniformly rich violet.

COMPANIONS Group pots of heliotrope with violet petunias, pale yellow argyranthemums and *Helichrysum petiolare* 'Limelight'.

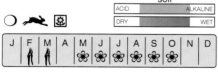

HELIOTROPIUM

HELLEBORUS ORIENTALIS

Lenten rose, a hardy evergreen perennial (Greece, 1839). Mature at 3 years: 45 x 45cm (18 x 18in).

The Lenten rose and *H. niger* AGM, the Christmas rose, both flower in winter. *H. niger* is earlier, but *H. orientalis* is easier to grow. Its handsome pointed dark green leaves, with smooth pale green stems, are dense enough to form weed-smothering ground cover. The single cupped flowers hang their heads beneath a little ruff of leaves. The colour range includes greenish-white through purple-pinks to dark plum, with the insides often prettily freckled. The faded flowers become papery and remain attractive until late spring.

USES Plant hellebores where they can be seen from your windows to cheer you up on dismal winter days. The flowers are beautiful close up, but most don't last long indoors.

CULTIVATION *H. orientalis* will grow in any reasonable soil, in sun or shade; *H. niger* needs retentive soil and shade. Both succeed in heavy clay. Plant with the crowns 5cm (2in) deep. When flower buds begin to push up, cut down all the previous season's leaves.

PROPAGATION Divide in spring. Hellebores self-seed, giving rise to an excitingly variable batch of seedlings.

PESTS AND DISEASES Hellebores may be attacked by rust and other fungal diseases; remove and burn infected leaves and spray the rest with fungicide.

OTHER VARIETIES *H. argutifolius* AGM, syn. *H. corsicus*, 60 x 90cm (2 x 3ft), has pale grey-green leaves with serrated edges and branching sprays of apple-green flowers in early spring. *H. foetidus* AGM is a native British plant with finely-cut leaves and green flowers.

COMPANIONS Plant in large informal groups under trees or shrubs, or in a north border; hellebores are set off by any red-purple foliage and associate well with hostas.

HELLEBORUS ORIENTALIS 'ELLEN TERRY'

H

HEMEROCALLIS

Day lily, hardy perennial. Mature at 2 years: from 40 x 45cm (16 x 18in) to 100 x 75cm (3ft x 2ft 6in).

More robust than their exotic-looking trumpet flowers would lead you to expect, each flower lasts one day, but the flowers are borne in long succession. There are early and late flowering cultivars, so that you can have day lilies in flower from late spring to early autumn. Clumps of arching strap-shaped or grassy leaves rise from fleshy roots. Several single or double flowers are carried at the top of each smooth leafless stem, in colours from nearly white to nearly black, with every shade of yellow, orange and maroon red on the way. Many yellow forms are scented.

USES Hemerocallis make good ground cover and are well-suited to the herbaceous border, as well as to the more wild parts of the garden.

CULTIVATION Plant in autumn or spring in almost any soil that is not too dry, in sun or partial shade. Cut down dead stems and leaves in autumn or winter.

PROPAGATION Increase stock by dividing roots in autumn or spring.

PESTS AND DISEASES Slugs and snails may eat the emerging young shoots.

GOOD VARIETIES There are some 600 or more cultivars, so choose by visiting gardens to see them in flower, or study lists from specialist nurseries. Outstanding species include *H. lilioasphodelus* AGM, syn. *H. flava*, one of the earliest, with delicate clear yellow flowers and a lovely fragrance; *H. citrina* has slender trumpet-shaped, rich lemon yellow flowers that open at night; 'Marion Vaughn' AGM, lemon yellow; and 'Stella d'Oro' AGM, with golden flowers over a very long period.

COMPANIONS Day lilies are most useful after midsummer, when they flower with border phloxes, deciduous ceanothus and eryngium.

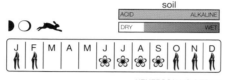

HEMEROCALLIS CITRINA

HEMEROCALLIS LILIOASHODELUS 'LINDA'

HESPERIS MATRONALIS

Sweet rocket, dame's violet, a hardy biennial or short-lived perennial (S. Europe, late 16th century). Mature at 12 months.

Sweet rocket (do not confuse with salad rocket, *Eruca sativa*) is a robust plant grown mainly for its scent – sweet and strong in the evenings, though you can sniff in vain earlier in the day. The plants have lance-like, pointed dark green leaves and a rather untidy floppy habit. The flowers, borne in clusters on branching stems, are like those of stocks, and are single or double, white, or pale to dark mauve-pink. With regular dead-heading, they last for six weeks or more.

USES Although quite pretty, the flowers are nothing special to look at. They are grown for their scent, so plant them near a door into the house, under a window, or where you sit in the garden in the evening.

CULTIVATION Sweet rocket needs sun and will tolerate quite poor soil as long as it is well-drained. It is happy on alkaline soil. Plant in autumn or spring. Dead head regularly to prolong flowering, and cut down stems and leaves in autumn.

PROPAGATION The plants become straggly and woody at the base after two years or so, so it is worth the effort of renewing the stock regularly. Sow seeds in spring and set young plants into their final positions in autumn. Double forms will not come true from seed; take basal cuttings of these during the spring.

GOOD VARIETIES The species usually has single mauve-pink flowers; var. *albiflora* has single white flowers and 'Lilacina Flore Pleno' has double mauve-pink flowers. Double forms are said to be more difficult to please than the single, preferring a moisture-retentive soil.

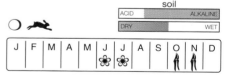

HESPERIS MATRONALIS

HEUCHERA

Hardy perennial (N. America). Mature at 3 years: 45-75 x 30-45cm (18-30 x 12-18in).

Rounded leaves with hairy surfaces, and sometimes with scalloped margins, form slowly spreading clumps on woody roots. The leaves of some species are bronzed or marbled with grey. Slender but strong wiry stems rise up and bear sprays of tiny flowers in pink, red, white or green.

USES Heucheras are among the very best ground cover plants. The flowers are very good for cutting.

CULTIVATION Although they will grow almost anywhere, heucheras prefer to be in semi-shade, in a moisture-retentive but well-drained soil. Plant them quite deeply, in autumn or spring, 40cm (16in) apart for ground cover. When the plants look tired, divide and replant them.

PROPAGATION Increase by dividing established clumps in spring.

PESTS AND DISEASES Generally trouble free.

GOOD VARIETIES *H. cylindrica* 'Greenfinch' makes rosettes of handsome heart-shaped leaves. In summer the tall spikes of cream-green flowers are much sought-after by flower arrangers. *H. micrantha* 'Palace Purple' AGM has glistening, dark purple-red, vine-like leaves and clouds of tiny white flowers on dark stems. 'Pewter Moon' and 'Rachel' both have pink flowers and leaves well marked with silver-grey.

'Strawberry Swirl' has profuse sprays of pink flowers and ruffled silver-green leaves. x *Heucherella* is similar to *Heuchera,* but the leaves are a fresh green.

COMPANIONS Heucheras have a woodland look to them, and look well planted in interlocking drifts with tiarella, pulmonaria, epimedium and other woodland ground cover plants.

HEUCHERA 'PALACE PURPLE'

HEUCHERA 'GREEN FINCH'

HIBISCUS SYRIACUS

H

Rose mallow, a deciduous shrub (India, China, 16th century). Mature at 20 years: 1.5 x 1m (5 x 3ft) after 10 years; up to 3 x 2m (10 x 6ft) at maturity.

Although quite hardy, hibiscus need long periods of warmth and light to bring them into flower, so they flower less well in northern Britain. They are slow-growing, densely branched shrubs with triangular toothed green leaves that emerge late. They flower from late summer into early autumn, the flowers being broadly trumpet-shaped with five overlapping petals. Some cultivars have semi-double or double flowers in white, pink, crimson or violet-blue.

USES Plant hibiscus in sheltered borders to prolong the garden's flowering season into autumn. They do well in containers and can survive in a polluted atmosphere.

CULTIVATION Sun and shelter from cold winds are the main requirements. In mild areas hibiscus can be planted in the open, but in cold districts it is wise to provide the shelter of a south-facing wall, fence or hedge. The soil should be fertile and well-drained. Prune in spring, cutting back the tips of young plants to encourage bushy growth. If necessary, cut old plants hard back to renew and improve their shape.

PROPAGATION Increase by taking semi-ripe cuttings in the summer.

PESTS AND DISEASES Whitefly can attack.

GOOD VARIETIES Double-flowered varieties can look bedraggled after rain. Good single-flowered kinds include 'Blue Bird', syn. 'Oiseau Bleu' AGM, with violet-blue flowers; 'Red Heart' AGM, with white flowers with red centres; 'Diana' AGM, pure white with pale green leaves; 'Russian Violet', dark violet-blue; 'Woodbridge' AGM, rose-crimson with a darker throat.

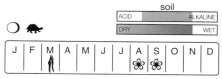

HIBISCUS 'BLUE BIRD'

H

HIPPOPHAE RHAMNOIDES

Sea buckthorn, a deciduous shrub (Europe, including Britain). Mature at 15 years: 4 x 3.5m (13 x 11ft) after 10 years, 6 x 5m (20 x 16ft) at maturity. AGM

These sturdy fast-growing shrubs have elegant, narrow silvery leaves and sharp spines on the branches. The flowers are insignificant, but in autumn there is a fine display of orange-yellow berries in large clusters. They are retained all winter because they are unpalatable, so birds will not take them. In order to produce berries a female plant needs a male nearby.

USES These are large plants and, as at least two are needed for a display of berries, they are plants for large gardens. If space is available their dense thorny growth and their ability to resist wind makes them ideal boundary plants, either growing naturally or tamed as a hedge; they are particularly useful by the sea, as they are tolerant of salt.

CULTIVATION Hippophae will grow in any soil that is not waterlogged, especially dry sandy soils. Plant between autumn and spring, including at least one male plant to every six females. For hedges plant 60cm (2ft) apart. Cut newly planted hedges back by one-third to encourage bushy growth. Trim hedges annually in spring. Bushes grown naturally need no pruning except when it becomes necessary to restrict their size. Old neglected bushes can be cut right down to 15cm (6in) above ground and will shoot again.

PROPAGATION *Hippophae* can be increased by sowing seeds and by taking cuttings, but it seeds itself freely and is also a suckering shrub; by far the easiest way is to transplant seedlings or rooted suckers.

PESTS AND DISEASES Trouble-free.

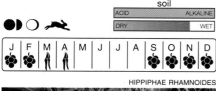

HIPPIPHAE RHAMNOIDES

HOSTA

Plantain lily, a hardy perennial (China, Japan, late 18th century onwards). Mature at 3 years: from 45 x 45cm (18 x 18in) to 1.2 x 1.5m (4 x 5ft).

Hostas, foliage plants *par excellence*, used to go by the funkier name of *Funkia*. Their broad smooth ribbed leaves are coloured blue, green, yellow and some startling variegations. By the end of the summer some of them may begin to look a little crude, but earlier in the year it is a pleasure to watch the chubby leaf buds push up and gradually unfurl. The leaves arch outwards from the clump and smooth flower stems emerge in summer to produce pendent, hyacinth-like white or mauve flowers.

USES Hostas make completely reliable ground cover, shading out the area beneath the leaves so that no weed can stand a chance. They look appropriate planted beside water, and are therefore invaluable plants for the dry ground often encountered on the banks of ponds and streams.

CULTIVATION Although they look lush enough to be bog plants, hostas will thrive in quite dry soil as well as in their preferred moist, well-drained, well-manured soil. Although they will grow in full sun and flower there more prolifically, the foliage is lusher in shade and the variegated forms do better in shade. Plant in autumn or spring and mulch thoroughly every spring.

PROPAGATION Divide and replant in early spring, chopping the roots into wedges with a sharp spade.

PESTS AND DISEASES Slugs and snails are the enemies. It is essential to protect hostas against them at all stages of growth.

GOOD VARIETIES With more than 600 cultivars on the market, the gardener is spoilt for choice. Many hostas, however, are very difficult to tell apart. To make choosing easier, the following selection offers a few of each colour.

Blue: the largest and one of the most popular of all hostas is *H. sieboldiana* var. *elegans* AGM. At 80cm x 1m (2ft 8in x 3ft) it does need space. Coming down a size, 'Big Daddy' and 'Blue Umbrellas' are 60 x 60cm (2 x 2ft), and the baby of the blues is 'Blue Moon', just 12 x 30cm (5 x 12in).

Yellow variegation: *H. fortunei* 'Aureomarginata' AGM has mid-green leaves with yellow margins and lavender flowers. 'August Moon' and 'Gold Standard' are yellow all over, fading to light yellow-green; 'Gold Standard' has dark green margins. *H. ventricosa* 'Aureomaculata' has big yellow splashes and stripes on green leaves.

White variegation: *H. fortunei* 'Albomarginata' has green leaves with narrow white margins and spikes of mauve flowers. *H. undulata* var. *univittata* has curled leaves with a central splash of cream.

Plain green: 'Royal Standard' AGM, 45 x 45cm (18 x 18in), has scented white flowers held well above deeply veined, rich green leaves. 'Honeybells' AGM, 80 x 60cm (2ft 8in x 2ft) is also fragrant, with long, light green leaves and mauve flowers. *H. plantaginea* 'Grandiflora' syn. var. *japonica* AGM, 60cm x 1.2m (2 x 4ft) is a Gertrude Jekyll favourite with shiny soft yellow-green leaves and richly scented flowers in early autumn. It needs a sunny position to bring on the late flowers.

COMPANIONS Hostas help almost any planting scheme by anchoring it firmly to the ground with their bold, architectural foliage. In a north border, plant them to follow on after hellebores and to accompany *Anemone* x *hybrida* and hemerocallis.

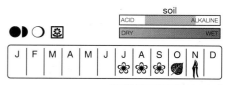

HOSTA FORTUNEI

HOSTA FORTUNEI 'ALBO PICTA'

HUMULUS LUPULUS 'AUREUS'

Golden hop, a hardy perennial climber (Europe, including Britain, Asia, America). Mature at 3 years: up to 6m (20ft). AGM

The golden hop is a less rampant version of the species that has supplied the brewing trade with flowers to flavour beer for centuries. It climbs by means of its stems which will twine around any support that is provided. It is grown mainly for its greenish yellow leaves which are a beautiful vine-leaf shape, with three or five lobes with serrated edges. They grow in pairs and are well-poised on smooth red stems. The flowers of the female plant hang in long clusters of papery cones in autumn.

USES Its rapid growth makes the golden hop excellent for making quick, attractive cover on a fence, shed or tree stump.

CULTIVATION It will grow in sun or light shade, but the yellow colouring is strongest in full sun. In shade it fades to lime green. It thrives best in a rich, moisture-retentive soil, but will tolerate quite poor conditions provided the drainage is good. Plant in early spring, with a cane to support the stems until they take hold. Water in dry spells and mulch every spring. Cut the stems down to the ground in autumn.

PROPAGATION Dig up and divide the roots in early spring.

PESTS AND DISEASES Generally trouble free.

OTHER VARIETIES If flowers are wanted to dry for winter decoration, plant the otherwise less decorative *H. lupulus* in an out-of-the-way corner.

COMPANIONS Try planting the golden hop with its leaves weaving through one of the evergreen ceanothus – a pretty contrast of blue and soft yellow.

HUMULUS LUPULUS 'AUREUS'

HYACINTHOIDES NON-SCRIPTA

Syn. Endymion non-scriptus, Scilla non-scripta, bluebell, a perennial bulb (W. Europe, including Britain). Mature at 6 months: 30 x 10cm (12 x 4in).

The bluebells that cover the woodland floor with a blue haze in late spring hardly need describing; the clump of narrow, strap-shaped, arching leaves is followed by smooth, sappy stems with their tips arching under the weight of the narrowly tubular flowers. They are violet-blue with petals curled at the ends. When growing en masse, their sweet scent is quite pronounced, even from the open window of a passing car. But from a single clump the scent is undetectable.

USES To be able to grow bluebells you need a large enough garden to have a woodland area, or an orchard where the grass can be allowed to grow long so that the bulbs can be left undisturbed.

CULTIVATION They flower best in dappled shade in woodland clearings, and will do equally well in acid or alkaline soils, given good drainage. Plant the bulbs in early autumn, 10-15cm (4-6in) deep, in clumps at random spacing, but approximately 10cm (4in) apart. Allow the leaves to die down naturally to build up food for next season.

PROPAGATION Dig up congested clumps and separate the bulbs. Seed sown when ripe germinates freely, but will take five years or so to produce flowering bulbs.

PESTS AND DISEASES Generally trouble free.

OTHER VARIETIES *H. hispanica*, syn. Scilla campanulata, S. hispanica, the Spanish bluebell, is bigger and more showy and seeds itself to the point of being a nuisance. It lacks the grace of the bluebell, but it hybridizes freely, so if you want to keep a pure stock of bluebells do not allow *H. hispanica* into your garden.

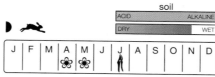

HYACINTHOIDES NON-SCRIPTA

HYACINTHUS ORIENTALIS

Hyacinth, a perennial bulb (Mediterranean region, late 16th century). Mature at 4 months: 30 x 10cm (12 x 4in).

Large bulbs in a papery outer skin produce broad strap-shaped, glossy bright green leaves. The flower stems are succulent and bear outward-pointing, bell-shaped flowers in white, pink, or blue. Cultivars described as yellow are, in fact, nearer to cream, and those described as red are deep pink. They have a sweet heady scent.

USES Hyacinths are the easiest and most satisfactory house plants; if planted early enough they can be brought into flower for Christmas. Outside, they are excellent in pots, window boxes and bedding.

CULTIVATION For winter-flowering indoors, buy bulbs prepared for forcing. Plant in soil-less compost in early autumn, with half the bulb above the surface. Plunge the pots in a cold frame outside, and cover with ashes or compost. Alternatively, put them in a cool, dark place indoors. Begin watering as the shoots show, and move into light and gradually warmer conditions. After flowering plant out, or put the pots outside and feed and water until the leaves die down, then store for planting out in autumn. Plant them 10cm (4in) deep. They will grow well outdoors for years in ordinary soil.

PROPAGATION Separate offsets from established bulbs.

PESTS AND DISEASES Generally trouble free.

GOOD VARIETIES Dependable kinds are 'Delft Blue' AGM and 'Ostara' AGM (blue), 'Carnegie' and 'L'Innocence' AGM (white), and 'Pink Pearl' AGM.

COMPANIONS Interplant hyacinths with herbaceous plants such as *Anemone* x *hybrida,* or *Hemerocallis*, or under shrubs and trees that come late into leaf.

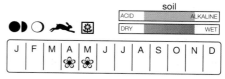

HYACINTHUS 'BLUE JACKET'

H

157

H HYDRANGEA

Deciduous shrub (N. America, E. Asia).
Mature at 10 years: from 60 x 90cm
(2 x 3ft) up to 3 x 2.5m (10 x 8ft).

Hydrangeas divide into three categories: species, mopheads (also called hortensias) and lacecaps. They have in common domed or flattened flower heads composed of showy, petal-like sepals surrounding tiny, insignificant fertile flowers, borne from late summer into autumn. The flower heads dry on the plant, remaining attractive for weeks after they have faded. Some of the species have handsome leaves, dark grey-green and velvety (*H. aspera* ssp. *sargentiana*) or colouring red and purple in autumn (*H. quercifolia*, *H. serrata*).

USES Hydrangeas tolerate atmospheric pollution. The mopheads and lacecaps do well in containers and the mopheads have a suitably formal style for pots or tubs on patios or terraces. The flower heads dry well, retaining their colour.

CULTIVATION It is no use trying to grow hydrangeas unless the soil is moisture-retentive or you can water the plants regularly. In dry conditions the leaves droop. At this signal, water copiously. Although hydrangeas are hardy they need a position

HYDRANGEA VILLOSA

HYDRANGEA MACROPHYLLA 'PRECIOSA'

sheltered from cold winds and from the midday sun. Cultivars with blue flowers have the peculiar habit of only revealing their truest blues in acid soil. In a pH above 5.5, they are dingy mauve-pink, but they can be treated with blueing compound. Blueing compound becomes less effective as the pH increases. White flowers are not influenced by soil pH. Plant in autumn or spring; mulch every spring with a thick layer of manure, garden compost or granulated bark; in early spring prune out any dead or straggly branches and remove dead flower heads. Prune *H. arborescens* and *H. paniculata* to within 5cm (2in) of their base. Neglected mopheads and lacecaps can be renovated by the same treatment, thereby sacrificing one season's flowers.

PROPAGATION Take softwood cuttings in summer or hardwood cuttings in winter.

PESTS AND DISEASES Generally trouble free.

CULTIVARS The various species may be difficult to find under their familiar names, as botanists have recently transferred the former *H. sargentiana* to a subspecies of *H. aspera*, but nurseries probably still list it under its old name. *H. villosa* has been

HYDRANGEA MACROPHYLLA

HYDRANGEA PANICULATA

ascribed to *H. aspera* Villosa Group and back again to *H. villosa*. *H. aspera* ssp. *sargentiana* AGM, and *H. villosa*, are 2m (6ft) or more, with large leaves and lacecap flowers, mauve-pink and lavender-blue respectively. *H. villosa* will grow in chalky soil. Both need sun; they grow gaunt and leggy in deep shade. *H. arborescens* 'Annabelle' AGM, 1.2 x 1.5m (4 x 5ft) has large mopheads of small greenish-white flowers. *H. quercifolia* AGM, 1.2 x 1.2m (4 x 4ft), has long cones of cream-white flowers and large, oak-shaped leaves with good autumn colour. *H. paniculata* has similar flowers but more upright growth and is good trained as a standard. The species *H. macrophylla* contains the mopheads and the lacecaps. Good mopheads include 'Mme Emile Mouillère' AGM, with white flowers fading to pale pink; 'Générale Vicomtesse de Vibraye' AGM, sky blue on the right soil; 'Preziosa' AGM, smaller pink flower heads becoming glowing red in autumn. 'Lanarth White' AGM, 'Blue Wave' syn. 'Mariesii Perfecta' AGM (blue or pink) and 'Geoffrey Chadbund' AGM (brick red) are a representative selection of lacecaps.

soil

ACID		ALKALINE
DRY		WET

J	F	M	A	M	J	J	A	S	O	N	D

HYDRANGEA ARBORESCENS 'ANNABELLE'

HYDRANGEA PETIOLARIS

Syn. H. anomala ssp. petiolaris, a deciduous woody climber (Japan, 1878). Mature at 12 years: 3 x 4m (10 x 13ft) but can reach 15m (50ft).

One of the most decorative self-clinging climbers, this hydrangea clings by means of adventitious roots in the same way ivies do. Young pale green shoots mellow to red-brown with peeling bark, pleasant to see in winter. The leaves hang downwards; they are oval and pointed, making a dense vivid green background for the wide flat heads of white lacecap flowers at midsummer.

USES This is the perfect cover for high walls and fences of any aspect except south. The climbing hydrangea will also make excellent ground cover, a quality not often exploited.

CULTIVATION Like all hydrangeas it needs a moisture-retentive soil and is inclined to scorch in full sun. So its needs are best satisfied on a north-, east- or west-wall or fence. Plant between autumn and spring, at least 45cm (18in) out from the wall with the shoots tied to a cane leaning against the wall. As with other self-clinging climbers, don't be tempted to buy large specimen plants for quick results; only the new growth will be induced to cling, so small plants with sturdy young shoots get off to a better start. For the first few years water in dry spells. No pruning is needed except occasionally to trim back outward-pointing shoots close against the wall, or to stop climbing shoots at the required height and width. If grown as ground cover, the climbing hydrangea will get off to a good start if it can cling to a tree stump or rock.

PROPAGATION Take softwood cuttings in summer or hardwood cuttings in winter.

PESTS AND DISEASES Generally trouble free.

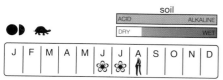

HYDRANGEA PETIOLARIS

HYPERICUM 'HIDCOTE'

Semi-evergreen shrub. Mature at 7 years: 1.5 x 2m (5 x 6ft). AGM

This hypericum makes a dense bushy mound of smooth mid- to dark green leaves. It comes into flower after midsummer when the bushes are smothered in golden yellow, saucer-shaped flowers, and continues to flower, though not so prolifically, until autumn.

USES This shrub makes good dense ground cover in almost any sunny situation. It is tolerant of atmospheric pollution and can cope with droughty conditions.

CULTIVATION Plant in autumn or spring in full sun, in any soil that is not waterlogged. Choose a position sheltered from cold winter winds. Pruning is not necessary, but if the plant grows too large for its position it can be cut back or clipped over in spring; take care to maintain its rounded shape.

PROPAGATION Take semi-ripe cuttings in late summer or autumn.

PESTS AND DISEASES Generally trouble free but *H.* 'Hidcote' may succumb to a virus that makes leaves narrow and variegated. *H. calycinum* may suffer from rust.

OTHER VARIETIES *H. calycinum*, the rose of sharon, has become such a successful ground cover plant for public landscaping that gardeners have begun to despise it. But for cheap and cheerful effect in difficult soils in sun or shade there is nothing to beat it. It spreads by underground suckers, so it can be a nuisance if used among other plants. Every year, or every second year, cut the growth down to the ground in spring or after flowering, using shears or, over large areas, a strimmer.

COMPANIONS With *H.* 'Hidcote' plant *Thalictrum delavayi, Ceanothus* 'Gloire de Versailles' or any of the eryngiums.

HYPERICUM 'HIDCOTE'

HYSSOPUS OFFICINALIS

Hyssop, a semi-evergreen or deciduous shrub (Mediterranean region and W. Asia, pre-1548). Mature at 3 years: 45 x 45cm (18 x 18in).

Hyssop is a dense leafy bush with upright stems covered with small, rich green narrow pointed leaves. After midsummer, flower spikes appear covered in tiny lipped bright blue flowers.

USES Its bushy habit and attractive leaves make hyssop a good plant to use for a low hedge, edging or component in a knot. The leaves, used sparingly, are said to aid digestion of fatty foods and can be used to flavour salads and stews. The flowers are much visited by bees and butterflies.

CULTIVATION Plant in spring in a light well drained soil. Hyssop does well on chalk or limestone. Group plants in threes or fives, 30cm (12in) apart. For hedges plant 23cm (9in) apart. To prevent the plants becoming leggy, cut the stems back each year to 20cm (8in) above ground. In mild areas, this can be done in autumn after flowering, but in cold districts wait until late spring.

PROPAGATION Take softwood cuttings in summer, divide or sow seeds in spring.

PESTS AND DISEASES Generally trouble free.

OTHER VARIETIES Forms with pink or white flowers are available as well as the blue forms. *H. officinalis* ssp. *aristatus* is more compact and a richer shade of blue, so on both counts is more desirable.

COMPANIONS The green-yellow fluff of *Alchemilla* flowers contrasts well with hyssop's blue spikes. *Achillea* 'Taygetea' is another good yellow with an overlapping flowering season. Alternatively, for a really vivid combination in the herb garden, try pot marigolds.

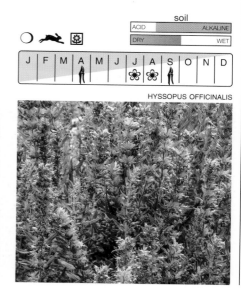

HYSSOPUS OFFICINALIS

H

I

IBERIS SEMPERVIRENS

*Candytuft, evergreen sub-shrub
(S. Europe and W. Asia, 1731). Mature at
3 years: 15-30 x 45-60cm (6-12 x 18-24in).
AGM*

A very hardy plant, this perennial candytuft
makes a low spreading cushion of linear
dark green leaves on thin, woody stems.
During spring and early summer the plant is
densely covered with clusters of small
brilliant white flowers in flattish domes.

USES This is a plant for the rock garden
where it can be tucked into a crevice or
fissure. Alternatively, use it in cracks
between flagstones, for formal or informal
edging to a sunny border or for the margins
of gravel paths or terraces. It makes good
ground cover.

CULTIVATION Iberis is easily satisfied in
any reasonable, well-drained soil and in full
sun. Plant in autumn or spring. After
flowering, clip over the plants to keep them
neat and bushy.

PROPAGATION The plants usually layer
themselves so that it is possible to divide
the roots easily. If there is not enough
suitable material, try covering the plant
with a thin layer of compost into which the
spreading branches can root. Or semi-ripe
cuttings can be taken in late summer.
I. sempervirens, like the annual candytufts,
can also be grown from seed.

PESTS AND DISEASES Generally trouble free.

OTHER VARIETIES 'Snowflake' is a variety
with slightly larger flowers.

COMPANIONS Make iberis part of the
kaleidoscopic display of colourful alpines
in a rock or gravel garden, with alpine
phloxes and helianthemums.

	soil	
ACID		ALKALINE
DRY		WET

J	F	M	A	M	J	J	A	S	O	N	D

IBERIS SEMPERVIRENS

ILEX AQUIFOLIUM

*Holly, evergreen tree (Europe including
Britain, W. Asia). Mature at 30 years:
3 x 1.5m (10 x 5ft) after 10 years; 20 x 6m
(70 x 20ft) at maturity.*

Holly grows slowly into a pyramid of glossy
dark green or variegated leaves. The leaves
at the base of the tree are usually very
prickly, becoming less so higher up the tree.
As they are out of reach of browsing
animals, the higher branches have no need
for defence. The flowers are greenish-white
and hardly noticeable, but the large clusters
of red (or yellow) winter berries are very
decorative. Most varieties need male and
female plants to produce berries.

USES Hollies are among the most adaptable
plants, as they are very hardy and tolerant
of salt spray and industrial pollution. They
make excellent hedges, will grow in
containers and can be trained as standards
or other forms of ornate topiary. Branches
are cut to decorate the house and make
wreaths at Christmas.

CULTIVATION Plant in early autumn or late
spring in any reasonable soil including
chalk, in sun or light shade. Hollies will
grow in quite dense shade but will then be
straggly. They dislike being transplanted –
fairly small container grown plants
establish most easily. For a hedge, plant
90cm (3ft) apart. Trim hedges and topiary
in early spring, removing any green shoots
on variegated plants. Trees that have
outgrown their present position may be
stooled or pollarded.

PROPAGATION Take cuttings in early autumn
or layer the roots. Hollies seed themselves
but the seedlings do not come true.

PESTS AND DISEASES Hollies may be
attacked by aphids or by leaf miners, which
make large yellow spots on the leaves. Pick
off and burn affected leaves. Tolerant of
honey fungus.

ILEX AQUIFOLIUM 'ARGENTEA MARGINATA'

GOOD VARIETIES *I. aquifolium*
'Pyramidalis' AGM and 'J.C. van Tol'
AGM (almost thornless) are self-fertile,
producing berries alone. Of the rest, *I. a.*
'Handsworth New Silver' AGM has leaves
with creamy white margins and orange
berries. *I. x altraclerensis* 'Lawsoniana'
AGM has leaves splashed with yellow, and
red berries. *I. aquifolium* 'Golden Queen'
AGM and 'Silver Queen' AGM, despite
their names, are male plants with no
berries. *Ilex x meserveae* 'Blue Angel'
AGM has dark blue-green leaves and dark
red berries.

	soil	
ACID		ALKALINE
DRY		WET

J	F	M	A	M	J	J	A	S	O	N	D

ILEX AQUIFOLIUM 'J.C. VAN TOL'

ILEX MESERVEAE 'BLUE ANGEL'

I

IMPATIENS

Busy lizzie, half-hardy evergreen perennial grown as an annual (E. Africa). Mature at 6 months or less: 30 x 30cm (12 x 12in).

Busy lizzies grow into tidy mounds of fresh green leaves on pale succulent, rather brittle stems. The leaves are oval and pointed. The flowers are flat and open with wide, rounded petals and last from spring to autumn. Double and semi-double varieties are available; as well as red and white they come in every shade in between, from salmon to mauve.

USES One of the most popular bedding plants, impatiens can be planted in formal schemes, but they also look right used as gap fillers in mixed beds and borders. They are also good for containers and hanging baskets as well as shady situations.

CULTIVATION When all danger of frost is past, set out young plants in ordinary garden soil in sun and shade. If you are growing them in containers or hanging baskets, use general-purpose soil-less compost with slow-release fertilizer added. The roots must not be allowed to dry out so it may be useful to add water-retentive granules to the compost mix. In any case, water containers and hanging baskets daily during dry weather, and water plants grown in borders as necessary.

PROPAGATION Raise from seed sown under glass in late winter or early spring, or buy plugs or young plants and grow them on under glass until planting outside.

PESTS AND DISEASES White fly and red spider mite can be a problem while the young plants are still under glass.

GOOD VARIETIES Make your selection of seeds from an illustrated catalogue or buy plants that are just coming into flower in the colours you like.

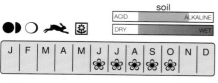

	soil	
	ACID	ALKALINE
	DRY	WET

J	F	M	A	M	J	J	A	S	O	N	D

IMPATIENS

IRIS GERMANICA

Flag iris, bearded iris, hardy rhizomatous perennial (S. Europe). Mature at 3 years: 45cm-1.2m x 23cm (18in-4ft x 9in).

There are many lovely species and varieties of iris, and of them all, the bearded flag iris is the most familiar; it has been grown in gardens since before records began. Handsome grey-green leaves, ribbed and sword-shaped, rise out of dry light brown rhizomes. In early summer strong, smooth stems carry pointed buds, which open into large stately flowers. Each flower has three up-standing petals (the standards), curving inwards at the top. Three more petals (the falls), each with a ridge of soft hairs along its centre, curve outwards and downwards. All the petals have slightly wavy margins and in some varieties this ruffling is exaggerated. Flower colours include white, yellow, orange, pink, mauve, purple, violet blue, red, brown and almost black, and two-tone mixtures of these.

USES The strong vertical line of the leaves is an excellent contrast with other plant shapes. The enormous range of flower colours means that you can find an iris to suit almost any colour scheme.

CULTIVATION A position where the rhizomes can bake in the sun is the first requirement. Plant irises in autumn, spring or after flowering, with the rhizomes half above ground and pointing south, in neutral or slightly alkaline soil. Ideally, feed with a fertilizer low in nitrogen in spring and again after flowering. To keep stock healthy, divide and replant every three years.

PROPAGATION Dig up and divide rhizomes into rooted pieces. Discard the old parts at the woody centre.

PESTS AND DISEASES Generally trouble-free.

GOOD VARIETIES Available varieties run into hundreds. The best way to choose is from a specialist nursery's illustrated catalogue. Look out for varieties with the AGM and for winners of the Dykes Medal in the USA and Britain. Irises flower for a relatively short time, so it makes sense to extend their season by mixing tall bearded irises, which flower from early to mid summer, with intermediates, which flower in from late spring to early summer and dwarfs which start the season in spring.

COMPANIONS Where there is enough space irises are stunning with a border all to themselves. But they also make a strong contribution to mixed planting schemes with shrub roses, peonies and hardy geraniums.

	soil	
	ACID	ALKALINE
	DRY	WET

J	F	M	A	M	J	J	A	S	O	N	D

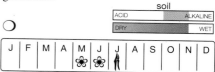

IRIS

IRIS 'APOGEE'

I

IRIS SIBIRICA

Hardy rhizomatous perennial (Europe, N. Asia, 16th century). Mature at 3 years: 90 x 45cm (3ft x 18in).

Strong clumps of grass-like, mid-green leaves rise from narrow hairy rhizomes in early spring. The flowers are elegant – smaller than those of bearded irises and poised on slender but strong stems. They bloom for just two or three weeks at midsummer but earn a place in this list for their good foliage and their adaptability. The colours are white, blue and violet.

USES These are excellent waterside plants.

CULTIVATION Plant in autumn or spring in any except very dry soil, in boggy areas and pool margins, in sun or partial shade. Cut down to the ground in autumn or winter.

PROPAGATION Divide established clumps.

PESTS AND DISEASES Generally trouble free.

OTHER SPECIES *Iris ensata* (syn. *I.kaempferi*) and *I. laevigata* are choice Japanese waterside irises. Easier and more robust for large ponds are *I. pseudacorus* and *I. p. variegata*. The iris that will grow in quite dense dry shade where virtually nothing else will, is *I. foetidissima*, the stinking or Gladwyn iris. Its boring little

yellowish-mauve flowers are followed by pods that burst open to reveal tightly packed bright orange seeds. Among the most beautiful of all irises are the little winter-flowering *I. reticulata* varieties, with white, blue or rich, deep violet flowers. They are not difficult to grow initially but often disappear after a few seasons.

IRIS RETICULATA

IRIS SIBIRICA

ITEA ILICIFOLIA

Evergreen shrub (W. China, early 18th century). Mature at 15 years: 90 x 90cm (3 x 3ft) after 5 years; 3 x 3m (10 x 10ft) at maturity. AGM

The small, pale yellow-green flowers are borne in late summer and early autumn on remarkable drooping catkins, sometimes as much as 30cm (12in) long. A plain green background is provided by shiny green leaves with prickly margins like holly, on rather lax twiggy branches.

USES Itea's lax habit of growth makes it well suited to train against a south or west-facing wall or trellis. It can also be grown successfully in a container on a sheltered patio or a terrace.

CULTIVATION Plant in spring in good well-drained soil in a position sheltered by walls, fences or other shrubs. To be on the safe side, protect young plants from winter frost by wrapping them in horticultural fleece. If you grow itea in a pot or tub, wrap the container in bubble polythene for the winter. Cut out any frost-damaged growth in late spring.

PROPAGATION Cuttings can be taken in summer and placed in a propagator with bottom heat.

PESTS AND DISEASES Generally trouble free.

OTHER VARIETIES *Itea virginica* is deciduous and is more reliably hardy, but lacks the spectacular catkins.

COMPANIONS The overall colouring makes this a good background shrub for red and orange flowers. It is excellent too as part of a gentle green and white colour scheme.

ITEA ILICIFOLIA

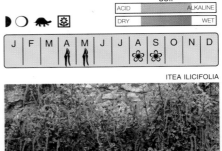

JASMINUM HUMILE 'REVOLUTUM'

Evergreen shrub (W. China, 17th century). Mature at 12 years: 2.5 x 3m (8 x 10ft). AGM

If this jasmine has any scent it is so slight as to be undetectable. But it is a good bushy shrub with elegant leaves divided into five or seven oval, pointed leaflets. The typical jasmine flowers are borne in clusters throughout the summer. They are yellow with long narrow tubes opening at the end into flat, five-petalled faces.

USES A good bulky shrub for background use or for screening.

CULTIVATION As long as it has sun and some shelter from cold winds, it is not fussy about soil. No pruning is needed.

PROPAGATION Semi-ripe cuttings will root fairly easily.

PESTS AND DISEASES Generally trouble free.

OTHER SPECIES We are more familiar with jasmine as a climbing plant. *Jasminum nudiflorum* AGM, the winter-flowering jasmine, which also has yellow flowers, is deciduous but the stems remain green all winter, providing a good background for the flowers. These also appear throughout winter, particularly during mild spells. It is difficult to train as a climber and usually looks uncomfortable hitched up to a wall or trellis. It seems more natural and at home trailing down from the top of a retaining wall or sprawling on a bank. *J. officinale* AGM is the summer-flowering jasmine with sweet-scented white flowers. It climbs with twining stems and needs a south- or west-facing wall and plenty of space: it can produce new stems 2m (6ft) long and more in a season, so it soon overwhelms the average pergola or arch. *J. x stephanense* likes the same conditions; it has fragrant pink flowers at midsummer.

◖ ○ 🐰

		soil		
ACID				ALKALINE
DRY				WET

J	F	M	A	M	J	J	A	S	O	N	D
		🌱	🌱	🌱	✿	✿	✿				

JASMINUM HUMILE 'REVOLUTUM'

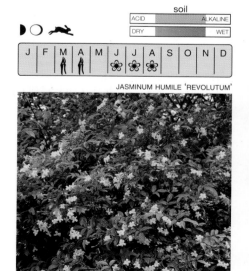

JUGLANS REGIA

J

Walnut, deciduous tree (S.E. Europe, W. and Central Asia, 16th century). Mature at 60 years: 8m (27ft) tall after 20 years; 20 x 15m (70 x 50ft) at maturity. AGM

A noble tree to consider if you are planting for posterity – walnuts live for about 300 years. They also grow fast initially, soon developing a broad domed crown. If a wet spring is followed by a warm summer, strong new shoots 90cm (3ft) long may be produced. The bark is light grey and the leaves, which are late to break, are large and divided into separate leaflets. They are light green with a slightly rough, sheeny texture. The nuts are encased in a bitter-tasting fleshy green outer skin and can be pickled if they are harvested before the inner shell hardens. It is about twelve years before the trees start to bear fruit.

USES The nuts are edible and the timber is highly valued for its density and decorative grain. It is the best wood for gun stocks and is used as a veneer in furniture making. In parks and gardens it makes a fine shade tree and, being late to come into leaf, its canopy provides the right conditions for shrubs and other plants that enjoy light shade.

CULTIVATION Walnuts dislike being moved so they should be planted while still small.

Plant them carefully in early spring in deep, free-draining soil over chalk or limestone; they dislike acid sandy soils or heavy clay. They need full sun, and young trees are susceptible to frost, so provide a site which is sheltered. For the first two seasons water in drought conditions. Any pruning to achieve a shapely tree should be done very early in the tree's life because when large branches are cut the wound 'bleeds' profusely, literally sapping the tree's strength and sometimes killing it. If you have to prune do it on a hot day in summer: heat helps to stop the flow of sap.

PROPAGATION Grow from seed sown 5cm (2in) deep outdoors in autumn. Named varieties are grafted.

PESTS AND DISEASES Generally trouble free but notably susceptible to honey fungus.

OTHER VARIETIES *J. regia* 'Franquette' has large, well-flavoured nuts. *Juglans nigra* AGM, the black walnut, is much more ornamental and has larger leaves, but the nuts are not edible.

○ 🐰

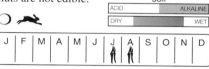

		soil		
ACID				ALKALINE
DRY				WET

J	F	M	A	M	J	J	A	S	O	N	D
						🧑 🧑					

JUGLANS REGIA

J

JUNIPERUS

Juniper, evergreen coniferous trees and shrubs (northern hemisphere). Mature at 25 years and over.

This is a variable and versatile species; some junipers form slender spires, others make ground-hugging mats. The leaves are needle-like or thread-like and can be green, grey-green, blue-grey, or yellow-green. In most forms the leaves are aromatic: when crushed they smell of gin.

USES The tall varieties make excellent exclamation marks in planting schemes, and those with a horizontal habit make impenetrable ground cover.

CULTIVATION Junipers will grow in almost any soil and have no aversion to lime or chalk. They are drought resistant and will tolerate shade, although they do best in sun. Plant them in early autumn or late spring. Horizontal forms can be pruned in spring or late summer to make the growth denser, and if necessary, to reduce the spread.

PROPAGATION Take cuttings in autumn.

PESTS AND DISEASES Generally trouble free. Tolerant of honey fungus.

GOOD VARIETIES Vertical: *J. communis* 'Hibernica' AGM grows to 1.8m x 60cm (6 x 2ft) after ten years and may eventually reach 5m (15ft) in height. It is grey-green and dense textured. *J. scopulorum* 'Skyrocket' is faster growing than most conifers, forming a slim column of feathery blue-grey fronds 2m x 30cm (6 x 1ft) after ten years, 8m x 75cm (25 x 2ft6in) at maturity. *J. chinensis* 'Aurea' AGM and *J. chinensis* 'Obelisk' AGM are broadly columnar.
Horizontal: *J. communis* 'Hornibrookii' AGM starts off prostrate and later on mounds up in the centre. Eventually it covers a wide area, moulding its shape to rocks or other obstacles. The leaves are green, becoming bronze. *J. horizontalis* 'Blue Chip' spreads to 1.2m (4ft) and has silver-blue feathery leaves; *J. h.* 'Emerald Spreader' is similar with bright green leaves; and *J. h.* 'Hughes' is grey-green with branches raised to 25cm (10in). *J. squamata* 'Blue Carpet' AGM, 30cm x 2m (1 x 6ft) is faster than most. *J. virginiana* 'Grey Owl' AGM 60cm x 2m (2 x 6ft) has open-textured grey foliage. Shrubs: *J. x media* 'Pfitzeriana' 1.5 x 2m (5 x 6ft) and more is a handsome plant with grey-green leaves on strong branches pointing upwards and outwards with arching tips. It does well in shade.

soil	
ACID	ALKALINE
DRY	WET

J	F	M	A	M	J	J	A	S	O	N	D

JUNIPERUS HORIZONTALIS

JUNIPERUS COMMUNIS 'HIBERNICA'

KERRIA JAPONICA 'PLENIFLORA'

K

Deciduous shrub (Japan, 1804). Mature at 7 years: 3 x 3m (10 x 10ft). AGM

This, the double form of kerria, was introduced by William Kerr, a young gardener sent from Kew to China on a plant hunting expedition. Kerria is among the easiest and most obliging of all shrubs. The double golden yellow pompon flowers are born in spring along green stems, which arch up from the base of the plant. The bright green, pointed and toothed leaves are rather sparse.

USES Reserve kerria for those difficult positions where nothing else will thrive. It is completely hardy and will grow on a north wall, under dripping trees or on a dry bank, on cold windy sites and even in polluted and industrial atmospheres.

CULTIVATION Plant kerria between autumn and spring in any soil including chalk and clay in sun or shade. Prune after flowering to encourage vigorous new shoots from the base: cut out one stem in three. Unwanted suckers may sprout up at some distance from the plant; pull them off or dig them out as they appear. If you grow the variegated form, it needs no regular pruning, but watch out for all-green shoots and remove them.

PROPAGATION Dig up suckers and replant them, or take hardwood cuttings in late autumn and insert them in a trench in the open. They should be ready to plant out by the following autumn.

PESTS AND DISEASES Generally trouble free.

OTHER VARIETIES *Kerria japonica*, the species, is more compact and bushy than 'Pleniflora', and has single flowers like buttercups. On *K. j.* 'Golden Guinea' AGM the flowers are larger. *K. j.* 'Picta' is a pretty form with cream variegated leaves and single flowers. It forms a dense little bush 90 x 90cm (3 x 3ft).

COMPANIONS Underplant kerria with *Euphorbia robbiae* and *Scilla non-scripta* (bluebells).

soil

	ACID	ALKALINE
	DRY	WET

J	F	M	A	M	J	J	A	S	O	N	D

KERRIA JAPONICA

KNAUTIA MACEDONICA

Syn. Scabiosa rumelica, hardy perennial (Macedonia). Mature at 3 years: 60 x 60cm (2 x 2ft).

This close relation of scabious has small pincushion flowers of dark crimson, a colour rarely found among herbaceous plants. They are carried from midsummer until early autumn on slender, branching stems springing from a basal clump of grey-green, deeply divided leaves.

USES Knautia provides dots of vibrant colour to save pale schemes from appearing too uniform and insipid.

CULTIVATION Plant in autumn or spring in any ordinary garden soil in full sun. The flower stems tend to flop forwards and in tidy gardens need the support of pea sticks or netting stretched horizontally. Cut the stems to the ground in autumn or winter.

PROPAGATION Divide established clumps or grow from seed.

PESTS AND DISEASES Generally trouble free.

OTHER VARIETIES One or two nurseries offer pink forms. The colour of the species is rather variable and can veer towards magenta. The only way to be sure of getting a good dark crimson form is to buy the plant while it is in flower.

COMPANIONS The crimson flowers associate well with almost any other colour except, perhaps, orange. They make a good contrast with any shade of yellow, especially yellow roses, pale yellow day lilies or *Achillea* 'Moonshine'.

soil

	ACID	ALKALINE
	DRY	WET

J	F	M	A	M	J	J	A	S	O	N	D

KNAUTIA MACEDONICA

K

KNIPHOFIA

Red hot poker, torch lily, evergreen and deciduous hardy and tender perennials (S. Africa). Mature at 3 years: from 60 x 45cm (24 x 18in) up to 2 x 1m (6 x 3ft).

The pokers bring a tropical look to the garden from early summer well into the autumn, depending on the type chosen; those mentioned below are all hardy. They form clumps of grassy or strap-shaped leaves, green or grey, and produce upright succulent stems with poker-like tops densely set with small tubular flowers. The flowers may be fiery orange, yellow paling almost to white, or two-tone orange and yellow.

USES Use them to extend the season in herbaceous and mixed plantings, specially in front of copper or purple foliage. They look good grouped alone in a semi-wild part of the garden.

CULTIVATION Kniphofias need full sun and, although they have a desert-dwelling look about them, soil which remains moist in summer. Plant them in spring, water in dry weather and mulch every spring with manure or compost. If you are in doubt as to their hardiness in your local climate,

cover them in winter with a 15cm (6in) layer of dry leaves or straw.

PROPAGATION Divide established clumps during the spring.

PESTS AND DISEASES Generally trouble free.

GOOD VARIETIES 'Little Maid' is early to flower, 45 x 30cm (18 x 12in) AGM, with creamy-yellow flowers emerging from green buds. 'Brimstone' AGM is a reliably hardy, taller yellow. *K. galpinii* 60 x 45 (24 x 18in) is a beautiful clear shade of orange flowering in late summer and early autumn. Tall and dramatic 'Fiery Fred' carries orange torches in later summer. 'Ice Queen' is tall with cream flowers, green in bud.

COMPANIONS Pokers with their strong shapes are a good antidote to the daisy-flowers that tend to dominate the garden in late summer. Both orange and yellow kinds look good with tawny gaillardias and heleniums or soft blue-mauve Michaelmas daisies.

KNIPHOFIA 'LITTLE MAID'

KOLKWITZIA AMABILIS 'PINK CLOUD'

Beauty bush, deciduous shrub (Central China 1901). Mature at 10 years: 1.8 x 1.8m (6 x 6ft) after 10 years, 3 x 3m (10 x 10ft) at maturity. AGM

Kolkwitzia is a graceful shrub with many widely arching branches with oval, pointed grey-green leaves that turn yellow in autumn. The wood matures to a warm brown with peeling bark, attractive in winter. In late spring and early summer the branches are weighed down by masses of pale pink flowers like wide-flared bells, borne in clusters.

USES Kolkwitzia is a good plant for mixed borders or shelter belts.

CULTIVATION Plant between autumn and spring in any reasonable soil and in full sun. Kolkwitzia thrives in chalk. To keep the plants flowering well take out one stem in three immediately after flowering. If necessary stems can be shortened at the same time to restrict the plant's height and spread, but it is a pity to have to spoil it's arching shape, so try and give it space to develop unhindered to its full size.

PROPAGATION Semi-ripe cuttings taken in late summer root easily and should be ready to plant out the following spring.

PESTS AND DISEASES Generally trouble free.

GOOD VARIETIES *K. amabilis* 'Pink Cloud' is the only variety available. It is important to be sure that you buy this variety, and not the species *K. amabilis*, which is variable; you may end up with a plant that has few flowers, whereas with 'Pink Cloud' you can be sure of a prolific display.

COMPANIONS To be appreciated to the full, Kolkwitzia benefits from the dark background of a copper beech hedge or a group of *Cotinus coggygria* 'Foliis Purpureis' or red-leaved berberis.

KOLKWITZIA AMABILIS 'PINKCLOUD'

LABURNUM X WATERERI 'VOSSII'

A hybrid between **L. alpinum** *(Southern Alps) and* **L. anagyroides** *(Central and S. Europe), deciduous tree (Holland, late 19th century). Mature at 25 years: 8 x 8m (25 x 25ft). AGM*

In early summer laburnum is a familiar sight in gardens the length and breadth of Britain. It has an elegant shape; the branches arch upwards and outwards to form a broad canopy, and the leaves, composed of triple leaflets, are rich deep green. In early summer before the leaves are fully developed and while they are still pale in colour, fragrant racemes of clear yellow pea flowers cascade from the branches, some as long as 60cm (24in). They are followed by pods containing very poisonous seeds which can kill if eaten by children.

USES Laburnum is most often seen as part of a mixed shrub and tree planting on the boundaries of small front or back gardens. But it deserves to stand alone and, if the canopy is kept high, makes a good shade tree on a lawn. Laburnum trained to form an arched tunnel became an immensely fashionable garden feature in the 1970s and 1980s, and is still popular. It can also be trained to make an arbour or, espalier fashion, to cover a high wall. It is an excellent small tree for cold exposed sites and for areas of industrial pollution.

CULTIVATION Plant between autumn and spring in any reasonable soil, including chalk and clay. If children are at risk remove the faded flower racemes before the seed pods form. When trees are trained on arches or pergolas, prune and tie in new shoots in late summer.

PROPAGATION Sow seeds in spring or graft buds in autumn.

PESTS AND DISEASES Generally trouble free.

COMPANIONS Laburnum is often seen in flower with mauve-pink lilacs, and this unappealing colour combination has contributed to a snobbish rejection of laburnum by design-conscious gardeners. Avoid pink flowers near laburnum: more compatible are the blues of evergreen ceanothus or *Clematis macropetala,* or the orange reds of *Euphorbia griffithii* 'Fireglow' and mixed helianthemums.

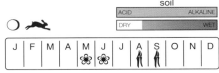

LABURNUM X WATERERI 'VOSSII'

LAMIUM MACULATUM

Deadnettle, semi-evergreen hardy perennial. Mature at 3 years: 20 x 90cm (8in x 3ft).

Low-growing weed-smothering plants creeping by underground runners, these lamiums are grown mainly for their foliage. The small, heart-shaped leaves have finely scalloped edges and spread horizontally from short stems, making total cover. The leaves are dark, greyish green, marked with a broad central silver-white stripe. In some varieties this colour covers almost the entire leaf. Spikes of hooded, lipped, dead-nettle flowers appear in late spring, and may be pink, mauve or white.

USES Lamiums are among the most dependable of all ground cover plants in sun or shade.

CULTIVATION Plant lamiums in dry shade or any other difficult area except bog. No aftercare is needed, but after flowering the plants can be clipped over with shears or, in large plantings, with a strimmer, to keep up a supply of fresh young leaves.

PROPAGATION Divide the roots during the autumn or the spring.

PESTS AND DISEASES Generally trouble free.

GOOD VARIETIES 'Aureum' has yellow-green leaves with a lighter central stripe; 'Beacon Silver' has leaves silvered right up to the narrowest of dark green margins and mauve-pink flowers; 'Pink Pewter' and 'James Boyd Parselle' are similar with pale pink flowers, and 'White Nancy' AGM has silvery leaves and white flowers. *L. m. roseum* has green leaves and pink flowers.

COMPANIONS All these varieties combine well together if planted in interlocking groups to make a tapestry carpet. Both gold and silver-leaved kinds contrast well with *Viola labradorica.*

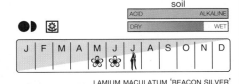

LAMIUM MACULATUM 'BEACON SILVER'

L

LATHYRUS LATIFOLIUS

Everlasting pea, hardy perennial climber (Europe, 1596). Mature at 3 years: up to 3m (10ft) high. AGM

This plant has the same grey-green smooth, rounded leaves and thread-like twining tendrils as the edible garden pea and the annual sweet pea (see 'Other varieties' below). The magenta-pink flowers are prolific and long-stemmed but have no scent. They continue from midsummer until early autumn.

USES Gertrude Jekyll used to plant this pea in its white form towards the back of her borders and train it forwards to cover the spent stems of plants which had flowered earlier. It will also clothe arches and trellises on a seasonal basis, ramble through hedges and sprawl down banks.

CULTIVATION Plant in autumn or spring in any reasonable soil in a sunny position. Provide twiggy supports or regularly coax the stems in the direction you want them to take, tying them in if necessary. In autumn cut the stems down to the ground. For edible garden peas and sweet peas push a double line of twiggy pea sticks into the ground or stretch strong netting vertically between canes for the plants to climb up. Alternatively, make bamboo wigwams. Pick sweet peas every day to keep them coming.

PROPAGATION Divide the roots in early spring or grow from seed. 'White Pearl' usually comes true from seed. Seeds of these and of annual garden peas and sweet peas *(L. odoratus)* can be sown under glass in small pots in late winter and planted out in spring. They can also be sown outdoors in flowering positions in autumn or spring.

PESTS AND DISEASE Generally trouble free.

OTHER VARIETIES The prettiest forms are 'White Pearl' AGM and 'Rosa Perle' ('Pink Pearl'). Sweet peas can be chosen according to the colours you prefer from a supplier's catalogue. Be aware that some varieties are grown for their showy flowers, not for their scent, and look for those which are described as strongly scented.

COMPANIONS Following the Jekyll principle, plant *L. latifolius* behind early flowering perennials or shrubs such as osmanthus, skimmia or *Spiraea x arguta*.

	soil	
	ACID	ALKALINE
	DRY	WET

J	F	M	A	M	J	J	A	S	O	N	D
						❀ ❀	❀	❀	✂	✂	

LATHYRUS ODORATUS

LATHYRUS LATIFOLIUS

LAURUS NOBILIS

Bay laurel, poet's laurel, sweet bay, evergreen tree or shrub (Mediterranean pre-16th century). Mature at 20 years: 2.5 x 1.5m (8 x 5ft) after 10 years, 12 x 10m (40 x 30ft) at maturity. AGM

Bay, left unpruned, will slowly form a dense pyramid of glossy dark green and aromatic leaves, oval and pointed with slightly wavy margins. The flowers are not very noticeable; they are small and yellow-green, held in clusters tight within the leaf axils. They are followed by black berries.

USES The leaves, fresh or dried, are used to flavour soups, stews, puddings and sauces. In the garden bay is an excellent subject for architectural topiary either in the ground or in containers. It does well in seaside and town gardens.

CULTIVATION Although *Laurus nobilis* is hardy the leaves can be damaged by cold winds, so a sheltered position is needed in sun or light shade. Plant in spring in good, well-drained soil or in loam-based compost in a pot or tub with a layer of drainage material at the bottom. Feed pot grown bay trees with a slow-release fertilizer every spring. Clip to the desired shape during summer. Bay trees grown as standards (lollipop heads on a single stem) are expensive to buy. With patience you can train your own by tying the main stem to a stake and rubbing out the buds of side shoots as they appear.

PROPAGATION Take cuttings in late summer or layer in early autumn.

PESTS AND DISEASES The leaves may get scorched by frost or wind, or turn yellow from lack of nitrogen. Pick off the affected leaves and apply a foliar feed to the rest.

OTHER VARIETIES There is a form with yellow leaves, *L. n.* 'Aurea'.

	soil	
	ACID	ALKALINE
	DRY	WET

J	F	M	A	M	J	J	A	S	O	N	D
						✂	✂				

LAURUS NOBILIS

LAVANDULA

Lavender, evergreen shrub (Mediterranean, mid 16th century). Mature at 5 years: from 30 x 45cm (12 x 18in) to 1 x 1.5m (3 x 5ft).

Lavenders vary in size, their hardiness, the colour of leaves and flowers, and the quality of their perfume. All have narrow, spikey, aromatic grey-green leaves in branching clusters above older, gnarled, woody stems. At midsummer or late summer, depending on the variety, stiff thin stems bear at their tips clusters of small, scented flowers of blue, mauve, pink or white.

USES Lavender is one of the most important plants in herbal medicine and aromatherapy as well as in the perfume trade. In the garden the more compact varieties make pretty low hedges or edging.

CULTIVATION A sunny position and good drainage are essential, so add plenty of rubble and grit if you want to grow lavender in heavy soil. Plant in groups of three or more. For hedges plant 30cm (12in) apart. Every year after flowering trim over the plants with shears and trim again in spring. Even if you observe this pruning regime meticulously, after four or five years the plants will become leggy and will need replacing.

PROPAGATION Take cuttings to grow outdoors in late summer or early autumn.

PESTS AND DISEASES Generally trouble free, but there is an outside chance your plants may catch the rare disease 'Lavender scab'. The young shoots wilt and flower heads curl up. There is no cure, so dig up and burn the plants.

GOOD VARIETIES *Lavandula angustifolia* AGM is a tall, strongly scented species. More compact varieties are *L. a.* 'Twickel Purple' AGM, 'Munstead' and the deservedly popular 'Hidcote' AGM. *Lavandula stoechas* is definitely not reliably hardy but so distinctive with its erect ears that it is worth growing in a pot and bringing inside for the winter.

COMPANIONS Lavender is an 'enabling' plant, which enhances almost any neighbour, but specially *Alstroemeria*, *Hypericum*, *Romneya* and roses.

soil		
ACID		ALKALINE
DRY		WET

J	F	M	A	M	J	J	A	S	O	N	D

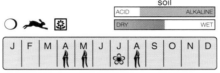

LAVANDULA STOECHAS

LAVANDULA AGUSTIFOLIA 'HIDCOTE'

LAVATERA

Tree mallow, hardy sub-shrub and annual. Mature at 3 years: 1.5 x 1.5m (5 x 5ft) or more. AGM

Although the plant is cut to the ground by frost in most years, it survives to throw up numerous long stems. For this reason it is sometimes listed in catalogues as a herbaceous perennial. It has large, shallowly lobed leaves, greyish-green. From midsummer until autumn plentiful flowers like single hollyhocks are borne in clusters.

USES The shrubby mallows are fast growing and have a long flowering season.

CULTIVATION Plant in spring in a sunny position, if possible sheltered from the wind, in any well-drained soil. On windy sites cut all the stems back by one-third in autumn. In spring cut back all branches to 10cm (4in) from the base.

PROPAGATION Take cuttings in autumn and root in a cold frame or frost-free greenhouse. Sow seeds of *L. trimestris* in autumn or spring in the site where they are intended to flower.

PESTS AND DISEASES Generally trouble free.

GOOD VARIETIES The flowers of *Lavatera* 'Barnsley' are white with a deep pink eye at the centre, and they fade to pale pink. The original garden plant, *Lavatera* 'Rosea' is still excellent and can be trusted to put on a spectacular performance. But it is quite variable. Look out for a specimen with leaves as grey as possible and flowers of a soft rather than hard shade of pink. Few of the more compact named varieties can be trusted for hardiness, but 'Burgundy Wine' with purple-red flowers and dark grey-green leaves should be all right except in the very coldest districts. *Lavatera trimestris* (up to 60 x 45cm, 2ft x 18in), a hardy annual, has the same funnel-shaped flowers.

soil		
ACID		ALKALINE
DRY		WET

J	F	M	A	M	J	J	A	S	O	N	D

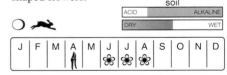

LAVATERA THURINGIACA 'BARNSLEY'

L

L

LEUCOJUM AESTIVUM

Summer snowflake, bulb (Europe including Britain). Mature at 6 months: 30-60 x 23cm (1-2ft x 9in).

Although it is called the summer snowflake, this giant snowdrop flowers in late spring. The long glossy green leaves are strap-shaped and upright. The white bell-shaped flowers are green-tipped and resemble snowdrops, hanging their heads from the tips of juicy green stems.

USES They are best planted in the wilder, naturalistic parts of the garden to follow on after earlier spring bulbs.

CULTIVATION Plant the bulbs in late summer or autumn in good soil in sun or under trees. Set them about 10cm (4in) deep and 7cm (3in) apart. Don't worry if the bulbs fail to flower their first season. They take a year or two to settle down. After flowering wait for the leaves to turn yellow before cutting them down.

PROPAGATION Every five years or so, clumps can be dug up and divided in autumn.

PESTS AND DISEASES Generally trouble free.

GOOD VARIETIES *L. aestivum* 'Gravetye Giant' AGM is the one to go for. *Leucojum vernum* is a smaller plant flowering in early spring and *L. autumnale* is also small, flowers in autumn and is less hardy.

COMPANIONS In an informal woodland setting, plant *L. aestivum* with erythroniums.

soil

ACID	ALKALINE
DRY	WET

J	F	M	A	M	J	J	A	S	O	N	D

LEUCOJUM AESTIVUM

LEYCESTERIA FORMOSA

Pheasant berry, flowering nutmeg, Granny's curls, deciduous shrub (the Himalayas, 1824). Mature at 7 years: 2 x 2m (6 x 6ft).

This shrub throws up a thicket of bloomy sea-green stems that keep their colour during the winter months. The stems are hollow and covered with leaves like elongated hearts, ending in long, tapering, slightly twisted points. Some leaves have toothed margins but most are smooth. From midsummer the stems arch under the weight of the flowers. They hang from the stems in tiers and are surrounded by pointed wine-red bracts. In autumn small purple-red berries are sheltered by the bracts.

USES Leycesteria berries provide food for birds including pheasants, and the plant is sometimes grown as game covert.

CULTIVATION It grows in almost any soil including wet clay, and is shade tolerant, although it does flower better in full sun. Plant it between autumn and spring. In the first spring, cut all the stems down to a few centimeters above the ground to encourage initial strong growth from the base. In the years that follow, cut out any frost-damaged stems at the base every spring, and thin out the rest by removing about one shoot in every three, taking the oldest wood. If the whole plant succumbs to severe winter weather, cut down all the stems and it will probably sprout again from below ground.

PROPAGATION Take cuttings in winter or sow fresh seed in late summer. It germinates easily and often seeds itself freely.

COMPANIONS Leycesteria looks at home in the partial shade of deciduous trees or grouped at the edge of woodland with hydrangeas. It would also be attractive arching over water.

soil

ACID	ALKALINE
DRY	WET

J	F	M	A	M	J	J	A	S	O	N	D

LEYCESTERIA FORMOSA

LIGULARIA DENTATA

Hardy perennial (China, 1900). Mature at 3 years: 120 x 60cm (4 x 2ft).

The ligularias are plants of forceful character. One would call them handsome rather than beautiful. This one has large, coarse-textured heart-shaped dark green leaves held on 30cm (12in) high stalks. In late summer stout branching stems carry large startling yellow-orange daisy flowers. *L. d.* 'Desdemona' AGM is the form usually available. It is more compact and the leaves are richly coloured.

USES This is a plant for dramatic waterside planting schemes.

CULTIVATION A place in the sun in rich moist and even boggy soil suits ligularias best but they will tolerate partial shade. Plant them in spring and mulch with manure or compost every year. In autumn cut them to the ground.

PROPAGATION Divide in spring.

PESTS AND DISEASES Slugs and snails.

OTHER VARIETIES *Ligularia* 'Gregynog Gold' AGM grows to 1.8m (6ft) and has huge leaves and orange daisy flowers arranged on tall cones. It needs full sun. *L.* 'The Rocket' AGM 180cm x 90cm (6 x 3ft) is rather different. The large round leaves are deeply cut to give a starry effect and tall black stems carry narrow spires of spidery yellow flowers.

COMPANIONS It is difficult to place such harsh yellow-orange shades in the garden. Graham Stuart Thomas recommends the bold combination of *L.* 'Gregynog Gold' with purple phloxes as 'quite sumptuous'. The less bold could take their cue from the foliage of 'Desdemona' to provide a background of purple. Add some late-flowering day lilies in golden yellow or mahogany shades.

soil

ACID	ALKALINE
DRY	WET

J	F	M	A	M	J	J	A	S	O	N	D

LIGULARIA DENTATA 'DESDEMONA'

LIGUSTRUM QUIHOUI

Deciduous shrub (China, 1862). Mature at 15 years: 2.5 x 2.5m (8 x 8ft). AGM

Privet has acquired a name for dreariness, but this one redresses the balance. It is not easy to come by, but it is worth tracking down for its elegant shape and late autumn flowering. The thin wiry branches spread to form a light canopy of dark green oval leaves. The panicles of little white flowers are quite substantial, up to 20cm (8in) long and 7cm (3in) wide.

USES Plant this shrub where it can form part of the background until its flowering time.

CULTIVATION Like all privets, *L. quihoui* is easily satisfied in ordinary garden soil in sun or light shade. Plant it between autumn and early spring. Pruning should not be necessary but if you want to improve the shape of the plant, prune in autumn.

PROPAGATION Take cuttings in autumn.

PESTS AND DISEASES Generally trouble free but susceptible to honey fungus.

OTHER VARIETIES The only other privet likely to be grown for its flowers is *L. sinense*. Almost evergreen, it can be treated as a shrub or encouraged to become a small tree up to 5 x 5m (16 x 16ft). After midsummer it produces flowers in fluffy clouds, followed by clusters of purple-black berries; which last well into winter. *L. s.* 'Variegatum' has grey-green leaves with white variegation. *L. ovalifolium* 'Aureum', the golden privet, is a splendid plant for giving a splash of colour among sober green-leaved shrubs but think twice before planting it as a hedge – *en masse* it is altogether too dazzling. The despised plain green *L. ovalifolium* is the quickest way to a background or boundary hedge, its one disadvantage being greed: it robs neighbouring plants of nourishment.

soil

| ACID | | | | | | | | | | | ALKALINE |
| DRY | | | | | | | | | | | WET |

| J | F | M | A | M | J | J | A | S | O | N | D |

LIGUSTRUM QUIHOUI

LILIUM

Lily, bulb. Mature at 1 year: from 30 x 30cm (12 x 12in) to 3m x 30cm (10ft x 12in).

Lilies grow from bulbs composed of layers of fleshy scales, throwing up a single stem with linear or strap-shaped leaves along its length. The flowers grow in outward-facing clusters along the top of the stem and are trumpet shaped.

USES Lilies can be grown in groups in beds and borders to fill the gap between roses and the flowers of late summer. They also do very well in pots.

CULTIVATION Most lilies need a sunny position and ordinary well-drained soil, but a few need acid soil and some shade. These are noted in the list of varieties below. Plant *L. candidum* in late summer just beneath the soil surface, the rest in autumn, stem-rooting kinds 15cm (6in) deep, the rest 10cm (4in) deep. In pots, plant into general purpose compost. Most tall lilies need a cane to support each stem. After flowering, dead head but leave the stems until the leaves have died. Mulch established groups every spring and water in dry spells.

PROPAGATION Plant offsets or bulb scales in sandy soil.

PESTS AND DISEASES Mottled or deformed leaves are a sign of virus disease and the plants should be burned to prevent the infection spreading. Red lily beetles feed on the leaves from early spring to autumn.

GOOD VARIETIES The following are easy to grow in pots: *L. regale* AGM with highly scented white trumpets; *L. regale* Royal Gold Group, the yellow version; *L. henryi* AGM, tall with soft apricot-orange trumpets; 'Rosita', dusky pink, 'Pink Tiger', dusky pink turk's cap.

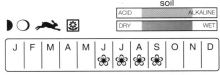

soil

| ACID | | | | | | | | | | | ALKALINE |
| DRY | | | | | | | | | | | WET |

| J | F | M | A | M | J | J | A | S | O | N | D |

LILIUM 'GOLDEN MELODY'

LILIUM REGALE

L

LIMNANTHES DOUGLASII

Poached egg flower, meadow foam, hardy annual (N.W. America, early 19th century). Mature at 6 months: 15 x 20cm (6 x 8in). AGM

The fresh light green leaves are very deeply cut giving a feathery effect. They form a loose rosette from which masses of flowers appear from early to late summer on brittle succulent stems. They are open and cup-shaped, with petals white at the margins and yellow at the centre, in roughly the same proportion as they are in a poached egg. The flowers are slightly fragrant.

USES Limnanthes are good early gap fillers between emerging herbaceous plants or under roses, to be pulled out as soon as their leaves fade.

PROPAGATION and CULTIVATION Sow directly into their flowering position in any reasonable soil in sun or partial shade, in autumn or early spring. You only need to do this once; your plants will seed themselves freely in subsequent years. They may become a nuisance, appearing in unwanted places, but in that case they are easy to pull out.

PESTS AND DISEASES Generally trouble free.

OTHER VARIETIES There are no others, this is a one-off.

COMPANIONS Myosotis (Forget-me-not) flowers at the same time and behaves in the same way, seeding itself around with abandon. The combination of forget-me-not blue with the yellow and white of Limnanthes gives a very fresh and bright impression.

soil

		ACID						ALKALINE
		DRY						WET

J	F	M	A	M	J	J	A	S	O	N	D
					✽	✽	✽				

LIMANTHES DOUGLASII

LIMONIUM PLATYPHYLLUM

Syn. **Limonium latifolium, Statice latifolia.** *Sea lavender, evergreen hardy perennial (Bulgaria, S. Russia, 1791). Mature at 3 years: 30 x 45cm (12 x 18in)*

From a clump of dark grey-green leathery leaves, a cloud of tiny violet-blue flowers hovers on wiry much-branched stems, in the manner of gypsophila. Limonium comes into flower in late summer and lasts into autumn.

USES Limonium is a useful contributor to planting schemes towards the end of the summer. It is an excellent cut flower and can be dried successfully. The large leaves qualify it as ground cover too.

CULTIVATION Plant limoniums in groups of three or more 30cm (12in) apart. They need to be in full sun and they are happy in any ordinary garden soil provided it is well-drained. To dry the flowers cut the stems just as they come into flower.

PROPAGATION Divide and replant the roots of established clumps in spring, or sow seeds in early spring.

PESTS AND DISEASES Generally trouble free.

GOOD VARIETIES In the named forms available the colour of the flowers is more intense. 'Violetta' is fairly easy to come by.

COMPANIONS Limoniums coincide with the second flowering flush of roses and go well with those of red or crimson colouring. A similar colour combination can be achieved by planting them with red and violet fuchsias such as *F.* 'Mrs Popple', 'Riccartonii' or 'Tom Thumb'.

soil

	ACID							ALKALINE
	DRY							WET

J	F	M	A	M	J	J	A	S	O	N	D
						✽	✽	✽			

LIMONIUM PLATYPHYLLUM

LINUM NARBONENSE

Flax, hardy perennial (S. Europe, 1759). Mature at 2 years: 45 x 45cm (18 x 18in).

This flax has larger flowers than other blue-flowered species. The slender stems are clothed in small narrow grey-green leaves. The flowers are carried in clusters at the end of the stems. They are shaped like small saucers with silky textured petals that reflect the colour of the summer sky from early to midsummer.

USES This is not the flax used to produce linen thread. That plant is an annual *L. usitatissimum. L. narbonense* is purely decorative and, although short-lived, makes an excellent front-line plant or filler among taller perennials or small shrubs.

CULTIVATION Plant in groups of five or more 25cm (10in) apart in any well-drained soil in full sun and in a position sheltered from extreme cold. As the plants are rather vulnerable to cold wet weather it is wise to plant them in spring rather than autumn. After flowering cut the flowered stems down or leave them in the hope that they may seed themselves.

PROPAGATION As the perennial linums are short-lived it is wise to propagate them frequently to keep up a supply of young plants. They grow easily from seed but the plants will be variable, so if you don't want to take chances, divide your plants in early spring.

PESTS AND DISEASES Generally trouble free.

OTHER VARIETIES *Linum perenne* has smaller flowers and is altogether a less substantial plant but it is still worthwhile. It grows to 30 x 15cm (12 x 6in), has very thin leaves and stems and flowers in succession throughout the summer.

COMPANIONS For a very pure colour contrast, plant blue flax with the scarlet-flowered *Lychnis chalcedonica* or *L. x arkwrightii* or scatter a pool of flax with a few field poppies.

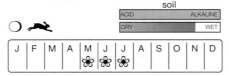

LINUM NARBONENSE

LIQUIDAMBAR STYRACIFLUA

L

Sweet gum, deciduous tree (Eastern USA, Mexico and Guatemala, 17th century). Mature at 50 years: 6m (20ft) tall after 20 years, 20 x 12m (65 x 40ft) at maturity.

Liquidambar slowly forms a symmetrical tree with an erect trunk with slender branches radiating from it to form first a pyramid and later a tall dome. The leaves are maple-like, but the flowers and seed clusters are not remarkable. The tree's moment of glory comes in autumn when the leaves take on shades of purple, crimson and orange.

USES The tree produces scented resin known as 'sweet gum' and the timber is used in furniture making under the description 'satin walnut'. It will tolerate industrial pollution.

CULTIVATION Because it is relatively slow growing it is tempting to plant liquidambar in too small a space. Make sure it has room to develop to its full spread. Plant between autumn and spring in sun or partial shade and in deep soil that does not dry out. The leaves colour best in neutral or acid soil and liquidambar is not a suitable tree for chalk or stony alkaline soils. Choose a sheltered position so that the leaves do not blow away too soon in autumn. For the first few years mulch every spring with manure or compost and water thoroughly in dry spells. If any pruning is needed to improve the shape, do it in late autumn.

PROPAGATION Layering is the easiest method for increasing stock.

PESTS AND DISEASES Generally trouble free. Tolerant of honey fungus.

GOOD VARIETIES *L. s.* 'Lane Roberts' AGM is a good form with reddish-purple autumn leaves, and 'Worplesdon' AGM has particularly red autumn colouring.

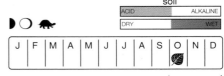

LIQUIDAMBER STYRACIFLUA 'WORPLESDON'

L

LIRIODENDRON TULIPIFERA

Tulip tree, deciduous tree (N. America, before 1688). Mature at 50 years: 12m (40ft) tall after 20 years, 25 x 12m (80 x 40ft) at maturity. AGM

This is a noble tree forming a massive columnar trunk up to 3m (10ft) in diameter. The leaves are bright light green and very distinctively shaped – broad with four shallow lobes, the tip having been squared off. They turn a uniform rich yellow in autumn. Adult trees bear plentiful large, greenish-white tulip-shaped flowers in summer. They are beautiful but not very noticeable from ground level as their colour blends with the foliage, and they are often partly hidden by the leaves.

USES In North America the tulip tree is valued for its timber, which is yellowish smooth and fine-grained and has the merit of not splitting easily. In parks and gardens it is planted as a specimen to be admired for its handsome shape and unusual leaves.

CULTIVATION Be sure that you have enough space for such a large tree to develop to its full size. Tulip trees dislike being moved and very young specimens 60cm (2ft) high will settle down quickly and soon catch up with trees planted when larger. Plant container grown specimens in late spring in good deep soil, preferably neutral or acid with a position in the sun.

PROPAGATION Sow seeds during the autumn but don't expect more than 10 per cent to germinate.

PESTS AND DISEASES Generally trouble free.

OTHER VARIETIES Where space is limited, consider *L. t.* 'Fastigiatum' AGM, a narrow, columnar form, or *L. t.* 'Aureomarginatum' AGM, a much smaller tree reaching 18 x 10m (55 x 30ft) with yellow margins to the leaves. But neither variety has quite the same dignity as the species.

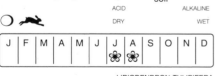

soil

| | ACID | | ALKALINE |
| | DRY | | WET |

J	F	M	A	M	J	J	A	S	O	N	D
					❀	❀					

LIRIODENDRON TULIPIFERA

LIRIOPE MUSCARI

Evergreen hardy perennial (China and Japan, early 19th century). Mature at 3 years: 30 x 45cm (12 x 18in). AGM

There is no other plant quite like this. Slowly spreading clumps of very dark green, glossy grass-like leaves colonize the ground. In late summer and autumn erect, thick stems appear, which are covered in little globular flowers that are a bright, shade of mauve.

USES The dense colonizing mats of evergreen leaves make it a good ground cover plant. Liriope is also very suitable for edging beds and borders.

CULTIVATION Plant in autumn or spring in any free-draining soil that is not too limey. Liriope will grow in sun or shade but will flower best in full sun. Tidy up the plants in spring by cutting back the old flower stems and leaves to give new growth a chance to come through.

PROPAGATION Divide and replant the roots of established plants in autumn or spring.

PESTS AND DISEASES Generally trouble free.

OTHER VARIETIES Named varieties include 'Monroe White' with white flowers. 'Variegata' has cream striped leaves but is less robust than the plain leaved species.

soil

| | ACID | | ALKALINE |
| | DRY | | WET |

J	F	M	A	M	J	J	A	S	O	N	D
								❀	❀	❀	❀

LIRIOPE MUSCARI

LOBELIA ERINUS

Half-hardy perennial treated as an annual (S. Africa, early 17th century). Mature at 6 months: 10 x 15cm (4 x 6in).

Bedding lobelias vary in habit from neat cushions of small oval or lance-shaped leaves to sprawling trailers. All through the summer and in autumn until the first frost they carry masses of little flowers with a shape somewhere between a miniature pansy and a miniature snapdragon. The colour range covers numerous shades of blue, white, mauve and red-purple. Those described in catalogues as red are very definitely on the purple side of red. Some varieties with deep blue flowers have bronzed leaves.

USES Lobelias are great favourites among bedding plants. The more compact varieties are ideal edging plants or components of complex patterns of carpet bedding, and the trailing kinds with their clouds of small flowers add a light, airy effect to hanging baskets and containers.

CULTIVATION Plant out lobelias in early summer when the danger of frost is past, in ordinary soil, setting them 7-15cm (3-6in) apart. Water during dry spells. In containers and hanging baskets use general purpose compost to which you add a slow-release fertilizer. Water daily unless it rains.

PROPAGATION Sow seeds in heat in late winter. You may be able to keep plants going through the winter if you cut back the flower stems in late summer and pot up the plants in a frost-free greenhouse. You can then increase them by division in spring.

PESTS AND DISEASES Generally trouble free.

GOOD VARIETIES Make your choice from seed catalogues or from plants already beginning to flower in the nursery or garden centre. Besides the bedding lobelias there are some splendid tall herbaceous kinds for damp soil in a warm, sheltered position. *L. cardinalis* AGM has dark green leaves, in some varieties suffused with red, and spires of brilliant scarlet flowers. They are not the easiest of plants to keep going.

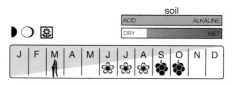

soil											
ACID									ALKALINE		
DRY									WET		

J	F	M	A	M	J	J	A	S	O	N	D
					❀	❀	❀	❀	❀		

TRAILING LOBELIAS

LONICERA PERICLYMENUM

L

Honeysuckle, woodbine, deciduous woody climber (Europe including Britain, and N. Africa). Mature at 7 years: up to 7m (22ft).

Honeysuckle leaves are light to mid green. The sweet scented tubular flowers are yellow and white streaked or suffused with red on the outside. They are borne in clusters in summer and develop into shiny translucent red berries. The scent is strongest early in the morning and in the evening.

USES Honeysuckle will quickly cover a trellis screen, arch or pergola.

CULTIVATION Plant between autumn and spring, if possible in a position where the roots can remain in shade and the stems reach sunlight. If you are planting honeysuckle against a wall or fence, a west or northwest aspect is ideal. Support the young shoots with canes leaning against the trellis or wires that they are intended to climb. Keep the roots moist with a thick mulch and water in dry spells. No pruning is necessary except occasionally to restrict size or remove dead wood. It should be done in early spring.

PROPAGATION Take cuttings in summer or layers from late summer to autumn.

PESTS AND DISEASES Aphids almost invariably infest the plants in summer and are at their worst in hot, dry weather.

GOOD VARIETIES *L. p.* 'Belgica' AGM (Early Dutch honeysuckle) flowers from early to midsummer and is followed by 'Serotina' AGM (Late Dutch). 'Graham Thomas' AGM flowers mid-way between them. *L. japonica* 'Halliana' AGM is the best all-purpose honeysuckle with the advantage of evergreen leaves. The flowers start white and fade to yellow. There are some beautiful unscented honeysuckles including *L. x brownii* 'Dropmore Scarlet'.

soil											
ACID									ALKALINE		
DRY									WET		

J	F	M	A	M	J	J	A	S	O	N	D
						❀	❀	❀	❀	❀	

LONICERA PERICLYMENUM

L

LONICERA NITIDA 'BAGGESEN'S GOLD'

Evergreen shrub. Mature at 10 years: up to 1.5 x 1.5m (5 x 5ft). AGM

This is a surprising cousin for a honeysuckle. It is the yellow-leaved form of a tough and tolerant evergreen that has been in circulation since it was introduced from China in 1908. Both shrubs have very small oval leaves densely and symmetrically arranged on straight much-branched stems. Left unpruned the bushes look like giant heads of untidy but well-cut hair. There are flowers and berries but they are hardly noticeable and usually lost by pruning.

USES 'Baggesen's Gold' adds colour to the winter scene in foliage planting schemes. It can also be used for topiary, as can the green *L. nitida*. For anyone in a hurry for an evergreen hedge, *L. nitida* gives results just as quickly as privet.

CULTIVATION For a hedge, plant *L. nitida* 30cm (12in) apart in any reasonable soil in sun or shade. Yellow and variegated forms need to be in the sun; in shade 'Baggesen's Gold' is pale lime green. Clip hedges and topiary severely in spring and again later in the year if they look shaggy. Neglected hedges or single specimens can be renovated by cutting them almost down to ground level.

PROPAGATION Take semi-ripe cuttings in midsummer or hardwood cuttings during the late autumn.

PESTS AND DISEASES Generally trouble free. Tolerant of honey fungus.

OTHER VARIETIES *L. nitida* 'Silver Beauty' is a pretty variegated form. *L. pileata* has green leaves and a horizontal habit of growth. It grows slowly to 60 x 150cm (2 x 8ft) and makes good ground cover in sun or light shade.

LUNARIA ANNUA

Syn. L. biennis. Honesty, hardy biennial (Europe including Britain). Mature at 2 years: 75 x 30cm (30 x 12in).

Despite being called *L. annua*, honesty is in fact a biennial, making bold clumps of leaves in its first season and flowering the following spring. The wide pointed leaves have serrated edges and are dark green. The flower spikes are stout enough to stand up without staking. They make a pyramid of magenta, or occasionally white flowers, single, with open four-petalled faces. The seed pods are a bonus: they are thin discs with a papery covering, which falls away to reveal a surface of translucent pearl.

USES The seed pods are excellent for winter flower arrangements and for drying.

CULTIVATION Honesty will grow in any reasonable soil in sun or shade, though its preferred situation is partial shade. Buy plants or move them from their self-seeded site to the position in which you want them to flower. Set out the plants in late summer or early autumn 30cm (12in) apart.

PROPAGATION Honesty seeds itself so freely that once you have it you will never have to do more than dig up and move the seedlings. To get the cycle started buy seed and sow outdoors in spring.

PESTS AND DISEASES Generally trouble free but the plants can be attacked by fungal diseases in a dry summer.

OTHER VARIETIES *L. rediviva* is a perennial, 60 x 30cm (2 x 1ft) with very pale pink-mauve flowers and oval rather than round seed pods. *L. annua variegata* has cream variegation at the leaf margins.

COMPANIONS For a vibrant contrast plant honesty in drifts with the lime green flower bracts of *Euphorbia amygdaloides robbiae*.

LUPINUS

Lupin, hardy perennial (N. America, 1826). Mature at 3 years: 120 x 60cm (4 x 2ft)

Lupin's soft-textured, fingered leaves and tall spikes, closely set all around with miniature scented pea flowers, are very distinctive. Many of the flowers are two-tone, the upper and lower half of each separate flower being a different colour. They come in a very wide range of colours from white and yellow to blue, violet and purple and from apricot to brick red.

USES Lupins can almost always supply the right colour to complete a scheme, as well as adding the invaluable vertical line.

CULTIVATION Lupins do best in well-drained alkaline soils, but any reasonable soil in sun or partial shade will satisfy them. Plant them in autumn or spring and mulch the plants with manure or compost every spring. If you cut off the flower stems before seed pods develop you may get a second crop of smaller flowers. Cut the plants to the ground in autumn.

PROPAGATION Lupins are easily grown from seed sown outdoors in spring, but colours will be unpredictable. To increase a particular variety take cuttings of the new young growth in early spring, before the stems have become hollow. Root them in a cool greenhouse.

PESTS AND DISEASES Aphids may attack the flower stems after the flowers have faded.

GOOD VARIETIES Before you choose, visit a horticultural show or a demonstration garden. If that is not possible, consult the catalogue of a specialist nursery. The tree lupin, *Lupinus arboreus*, is a short-lived shrub 90 x 90cm (3 x 3ft) with smaller leaves and flowers than the herbaceous lupin. The flowers are yellow or white, and fragrant.

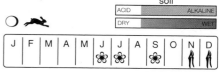

LONICERA NITIDA 'BAGGESEN'S GOLD'

LUNARIA REDIVIVA

LUPINUS

LYCHNIS CHALCEDONICA

Maltese cross, Jerusalem cross, hardy perennial (E. Russia, 1593). Mature at 3 years: 90 x 30cm (3 x 1ft). AGM

This lychnis forms a clump of stiff erect stems with oval pointed leaves. In early summer at the top of each stem it carries a flat cluster of small flowers of brilliant scarlet red.

USES The flower colour is useful in mixed plantings. The flowers last well as cut flowers.

CULTIVATION Plant in any reasonable soil in a sunny position. Cut the stems down after flowering.

PROPAGATION Divide the roots in late summer and autumn or in late winter and early spring.

PESTS AND DISEASES Generally trouble free.

OTHER VARIETIES *L. coronaria* or dusty miller, 60 x 45cm (24 x18in), is another easy perennial, flowering a little later over a long period. The magenta velvet colour of the single flat flowers is not to everyone's taste, but it is enhanced by attractive felted grey leaves and grey branching stems. White and pink forms are available.

COMPANIONS The scarlet flowers of *L. chalcedonica* and the magenta flowers of *L. coronaria* are both effective as accents to pep up pale yellow and blue or lavender colour schemes – for example with *Achillea* 'Moonshine' and blue *Campanula persicifolia*.

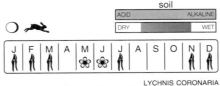

LYCHNIS CHALCEDONICA

LYSICHITON AMERICANUS

L

Bog arum, skunk cabbage, hardy perennial (Western N. America, 1901). Mature at 3 years: 1.2 x 1.8m (4 x 6ft). AGM

A giant bog plant, in early spring *Lysichiton* produces yellow arum flowers 30cm (1ft) high with green-yellow central spadices. They look splendid, but if you get too close to them your nose will be assailed by a strong unpleasant scent. The flowers are followed by very large shiny pea green leaves, giving the whole plant the appearance of a giant Cos lettuce, and remaining handsome until the autumn.

USES *Lysichiton* is an excellent weed smotherer for wet soil or along the margins of a stream.

CULTIVATION Plant single specimens in rich permanently wet soil in a bog or beside a stream or pond. Do not allow the soil to dry out. The plants take a while to become established.

PROPAGATION Sow fresh seed in late summer. Established plants will seed themselves around freely, and the seedlings sometimes become a nuisance.

PESTS AND DISEASES Generally trouble free.

OTHER VARIETIES *Lysichiton camtschatcensis* AGM, 75 x 60cm (30 x 24in), is smaller in all its parts and has white sweetly scented flowers with pale green spadices. It enjoys the same conditions as *L. americanus* and the two sometimes hybridize to produce creamy yellow flowers.

COMPANIONS In the largest scale waterside planting schemes, only *Gunnera manicata* can compete with this plant. In smaller spaces plant primulas and astilbes to follow *Lysichiton* in flower.

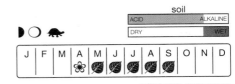

LYSICHITON AMERICANUS

L

LYSIMACHIA NUMMULARIA 'AUREA'

Creeping jenny, moneywort, hardy perennial (Britain). Mature at 3 years: 22.5-5cm (1-2in) x indefinite spread.

This is the yellow-leaved form of a ground cover plant that will grow in most conditions. It is very prostrate and increases by sending out rooting stems up to 60cm (2ft) long. The leaves are round, like coins, and cheerful buttercup flowers cover the plant in summer.

USES This is one of the most reliable ground cover plants for almost any situation including dry shade.

CULTIVATION Plant 30cm (12in) apart between late summer and spring in any reasonable soil, in sun or shade. Keep the site weeded until cover is established.

PROPAGATION Detach the rooted stems and replant.

PESTS AND DISEASES Generally trouble free.

OTHER VARIETIES *Lysimachia punctata* (yellow loosestrife), 60-75cm (2ft-2ft6in) tall, is also a good ground cover plant. From mid- to late summer it carries stiff spikes of brassy yellow starry flowers. It spreads too vigorously in beds and borders, but looks right beside water.

COMPANIONS Plant *Lysimachia nummularia* 'Aurea' in drifts with *Viola labradorica* or *Ajuga reptans* 'Purpurea'.

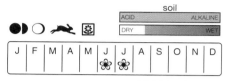

soil

| ACID | | ALKALINE |
| DRY | | WET |

| J | F | M | A | M | J | J | A | S | O | N | D |

LYSIMACHIA PUNCTATA

LYSIMACHIA NUMMULARIA 'AUREA'

LYTHRUM SALICARIA

Purple loosestrife, hardy perennial (Europe including Britain). Mature at 3 years: 75 x 45cm (30 x 18in) or more.

In the wild, purple loosestrife is a bog or waterside plant, but it is equally at home in a border provided the soil stays moist. From a clump of lance-shaped leaves numerous stems spring up covered in magenta, rose-red or pink flowers, from mid to late summer. Sometimes the leaves colour red and orange in autumn.

USES Loosestrife is easy to naturalize in wet soil; a good plant for the wild garden, it is a late source of nectar for butterflies and bees. The emperor moth and the small elephant hawkmoth feed on the leaves.

CULTIVATION Plant between late summer and spring in any reasonable soil, preferably moist or even boggy, in sun or shade. Cut down the flower stems before they go to seed, unless you want to encourage the plants to naturalize.

PROPAGATION Sow seeds in early spring or early autumn, or divide the roots.

PESTS AND DISEASES Generally trouble free.

GOOD VARIETIES *L. salicaria* 'Feuerkerze' ('Firecandle') AGM is an old favourite. It has intense rose-red flowers. More recent introductions include 'Dropmore Purple' with deep pink-purple flower spikes and dark green leaves.

COMPANIONS A strong colour lcombination can be achieved by planting purple loosestrife and yellow loosestrife together: a sight best seen from a distance across water.

soil

| ACID | | ALKALINE |
| DRY | | WET |

| J | F | M | A | M | J | J | A | S | O | N | D |

LYTHRUM SALICARIA

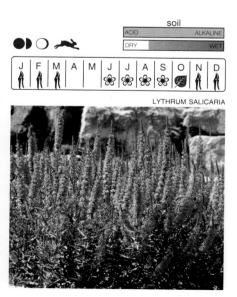

MAGNOLIA X SOULANGEANA

A hybrid between **M. denudata** *and* **M. liliiflora** *(both from China, 1820s), deciduous shrub or small tree. Mature at 40 years: 3 x 1.8m (10 x 6ft) after 10 years, 6 x 6m (20 x 20ft) at maturity.*

This is a wide spreading, low branching tree. In spring the bare branches are covered in large goblet-shaped satiny flowers, white inside and flushed with soft red-purple on the outside. A fresh supply of fragrant flowers continues until midsummer while the green glossy oval leaves unfurl. All magnolias are slow growing; *M. x soulangeana* takes up to five years to flower, and other species may take even longer.

USES Magnolias make lovely specimens on lawns or in other situations where they can be appreciated without distraction. They are tolerant of air pollution.

CULTIVATION Most magnolias prefer neutral or acid soil but do quite well on alkaline soil provided it is not dry. On hot, dry chalk, *M. kobus*, *M. sieboldii* and *M. wilsonii* AGM may be grown successfully, but moisture is important on chalk or sandy soils and leaf mould or compost should be added when planting, and used to mulch the root area. Give magnolias a sheltered position in sun or partial shade. The best time to plant is late spring or early summer. Pruning should not be necessary but damaged or straggly branches can be cut back in early spring.

PROPAGATION Take semi-ripe cuttings in summer or sow seeds in autumn, but they may take more than a year to germinate.

PESTS AND DISEASES Generally trouble free.

GOOD VARIETIES *M x s.* 'Brozzoni' AGM is a vigorous late flowering form with white flowers. *M x s.* 'Lennei' AGM is vigorous with plenty of large pink flowers; 'Rustica Rubra' AGM is purple-pink and *M. liliiflora* 'Nigra' AGM is the darkest. *M. stellata* AGM and its several varieties are compact shrubs up to 3 x 3m (10 x 10ft) with starry white or pink flowers. *M. grandiflora* 'Exmouth' is the evergreen magnolia often trained against the walls of large houses, and it does need a large house to develop to its full potential. The dark green glossy leaves have rusty down on their undersides, and the huge cream, highly scented flowers appear at intervals from midsummer till autumn.

COMPANIONS The roots of magnolias are vulnerable, so avoid planting anything which involves much digging. A low ground cover such as *Viola labradorica* or *Ajuga*, or a carpet of small blue or white spring bulbs such as *Anemone blanda* is all that is needed. Avoid yellow flowers or foliage near pink or purple magnolias.

MAGNOLIA X SOULANGEANA 'LENNEI ALBA'

MAHONIA AQUIFOLIUM

Oregon grape, evergreen shrub (N. America, 1823). Mature at 15 years: 90 x 120cm (3 x 4ft)

A real toughie, this mahonia is as hardy as they come. It spreads by means of suckers, slowly forming a dense low thicket. The leaves are glossy and prickly like holly. At the tip of each shoot erect clusters of tightly packed little scented flowers appear, a few in late winter and many more in spring. They are a cheerful yellow and develop into bunches of black berries with a blue grapey bloom. The leaves turn purplish in frost.

USES *Mahonia aquifolium* makes one of the most effective and dependable ground covers in the open or under deciduous trees or shrubs. It tolerates pollution.

CULTIVATION Plant between autumn and spring, setting plants 60cm (2ft) apart for ground cover. They will grow in almost any soil in sun or shade. To keep the growth dense, prune hard every second year in early summer.

PROPAGATION Dig up rooted suckers and replant between late summer and spring, or take cuttings in early autumn.

PESTS AND DISEASES The plants sometimes suffer from rust. If it appears, cut off and burn affected branches and spray the plants with a systemic fungicide. Mahonias are tolerant of honey fungus.

OTHER VARIETIES *Mahonia aquifolium* 'Apollo' AGM has larger flowers and more scent than the species. There are several tall mahonias with long racemes of sweetly scented flowers in midwinter. *M. japonica* AGM is the hardiest and *M. x media* 'Charity' comes next.

COMPANIONS Informal planting suits mahonias best, such as a foreground of naturalized spring bulbs or dark hellebores.

MAHONIA AQUIFOLIUM

M

MALUS CORONARIA 'CHARLOTTAE'

MALUS 'JOHN DOWNIE'

Crab apple. Mature at 30 years: 5.5 x 2.5m (18 x 8ft) after 10 years, 8 x 5m (26 x 16ft) at maturity.

This is one of the last of the crab apples to come into flower, from late spring to early summer. The shell pink semi-double flowers are larger than most and sweetly scented. The fruit is inconspicuous but the maple-like leaves colour well in autumn. Other crabs spectacular in flower but without showy fruit include the popular *Malus floribunda* AGM flowering in early spring with attractive spreading branches. Shapely *Malus tschonoskii* AGM has leaves that turn scarlet and orange in autumn.

USES Crab apples are amenable to training on walls and as espaliers and cordons to make divisions within the garden. They tolerate industrial pollution. The fruit is too sour for puddings and pies but can be used to make crab apple jelly.

CULTIVATION Plant in autumn in any soil that is not waterlogged. Prune in winter to remove diseased or weak growth and maintain a good shape.

PROPAGATION Increase your stock by budding or grafting.

PESTS AND DISEASES Aphids, caterpillars and red spider mite can attack trees, also fireblight and apple scab. Malus are all susceptible to honey fungus.

OTHER VARIETIES For orchard fruit, see under 'Apples' on page 74. There is a wide choice of ornamental crab apples. The following list suggests some of the most reliable varieties.

MALUS 'ROYALTY'

MALUS BACCATA

'Evereste', 3 x 2m (10 x 6ft) after 10 years, 5 x 4m (16 x 13ft) at maturity; compact with a rounded crown and deep pink buds opening to white flowers in mid spring. The orange-red apples ripen in mid autumn and are retained through the winter. This also applies to 'Red Sentinel', a fine, larger tree – 8 x 6m (26 x 19ft) – with deep red apples, but 'Evereste' has the bonus of autumn leaf colour. 'Profusion', 6 x 3m (19 x 10ft) after ten years, 7 x 5m (23 x 16ft) at maturity; crimson flowers, purple leaves and dark red fruit make a distinctive contribution to the garden, but trees with this colouring are particularly prone to scab and canker. 'Profusion' is the healthiest. The flowers are red-purple in bud, fading to dark pink. 'Royalty' is a similar variety with glossy purple leaves, crimson to purple flowers and crimson fruit. *M.baccata* is a large tree to 15m (50ft), with tiny red or yellow fruit. 'Golden Hornet' is smaller, with white flowers and golden yellow apples. The popular 'John Downie' has white flowers followed by reddish-orange fruit. 'Winter Gold' 5 x 3.5m (16 x 11ft) after ten years, 8 x 5m (26 x 16ft) at maturity is a rounded tree with typical pink and white apple blossom in late spring. 'Winter Gold' retains its fruit longer than any of the other yellow-fruited crabs, for up to fifteen weeks. *Malus x robusta* 'Yellow Siberian' is next best in this respect. It is a smaller tree, 5 x 6m (16 x 19ft), flowers earlier and has good autumn colour.

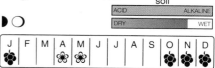

soil	
ACID	ALKALINE
DRY	WET

J	F	M	A	M	J	J	A	S	O	N	D

MALUS 'GOLDEN HORNET'

MALVA MOSCHATA ALBA

Musk mallow, hardy perennial (Europe including Britain). Mature at 1 year: 60 x 60cm (2 x 2ft).

A basal clump of rounded leaves throws up stout stems with different, finely-cut lacy leaves. The stems are studded with open bowl-shaped white flowers from midsummer to early autumn. The seed pods are like pointed quartered buttons starting pale green and turning black.

USES The leaves are said to be edible if cooked. In the garden, use this mallow to colonize difficult ground or to soften areas of gravel or paving.

CULTIVATION Plant betweeen autumn and spring in any soil that is not waterlogged, from slightly acid to very alkaline, in sun or light shade. In good rich soil the flower stems will grow to 75cm (30in) or taller, and will need the support of pea sticks or canes. In poor dry situations they will be shorter and self-supporting. If you do not want the plants to self-seed, be vigilant and remove the flower stems before the seeds ripen. Musk mallows are in flower for a very long season and you can make it still longer by regular dead-heading. In autumn cut the stems to the ground.

PROPAGATION Take cuttings of basal shoots in spring or sow seeds early in the spring. The plants are not long-lived, so propagate often.

PESTS AND DISEASES Generally trouble free.

OTHER VARIETIES The form of *Malva moschata* usually found in the wild has flowers of pale clear pink.

COMPANIONS In the wild the musk mallow can sometimes be seen in hedgerows with *Geranium pratense*, the meadow cranesbill, and they look good together in the garden.

MATTEUCCIA STRUTHIOPTERIS

Ostrich plume fern, shuttlecock fern, hardy deciduous rhizomatous fern (northern hemisphere, 1766). Mature at 3 years: 90 x 45cm (3ft x 18in).

This is the only hardy fern to make a single central stem. It grows to about 23cm (9in) and from it a shuttlecock of fronds emerges each spring, pale green and intricately cut, giving a delicate lacy effect. These sterile fronds remain beautiful until late summer when they begin to give way to the fertile central fronds, which are dark brown and remain erect through the winter.

USES This is a beautiful fern particularly suitable for the waterside.

CULTIVATION *Matteuccia struthiopteris* must have damp soil and shelter from cold winds. It is quite happy when planted in a bog or at the margin of a stream or pond. Plant in spring in a sheltered lightly shaded site, adding leaf mould or garden compost to the planting hole. Remove old fronds as they fade.

PROPAGATION Divide the rhizomes of crowded clumps in autumn or winter.

PESTS AND DISEASES Generally trouble free.

OTHER VARIETIES This is the only type that is generally available.

COMPANIONS This is a plant to use in a restful, all-green colour scheme. Its fresh light green colouring shows to advantage against a background of dark ivy ground cover; the spikey leaves of irises would make an effective contrast in form.

MATTHIOLA

White perennial stock, evergreen hardy perennial (S. Europe, 18th century). Mature at 2 years: 60 x 45cm (2ft x 18in)

This short-lived perennial is a close relation of the biennial Brompton stock and has similar lance-shaped grey leaves carried in symmetrical whorls. At the centre of each whorl there are clusters of white flowers with a heady scent, especially in the evening. They bloom from early to midsummer then develop into long, smooth grey seed pods. Most stocks are treated as annuals, fresh stock being raised from seed each year. This one is a short-lived perennial but it is worth keeping it going for two or three years, after which it deteriorates, the main stem becoming bare, woody and fibrous like a cabbage stalk, and the flowers sparse.

USES Planted by a door or beneath a window, the perennial stock will waft its scent into the house, particularly at dusk. The flowers are good for cutting.

CULTIVATION Plant in autumn or spring in sun or partial shade in any reasonable garden soil, but stocks are particularly happy in limey soil. During the flowering season dead-head regularly to keep up a supply of new flowering stems.

PROPAGATION Take semi-ripe cuttings in summer or sow seeds under glass during early spring. Seeds can also be sown a little later outdoors.

PESTS AND DISEASES Generally trouble free but there is risk of aphids, flea beetle, club root, downy mildew and botrytis.

OTHER VARIETIES Brompton stocks, ten-week stocks and night-scented stocks are all worth growing as annuals to fill gaps in beds and borders, to fill containers and to provide cut flowers.

MALVA MOSCHATA

MATTEUCCIA STRUTHIOPTERIS

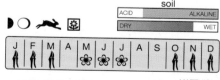

MATTHIOLA

M

MECONOPSIS CAMBRICA

Welsh poppy, hardy perennial (Europe including Britain). Mature at 1 year: 30 x 30cm (12 x 12in).

This easy poppy forms clumps of fresh looking, ferny bright green leaves. The single cup-shaped flowers are bright lemon yellow or clear light orange. Their petals have the same crumpled fragility as those of field poppies. Double flowered forms are also available.

USES Welsh poppies seed themselves freely and are apt to become a nuisance in borders, but where there is space they are lovely naturalized in wilder parts of the garden.

CULTIVATION Plant in groups of five or more in light shade in any reasonable soil that does not dry out. If you don't want the plants to seed themselves, be vigilant about removing the seed heads before they ripen. But the best policy is to plant them where they can increase to their heart's content.

PROPAGATION Scatter the seed where you want it to grow as soon as it is ripe, or in early spring.

PESTS AND DISEASES Generally trouble free.

OTHER VARIETIES The Himalayan blue poppies, *M. betonicifolia* and *M. grandis* are sadly not for the average garden. They need soil that is lime-free and permanently moist in a sheltered, partly shaded position, with a cool atmosphere.

COMPANIONS Both the orange and the yellow Welsh poppies look wonderful when flowering among bluebells.

soil

ACID		ALKALINE
DRY		WET

J	F	M	A	M	J	J	A	S	O	N	D

MECONOPSIS CAMBRICA

MELISSA OFFICINALIS 'AUREA'

Golden balm, hardy perennial (Europe including Britain). Mature at 3 years: 60 x 60cm (2 x 2ft).

Balm or lemon balm forms a dense rounded clump of broadly oval, soft hairy leaves. They give off a lemony scent when crushed. In the form 'Aurea' the leaves have a yellow variegation. The flowers are small and insignificant.

USES Balm is an ancient medicinal herb, used as an antidepressant and said to have contributed to the longevity of one John Hussey, who lived to one hundred and sixteen years having breakfasted on balm tea with honey for fifty of those years. It is also said to bring relief from insect bites and to relieve the symptoms of bronchial catarrh and colds.

CULTIVATION Plant balm in autumn or spring 30cm (12in) apart. It will grow in any reasonable soil in sun or light shade, but the variegated and golden forms need shade to prevent the leaves scorching. If you want to dry the leaves, cut the stems when the flowers are just beginning to open. After flowering, cut the stems to the ground to encourage fresh new growth.

PROPAGATION Balm seeds itself all too freely, and seedlings of 'Aurea' revert to plain green. Otherwise it is easily increased by division.

OTHER VARIETIES There is another form that has leaves that are yellow all over, called 'All Gold'.

COMPANIONS Nearly all culinary and medicinal herbs seem to have an affinity with each other and this is no exception. Planted in the herb garden golden balm's soft mound of foliage will contrast well with feathery fennel and spikey lavender. In borders it provides a good foil to magenta and purple phlox.

soil

ACID		ALKALINE
DRY		WET

J	F	M	A	M	J	J	A	S	O	N	D

MELISSA OFFICINALIS 'AUREA'

MENTHA

Mint, hardy perennial (Europe including Britain). Mature at 3 years: from 1cm ($^1/_2$in) to 1m (3ft) tall with indefinite spread.

Most mints are aggressive colonizers by means of running roots, and all have distinctively scented leaves. If you grow mint for the kitchen it makes sense to choose the more decorative varieties: for descriptions see 'Good Varieties' below.

USES The traditional English dish of roast lamb with mint sauce is rather out of favour now, but there are plenty of other culinary uses for mint: chopped into a yoghurt dressing for cucumber, flavouring new potatoes, baby carrots and peas, with fruit drinks and salads.

CULTIVATION Plant mint in any soil that doesn't dry out, in sun or shade. At midsummer cut the stems to the ground to stimulate a second crop of young leaves (leave a clump for use until the new shoots grow). For winter use pot up a few roots for the kitchen windowsill.

PROPAGATION Divide the roots during autumn or spring.

PESTS AND DISEASES Generally trouble free.

GOOD VARIETIES The smallest is *M. requienii* creeping along the ground with tiny peppermint leaves and tiny mauve flowers in summer. It does best in shade. *M. suaveolens*, syn. *M. rotundifolia* is apple mint. It is the most decorative of the culinary mints and has rounded woolly light green leaves on 60cm (2ft) stems. Its variegated form, *M. s.* 'Variegata' is the prettiest of mints, with creamy-white splashed leaves. It is a useful ground cover plant for light shade.

COMPANIONS Rather negative but important advice: keep mint well away from any precious little plants.

soil

ACID		ALKALINE
DRY		WET

J	F	M	A	M	J	J	A	S	O	N	D

MENTHA SUAVEOLENS 'VARIEGATA'

MESPILUS GERMANICA

Medlar, deciduous tree (Europe and Asia Minor, naturalized in S. England). Mature at 30 years: up to 6 x 6m (20 x 20ft).

The medlar is a very hardy, attractive, old-fashioned small tree with spreading, crooked branches which make a canopy like a broken umbrella. The leaves are broad, oval and bright green with minutely toothed margins. In early summer flowers are borne singly at the end of short branches. They have five large white petals, sometimes tinged with pink, and red anthers at the centre. In autumn small brown apple-shaped fruit develop and the leaves turn orange-brown before falling.

USES At maturity medlars are excellent shade trees for small gardens. The fruit, if left on the tree during the autumn and then stored until half-rotted, are edible: an acquired taste, but medlar jelly is good, specially with game dishes.

CULTIVATION Plant medlars between autumn and spring in any reasonable soil in a sunny or semi-shaded position. The only pruning necessary is to remove weak or overcrowded branches during the winter. Pick the fruit before the first frosts and store it until it is over-ripe (bletted), for about a month.

PROPAGATION Sow seeds of the species during the autumn. Named forms must be budded or grafted.

PESTS AND DISEASES Generally trouble free.

GOOD VARIETIES *Mespilus germanica* 'Nottingham' is the one usually grown for the size and flavour of its fruit.

COMPANIONS Best grown as an isolated specimen on a lawn or patio with small naturalized spring bulbs at its base, and perhaps a carpet of *Cyclamen coum* too.

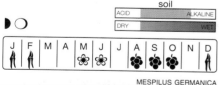

MESPILUS GERMANICA

METASEQUOIA GLYPTOSTROBOIDES

Dawn redwood, deciduous coniferous tree (China, 1948). Mature at 30 years: 5m (16ft) tall after 10 years; height at maturity up to 40m (131ft) in the wild; it is too early to know what height it may reach in European gardens.

One of the fastest growing trees available, the metasequoia is a tall columnar conifer with soft light blue-green leaves and fibrous red-brown bark. It is not planted nearly as often as the leyland cypress when a quick screen is needed, presumably because it is not evergreen. But it makes up for that deficiency by producing glowing yellow, pink and red autumn colour.

USES Plant metasequoias to lighten a group of darker conifers, as a handsome single specimen or as part of a quick-growing screen. It tolerates industrial pollution.

CULTIVATION Plant in early autumn or late spring in any ordinary soil. It prefers soil that does not dry out, growing more slowly on sandy or chalky soil. Avoid frost pockets, choosing a site in sun or light shade, sheltered from cold winds.

PROPAGATION Take half-ripe cuttings in summer and place in bottom heat, or later on place hardwood cuttings in a cold frame.

PESTS AND DISEASES Generally trouble free.

OTHER VARIETIES One or two named varieties have appeared; however they are not easily available and it is too early to know if they are significantly different from the species.

COMPANIONS It is useful for bridging the gap between conifers and hardwoods in groups of trees.

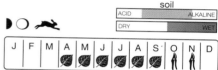

METASEQUOIA GLYPTOSTROBOIDES

M

MIMULUS GUTTATUS

*Monkey musk, hardy perennial
(N.America, 1826). Mature at 3 years:
60 x 60cm (2 x 2ft).*

This plant has become naturalized in wet
places in Britain. It produces lush green
growth with oval leaves and a succession of
yellow flowers dappled with red-brown,
like large flatter snapdragons, from
midsummer until autumn. Some of the
hybrid forms are very attractive (see 'Good
varieties' below).

USES Monkey musk is rather invasive, so
use it in difficult damp spots where other
plants will not do well. The hybrid forms
can be used in more prominent positions,
the perennials in a bog garden, annuals in
pots and hanging baskets.

CULTIVATION Plant in spring in full sun in
soil that does not dry out, including boggy
soil. Cut down stems after flowering.

PROPAGATION Divide *M. guttatus* in spring.
Sow seeds of perennials treated as annuals
in early spring in heat.

PESTS AND DISEASES Generally trouble free.

OTHER VARIETIES M. Calypso hybrids
AGM, 15 x 30cm (6 x 12in), are half-hardy
perennials treated as annuals. Branching
stems carry tubular flared flowers in
yellow, orange and red all summer.
'Whitecroft Scarlet' is a short-lived half-
hardy perennial 20 x 30cm (8 x 12in), with
masses of vibrant scarlet snapdragon
flowers all summer.

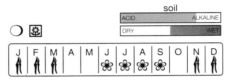

MIMULUS GUTTATUS

MISCANTHUS SINENSIS

*Hardy perennial grass (China, Japan
1875). Mature at 5 years: 1.8m x 60cm
(6 x 2ft).*

This tall grass forms an elegant clump of
erect stems with narrow, ribbon-like leaves.
Only two forms, 'Silberfeder' ('Silver
Feather') and 'Zebrinus' (the Tiger grass)
produce flowers regularly in Britain.

USES These distinctive graceful grasses are
valuable in the garden as an antidote to the
different shapes and textures of more
colourful plants. Both the leaves and
flowering stems provide material for flower
arranging and for drying.

CULTIVATION Plant during spring in any
ordinary soil, moist or dry, in sun or shade.
Leave the dry leaves and flower stems (if
any) on the plant during the winter months
and cut them down as soon as there is a
sign of new growth in spring.

PROPAGATION Divide established clumps
during the spring.

PESTS AND DISEASES Generally trouble free.

OTHER VARIETIES 'Silberfeder' is similar to
the species but with the bonus of graceful
arching stems with silky plumes of pale
buff pink appearing in early autumn.
'Zebrinus' makes a fountain of green leaves
with horizontal yellow stripes, and may
produce feathery pinky-brown flower
sprays in autumn.

COMPANIONS Gertrude Jekyll thought it
desirable to use plants with bold foliage
next to grasses, and suggested bergenias.
Hostas would be good too.

MISCANTHUS SINENSIS 'KLEINE SILBERSPINNE'

MOLINIA CAERULEA

Ssp. caerulea 'Variegata', variegated purple moor grass, hardy perennial grass (Europe including Britain). Mature at 3 years: 60 x 30cm (2 x 1ft). AGM

This grass makes short neat tufts of arching narrow leaves, bright green with lengthwise cream stripes. In late summer buff flower plumes with purple spikelets are held on cream stems. The whole plant fades to pale buff in winter.

USES It could be part of a group planned for winter effect, and is tidy enough to be used for edging.

CULTIVATION Although the species is a native of acid moorland, this variety seems to grow happily in any soil, when planted in a sunny position.

PROPAGATION Divide established clumps during the spring.

PESTS AND DISEASES Generally trouble free.

GOOD VARIETIES *M. c.* ssp. *c.* 'Heidebraut' is another, taller grass for winter effect, with stiff straw-coloured stems topped with multiple seed heads. It reaches 1.2-1.5m (4-5ft) in height. 'Moorhexe' forms a stiff upright column of needle-like flower stems 45cm (18in) high.

COMPANIONS Grasses always look right grouped with other grasses, but recently they have also become popular components of mixed plantings, used as accents in drifts of herbaceous plants such as achilleas or hardy geraniums, or planted in drifts themselves to interlock with other groups.

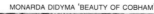

MOLINA CAERULEA SSP. CAERULEA 'VARIEGATA'

MONARDA

Bee balm, bergamot, Oswego tea, hardy perennial (N. America, 1744). Mature at 3 years: 60-100 x 45cm (2-3ft x 18in).

From a basal clump of oval pointed leaves, erect square leafy stems grow, topped with tightly packed circles of sage-like hooded flowers, giving a shaggy effect from mid- to late summer. Colours are reds, pinks, purples, mauves and white.

USES Apart from their decorative qualities in mixed and herbaceous planting schemes, monardas have herbal uses. The leaves are used to flavour tea, jellies and jams, and a steam inhalation is said to relieve bronchitis and sore throats.

CULTIVATION Plant in spring in moist soil and in a sunny position, preferably in groups of five or more, setting the plants 45cm (18in) apart. Mulch every spring with manure or compost and water in dry spells. Cut the stems to the ground any time between autumn and spring.

PROPAGATION Divide established clumps in spring, discarding the old centre of the plant.

PESTS AND DISEASES Many varieties suffer from mildew, particularly older kinds. As soon as mildew appears, spray with a systemic fungicide.

GOOD VARIETIES Old favourites include 'Cambridge Scarlet' AGM, 'Croftway Pink' AGM, and 'Beauty of Cobham', soft pink and mauve. Unfortunately they are all liable to suffer from mildew. Newer varieties are mildew resistant. 'Aquarius' is pale lilac, 'Capricorn' purple and 'Pisces' pink. 'Squaw' is a mildew resistant variety.

COMPANIONS For flowers in a similar colour range, plant penstemons and phlox with monardas. For contrast choose pale yellow hemerocallis or evening primrose.

MONARDA DIDYMA 'BEAUTY OF COBHAM'

MORUS NIGRA

Black mulberry, deciduous tree (the Orient, introduced before the early 16th century). Mature at 60 years: 4 x 4m (17 x 17ft) after 20 years, up to 12 x 15m (40 x 50ft) at maturity. AGM

Mulberry trees branch from low down to make a dense spreading crown, usually wider than it is high. Although mulberries are slow growing, the rough trunk and much-branched habit result in an attractive appearance quite early in the tree's life. The leaves are broad and heart-shaped with toothed margins, glossy bright green, turning yellow in autumn. The fruits ripen in late summer or early autumn. They look like large dark red-black raspberries and have a pleasant, distinctive flavour. The juice stains clothes indelibly.

USES Although the fruit can be used for puddings, tarts and jam, the trees are planted for their attractive character rather than for their produce. The leaves can be used to feed silkworms, but *Morus alba* is the tree usually grown for that purpose.

CULTIVATION Plant in autumn or spring in ordinary soil in a sunny position. Mulch the root area for the first few years. If pruning is needed to shape the tree, do it in winter. The dropping fruit may be a nuisance, staining paving outdoors or carpets inside if carried on the soles of shoes. If this is a problem, polythene sheets can be laid on the ground to catch the falling fruit.

PROPAGATION Summer cuttings root easily. Branches that touch the ground usually root down.

PESTS AND DISEASES Generally trouble free.

OTHER VARIETIES *Morus alba*, the white mulberry, is grown in China to provide food for silkworms. There is a weeping form, *M. alba* 'Pendula'.

MORUS NIGRA

M

MUSCARI ARMENIACUM

Grape hyacinth, hardy bulb (Europe). Mature at 6 months: 15-20 x 8-10cm (6-8 x 3-4in). AGM

Grape hyacinths make rather untidy clumps of narrow, strap-shaped leaves which tend to flop over. In spring upright smooth pale green stems emerge from the tangled leaves with densely packed spikes of small round blue flowers. They are intense cobalt blue with thin white rims.

USES They are sometimes used for edging beds but the untidy leaves are a problem. They are quite robust enough to naturalize in thin grass where the leaves are unobtrusive, and this seems to me to be the best way to use them.

CULTIVATION Plant the bulbs from late summer to autumn, 5cm (2in) deep in heavy soil, 10cm (4in) in light sandy soil. They should be planted in generous drifts, at random spacing between 2.4 and 10 cm (1in and 4in) apart. After the bulbs have flowered, allow the leaves to fade before cutting them down. To grow in pots for the house, plant in general purpose compost 2.5cm (1in) deep. Leave the pots outdoors under a layer of ashes or bark mulch until growth starts, then bring them indoors, acclimatizing them gradually. After flowering leave the pots outside in a sunny position until the leaves fade or plant the bulbs outside immediately.

PROPAGATION Lift and divide established clumps. When they are suited, muscari will seed themselves freely. It takes a seedling three or four years to reach flowering stage.

PESTS AND DISEASES Mice and other small creatures may eat the bulbs.

OTHER VARIETIES There are several named varieties including a white one, 'Album', which is pretty but not as robust as the blue.

COMPANIONS In wild areas the blue makes a lovely contrast with pale yellow dwarf narcissi. In containers or formal beds try planting them as a background to yellow or white tulips.

MUSCARI ARMENIACUM

MYOSOTIS

Forget-me-not, hardy perennial treated as a biennial (Europe). Mature at 2 years: 25 x 25cm (8 x 10in).

Forget-me-nots grow from ground-hugging clumps of soft greyish-green lance-shaped leaves with rounded tips. In late spring and early summer branching stems carry clusters of little star-shaped flowers, intense sky blue with yellow centres.

USES A great standby for filling spring gaps which will later be taken over by herbaceous plants, forget-me-nots are also used in formal bedding schemes and in containers. They are used in homeopathy.

CULTIVATION In autumn plant in groups 15cm (6in) apart, preferably in light shade, but they can also cope with full sun. After flowering pull them out as soon as the flowers fade, leaving a few plants to seed themselves if you want.

PROPAGATION Sow seed outside in rows from spring to midsummer, thin out as they develop and transplant into final positions in early autumn to flower the following season. Alternatively, in summer take plants that have gone to seed and shake them over the areas you want colonized.

PESTS AND DISEASES Almost invariably, myosotis suffer from mildew towards the end of their flowering life. Pull up affected plants and put them on the bonfire.

OTHER VARIETIES Different seed merchants have different named varieties. There are kinds with pink flowers and white. *Myosotis scorpioides* is the water forget-me-not, to be grown at the margins in mud or very shallow water.

COMPANIONS Forget-me-nots are often planted with tulips or wallflowers in spring bedding. They are also useful under roses and other summer-flowering shrubs.

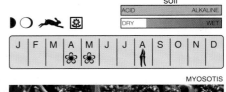

MYOSOTIS

MYRRHIS ODORATA

MYRTUS COMMUNIS

M

Sweet cecily, hardy perennial (Europe including Britain). Mature at 2 years: 60 x 60cm (2 x 2ft).

This is like an elegant version of cow parsley, with aromatic fresh green, finely-cut ferny leaves. The tiny white flowers are carried on umbrella-shaped heads at the top of branching stems in early summer. The immature seeds are light green, oblong and ridged; they turn black as they ripen.

USES The seeds can be eaten in salads or with ice cream while they are still green. They taste of aniseed and have a nutty texture. The leaves are used to flavour soups and stews and to cut the acidity of fruit such as rhubarb and gooseberries, reducing the need for sugar to sweeten them. The root can be eaten cooked or raw. As sweet cecily grows in shade it is useful to lighten dark corners of the garden.

CULTIVATION Plant in autumn or spring in any ordinary soil in sun or shade. Set the plants in groups of three or more, 60cm (2ft) apart. If you don't want the plants to self-seed, cut down the stems as the flowers fade. Otherwise cut down the whole plant in autumn or winter.

PROPAGATION Sow seeds outdoors in late summer or spring or divide the roots in autumn or spring.

PESTS AND DISEASES Generally trouble free.

COMPANIONS In the shade, plant *Anemone x hybrida* with sweet cecily to carry on the white theme later in the season.

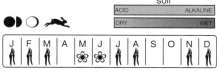

MYRRHIS ODORATA

Myrtle, tender evergreen shrub (W. Asia). Mature at 20 years: 90 x 90cm after 5 years; 4 x 2m (12 x 6ft) at maturity.

Myrtle is a dense and bushy evergreen with shiny oval pointed leaves and fragrant single white flowers with a boss of fluffy stamens from mid- to late summer, followed by purple-black berries. The leaves are scented when crushed.

USES Myrtle will only survive winter in mild areas or in very sheltered situations, and in other conditions is best grown in a pot and brought in during the coldest months. But it is wind resistant and can be used in hedges or windbreaks in mild seaside gardens. Myrtle responds well to training and can be grown as a standard or clipped into formal shapes. Whether used formally or informally, it is an excellent pot plant for patios and terraces.

CULTIVATION Plant in sun or partial shade in a sheltered position, for example against a south-facing wall, in any well-drained soil including chalk. Cover young plants with horticultural fleece in winter to protect them from frost. Frost-damaged shoots can be pruned out in spring, and hedges or topiary cut in early summer.

PROPAGATION Cuttings can be taken in late autumn and rooted in a propagator or a frost-free greenhouse or frame.

PESTS AND DISEASES Generally trouble free.

OTHER VARIETIES *Myrtus communis* ssp. *tarentina* AGM is smaller in all its parts, eventually reaching 2 x 2m (6 x 6ft). *M. c.* 'Variegata' is tender and will not survive outdoors except in the mildest climates.

MYRTUS COMMUNIS

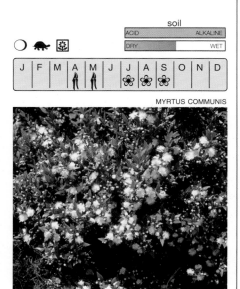

N

NANDINA DOMESTICA 'FIREPOWER'

Sacred bamboo, evergreen shrub (China, Japan, 1804). Mature at 7 years: 1.5 x 1m (5 x 3ft).

This elegant bamboo-like shrub is almost hardy but needs a sheltered position. The deeply divided leaves are stained with red when they first open and become pale to mid-green as they mature. In autumn they become brilliant shades of orange, red and pink. Small delicate star-shaped white flowers are carried in loose clusters after midsummer; in warm areas they may be followed by scarlet berries, which ripen in late summer and persist through winter.

USES Plant nandina for the sake of its dazzling autumn colour.

CULTIVATION Plant in rich moist well-drained soil between spring and early summer in a sunny sheltered position. In severe winters the leaves may be scorched and the tips of the branches killed by frost, but the plant usually recovers. No pruning is needed except to remove dead wood and weak shoots after flowering and, on mature plants, to take out some of the oldest stems to let some light in to the plant's centre.

PROPAGATION Take semi-ripe cuttings of *N. d.* 'Firepower' in summer. The species can be grown from seed.

PESTS AND DISEASES Generally trouble-free.

OTHER VARIETIES The species is a larger plant, 2 x 2m (6 x 6ft).

COMPANIONS Plant nandina with white *Anemone* x *hybrida* and with blue *Aster thomsonii* 'Nanus'.

soil

| ACID | | | | | | | | | | | ALKALINE |
| DRY | | | | | | | | | | | WET |

J	F	M	A	M	J	J	A	S	O	N	D

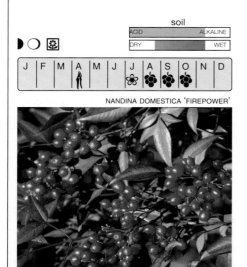
NANDINA DOMESTICA 'FIREPOWER'

NARCISSUS

Daffodil, jonquil, hardy bulb (Europe including Britain, N. Africa). Mature at 6 months: various heights.

Daffodils, the inspiration of poets and a familiar sight in every park and garden in spring, hardly need describing. Their grassy leaves and skirted, trumpet-shaped flowers come in a wide range of shapes and sizes with many variations on the colour themes of yellow, white and orange.

USES Daffodils can be naturalized in grass, grown in pots, troughs and window boxes indoors and out, and cut for flower arranging. The miniature varieties can be planted in rock gardens or alpine beds.

CULTIVATION Plant the bulbs in any reasonable soil that is not waterlogged, in sun or partial shade in late summer or early autumn. However, it does not seem to matter if you are late. I have planted daffodils already sprouting in early spring and they have still flowered. If you are planting large numbers in grass it is worth using a bulb planter. The hole should be three times the depth of the bulb. Let the leaves fade and turn yellow before removing them, so the foliage can feed the bulbs. Don't tie the leaves in knots: it weakens the bulbs by reducing the leaf surface exposed to the sun, thus preventing the formation of food reserves in the bulb. Split up established clumps in summer when the leaves have turned yellow and you can still see where the bulbs are. You can either replant them immediately or dry them off and store them until later.

PROPAGATION Lift clumps and remove bulb offsets, planting them separately to grow into flowering size in one or two years.

PESTS AND DISEASES Generally trouble free, although stem and bulb eelworm, tarsonemid mites, narcissus fly and slugs may all attack the bulbs. They are also vulnerable to mosaic viruses. The ordinary, robust varieties are usually able to fight back.

GOOD VARIETIES In most gardens large drifts of fairly short varieties with small flowers are more effective than those with huge bright yellow trumpets. 'February Gold' and 'February Silver', 32cm (13in) tall, are cyclamineus daffodils with one or two flowers on each stem. 'Gold' has golden petals and darker trumpets; 'Silver' has creamy petals and lemon to creamy-yellow trumpets. The flowers of both are long lasting and, as their names suggest, appear early in the year.

soil

| ACID | | | | | | | | | | | ALKALINE |
| DRY | | | | | | | | | | | WET |

J	F	M	A	M	J	J	A	S	O	N	D

NARCISSUS 'FEBRUARY SILVER'

NARCISSUS 'FEBRUARY GOLD'

NASTURTIUM

Tropaeolum majus, hardy perennial treated as annual (S. America). Mature at 6 months: from 20 x 30cm (8 x 12in) to 1.8m x 45cm (6ft x 18in).

The larger more robust nasturtiums will use their twining stems to climb a fence or trellis, but there are also much more compact varieties, suitable for edging. The smooth leaves are completely circular with waved edges and pale to mid-green; some varieties are variegated with cream or yellow streaks and splashes. Faintly scented yellow, orange or red flowers with a long spur are carried from midsummer till early autumn. The leaves and stems have a pungent smell when crushed. The seed heads are green and nutty.

USES Nasturtiums give quick cover on poor soil. The trailing kinds can be planted in pots and hanging baskets, on banks or at the top of a retaining wall, and the climbers on trellises and fences. The flowers, leaves and seeds can be eaten in salads.

CULTIVATION Sow the seeds in a permanent planting position, in full sun and in poor soil which is on the dry side. In rich, moist soil lush leaves will develop at the expense of flowers.

PROPAGATION Sow seeds in spring and thin the seedlings to 20cm (8in) apart or more. For pots and hanging baskets sow the seeds in late winter under cover; harden the seedlings off and plant them out in spring.

PESTS AND DISEASES The plants are invariably spoiled by infestations of aphids after midsummer: usually more of them than the ladybird population can cope with, so spraying with insecticide or turning a blind eye are the only alternatives.

GOOD VARIETIES Choose from a reliable seed supplier, according to your colour scheme and preference.

NASTURTIUM

NECTAROSCORDUM SICULUM SSP.BULGARICUM

Syn. Allium bulgaricum, hardy bulb (the Balkans). Mature at 12 months: 90 x 30cm (3 x 1ft).

The long narrow grey-green leaves are like those of an onion, and they smell of onions if they are bruised. The bell-shaped pale purplish-greenish-white flowers are carried in arching clusters at the top of tall, smooth stems in early summer. The downward-hanging bells turn upwards after they have been fertilized and develop into seed heads with buff, papery cases that open into shuttlecocks to throw out the seeds.

USES These are good plants for the wilder parts of the garden, where they can be naturalized in grass, and they are also attractive planted in groups running between shrubs in the border.

CULTIVATION *Nectaroscordum* grow in any reasonable soil in sun or shade, but prefer a site in partial shade. Plant them in early autumn covering the bulbs to three or four times their own depth. Leave them until the clumps are so thick that flowering is stifled. The flower stems may need staking on exposed sites, but that will spoil the effect, so it is best to plant them where they are sheltered from the wind. Remove the dead leaves and stems in autumn.

PROPAGATION They can be grown from seed, the bulbs, which increase quickly, can be dug up and divided.

PESTS AND DISEASES Generally trouble free, but slugs may be a nuisance.

COMPANIONS The subtle colouring of the flowers goes well with the leaves of *Rosa glauca* (syn. *R. rubrifolia*).

NECTAROSCORDUM SICULUM BULGARICUM

NEMESIA STRUMOSA

Half-hardy annuals (S. Africa, mid 18th century). Mature at 6 months: 20-45 x 15cm (8-18 x 6in).

These bushy little plants have small light green, lance-shaped toothed leaves. The flowers are broadly funnel-shaped with pouched bases and often with spotted and bearded throats. They flower from mid- to late summer and are available in a wide range of colours.

USES Nemesias are good subjects for filling gaps at the front of borders and for growing in pots and hanging baskets.

CULTIVATION Nemesias will grow in any reasonable soil, but their ideal situation is a sunny position in a medium to light, slightly acid soil that contains plenty of organic matter. Plant them after all danger of frost is past and water well in hot dry weather. If you cut back the stems after the first flowering you may induce a second flush of flowers.

PROPAGATION Sow the seeds under glass in early spring, barely covering them with compost. Harden them off before planting them out in late spring or early summer.

PESTS AND DISEASES Generally trouble free.

GOOD VARIETIES Each seed supplier offers a different selection. Whether you grow your own plants from seed or buy young plants from a nursery, make your own choice according to your colour schemes.

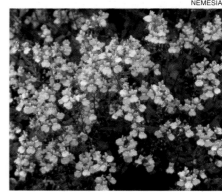

NEMESIA

N

N

NEPETA 'SIX HILLS GIANT'

Catmint, hardy perennial. Mature at 3 years: 60 x 90cm (2 x 3ft).

The large version of catmint can be trusted to put up a good performance with very little help from the gardener. The soft grey-green hairy leaves are oval, toothed and pointed, and a clump gives an overall impression of silvery-grey. Loosely branching stems carry narrow spikes of small lavender-blue hooded and lipped flowers from late spring until late summer and, if the plants are cut back, again well into the autumn.

USES The clumps of good foliage and long flowering season make this a prime candidate for the front of a border.

CULTIVATION Plant nepeta from autumn to spring in ordinary well-drained soil, preferably in full sun, though it will tolerate partial shade. After midsummer cut the whole plant back to induce new growth. Regrowth occurs very quickly, and the second flowering will continue until frost kills the stems. When that happens cut flower and leaf stems to the ground.

PROPAGATION Divide and replant during the early spring.

PESTS AND DISEASES Generally trouble free. Powdery mildew sometimes attacks the plants and is unsightly but it does no permanent damage.

OTHER VARIETIES *N. x faassenii* is smaller in all its parts, and a tidier plant more suitable for edging. But it is not as hardy as 'Six Hills Giant'. *N. govaniana* has airy heads of long, tubular pale yellow flowers and thrives in very different conditions, preferring a cool, moist site.

COMPANIONS Plant *N.* 'Six Hills Giant' or *N.* x *faassenii* in front of red or yellow roses to hide their bare legs.

soil		
ACID		ALKALINE
DRY		WET

J	F	M	A	M	J	J	A	S	O	N	D

NEPETA 'SIX HILLS GIANT'

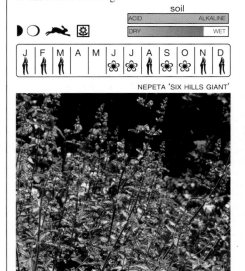

NICOTIANA ALATA

Syn. **N. affinis.** *Tobacco plant, perennial often treated as an annual (Brazil mid 16th century). Mature at 6 months: 75 x 30cm (30 x 12in).*

The flowers of this tobacco plant are sweetly scented at night. They are shaped like long narrow funnels opening into flat stars at the ends. In late summer they are borne in clusters at the top of tall stems rising out of a basal rosette of large fresh green, soft textured oval leaves.

USES Plant this and the other scented varieties in a position where you can enjoy the scent in the evenings.

CULTIVATION Plant nicotianas in early summer when the risk of frost is past, in groups of at least three. They will grow in ordinary soil in sun or partial shade.

PROPAGATION Sow the seeds in a cool greenhouse or similar situation indoors in early spring.

PESTS AND DISEASES Generally trouble free.

OTHER VARIETIES *N. a.* 'Lime Green' is scented and an unusual colour. *N. sylvestris* is also very fragrant with large leaves and long tubular flowers, but at 1.5m (5ft) tall it demands space. Compact varieties 30cm (12in) or so high include 'Domino' or 'Havana' series. They are not scented but are good plants in pretty, subtle colours.

soil		
ACID		ALKALINE
DRY		WET

J	F	M	A	M	J	J	A	S	O	N	D

NICOTIANA ALATA

NIGELLA DAMASCENA

Love-in-a-mist, hardy annual (S. Europe, mid 16th century). Mature at 6 months: 60 x 30cm (2 x 1ft).

The flowers rise out of a mist of bright green very finely-cut feathery foliage, on slender wiry stems. They are blue, white or mauve pink and are surrounded by thread-like bracts. The flowers bloom from mid- to late summer and are succeeded by attractive, inflated pale green seed pods, which become brown with red bars.

USES A promiscuous self-seeder, love-in-a-mist can be allowed to wander through beds and borders: just pull it up where it is not wanted. The flowers last well in water and both they and the seed heads are excellent for drying.

CULTIVATION Sow the seeds in the intended flowering position in spring or early autumn in any well-cultivated soil in a sunny position. Regular dead-heading will prolong the flowering season and increase the size of later flowers. If the soil is left undisturbed and some seed heads are left to ripen, a colony will survive year after year.

PROPAGATION Sow the seeds in the flowering site in spring or early autumn just covering them with soil. An autumn sowing usually results in larger plants and in much earlier flowers.

PESTS AND DISEASES Generally trouble free.

GOOD VARIETIES *N. d.* 'Miss Jekyll' is a good sky blue form, and 'Persian Jewels' is a form with mixed colours.

soil

ACID			ALKALINE
DRY			WET

J	F	M	A	M	J	J	A	S	O	N	D
					✿	✿	✿	✿			

NIGELLA

NYMPHAEA 'JAMES BRYDON'

Waterlily, perennial water plant. Mature at 7 years: leaves 20cm (8in), spread 90cm (3ft), planting depth 20cm-1m (6in-3ft). AGM

'James Brydon' is one of the most reliable and most attractive waterlilies. The round glossy leaves are maroon when young, later becoming dark green splashed with maroon. The deep pink to rose-crimson flowers, 13-16cm (4-5in) wide, bloom from midsummer until early autumn. Each flower lasts between three and five days, opening at about 10am and closing at about 4pm. In dull weather the flowers remain closed all day.

USES Apart from their ornamental value, waterlilies provide shade for fish and help to prevent the growth of the algae which can cause a number of problems in ponds and lakes.

CULTIVATION Plant waterlilies in good ordinary soil either directly in the base of a pool or in black plastic baskets. To keep the young plants near the surface initially, the containers can be propped on bricks or breeze-blocks, which are removed when the plants are growing strongly. Plant the tubers in late spring or early summer, keeping the water as clear as possible to allow light and warmth to penetrate to the plants. Once the plants are established, remove dead or untidy leaves from time to time and thin out any overcrowded plants during late spring.

PROPAGATION Divide established clumps.

PESTS AND DISEASES Generally trouble free but aphids, waterlily beetles and caterpillars may be a nuisance. Plants occasionally suffer from leaf spot or stem rot.

OTHER VARIETIES There are many beautiful waterlilies available: the choice depends on the area of the pool and its depth. If yours is a small pool, do not be tempted to buy plants that will end up covering the whole surface. It is worth visiting a nursery specializing in aquatic plants and taking expert advice.

soil

ACID			ALKALINE
DRY			WET

J	F	M	A	M	J	J	A	S	O	N	D
							✿	✿	✿		

NYMPHAEA

O

OENOTHERA MACROCARPA

Syn. O. missouriensis, evening primrose, hardy perennial (Southern USA, 1811). Mature at 2 years: 10 x 40cm (4 x 16in). AGM

This evening primrose is almost prostrate with long oval leaves and wide, clear yellow open funnel-shaped flowers all summer long. Each flower is up to 10cm (4in) across. They don't open till sunset, but they shine gently in the dusk and so are worth waiting for.

USES Plant evening primroses where you can see them at night from the house. The seeds of *Oenothera biennis* contain gamma-linoleic acid, which has medicinal properties, the subject of important research.

CULTIVATION Plant from autumn until spring in groups in any well-drained garden soil, preferably sandy, setting the plants 30cm (12in) apart. They prefer an open sunny site. Water in very dry weather. Cut the stems down to ground level during autumn or winter.

PROPAGATION Sow seeds in spring or early summer. Plants grown in light soil will self-seed. Alternatively, divide and replant the roots in spring.

PESTS AND DISEASES Generally trouble free but plants are occasionaly affected by eel worm, powdery mildew and root rot.

OTHER VARIETIES *O. fruticosa* 'Fireworks' AGM, syn. *O. tetragona* 'Fireworks', 30 x 30cm (12 x 12in), has spikes of cup-shaped golden scented flowers opening from red-flushed buds from mid- to late summer. *O. speciosa*, the white evening primrose, is lovely but short-lived and not reliably hardy.

COMPANIONS The leaves of *Viola labradorica* set off the oenothera's yellow flowers well.

OLEARIA X HAASTII

Daisy bush, evergreen shrub (New Zealand, 1858). Mature at 10 years: 1.5 x 1.5m (5 x 5ft) or more.

This is not the prettiest olearia but it is the only reliably hardy one. The others can only be grown successfully in very mild areas. *O. x haastii* is a dense bushy and rounded shrub. The small leaves are broadly oval, with glossy mid-green surfaces. Clusters of small white daisy-like flowers are produced in great profusion after midsummer.

USES Olearias will stand up to salt-laden winds and to atmospheric pollution, but they need shelter from the cold. They are good shrubs for seaside and town gardens where the climate is mild. In more exposed inland areas they need the shelter of a sunny wall. A cold winter may cut them to the ground but they will usually bounce back.

CULTIVATION Plant in spring in any reasonable well-drained soil in a sunny, sheltered position or, in mild coastal climates, an exposed position to shelter other plants. Cut out any dead shoots in spring and shorten others to reduce the overall size of the plant if necessary.

PROPAGATION Take half-ripe cuttings in late summer.

PESTS AND DISEASES Generally trouble free.

OTHER VARIETIES If your climate is really mild, *O. x macrodonta* AGM makes a shrub up to 3.5m (12ft) tall. It has serrated grey-green leaves and large heads of scented daisies at midsummer. *O. stellulata* De Candolle AGM, syn. *O. x scilloniensis*, is more compact, making a rounded bush 1.5 x 1.5m (5 x 5ft) and flowering so prolifically from early to midsummer that the leaves are invisible under the encrustation of white daisies.

OMPHALODES CAPPADOCICA

Navelwort, hardy perennial (Turkey, early 17th century). Mature at 3 years: 15 x 60cm (6in x 2ft). AGM

This is a well-behaved, low-growing and clump-forming species with long-stalked oval, hairy bright green leaves. It spreads steadily by means of creeping underground stems. From late spring to early summer loose sprays of small flowers are held above the leaves. They are a vivid shade of blue: deeper than forget-me-nots, but not quite as intense as gentians.

USES *O. cappadocica* makes excellent ground cover, particularly in a woodland setting between shrubs or on a rock garden.

CULTIVATION Plant in spring in groups of three or more, set 45cm (18in) apart. In light soil add some leaf mould or garden compost to make the soil more moisture retentive. Choose a position in partial or full shade. Mulch every spring with manure or compost. Ideally, remove the faded flower stems in order to prolong the flowering period.

PROPAGATION Divide and replant during spring or after flowering in late summer. Alternatively, sow seeds in spring.

PESTS AND DISEASES Generally trouble free.

OTHER VARIETIES *O. verna* is similar in many ways, but the flowers are not as profuse and not such a brilliant shade of blue. *O. cappadocica* is the one to go for.

GOOD COMPANIONS *O. cappadocica* makes a pretty carpet under yellow-leaved shrubs such as *Lonicera nitida* 'Baggesen's Gold' or *Philadelphus coronarius* 'Aurea'. It also makes a good planting with the lime-green flowers of *Euphorbia polychroma*.

OENOTHERA FRUTICOSA 'FIREWORKS'

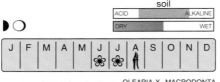

OLEARIA X MACRODONTA

OMPHALODES CAPPADOCICA

ONOPORDUM ACANTHIUM

O

Scotch thistle, cotton thistle, biennial (Europe including Britain). Mature at 2 years: 1.8m x 90cm (6 x 3ft).

This is one of the most dramatic garden plants. In the first summer it forms a basal rosette of large silver-white leaves covered with white cobweb-like hairs. The truly magnificent leaves are long and broadly oval, with wide white central ribs and serrated spiney margins. The following season erect branching and winged stems bear purple-pink thistle flowers during the late summer.

USES The Scotch thistle is an exceptionally fine architectural plant for the back of a border. Both the leaves and the flowers are much used in flower arranging, and the flower heads can be dried.

CULTIVATION Plant in any reasonable soil in full sun or partial shade. The richer the soil the larger the leaves and the taller the stems. If you don't want the plant to seed itself, remove the faded flower heads.

PROPAGATION Sow seeds during the autumn or spring.

PESTS AND DISEASES Generally trouble free but slugs and snails may eat the leaves.

ONOPORDUM ACANTHIUM

OPHIOPOGON PLANISCAPUS 'NIGRESCENS'

Evergreen hardy perennial. Mature at 3 years: 23 x 30cm (9 x 12in).

A strange plant, *O. p.* 'Nigrescens' looks like black grass. The colour of its narrow strap-shaped blades is very dark purple, about as near to black as any plant gets. They grow in spidery clumps, arching over in different directions. Minute mauve flowers appear in summer, followed by black seeds, which remain all winter.

USES It makes a tidy edging or ground cover for modern rather than traditional planting schemes.

CULTIVATION Plant in autumn or spring in any reasonable soil in sun or partial shade. Lift and divide every four or five years to keep fresh young stock.

PROPAGATION Divide established clumps in early spring.

PESTS AND DISEASES Generally trouble free.

COMPANIONS Plant it with other foliage plants such as contrasting grasses or ferns. Or repeat its colouring in a lighter vein with *Ajuga reptans* 'Purpurea' or *Viola labradorica*.

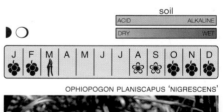

OPHIOPOGON PLANISCAPUS 'NIGRESCENS'

193 ■

O

ORIGANUM LAEVIGATUM 'HERRENHAUSEN'

Marjoram, hardy perennial (Turkey, Syria, pre-1960). Mature at 5 years: 40 x 40cm (15 x 15in). AGM

The leaves of this marjoram are hardly aromatic at all. They are dark green ovals with a purplish tinge and they form a dense, ground-hugging mat. Slender dark red-green branching stems rise up in late summer bearing an airy mass of tiny red-purple flowers.

USES Although this is a different plant from the culinary herb marjoram or oregano, it is at home in the herb garden. Its flowers are much visited by bees and butterflies. *Origanum vulgare* and its golden form 'Aureum' (see below) are culinary herbs.

CULTIVATION Plant in spring in a sunny sheltered position in ordinary well-drained soil, preferably alkaline. It is reasonably hardy but in cold districts protect it from winter wet by putting a cloche or pane of glass over it. *Origanum vulgare* can be cut back by two-thirds to keep it tidy before the plant dies down in winter. For the kitchen, pick shoots fresh as required. The flavour is best just before the flowers open and that is when the leaves should be gathered for drying or freezing. A second harvest may be taken in early autumn.

PROPAGATION Divide established plants during the spring.

PESTS AND DISEASES Generally trouble free.

OTHER VARIETIES *Origanum vulgare* 'Aureum' AGM is the yellow-leaved form of common or wild marjoram. It is 8cm (3in) high in leaf and spreads indefinitely. The leaves are small, rounded, slightly puckered and golden-yellow when young. They become pale greenish-yellow after midsummer. Some forms hardly have any flowers. Others have tiny tubular rose-purple flowers covering the stems in late summer. Golden marjoram is just as good for cooking with as the plain form.

ORIGANUM VULGARE VAR. 'AUREUM'

ORNITHOGALUM NUTANS

Star of Bethlehem, hardy bulb (Europe including Britain). Mature at 1 year: 30 x 10cm (12 x 4in).

This desirable plant should not be confused with *O. umbellatum*, which has pretty flowers but can become an ineradicable weed. *O. nutans* has mid- to dark green narrowly strap-shaped, grass-like leaves. The nodding bell-shaped flowers are like widely spaced hyacinth flowers. Their colouring is soft grey-white striped with pale green and they bloom in late spring or early summer.

USES It can be naturalized in grass among shrubs or in woodland. Plant it where the flowers can be seen close up.

CULTIVATION Plant in early autumn in a partially shaded position in ordinary well-drained soil, setting the bulbs 5-8cm (2-3in) deep. As with all bulbs, let the leaves fade naturally before cutting them down so that they can absorb light to store food and build up the bulbs' strength.

PROPAGATION Sow seeds in autumn or dig up established clumps and detach bulb offsets in autumn.

PESTS AND DISEASES Generally trouble free.

OTHER VARIETIES Avoid *Ornithogalum umbellatum*. It spreads with great rapidity and is difficult to get rid of.

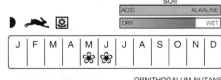

ORNITHOGALUM NUTANS

ORONTIUM AQUATICUM

Golden club, deciduous perennial water plant (N. America, mid 18th century). Mature at 5 years: spread 60cm (2ft).

The waxy blue-green leaves are oblong and pointed and float on the water's surface. In spring slender petal-less flower spikes white with gold tips, curve upwards, like the central spadix of an arum lily without the enfolding spathe.

USES As with waterlilies, the shade orontium makes over the water surface helps to keep the water cool so that algae will not breed. The plant also provides protective cover for fish.

CULTIVATION Plant between spring and early summer in full sun at the margin of a stream or pond or on the bottom, placing the roots between 15 and 30cm (6 and 12in) below the surface of the water. Remove the faded flower spikes.

PROPAGATION In autumn or spring divide the roots and replant, or sow seed in summer when it is fresh.

PESTS AND DISEASES Generally trouble free.

COMPANIONS Golden club is handsome enough to plant with waterlilies for contrasting foliage and earlier flowers.

soil

	ACID	ALKALINE
	DRY	WET

J	F	M	A	M	J	J	A	S	O	N	D

ORONTIUM AQUATICUM

OSMANTHUS X BURKWOODII

*Syn. x **Osmarea burkwoodii**, evergreen shrub. Mature at 20 years: 1.8 x 1.2m (6 x 4ft) after 10 years, 3 x 3m (10 x 10ft) at maturity. AGM*

In its quiet way this is one of the most attractive evergreen shrubs. The dark green glossy leaves are oval, pointed and slightly toothed. They are elegantly poised on a dense, bushy, rather slow-growing plant. In spring clusters of sweetly scented small white flowers open at the tips of the shoots.

USES This and other varieties of osmanthus are good border plants. They can also be planted as a hedge.

CULTIVATION Plant between autumn and spring in any reasonable soil including chalk, in partial shade in a position sheltered from north and east winds. For hedges set the plants 60cm (2ft) apart. No pruning is necessary but plants that outgrow their position can be cut hard back without harming them.

PROPAGATION Take cuttings of half-ripe shoots in summer, or layer the branches in early autumn.

PESTS AND DISEASES Generally trouble free.

OTHER VARIETIES *Osmanthus delavayi* AGM has smaller darker green leaves and masses of scented white flowers in spring. It reaches the same size eventually, but more slowly. *O. heterophyllus* and its variegated forms are also slow. They are tidy shrubs with prickly holly-like leaves and fragrant white flowers in autumn.

soil

	ACID	ALKALINE
	DRY	WET

J	F	M	A	M	J	J	A	S	O	N	D

OSMANTHUS X BURKWOODII

O

OSMUNDA REGALIS

Royal fern, deciduous fern (everywhere except Australasia). Up to 1.2m x 90cm (4 x 3ft). AGM

This splendid plant is the largest hardy fern that will grow in Britain. Elegant cut fronds unroll in crosier fashion in the spring. They start coppery-brown and become a bright fresh shade of green in summer, then yellow, then brown again in autumn.

USES This and other ferns are ideal for waterside planting, and bring a refreshing splash of cool green to shady parts of the garden – provided the ground can be kept damp for them.

CULTIVATION Plant in spring in humus-rich soil with the crown at soil level. Mulch thickly with leaf mould or compost every spring. Unlike most other ferns, which will only grow in shade, *O. regalis* is also happy in the sun. The dead leaves can be cut down in autumn or winter.

PROPAGATION Sow spores in summer as soon as they are ripe. They remain viable for only three days after being gathered, unless kept in a deep freeze. Alternatively, divide well-separated, multiple crowns in spring. If crowns that are closely set are cut they may not survive.

PESTS AND DISEASES Generally trouble free.

COMPANIONS Plant the royal fern with other lesser ferns, mosses and ivies.

	soil	
	ACID	ALKALINE
	DRY	WET

J	F	M	A	M	J	J	A	S	O	N	D

OSMUNDA REGALIS

OSTEOSPERMUM 'BUTTERMILK'

Syn. **Dimorphotheca** *'Buttermilk'. Tender sub-shrubby evergreen perennial (South Africa). Mature at 3 years: up to 60 x 30cm (24 x 12in). AGM*

This is one of the few tender perennial plants to wheedle its way into this list. Osteospermums offer a very wide choice of colours and, in sunny gardens, are covered in flowers from midsummer until autumn. The leaves are long, grey-green, hairy and serrated. The daisy-like flowers have long rays and dark centres. 'Buttermilk' has pale yellow petals deepening in colour towards the outer edges.

USES Use osteospermums as gap-fillers in sunny beds and borders. They make good cut flowers.

CULTIVATION Plant out in early summer in full sun in any reasonable well-drained soil, including sandy soil. Dead-head to keep up the supply of flowers.

PROPAGATION Take cuttings of the non-flowering shoots at midsummer and keep the young plants in a frost-free greenhouse through winter and spring.

PESTS AND DISEASES Generally trouble free.

OTHER VARIETIES There is a wide range to choose from, in colours from white and yellow to pink and purple.

	soil	
	ACID	ALKALINE
	DRY	WET

J	F	M	A	M	J	J	A	S	O	N	D

OSTEOSPERMUM

OSTEOSPERMUM 'BUTTERMILK'

PAEONIA DELAVAYI

Tree peony, deciduous shrub (China, 1908). Mature at 5 years: up to 1.8 x 1.2m (6 x 4ft).

Tree peonies are only in flower for a few weeks in early summer, but they also qualify as foliage plants. The leaves of *P. delavayi* are long, slender and pointed, deeply-cut and dark green above, glaucous beneath. The bowl-shaped flowers are blood red with golden anthers in the centre.

USES Plant tree peonies for their attractive foliage; consider the flowers a bonus.

CULTIVATION Plant between autumn and spring in any reasonable soil including chalk, in sun or partial shade. Peonies flower better in full sun but choose a site that is shaded from early-morning sun, as a quick thaw after frost will damage the buds. Dig a planting hole 90cm (3ft) deep and add well-rotted manure or compost. Plant the shrub 10cm (4in) deeper than the soil level in its container. On chalk or light sandy soil, mulch annually with manure or compost in spring.

PROPAGATION Tree peonies are difficult to propagate: it is best to buy new stock.

PESTS AND DISEASES Generally trouble free but there is a killer disease called peony blight or peony wilt. Spotting it early and cutting out and burning infected shoots may prevent it spreading. Honey fungus, leaf spot, grey mould, virus disease and physiological disorder may also attack.

OTHER VARIETIES *P. d.* var. *ludlowii* AGM is a handsome shrub up to 2.5 x 2.5m (8 x 8ft) with fine, deeply-cut fresh green leaves and big yellow single flowers. In some strains the flowers are almost completely hidden among the leaves. This only becomes apparent when it is too late, as it takes a few years for the plants to start flowering.

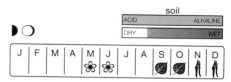

	soil	
ACID		ALKALINE
DRY		WET

J	F	M	A	M	J	J	A	S	O	N	D
				❀	❀						

PAEONIA DELAVAYI

PAEONIA LACTIFLORA

Syn. P. albiflora, P. japonica, P. sinensis. Peony, hardy perennial (Siberia, 1784, China, 1805). Mature at 5 years: 90 x 60cm (3 x 2ft).

This species is the parent of many of the garden hybrids. It has large single flowers with silky petals and yellow stamens at the centre in early summer. The leaves are dark reddish green. The hybrids are single, semi-double or double and come in dark red, cream-yellow and white and every possible shade that mixes these three colours. The young shoots of most varieties emerge rich dark crimson, slowly becoming green as the leaves unfurl. Some colour up again in autumn. Each variety flowers for about three weeks from late spring to midsummer.

USES In a large garden, a whole bed devoted to peonies looks stunning. But they are also greatly valued components of herbaceous and mixed borders. Indoors, they are a mainstay of early summer flower arrangements.

CULTIVATION Peonies flower best in a sunny position but will tolerate partial shade. They need to remain undisturbed for as long as possible, so the ground should be thoroughly prepared before planting. Dig in manure or compost and add a handful of bonemeal to each planting hole. Unlike tree peonies, herbaceous peonies may fail to flower if they are planted too deep; make sure the crown is barely covered, with 5cm (2in) of soil at the most. Top dress with bonemeal in autumn and in spring apply fertilizer and mulch.

PROPAGATION Divide the roots and replant making sure there are buds on each piece.

PESTS AND DISEASES Generally trouble free but there is a slight risk of peony wilt.

GOOD VARIETIES Choose from a specialist catalogue, giving preference to scented varieties and those described as free-flowering, robust and flowering over a long period. The following are trusty old favourites: 'Duchesse de Nemours' AGM double white, scented, flowering for a long period. 'Sarah Bernhardt' AGM double, scented, apple-blossom pink. 'Felix Krousse' AGM bright red double.

GOOD COMPANIONS Interplant peonies with early flowering small bulbs to flower among the emerging peony shoots.

	soil	
ACID		ALKALINE
DRY		WET

J	F	M	A	M	J	J	A	S	O	N	D
				❀	❀			🍃	🍃		

PAEONIA 'NICE GAL'

PAEONIA LACTIFLORA 'SARAH BERNHARDT'

P

PAPAVER SOMNIFERUM

Opium poppy, hardy annual (Greece and the Orient). Mature at 2 years: 75 x 30cm (30 x 12in).

The smooth, deeply lobed leaves are a striking pale grey-green. Single or double flowers in shades of purplish-red and dusky pink emerge from grey-green sepals carried on strong smooth stems. The round, flat-headed seed pods are still beautiful long after the petals have fallen. 'Pink Chiffon' is a named double variety.

USES Once you have the opium poppy in the garden you have it for life, seeding itself around to fill empty spaces in beds and borders. Just pull out unwanted seedlings. The seed heads can be dried for winter arrangements.

CULTIVATION Sow seeds in final positions, in any soil that is not water-logged, in sun. If you don't want the plants to self-seed, dead-head as the petals fall.

PROPAGATION Sow in spring in the final flowering position. Thin out the seedlings to 30cm (12in) apart.

PESTS AND DISEASES Downy mildew can form grey fungal growth on the undersides of the leaves. Pull out and then burn the affected plants.

OTHER VARIETIES *Papaver orientale*, the Oriental poppy, is a hardy perennial with long, toothed, hairy leaves and huge, mostly single flowers on leafless hairy

stems. 'Beauty of Livermere' AGM is rich glowing red with black blotches at the centre; 'Blue Moon' is pink tinged with blue-grey; 'Cedric's Pink' is pale grey-pink with purple blotches; 'Mrs Perry' AGM is

light salmon pink with black blotches; and 'Perry's White' has the faintest blush on its white petals and a black centre.

COMPANIONS The colouring of both leaves and flowers of *P. somniferum* blends beautifully with *Dicentra formosa*. The leaves of *P. orientale* die down after flowering so interplant with *Anemone x hybrida* to fill the gap.

soil		
ACID		ALKALINE
DRY		WET

J	F	M	A	M	J	J	A	S	O	N	D

PAPAVER ORIENTALE 'PERRY'S WHITE'

PAPAVER ORIENTALE 'BEAUTY OF LIVERMERE'

PARROTIA PERSICA

Persian ironwood, deciduous tree (Iran, Caucasus, 1841). Mature at 40 years: 4 x 4.5m (13 x 15ft) after 10 years, 8 x 10m (25 x 32ft) at maturity. AGM

The parrotia is completely hardy. It is grown for its autumn colouring of amber, crimson and gold and, although it is lime tolerant it usually colours best on neutral or acid soil. It has a solid, dignified shape with a rounded crown and wide-spreading branches sweeping the ground. The oval rounded leaves are like large soft beech leaves. On trees more than ten years old tiny flowers appear in early spring with red stamens and no petals, surrounded by hairy bracts.

USES This is a tree for large gardens, to be planted where not only its vivid autumn colour but also its shape can be appreciated.

CULTIVATION Plant between autumn and spring in well-drained soil, preferably neutral or acid, in sun or light shade. No pruning is needed except to remove any damaged branches or to reduce the size of plants that outgrow their space. It can be done at any time during winter.

PROPAGATION Seed can be sown in autumn. As the lowest branches often touch the ground they are easy to layer. Do this in late summer or early autumn and the layers should root well enough to sever from the parent after two years.

PESTS AND DISEASES Generally trouble free.

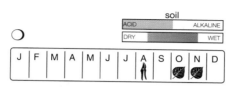

PARROTIA PERSICA

PARROTIA PERSICA

PARTHENOCISSUS TRICUSPIDATA

P

*Syn. **Ampelopsis veitchii**. Boston ivy, deciduous woody plant climbing by tendrils (Japan, China). Mature at 7 years: up to 20m (70ft). AGM*

Although the plant covers walls in the same fashion as a very vigorous ivy, the three-pointed leaves are not evergreen and are more like maple than ivy leaves. They turn brilliant crimson in autumn.

USES It is too large for the average house front, soon reaching the gutters and dislodging roof tiles. It is best where the long trails can hang to form a curtain, draped over a high garden wall for example. In large gardens it will make good ground cover over a steep bank.

CULTIVATION Plant at any time from autumn to spring in any soil that does not dry out, adding plenty of manure or compost. No pruning is needed except to remove unwanted growth during the summer months.

PROPAGATION Take hardwood cuttings in late autumn or sow seeds in autumn. Alternatively, layer long shoots in autumn.

PESTS AND DISEASES Generally trouble free but scale insects can attack the stems, making the plants sticky and sooty. Aphids may infest young shoots. The plant is susceptible to honey fungus.

OTHER VARIETIES *P. henryana* syn. *Vitis henryana* AGM has elegant fingered leaves with a velvety bronze-green surface and pale greyish-pink veins, turning red in autumn. *P. quinquefolia* syn. *Vitis quinquefolia* AGM (Virginia creeper) has five-fingered leaves, dull green in summer but glorious crimson in autumn.

COMPANIONS The red autumn leaves mingle well with the creamy variegations of *Hedera canariensis* 'Gloire de Marengo'.

PARTHENOCISSUS HENRYANA

P

PASSIFLORA CAERULEA

Syn. P. chinensis, P. mayana, passion flower, half-hardy evergreen woody climber (Brazil, 1609). Mature at 5 years: up to 10m (32ft).

Most passion flowers are greenhouse or conservatory plants, too tender to be grown outdoors. *P. caerulea* will survive most winters against a south- or west-facing wall. Even if the stems are cut to the ground by frost, the plant usually starts again with new shoots from the base. It is a fast growing plant climbing by tendrils. The leaves are deeply cut into five or seven fingers. The strangely constructed flowers are said to symbolize the elements of Christ's Passion. The overall impression is light blue-purple, from a band of this colouring on the white petals. They flower from midsummer until autumn and in a warm summer may produce orange-yellow egg-shaped edible fruits.

USES In mild areas, particularly in sheltered town gardens, use *Passiflora caerulea* to provide rapid cover on trelliswork, arbours and walls.

CULTIVATION Plant outdoors in areas with mild winters in late spring in any ordinary, well-drained soil; choose a sheltered site in sun or partial shade, preferably against a house wall where the warmth from indoors will help it through the winter. Provide trellis or wires for the tendrils to hold and tie in the young growths to start with. For the first few years, protect the plants in winter with brushwood, bubble plastic or polythene sheeting. Old tangled plants can be thinned out by cutting them to ground level or back to the main stem in late winter or early spring. Side shoots can be shortened to 15cm (6in) at the same time.

PROPAGATION Take cuttings in late summer or layers in spring.

PESTS AND DISEASES Generally trouble free but cucmber mosaic virus sometimes attacks the leaves.

OTHER VARIETIES *P. c.* 'Constance Elliott' AGM is a white-flowered form.

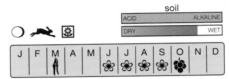

PASSIFLORA CAERULEA

PEAR

Pyrus communis, deciduous tree (Europe and Western Asia). Mature at 40 years: various sizes.

Pear trees grown for their fruit are usually grafted on to quince rootstocks. 'Quince A' is the best general-purpose stock producing trees up to 4 x 4m (12 x 12ft). Pear trees are covered in white blossom in spring and bear green, buff-brown or golden edible fruit in late summer and autumn. The leaves often colour well in autumn. Although some varieties are self-fertile they all crop better after cross-pollination.

USES Grow pears for their fruit, for dessert or cooking. Plants can be trained as cordons, fans or espaliers to make divisions within the garden or to decorate walls.

CULTIVATION Pears prefer well-drained deep soil that does not dry out. Avoid exposed inland or coastal situations and frost pockets. Pears are hardy but the blossom may be caught by frost, destroying that year's crop. Trees planted close to each other will give mutual protection. Plant during the autumn.

PROPAGATION Grafting on to quince rootstock is the usual method.

PESTS AND DISEASES The list is daunting but healthy plants in good soil should not be unduly troubled: birds, aphids, pear leaf blister mites; apple canker, brown rot, cracking, eye rot, fireblight, frost damage, honey fungus, mineral deficiencies, pear scab, physiological disorder turning leaves black, russetting.

GOOD VARIETIES Choose from the following for good crops of well-flavoured fruit: 'Beth', 'Concorde', 'Conference', 'Onward', 'Williams' Bon Chrétien'.

PEAR

PELARGONIUM

P

Geranium, tender evergreen shrubby perennials (S. Africa, 1632). Mature at 2 years: from 25 x 15cm (10 x 6in) to 1.5 x 1.5m (5 x 5ft).

Everyone continues to call perlargoniums 'geraniums' although they are completely different from the hardy geraniums or cranesbills. They are among the most colourful plants of summer. They divide into four basic groups and within each group there is a wide variety of forms and colours. *The RHS Plant Finder* lists over 2000 varieties. The groups are:

SPECIES AND SCENTED-LEAVED are grown more for their leaves than their flowers. The leaves may be grey-green velvet plates (*P. tomentosum*) or finely crimped and curled frills (*P. crispum* 'Variegatum'). The scent of the leaves when crushed may be rose, lemon or peppermint.

ZONAL plants have rounded leaves, each with a darker 'zone' running around it. The showy flowers are in clusters on straight bare stems, and may be double or single and any shade of red or pink, from magenta, scarlet or salmon to white.

PELARGONIUM 'RED ELITE'

IVY-LEAVED get their name from the trailing stems with slightly fleshy ivy-shaped leaves. The flowers are similar to those of zonal perlargoniums. Some varieties have flowers that are more delicate and airy in appearance.

REGAL PELARGONIUMS are larger, more shrubby plants with serrated leaves and large trumpet-shaped flowers. They are not weather-resistant and are best grown indoors.

USES Geraniums are much used in municipal summer bedding. In private gardens they can decorate every kind of pot, urn, tub, trough, window box or hanging basket.

PELARGONIUM 'APPLE BLOSSOM'

CULTIVATION Pot pelargoniums into general purpose compost. Keep the compost just moist in winter and early spring and water freely during the growing period. Outdoors, plant them from early summer, in compost in pots or in ordinary well-drained soil in full sun. The plants can be lifted in early autumn for overwintering in a frost-free greenhouse or room. Cut off one-third of the growth and pot up.

PROPAGATION Take cuttings in late summer or sow seeds in heat in late winter.

PESTS AND DISEASES The usual range of greenhouse problems may occur: leafhoppers, whitefly, vine weevils, root rot, grey mould, leafy gall, oedema, rust, virus diseases. Spray as soon as a problem is detected and get the plants out into the open air as soon as weather permits.

GOOD VARIETIES The type of pelargonium and the colours you choose are matters of personal preference. It is safest to make your selection from a nursery in early summer when the plants are coming into flower. Once you have a few plants it is quite easy to increase them from cuttings.

GOOD COMPANIONS In tubs and hanging baskets pelargoniums can be mixed with fuchsias, petunias, bidens, *Helichrysum petiolatum* and lobelias for strong, uninhibited colour schemes.

MIXED PELARGONIUMS

	soil	
ACID		ALKALINE
DRY		WET

J	F	M	A	M	J	J	A	S	O	N	D
					✿	✿	✿	✿	✿		

PELARGONIUM

P

PENSTEMON BARBATUS

Syn. **Chelone barbata.** *Semi-evergreen perennial (Colorado, 1784). Mature at 3 years: 90 x 30cm (3 x 1ft).*

A few mild summers in a row lull you into a false sense of security about penstemons. They are not reliably hardy and may succumb to hard frosts or to cold, dessicating spring winds. But they give such good value, flowering on and on, that they are worth risking. This species is among the hardiest of penstemons. It has a basal clump of mid-green, lanceolate leaves and branching stems of scarlet-pink flowers from mid-to late summer. In shape the flowers are somewhere between a snapdragon and a foxglove, but narrower than either. Penstemon varieties cover a range of sizes and colours from blue to purple to red, pink and white. In general those with large leaves and flowers are less hardy than smaller ones.

USES Penstemons flower just when there tends to be an awkward gap in the flower garden, towards the end of the summer, continuing into autumn.

CULTIVATION Plant in spring in well-drained garden soil in a sunny position sheltered from cold winds. In autumn cut the stems down to just above ground level and protect with cloches or a layer of straw or bracken during the winter.

PROPAGATION Take cuttings of non-flowering side shoots in late summer. Ideally, do this regularly as a precaution against a hard winter.

PESTS AND DISEASES Generally trouble free.

OTHER VARIETIES *Penstemon* 'Stapleford Gem' and the similar 'Sour Grapes' have flowers of opalescent purplish blue-green. 'White Bedder' and 'Heavenly Blue' are self-descriptive; 'Raven' is a good dusky red-purple.

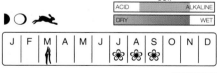

			soil			
			ACID		ALKALINE	
			DRY			WET

| J | F | M | A | M | J | J | A | S | O | N | D |

PENSTEMON

PEROVSKIA ATRIPLICIFOLIA

Russian sage, deciduous subshrub (Afghanistan to Tibet, 1841). Mature at 5 years: 1.2 x 1m (4 x 3ft).

It is quite hardy but it is easy to tell by looking at it that this is a plant for a hot dry position. The grey-green leaves are oval and deeply toothed. They smell of sage. In late summer airy branching spires covered in white down bear masses of violet-blue, tubular flowers. The plants tend to sprawl if not supported.

USES On chalk, sand or other light soils, perovskia takes over flowering when lavender leaves off, bringing a continuation of the silver and blue colouring that is so restful to the eye.

CULTIVATION Plant from autumn to spring in well-drained light soil and in a sunny position. Leave the stems during winter, and as soon as the new season's growth starts in spring, cut them down almost to ground level.

PROPAGATION Take cuttings in summer.

PESTS AND DISEASES Generally trouble free.

OTHER VARIETIES 'Blue Spire' AGM is a form with leaves more deeply and more intricately cut.

GOOD COMPANIONS Perovskia mixes well with other grey-leaved plants and doesn't object to the poor, stony conditions in which *Convolvulus cneorum* thrives.

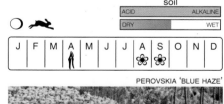

			soil			
			ACID		ALKALINE	
			DRY			WET

| J | F | M | A | M | J | J | A | S | O | N | D |

PEROVSKIA 'BLUE HAZE'

PERSICARIA AFFINIS

Syn. **Polygonum affine,** *knotweed, evergreen hardy perennial (Nepal). Mature at 3 years: 8-15 x 30cm (3-6 x 12in).*

These plants spread slowly making ground-hugging mats of small, glossy oval pointed leaves. In late summer and autumn lots of pinkish-red miniature poker-like flower spikes appear and in winter the leaves become bronze. The species is seldom grown, having been replaced by the varieties described below.

USES Unlike some persicaria species which are uncontrollable, this and the others described are excellent ground cover plants in sun or shade.

CULTIVATION Plant in autumn or spring in sun or shade and in any reasonable soil. Persicarias do particularly well and flower for a longer season in damp positions.

PROPAGATION Divide established clumps and replant in autumn or spring.

PESTS AND DISEASES Generally trouble free.

OTHER VARIETIES *P. a.* 'Darjeeling Red' AGM, height 20cm (8in) has deep red flowers; on 'Donald Lowndes' AGM the 15cm (6in) flowers start red and fade to pink. One of the very best persicarias is *P. bistorta* 'Superba' AGM. A form of the native British bistort, it makes a large clump of broad oval, light green leaves and carries plenty of pale pink pokers from early through to late summer. It grows to 60-75 x 60cm (2-2ft6in x 2ft). *P. vacciniifolia* AGM is a low carpeter with leaves tinged with red in autumn. The miniature flower spikes – 8cm (3in) – are longer, narrower and not as stubby as those of the other species. They appear in autumn.

			soil			
			ACID		ALKALINE	
			DRY			WET

| J | F | M | A | M | J | J | A | S | O | N | D |

PERSICARIA AFFINIS 'SUPERBA'

PHALARIS ARUNDINACEA VAR. PICTA 'PICTA'

Syn. P. a. 'Elegantissima', gardener's garters, ribbon grass, evergreen perennial grass (northern hemisphere, 1596). Mature at 3 years: up to 90cm (3ft) tall, indefinite spread. AGM

This grass is grown for its colourful leaves, pale green with a broad cream stripe down the centre. In summer it flowers with numerous stems carrying narrow green or purple panicles and in autumn and winter the whole plant fades and dries to pale buff. It spreads rapidly by invasive roots.

USES Plant gardener's garters in the wild garden where it can spread without being a nuisance, lightening a dark corner. It looks good beside water.

CULTIVATION Plant from autumn to spring in any reasonable soil in partial or full shade. It will grow in sun, but the sunny parts of the garden are best saved for plants that will not tolerate shade. Restrict the spreading rhizomes by digging up the plants and replanting them every three or four years.

PROPAGATION Divide and replant the roots from autumn till spring.

PESTS AND DISEASES Generally trouble free.

PHALARIS

PHILADELPHUS 'SYBILLE'

Mock orange, syringa, deciduous shrub (northern hemisphere). Mature at 10 years: 1.2 x 2m (4 x 6ft).

There are many hybrid philadelphus available in different sizes, some with single, some with double flowers. We grow them for their orange-blossom scent but not all varieties are strongly fragrant. Those described here are all sweetly scented and of reasonably compact habit. 'Sybille', a low arching shrub with mid-green oval leaves, is one of the best for small gardens. At midsummer it is covered with single white flowers, each with a pink stain at its centre.

USES Plant philadelphus in a position where you can enjoy its scent. It is tolerant of polluted atmospheres.

CULTIVATION Plant between autumn and spring in any reasonable soil in full sun or partial shade. A position sheltered from wind helps to entrap the scent. Prune about one-third of the oldest branches after flowering.

PROPAGATION Take cuttings of half-ripe side shoots in summer, or hardwood cuttings in the autumn.

PHILADELPHUS 'BELLE ETOILE'

PESTS AND DISEASES Generally trouble free.

OTHER VARIETIES *P.* 'Belle Etoile' is fairly upright to 2 x 2m (6 x 6ft); in summer the branches arch over with the weight of the cream-white single flowers. They have purple blotches at the base. The flowering season of all these shrubs is short, but the foliage of *P. coronarius* 'Aureus' AGM (up to 2.5 x 1.5m, 8 x 5ft) or *P. c.* 'Variegatus' AGM (slowly up to 2 x 2m, 6 x 6ft) helps to compensate. Both need to be in shelter and partial shade. They both have very fragrant single flowers. 'Manteau d'Hermine' AGM is a good double form of about the same size as 'Sybille'.

GOOD COMPANIONS Give philadelphus a dark background if possible: a yew hedge or a group of evergreen shrubs.

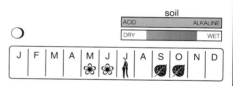

PHILADELPHUS CORONARIUS 'AUREUS'

PHILADELPHUS 'INNOCENCE'

P

PHLOMIS FRUTICOSA

Jerusalem sage, evergreen shrub (Mediterranean, 16th century). Mature at 5 years: 90 x 1.2m (3 x 4ft). AGM

This dense spreading shrub has oval, pointed, coarse-textured woolly grey-green leaves. At midsummer numerous white woolly stems rise up carrying whorls of yellow hooded and lipped flowers in the upper leaf axils. They flower at intervals up the stems, giving a tiered effect.

USES *Phlomis fruticosa* makes useful ground cover on dry sunny banks.

CULTIVATION Plant from autumn to spring in light well-drained soil in a sunny position. Phlomis will tolerate sandy soil or chalk. Pruning is optional. You can either cut back all the branches to within a few inches of the previous year's growth every spring, or you can leave the plant to fend for itself until it becomes ungainly, then cut it down to 15cm (6in) from the ground and let it start again.

PROPAGATION Phlomis tends to seed itself. If there are no seedlings to transplant, take cuttings in late summer.

PESTS AND DISEASES Generally trouble free.

OTHER VARIETIES *P. italica* is not so hardy but can be grown in a sheltered corner in mild areas. It has smaller leaves and mauve-pink flowers. *P. russeliana* AGM is a hardy perennial 90 x 60cm (3 x 2ft) making good ground cover with large leaves and tiers of yellow flowers at midsummer.

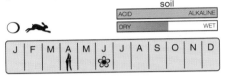

PHLOMIS ITALICA

PHLOMIS FRUTICOSA

PHLOX MACULATA 'OMEGA'

Hardy perennial (Eastern N. America, 1740). Mature at 3 years: 90 x 45cm (3ft x 18in). AGM

This phlox is less susceptible to eel worm than *P. paniculata* and its hybrids. It flowers earlier, producing its tall cylinders of scented white flowers from mid-to late summer.

USES Phlox are invaluable for bringing colour to beds and borders during the gap when roses have finished their first flowering, and not started their second.

CULTIVATION Plant in groups of at least five in autumn or early spring in a sunny or partially shaded position. The soil should be moisture-retentive but well-drained. Mulch every spring with manure or compost to preserve moisture round the roots. Older plants produce numerous shoots, and the weaker stems should be cut out in spring.

PROPAGATION Divide in autumn or spring. The crowns can be sliced off in late winter or early spring, leaving only the roots. Dig up young plantlets and replant separately.

PESTS AND DISEASES It may need protection against slugs and may suffer from leaf spot, leafy gall, a physiological disorder that turns the leaves yellow or brown, and powdery mildew.

OTHER VARIETIES *P. maculata* 'Alpha' AGM is lilac pink. *P. paniculata* hybrids come in numerous shades of pink. 'Fujiyama', a white variety, flowers later than the rest, prolonging the season. *Phlox divaricata*, *P. douglasii* and *P. subulata* are prostrate alpine phloxes with a mass of flowers in early summer.

GOOD COMPANIONS Some of the later-flowering yellow day lilies contrast with red and purple phlox. Plant those of softer colouring with hebes and *Ceanothus* 'Gloire de Versailles'.

PHLOX MACULATA

PHORMIUM COOKIANUM TRICOLOR

Mountain flax, evergreen perennial (New Zealand, 1868). Mature at 7 years: 90 x 30cm (3 x 1ft).

Phormiums are reasonably hardy once they are established. *P. cookianum* is more compact than *P. tenax* and so more suitable for small gardens. The handsome sword-shaped leaves are striped lengthways with green, red and yellow. Established plants bear dramatic stems of red-brown flowers.

USES The bold foliage provides a strong vertical accent. Phormiums are good seaside plants as they tolerate salt in the air, and they do well in containers in city courtyards. The fibre that makes up the dead leaves can be used as cord.

CULTIVATION Plant phormiums in spring in deep moist soil in a sunny position. For the first few years protect the plants in winter with straw or bracken. Remove the dead flower stems during the late summer or early autumn.

PROPAGATION Divide mature clumps and replant in spring, making sure each rooted piece has at least three or four leaves.

PESTS AND DISEASES Generally trouble free.

OTHER VARIETIES *P. cookianum* ssp. *hookeri* 'Cream Delight' AGM has a broad cream band down the centre of each leaf. *P. tenax* (New Zealand flax, introduced in 1789) is very large, growing up to 3 x 1.2m (10 x 4ft), with grey-green leaves. The form *P. t.* 'Purpureum' has leaves with a soft red-purple sheen.

COMPANIONS The contrasting shapes of plants with rounded or horizontal lines will set off the strong vertical leaves of a phormium: cistuses, or *Hypericum* 'Hidcote', or *Juniperus x media* 'pferzeriana'.

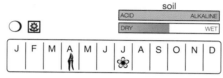

| J | F | M | A | M | J | J | A | S | O | N | D |

PHORMIUM COOKIANUM 'TRICOLOR'

PHORMIUM COOKIANUM 'TRICOLOR'

PHOTINIA X FRASERI 'RED ROBIN'

Evergreen shrub (a hybrid between two Chinese species raised in N. America, 1955). Mature at 12 years: 3 x 2.5m (10 x 8ft) after 10 years; 6 x 4m (20 x 12ft) at maturity.

This photinia is grown for the brilliance of the new young leaf shoots. They are bright red; in spring, from a distance, the shrub looks as if it is covered in red flowers. Later the oval pointed leaves turn bronze, then glossy dark green. New red shoots appear spasmodically through most of the year. Flowers are only produced in mild climates. They are white tinged with pink, scented like hawthorn, and followed by red berries that turn black.

USES Photinia is often planted in limy soil as a substitute for pieris, which will only grow on acid soil. (Pieris also has young red shoots.)

CULTIVATION Plant in any reasonable soil in sun or light shade in a position sheltered from cold winter winds, and not in a frost pocket. In the first spring prune back all the shoots by one-third to promote a strong, bushy framework. In subsequent years pruning is optional. Plants can be cut back by up to one-third in spring to control the size and encourage fresh young growth.

PROPAGATION Take semi-ripe cuttings during the summer.

PESTS AND DISEASES Generally trouble free.

OTHER VARIETIES *P. davidiana* (syn. *Stransvaesia davidiana*) is a tall shrub or small tree to 6m (20ft). It is easily confused with *Cotoneaster frigidus* 'Cornubia', and rivals it in the abundance of red berries in autumn and winter, but is rather sparsely branched. *P. d.* 'Fructu Luteo' has creamy yellow berries.

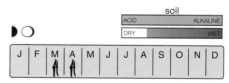

| J | F | M | A | M | J | J | A | S | O | N | D |

PHOTINIA X FRASERI 'RED ROBIN'

P

PHYGELIUS AEQUALIS 'YELLOW TRUMPET'

Subshrub treated as a perennial (S. Africa). Mature at 5 years: 90 x 90cm (3 x 3ft).

In milder areas and in sheltered positions, phygelius may develop into a shrub, but in most gardens it will be cut to the ground by frost every winter. It has branching stems of mid-green lance-shaped toothed leaves. Along the top of each stem slim butter-yellow trumpet flowers are strung, hanging in clusters from midsummer until autumn.

USES Phygelius will grow against a north wall provided it is not exposed to the wind.

CULTIVATION Plant in spring, preferably in a sunny sheltered position and in light soil. Leave the dead branches on the shrub in winter to give some protection against severe weather, and cut them down to ground level in spring.

PROPAGATION Divide and replant the roots during early spring or take cuttings during the summer.

PESTS AND DISEASES Generally trouble free.

OTHER VARIETIES *P. aequalis*, the species from which 'Yellow Trumpet' is derived, is similar, but produces soft buff-coral flowers. *P. capensis* AGM, Cape figwort, was introduced from South Africa in 1855. It bears masses of bright red tubular flowers from after midsummer until autumn and, against a wall, may grow to 2.5m (8ft).

soil

| | ACID | ALKALINE |
| DRY | | WET |

| J | F | M | A | M | J | J | A | S | O | N | D |

PHYGELIUS AEQUALIS 'YELLOW TRUMPET'

PHYSOSTEGIA VIRGINIANA 'VIVID'

Syn. Dracocephalum virginicum, obedient plant, perennial (Eastern N. America, 1683). Mature at 3 years: 60 x 60cm (2 x 2ft). AGM

Upright branching stems with sharply toothed lance-shaped leaves are closely set with narrow snapdragon-like, deep mauve-pink flowers in late summer and early autumn. If the individual flowers are pushed to one side they remain in that position, hence 'obedient plant'.

USES This physostegia and the white form 'Summer Snow' bring colour to borders late in the flowering season.

CULTIVATION Plant in autumn or early spring in ordinary garden soil in a sunny or partially shaded position. Mulch every spring with manure or compost to conserve water in the soil. During dry spells in summer water the plants at the first sign of wilting. In late autumn or winter cut the stems right down to the ground.

PROPAGATION Divide established clumps in autumn or early spring, replanting the vigorous outer roots and discarding the woody centre. Alternatively, take cuttings of young shoots in spring.

PESTS AND DISEASES Generally trouble free.

OTHER VARIETIES *P. v.* 'Summer Snow', the white-flowered variety, grows a little taller to 75cm (30in) and flowers a few weeks earlier. There is also a form with white leaf margins and pink flowers – *P. v.* 'Variegata', 90cm (3ft) tall.

GOOD COMPANIONS An autumn flowering group could be made with physostegias, Japanese anemones, sedums and Michaelmas daisies.

soil

| | ACID | ALKALINE |
| DRY | | WET |

| J | F | M | A | M | J | J | A | S | O | N | D |

PHYSOSTEGIA VIRGINIANA 'ALBA'

PICEA PUNGENS 'KOSTER'

Koster's blue spruce, evergreen coniferous tree (Rocky Mountains, 1862). Mature at 50 years: slowly reaching 10 x 4m (30 x 12ft). AGM

Other members of the spruce family include the Norway spruce *Picea abies*, the one usually sold as a Christmas tree. Don't be tempted to buy a Christmas tree with roots and plant it in the garden on Twelfth Night. It will become a large, ungainly thing taking up valuable space. *P. pungens* 'Koster' is a great deal more attractive. It slowly makes a narrow cone. Stiff prickly needles radiate from stout shoots, the youngest being grey-blue or nearly white, the inner ones shading to dark blue-green. The overall effect is soft silvery-blue. Cones are borne after about twenty years and ripen to a shiny pale brown.

USES Plant it as a lawn specimen or as part of a group of conifers.

CULTIVATION Piceas prefer deep moist soil on the acid side. They will struggle in alkaline conditions. Plant them during suitable weather from autumn to spring in sun or partial shade and preferably in a sheltered position; young trees are easily damaged by late spring frosts. On heavy soils delay planting until spring. To achieve rapid and shapely growth use young plants no taller than 60-90cm (2-3ft). No pruning is needed except to reduce forked trees to a single leader.

PROPAGATION The blue and silver-leaved forms are propagated by grafting.

PESTS AND DISEASES Aphids may attack.

OTHER VARIETIES There are several other attractive slow growing blue and silvery-leaved forms of *P. pungens* and *P. glauca*. *P. breweriana* AGM is a beautiful weeping tree slowly reaching 10 x 4m (30 x 12ft).

soil

| | ACID | ALKALINE |
| DRY | | WET |

| J | F | M | A | M | J | J | A | S | O | N | D |

PICEA PUNGENS 'KOSTER'

PIERIS 'FOREST FLAME'

Evergreen shrub. Mature at 12 years: 1.5 x 1.2m (5 x 4ft) after 10 years; 4 x 2m (12 x 6ft) at maturity.

Pieris are distinctive shrubs, not difficult to grow provided the very specific conditions that suit them can be provided. 'Forest Flame' is one of the hardiest forms, a bushy shrub densely covered with glossy, tapering lance-shaped leaves. The young leaf shoots start bright red and turn pink, cream and finally dark green. From mid to late spring long clusters of waxy lily of the valley-like flowers cover the plant.

USES Plant pieris in woodland gardens, or in sheltered town gardens where the same conditions prevail. They can be grown in pots or tubs.

CULTIVATION Plant in early autumn or in spring in moist lime-free soil, adding leaf mould or garden compost to the planting hole and choosing a sheltered position in partial shade. Mulch every spring with leaf-mould or compost and do not allow the soil to dry out during the summer. After flowering remove the faded flower heads and cut back any straggling stems.

PROPAGATION Layer shoots in autumn. Layers usually take a year to root. Alternatively take cuttings of half-ripe shoots at any time during August.

PESTS AND DISEASES Generally trouble free.

OTHER VARIETIES There are several good named varieties. *Pieris japonica* 'Blush' has masses of pink flowers in spring and bronze young leaves.

GOOD COMPANIONS Plant pieris varieties among rhododendrons and azaleas. They enjoy the same conditions and follow each other in flower.

PIERIS 'FOREST FLAME'

PILEOSTEGIA VIBURNOIDES

Syn. **Schizophragma viburnoides,** *evergreen climber (Japan). Mature at 20 years: up to 6m (20ft).*

A slow but steady self-supporting climber, *Pileostegia* hoists itself up walls or tree trunks by means of ariel rootlets. The evergreen leaves are oval and pointed; multiple, branching heads of tiny cream-white flowers with fluffy stamens bloom from late summer until autumn.

USES *Pileostegia* will grow in sun or shade and is therefore a good candidate for a north-facing wall or for climbing into a large tree. It is not one hundred per cent reliable for hardiness, so it is at risk in cold exposed situations.

CULTIVATION Plant in spring, in ordinary well-drained soil, setting the plant at least 45cm (18in) out from the wall or other support. Attach the shoots to canes leaning against the wall to start it climbing. For the first one or two seasons water during dry spells. Established plants may need pruning to keep them within bounds. This should be done in spring.

PROPAGATION Take semi-ripe cuttings in summer, and place in a cold frame or frost-free greenhouse during the winter.

PESTS AND DISEASES Generally trouble free.

OTHER VARIETIES This is the only one, but *Schizophragma integrifolium* is an interesting climber of the same family, with similar requirements. However it will grow twice as big so really does need plenty of space. Unlike *Pileostegia viburnoides* it is deciduous. Its small flowers are accompanied by large white bracts, giving it a very distinctive appearance.

PILEOSTEGIA VIBURNOIDES

PILEOSTEGIA VIBURNOIDES

P

PINUS MUGO

Mountain pine, evergreen coniferous tree (Central and S.E. Europe). 1 x 1m (3 x 3ft) after 10 years; 4 x 6m (12 x 20ft) eventually.

This pine is variable in habit and size, but always attractive, growing into a large shrub of gnarled appearance. It looks and is tough and hardy: in the wild it colonizes steep stony slopes. The leaves are long bright green needles and the seeds are carried in long brown cones.

USES *Pinus mugo* is a good plant for difficult stony soil, rocky sites or sites exposed to the wind. Its sculptural character would suit a minimalist garden.

CULTIVATION Plant in autumn or during mild spells in winter or early spring in well-drained soil, acid or limey, in full sun. For the first few seasons apply a general fertilizer in late spring. No pruning needed.

PROPAGATION Sow seeds in early spring.

PESTS AND DISEASES Generally trouble free, but the plant may be host to caterpillars of the pine shoot moth, and sawfly, and can suffer from rust. All pines are susceptible to honey fungus.

OTHER VARIETIES *P. mugo* 'Mops' is a tidier, compact rounded form of the tree, 1 x 2m (3 x 6ft).

COMPANIONS A few carefully chosen rocks and a piece of driftwood might be better companions than other plants, but prostrate junipers and thymes would be appropriate.

soil		
ACID		ALKALINE
DRY		WET

J	F	M	A	M	J	J	A	S	O	N	D

PINUS MUGO

PITTOSPORUM TENUIFOLIUM

Evergreen shrub (New Zealand). Mature at 20 years: 3 x 1.5m (10 x 5ft) after 10 years; 6 x 2.5m (20 x 8ft) at maturity. AGM

This is one of the few pittosporums that can be grown outdoors in Britain, and except in the mildest areas it needs the protection of a south- or west-facing wall. It is grown for its attractive evergreen leaves and the scent, but not the appearance, of its flowers, which are small and insignificant. The leaves, covering a dense bushy upright shrub, are a soft shade of pale green with gracefully undulating margins. The stems are almost black. In late spring small bell-shaped, dark chocolate-purple flowers appear in the leaf axils, smelling deliciously of vanilla.

USES In very mild areas *P. tenuifolium* is used for hedging. Cut branches are popular with flower arrangers.

CULTIVATION Plant in late spring in ordinary well-drained soil in a position sheltered from north and east winds. For hedges plant 45cm (18in) apart. Trim off the tips of all the shoots at least twice in the first season. When the hedge is large enough, clip it in spring and again after midsummer. Freestanding plants or plants grown against a wall can be shaped at the same times.

PROPAGATION Take cuttings of half-ripe side shoots in late summer.

PESTS AND DISEASES Generally trouble free.

OTHER VARIETIES *P.* 'Garnettii' AGM is one of the hardiest. The leaves have white margins, which become tinted with pink in winter. *P. t.* 'Silver Queen' AGM is a tidy plant with white and grey variegated leaves.

soil		
ACID		ALKALINE
DRY		WET

J	F	M	A	M	J	J	A	S	O	N	D

PITTOSPORUM TENUIFOLIUM

PLATYCODON GRANDIFLORUS

PLUM

P

Balloon flower, hardy perennial (China and Japan, 1782). Mature at 3 years: 30 x 40cm (12 x 15in). AGM

The leaves are oval and blue-green, forming a tidy clump. It is the flower buds that resemble balloons. They appear in late summer, clustered on leafy stems and open into light blue saucer-shaped flowers, rather like those of campanulas, to which platycodon is related. They continue to bloom from mid- to late summer.

USES As low-growing, front-row plants platycodons bring welcome shades of blue and white to late flowering borders.

CULTIVATION Plant in groups of at least three, in autumn or early spring in ordinary, well-drained soil and in a sunny position. The white fleshy roots are slow-growing but once the plants are established they are

long lived, resenting disturbance. Growth starts late each spring, so mark the plants' position to avoid accidental damage.

PROPAGATION Plants more than three or four years old can be divided in spring. Or sow seeds in spring.

PESTS AND DISEASES Generally trouble free.

OTHER VARIETIES *P. g. 'albus'* is soft grey-white with blue veins. *P. g. mariesii* AGM has larger blue flowers.

COMPANIONS Plant blue platycodons with *Achillea* 'Fanal' as a cool contrast to its vibrant red colouring.

PLATYCODON GRANDIFLORUS

Prunus domestica, deciduous tree. Mature at 30 years.

Plums and gages can be grown as orchard trees up to 6m (20ft) tall or trained against a wall or on a post-and-wire framework, or grafted on dwarfing rootstock. The stock 'Pixy' will produce a bush just 2m (6ft) high. On 'St Julien A', a general purpose rootstock, trees will grow up to 4m (12ft) high. If you only have room for one tree, choose a self-fertile variety or you will not have any fruit. The others need at least one other compatible variety to pollinate them.

USES Plums are grown for their fruit, which ripens in late summer or early autumn. Dessert fruit is sweet enough to eat raw.

CULTIVATION Plant plums between autumn and spring in a sunny site sheltered from hard frosts and cold winds. They like rich soil and appreciate a thick mulch of manure or compost every spring. Prune young trees and mature trained trees in early spring. In summer tie in trained trees and cut back unwanted side shoots. On freegrowing trees and bushes cut out overcrowded, weak or damaged branches in summer. If crops are very heavy, thin out the fruit.

PROPAGATION Plum trees are propagated by grafting on to the appropriate rootstock.

PESTS AND DISEASES Trees can be attacked by birds, wasps, aphids and winter moth caterpillars. The most serious diseases are silver leaf and bacterial canker. Summer pruning helps keep silver leaf at bay.

GOOD VARIETIES 'Oullins Gage', 'Golden Transparent' and 'Reine Claude de Bavais' are self-fertile desert varieties of good flavour. 'Czar' (early) and 'Marjorie's Seedling' (late) are self-fertile cookers and 'Prune' (syn 'Shropshire') is a good self-fertile damson.

PLUM

P

POLEMONIUM CAERULEUM

Jacob's ladder, hardy perennial (northern hemisphere including Britain). Mature at 3 years: up to 60 x 45cm (2ft x 18in).

Clumps of erect leafy stems grow up in spring, carrying rich green elegant, deeply divided leaves. In early summer each stem bears a cluster of bowl-shaped blue flowers with orange-yellow stamens. If they are regularly dead-headed, they continue to flower off and on until the end of summer.

USES Polemoniums contribute early colour to mixed borders and can be naturalized in the wild garden.

CULTIVATION Plant between autumn and spring in ordinary garden soil, in sun or partial shade. Polemoniums will grow in any soil but are at their best and flower more profusely in rich soil. They appreciate an annual spring mulch of manure or garden compost. Cut the faded flower stems down to the base as soon as flowering is over to encourage fresh leaves and flowers.

PROPAGATION Divide and replant established clumps from autumn to spring. It pays to do this every few years as the plants quickly become tired.

PESTS AND DISEASES Generally trouble free.

OTHER VARIETIES *P.* 'Lambrook Mauve' (syn *P. foliosissimum*) AGM has long-lasting pale mauve-pink flowers, and *P. reptans* 'Blue Pearl' is a low-growing variety with pale blue flowers.

COMPANIONS Grow the blue polemoniums among cream and yellow *Cytisus* varieties.

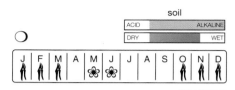

POLEMONIUM

POLEMONIUM CAERULEUM

POLYGONATUM X HYBRIDUM

Syn. P. multiflorum, Solomon's seal, hardy perennial (Europe including Britain, N. Asia). Mature at 3 years: 75 x 45cm (2ft6in x 18in). AGM

This is the garden form of a graceful woodland plant that is seldom found in the wild anymore. Pale green lance-shaped leaves, prominently ribbed, are poised horizontally all along elegantly arching stems. In late spring and early summer, it produces long green and white flowers that hang in pairs from each leaf joint.

USES Solomon's seal is a great standby for shady sites, making good ground cover and supplying attractive flowers for cutting.

CULTIVATION Plant between early autumn and spring in ordinary soil, in partial or full shade. Solomon's seal will grow almost anywhere but prefers peaty soil or leaf mould, so get your plants off to a good start by digging in leaf mould or compost. Give a good mulch every spring. Cut down the dead stems in autumn or winter.

PROPAGATION Divide and replant the spreading roots in autumn or spring, or sow seeds when they ripen in late summer or early autumn.

PESTS AND DISEASES Sawfly larvae can chomp their way through the leaves, stripping them down to skeletons. The plants will usually survive but serious infestations can be dealt with by spraying with an appropriate preparation.

OTHER VARIETIES *P. x hybridum* 'Striatum' has leaves striped lengthways with creamy white. It is less vigorous than *P. falcatum* 'Variegatum'.

COMPANIONS Use Solomon's seal in a cool, green and white foliage group with ferns, hostas and ivies.

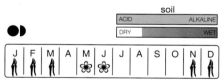

POLYGONATUM X HYBRIDUM

POLYSTICHUM SETIFERUM

Divisilobum Group, soft shield fern, evergreen hardy perennial fern (Europe including Britain). Mature at 3 years: 60cm x 45cm (2ft x 18in).

Like all ferns, this has a long period of interest, starting in the spring with the uncurling of its new fronds from shoots covered in pale brown scales. The fronds are soft-textured and the colour is soft mid green. They are intricately cut and deeply divided, arching when young but becoming prostrate in winter.

USES The soft shield fern is one of the few ferns that are tolerant of dry conditions, and can be used to give the illusion of moisture in dry shady parts of the garden.

CULTIVATION Plant in spring in the shade, preferably in a humus-rich soil, not acid, ideally containing lime or chalk. In dry soils add some compost or leaf mould when planting, and mulch every spring to be on the safe side.

PROPAGATION Sow the spores in spring or divide plants with multiple crowns in spring. Alternatively, detach bulbil-bearing fronds in autumn and peg them to the surface of a tray of compost mixed half and half with sand.

PESTS AND DISEASES Generally trouble free.

OTHER VARIETIES Ferns of *P.s.* Acutilobum Group are said to be very easy to grow in almost any conditions. The long pointed fronds are dark green in colour and are very lacy. They grow in a spiral around the crown of the plant.

COMPANIONS Plant these ferns with hostas on a steep pond bank – a site that is often dry although it looks as if it should be wet.

POTATOES

Solanum tuberosum, tender perennial with edible tuberous roots. Mature at 1 year: 60 x 60cm (2 x 2ft).

Potatoes are underground tubers; they only develop when the leafy shoots above the ground are growing vigorously. The flowers on a potato plant are small, drooping, green-white stars, similar to the flowers of the tomato.

USES If you have a small garden it is a waste of space to grow maincrop potatoes, but it is worth finding room for a row of early potatoes.

CULTIVATION Buy seed potatoes in late winter and set them to 'chit' in a light, cool but frost-free shed or room. After about six weeks they will have made shoots about 2cm (¾in) long and are ready to plant. In spring when the soil is warm plant them with their sprouts uppermost, about 2.5cm (1in) deep and 38cm (15in) apart. When the shoots are about 23cm (9in) high, earth them up by drawing soil up around them to a depth of about 10cm (4in). This ensures that the potatoes don't get exposed to the light and turn green (green potatoes are poisonous). Water copiously during dry weather. New potatoes are usually ready to dig and eat when the plants start to flower.

PESTS AND DISEASE Various pests and diseases attack potatoes. To prevent minor infestations becoming plagues, observe a three-year rotation. If infestations persist, give up growing potatoes completely for at least six years.

GOOD VARIETIES 'Accent', 'Arran Pilot' and 'Dunluce' are new potatoes with excellent flavour. 'Ratte' and the strangely shaped 'Pink Fir Apple' are later crops with the taste and texture of early poatoes.

POTENTILLA FRUTICOSA 'TANGERINE'

P

Deciduous shrub (northern hemisphere). 1.2 x 1.5m (4 x 5ft) after 5 years. AGM

A rounded shrub with small finely-cut mid-green leaves on dense twiggy branches. The single saucer-shaped yellow flowers are flushed with orange. Like other shrubby potentillas, 'Tangerine' is in flower for an exceptionally long period in summer.

USES The plants are dense enough to form weed-smothering ground cover or a low hedge. They will also grow in pots.

CULTIVATION Potentillas prefer light soil and a sunny position. In light shade there are fewer flowers but the flower colours are less likely to fade. Plant them between autumn and spring. After flowering or in early spring the bushes can be clipped over.

PROPAGATION Take half-ripe cuttings in early autumn.

PESTS AND DISEASES Generally trouble free.

OTHER VARIETIES Not all shrubby potentillas are wholly reliable. The following are among the best: *P. fruticosa* 'Abbotswood' AGM, 80 x 150cm (2ft6in x 5ft), is widespreading with masses of white flowers. 'Primrose Beauty' AGM with pale yellow flowers is the best yellow-flowered variety. There is also a group of herbaceous potentillas to brighten up the front of the border; *P.* 'Gibson's Scarlet' AGM 45 x 45cm (18 x 18in) has large scarlet strawberry flowers from mid- to late summer and plentiful strawberry-type, grey-green foliage.

COMPANIONS Many gardeners find orange a difficult colour to place in the garden. But cream variegated foliage cools it down and forget-me-nots, bluebells or borage provide a bright, clear contrast. To separate orange from more delicate colours, use white *Gypsophila paniculata*.

soil

| ACID | ALKALINE |
| DRY | WET |

| J | F | M | A | M | J | J | A | S | O | N | D |

POLYSTICHUM SETIFERUM DIVISILOBUM GROUP

soil

| ACID | ALKALINE |
| DRY | WET |

| J | F | M | A | M | J | J | A | S | O | N | D |

POTATO 'CRAIG'S ROYAL'

soil

| ACID | ALKALINE |
| DRY | WET |

| J | F | M | A | M | J | J | A | S | O | N | D |

POTENTILLA FRUTICOSA 'ABBOTSWOOD'

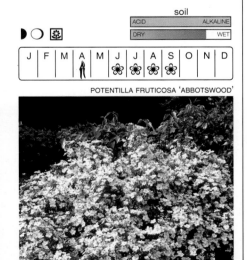

P

PRIMULA VULGARIS

PRIMULA VULGARIS

Syn. **P. acaulis,** *primrose, perennial (Britain). Mature at 2 years: 15 x 23cm (6 x 9in).*

The neat rosettes of light green corrugated, broadly lance-shaped leaves overwinter in sheltered shady places. In early spring the single pale yellow flowers appear on slender bare stems. Each flower has five heart-shaped petals, darker yellow at the centre. The flowers are lightly scented. There are single and double named varieties in white, dusky pink, purple-red and violet.

USES Plant drifts of primroses in the wild garden or in informal shrub borders. Use the more highly bred garden varieties as edging for shady beds.

CULTIVATION In the wild primroses thrive in sites sheltered from the midday sun, on west-facing banks at woodland margins or between the roots of trees. Equivalent positions in the garden are the shrubbery, the orchard or the base of a hedge. Plant between autumn and spring, adding manure or leaf mould. Water at times of drought.

PROPAGATION Primroses are unpredictable from seed but easily increased by division. After flowering dig them up, pull them apart and plant pieces with good roots straight into their final positions.

PESTS AND DISEASES Cutworms and vine weevils can destroy the roots. A number of different fungi attack other primulas, but *P. vulgaris* is generally trouble free.

COMPANIONS Planted under shrub roses and other deciduous shrubs, primroses provide interest in spring and die back unobtrusively when the shrubs come into leaf. Their natural woodland companions are *Anemone nemorosa* and *Helleborus foetidus*. For contrast plant *Chionodoxa* and *Scilla siberica* with primroses.

PRIMULA 'HUSKY MIXED'

OTHER VARIETIES There are some very pretty double forms: *P. v.* 'Lilacina Plena', 15 x 22cm (6 x 9in), has a compact rosette of bright green corrugated leaves and mauve-pink flowers; 'Miss Indigo' has very dark violet-blue flowers with a thread of white at the margin of each petal. Each flower is like a Victorian posy. 'Dawn Ansell' is a prolific variety with cream-white scented flowers.

	soil	
ACID		ALKALINE
DRY		WET

J	F	M	A	M	J	J	A	S	O	N	D

PRIMULA 'HUSKY MIXED'

PRIMULA 'HUSKY MIXED'

PRIMULA JAPONICA 'MILLER'S CRIMSON'

Candelabra primula, *hardy perennial (Japan, 1871). Mature at 3 years: 60 x 45cm (2ft x 18in).*

These are the primulas that are such a strong feature in waterside planting. Rosettes of pale green oblong, oval leaves produce stout stems each carrying several whorls of crimson-red flowers from early summer through midsummer.

USES These primulas are a mainstay of the bog garden, and of all waterside plantings.

CULTIVATION Although they revel in boggy conditions, candelabra primulas thrive in any soil that does not dry out in spring and summer. Plant them between autumn and early spring in full sun or partial shade. Before planting dig in compost or well-decayed manure. Keep the soil moist in dry weather, preferably by overhead spraying.

PROPAGATION Divide after flowering and plant directly into the new flowering positions. They can also be grown from seed, and usually self-seed freely.

PESTS AND DISEASES Fairly trouble free, but these plants are at risk from aphids, caterpillars and cutworms. Primulas can also be affected by cucumber mosaic, grey mould and leaf spot.

OTHER VARIETIES Reliable candelabras include *P. japonica* 'Postford White', *P. pulverulenta* AGM with crimson-purple flowers on stems covered in white down. *P. bulleyana* AGM and *P. aurantiaca* come in shades of orange. *P. florindae* AGM is not a candelabra and flowers a little later but overlaps and mixes well with them. It has drooping heads of scented lemon yellow bells liberally dusted with white down on 60cm (2ft) stems.

soil		
ACID		ALKALINE
DRY		WET

J	F	M	A	M	J	J	A	S	O	N	D

PRIMULA JAPONICA 'MILLER'S CRIMSON'

PRUNELLA GRANDIFLORA 'LOVELINESS'

Syn. **P. x webbiana,** *self-heal, hardy semi-evergreen perennial (Europe). Mature at 3 years: 20 x 30cm (8 x 12in). AGM*

Ground-hugging rosettes of oval mid-green leaves spread gradually to cover a wide area of earth. The pale mauve-blue flowers are tubular with spreading lobes, densely covering upright spikes from early summer to early autumn.

USES Plant prunellas as small-scale ground cover at the front of beds and borders.

CULTIVATION Plant in early spring in any ordinary soil that doesn't dry out, in sun or in partial shade. Dead-head the plants regularly throughout summer to avoid the growth of self-sown seedlings, which can become a nuisance.

PROPAGATION Divide in late summer, in autumn or in early spring, and replant directly into permanent positions.

PESTS AND DISEASES Generally trouble free.

OTHER VARIETIES Variations in flower colour are provided by *P. grandiflora* 'Blue Loveliness', 'White Loveliness' and 'Pink Loveliness'.

soil		
ACID		ALKALINE
DRY		WET

J	F	M	A	M	J	J	A	S	O	N	D

PRUNELLA GRANDIFLORA

P | PRUNUS

This versatile group includes flowering and fruiting almonds, cherries, plums (for fruiting varieties see under 'Plum'), and evergreen laurels. The Japanese cherries are lovely in flower but blossoms only last for a short time. Those described here have other attributes, such as autumn colour or beautiful bark. There is only space for a tiny selection of those available.

PRUNUS DULCIS

Syn *P. amygdalus*. Almond. Deciduous tree 8 x 8m (25 x 25ft). Single, clear pink flowers appear in clusters on the bare branches in very early spring. They are followed by mid-green lance-shaped leaves. 'Roseoplena' has double pink flowers.

USES In warm climates the almond is cultivated for its edible nuts, but in Britain for its blossom. It can be grown as a free-standing specimen, trained against a wall, fence or trellis, or grown in a container.

CULTIVATION Plant between early autumn and spring in any soil that is neither very dry nor waterlogged. No pruning is needed normally but if you need to shape the trees, do it in summer on a hot sunny day when the wounds will dry quickly. If you prune at other times the sap bleeds profusely and the tree may die.

PROPAGATION Seeds can be sown in autumn. Alternatively, bud in summer or graft in spring.

PESTS AND DISEASES Bullfinches and other birds sometimes eat the buds, and then there is no blossom. Aphids can infest young shoots. The fungus peach leaf curl can be a nuisance. Treat it by spraying with Bordeaux mixture in late winter and again two weeks later. Also spray just before leaf fall. Prunus species are susceptible to honey fungus, except for *P. laurocerasus*.

COMPANIONS Almond blossom is best seen against a blue sky or dark evergreens.

PRUNUS SARGENTII

PRUNUS

PRUNUS AVIUM 'PLENA'

Double-flowered gean, wild cherry, deciduous tree (W. Asia, Europe including Britain); 12 x 9m (40 x 30ft). This is the tree from which most of the cultivated sweet cherries are derived. It is fast-growing, making a tall, rounded crown of green leaves which colour orange and crimson in autumn. The white cup-shaped flowers are borne in pendulous clusters several centimeters long, and open with the leaves in spring. The fruits, ripening in late summer, are edible but small compared to those of cultivated varieties. It is a handsome quick-growing tree for shade or screening, tolerant of industrial pollution and useful for reclaiming consolidated ground.

PRUNUS 'SPIRE'

Syn. *P.* 'Hillieri Spire' 9 x 3m (30 x 10ft) AGM. A single-flowered cherry, 'Spire' starts as a narrow cone and broadens into a vase shape. In early spring it is smothered in a cloud of soft pink as the flowers open. The dark green leaves turn orange-red in autumn. Its compact, upright growth makes it ideal for small gardens.

PRUNUS SARGENTII

Japan, Korea 9 x 12m (30 x 40ft) AGM. Young, bronze-red leaves unfold very early in spring at the same time as the clusters of pale, clear pink flowers. This species is one of the first trees to change colour in the autumn, the leaves becoming a glorious, fiery mixture of orange and crimson.

PRUNUS X BLIREANA

Ornamental plum. Deciduous shrub or small tree 4 x 4m (12 x 12ft) AGM. This prunus is often used for hedges. The leaves are metallic coppery-purple; double rose-pink flowers appear in spring.

PRUNUS SUBHIRTELLA

This cherry blossoms in early spring, producing single pink, five-petalled flowers. The dark green leaves turn yellow in the autumn. The small fruit is reddish-brown.

PRUNUS LAUROCERASUS 'ZABELIANA'

Named form of cherry laurel, common laurel. Evergreen shrub 1.2 x 1.8m (4 x 6ft). Laurels have always been a great standby

PRUNUS AVIUM PLENA

PRUNUS LAUROCERASUS 'ZABELIANA'

for tall hedges or screens in difficult soil and in shade. 'Zabeliana' is one of a comparatively modern group which make excellent low, spreading ground cover. It is a vigorous shrub with very shiny narrow, almost willow-like leaves. They are mid-green above, pale green beneath. The branches are almost horizontal and upright spikes of white flowers are borne like candles crowding the stems in spring. They are followed by small red fruits which turn black. *P. l.* 'Otto Luyken' AGM is similar but the branches are more erect and the leaves not so narrow. *P. lusitanica* (Portugal laurel) has much smaller, less glossy foliage and red leaf stalks. It looks like a bay tree and is a good topiary subject.

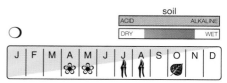

			soil								
ACID — ALKALINE
DRY — WET

J	F	M	A	M	J	J	A	S	O	N	D

PRUNUS SUBHIRTELLA FLORE-PLENO

PULMONARIA ANGUSTIFOLIA

Lungwort, hardy perennial (Central Europe, 1731). Mature at 3 years: 23 x 45cm (9 x 18in).

Plain dark green, bristly narrow lance-shaped leaves develop in spring at the same time as the flowers. The flowers, carried in clusters at the tips of short stems, are pink in bud, opening true blue, and are broadly funnel-shaped like borage flower buds. After flowering the leaves spread and flatten out to form dense clumps.

USES This and the varieties with spotted leaves described below are invaluable ground cover in shady places.

CULTIVATION Plant from autumn to early spring in a shady position in ordinary garden soil. Keep the roots moist by mulching in spring with manure or with garden compost.

PROPAGATION Divide and replant the roots in autumn or early spring.

PESTS AND DISEASES Generally trouble free but sawfly larvae sometimes eat the leaves.

OTHER VARIETIES *P. a.* 'Munstead Blue' is the earliest to flower and is very compact, just 15cm (6in) tall. *P.* 'Lewis Palmer' AGM has pure deep blue flowers and leaves spotted with silver. *P. officinalis* 'Sissinghurst White' AGM has white flowers and evergreen pale green leaves spotted with silver. *P. rubra* AGM has fresh looking green leaves and coral flowers. Then there is *P. saccharata* Argentea Group AGM; the leaves have such large silvery-grey spots that they merge to cover the entire surface. The flowers start pink and turn blue. Measuring 30 x 60cm (1 x 2ft), the whole plant is larger than most others.

GOOD COMPANIONS Interplant the blue pulmonarias with drifts of small yellow narcissi and groups of erythroniums, and follow them with Solomon's seal, then *Anemone x hybrida*.

J F M A M J J A S O N D

PULMONARIA SACCHARATA

PULMONARI ANGUSTIFOLIA

PULSATILLA VULGARIS

P

*Syn. **Anemone pulsatilla**, pasque flower, perennial (Europe including Britain). Mature at 3 years: 30 x 38cm (12 x 15in).*

The pasque flower is now rare in the wild and, lovely though it is, not seen very often in gardens. Finely-cut mid-green leaves form a tidy low mound. The dusky mauve-purple flowers open in spring from buds with a ruff of pale silky hairs. Later the seed heads are covered in the same silk fluff. There are named varieties with pale pink, white and red flowers, but they are generally not as robust as the species.

USES This is a plant to look at close up, in a raised bed, a pocket of the rock garden or the front of a border.

CULTIVATION Plant in late summer or early autumn in a sunny site in well-drained soil with added leaf mould or compost. It grows on chalk in the wild, so suits being grown in a limey soil.

PROPAGATION Sow seeds in summer.

PESTS AND DISEASES Generally trouble free.

COMPANIONS Plant *Salvia officinalis* 'Purpurascens' behind groups of pulsatilla and *Viola labradorica* for harmony; for contrast, but linked to the pulsatilla's yellow stamens, *Erysimum* 'Moonlight'.

soil
| ACID | | ALKALINE |
| DRY | | WET |

J F M A M J J A S O N D

PULSATILLA VULGARIS

P

PYRACANTHA ROGERSIANA

Firethorn, evergreen shrub or wall plant (China, 17th century). Mature at 15 years: 3 x 3m (10 x 10ft).

Pyracanthas are very hardy, with spiny branches of small glossy dark green leaves. At midsummer the bushes are smothered with clusters of small cream-white flowers, followed by bunches of red, orange or yellow berries in autumn until spring.

USES Pyracanthas are usually trained against a wall and thrive on a north or east aspect, but they are also good free-growing shrubs or hedging plants. Their vicious spines make them burglar-proof and vandal-proof, they tolerate industrial pollution and will grow in a wide range of soils.

CULTIVATION Plant between autumn and spring in any reasonable soil. If you are growing pyracanthas against a wall provide some support – hinged trellis panels, strong galvanized wire. Tie in vigorous growths each year in late summer. For a hedge, set plants 37-60cm (15-24in) apart and prune back the current season's growth by half. Pinch out the growing points of young shoots when they reach 15-20cm (6-8in) and repeat the process later in the year if necessary. Trim surplus growth from wall plants in early summer, leaving as many flower buds on the plant as possible. Clip established hedges to shape during the early summer.

PROPAGATION Take semi-ripe cuttings in late summer or hardwood cuttings in autumn, or grow from seed.

PESTS AND DISEASES There are two serious diseases: fireblight (rare but deadly) and pyracantha scab. The varieties recommended here are resistant to scab but not immune.

OTHER VARIETIES *P. rogersiana* 'Flava' has bright yellow berries, 'Soleil d'Or' golden yellow. 'Mohave' is disease-resistant with orange-red berries.

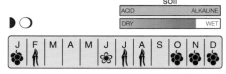

PYRACANTHA 'MOHAVE'

PYRACANTHA ROGERSIANA 'FLAVA'

PYRUS CALLERYANA 'CHANTICLEER'

Callery pear, deciduous tree. Mature at 50 years: 6m (20ft) tall after 20 years; 12 x 5m (38 x 17ft) at maturity. AGM

This pear is grown not for its fruit, which are insignificant, but for its elegant tall narrow shape, its mass of white blossom in spring and its fresh green leaves, which turn red and maroon-purple in autumn.

USES Its narrow shape and tolerance of air pollution make it a good front garden tree.

CULTIVATION Plant between autumn and spring in any ground including chalk, clay or waterlogged soil, in sun.

PROPAGATION Increase by budding in summer or grafting in winter.

PESTS AND DISEASES Pears are generally susceptible to fireblight, honey fungus and scab, but this tree is resistant to fireblight.

OTHER VARIETIES *Pyrus salicifolia* 'Pendula' AGM, the weeping silver pear, is a deservedly popular small garden tree, but eventually not as small as is generally thought. It can reach 8 x 6m (25 x 20ft). Some specimens are apt to remain low and squat, and in that case it helps to train a leading shoot up a pole to 4m (12ft).

PYRUS CALLERYANA 'CHANTICLEER'

PYRUS SALICIFOLIA

QUERCUS CERRIS

Turkey oak, deciduous tree (S. Europe, Asia Minor). Mature at 50 years: 12m (38ft) after 20 years; 30 x 25m (100 x 80ft) at maturity.

This is a tree for those with large gardens who would like to see a substantial handsome tree develop in their own lifetime. Turkey oaks are hardy, vigorous trees with domed heads, spreading with age. The mid- to deep green leaves are oval, sharply lobed and slightly rough in texture. The female flowers are generally insignificant, but male flowers are fluffy yellow catkins appearing with the new leaves in late spring. The fruits are acorns.

USES The Turkey oak is a fine shade tree for a large garden and will tolerate a wide range of soils.

CULTIVATION Plant between autumn and spring in any soil including clay and shallow soil over chalk; most trees develop a better shape in an open position and in full sun, but they will tolerate partial shade. Young plants up to 1.2m (4ft) high need no support. During the first few years an annual mulch of well-rotted manure, compost, peat or leaf mould helps to establish the trees. Remove lateral branches in winter when the trees are two or three years old, to maintain a clean stem.

PROPAGATION Acorns are short-lived and must be sown within two months.

PESTS AND DISEASES Trees can be affected by caterpillars, chafer beetles, gall wasps, oak phylloxera, fungal diseases including bracket fungi, canker, die-back, frost damage, honey fungus and powdery mildew.

OTHER VARIETIES If you are planting for posterity, *Quercus robur*, the common oak, reaching 25 x 25m (80 x 80ft) eventually, will live for centuries. It is a wonderful wild life plant, supporting an enormous number of insect, bird and small mammal species. For autumn colour on neutral or acid soil, *Quercus coccinea* 'Splendens' AGM, an improved form of the scarlet oak, 18 x 15m (55 x 45ft), is more reliable than *Q. rubra*, the red oak. The evergreen oak, *Quercus ilex*, should get a mention. It will grow on shallow chalk and makes good shelter on exposed, coastal sites. As a tree it slowly reaches 25 x 20m (80 x 70ft), but it can also be clipped into formal shapes.

soil	
ACID	ALKALINE
DRY	WET

J	F	M	A	M	J	J	A	S	O	N	D

QUERCUS CERRIS

RASPBERRY

R

Rubus idaeus, deciduous cane fruit. Mature at 3 years: 2-2.5m (6-8ft) tall.

Varieties of the edible raspberry are divided into two groups – summer fruiting and autumn fruiting. The fruit of the former are carried on shoots produced during the previous season; those of autumn fruiting varieties on shoots produced the same season. Both canes and leaves are prickly.

USES The texture and flavour survive freezing remarkably well as whole fruit or in ice cream or purée.

CULTIVATION Plant in autumn or winter, in well-drained but moisture-retentive soil. Grow in sun or partial shade and eradicate perennial weeds before planting. Mulch well in spring and water during dry spells. Canes can be tied into clumps to make them self-supporting, but they are easiest to harvest if they are supported on 12-13 gauge galvanized wires. If more than two rows are grown, allow 1.2m (4ft) between each pair of rows. At the end of the first season, leave the strong canes and cut out weak ones. On established plants, cut out the canes that have carried fruit and thin out the new shoots to five or six on each plant.

PROPAGATION Lift and transplant rooted suckers in autumn.

PESTS AND DISEASES Rather a daunting list: raspberry beetle, aphids; cane blight, cane spot, chlorosis, crown gall, grey mould, honey fungus, physiological disorders, raspberry virus diseases, spur blight. But in most gardens even if these problems occur, the crop will not suffer greatly.

GOOD VARIETIES These are chosen for flavour and resistance to diseases: 'Glen Moy', 'Glen Prosen', Malling Admiral', 'Malling Jewel', 'Autumn Bliss'.

soil	
ACID	ALKALINE
DRY	WET

J	F	M	A	M	J	J	A	S	O	N	D

RASPBERRY

R

RHAMNUS ALATERNUS 'ARGENTEOVARIEGATA'

Buckthorn, evergreen shrub (Southwest Europe). Mature at 15 years: 2.5 x 1.8m (8 x 6ft) after 10 years; 3 x 3m (10 x 10ft) at maturity.

This shrub has very pretty foliage. It makes a dense bushy pyramid of small grey-green leaves with white margins. The flowers are insignificant but after a warm summer it may produce red berries that later turn black. However, the berries are a bonus. The main attraction is the foliage and the tidy pyramidal habit of growth.

USES This shrub is tolerant of industrial pollution and of salt, so it is a good city or seaside plant. But it is not reliably hardy in cold, exposed areas, especially in its first few years. It does well in a container, and can be clipped into simple but elegant architectural shapes.

CULTIVATION Plant in spring in a sheltered corner, unless your local climate is mild. This rhamnus will grow in any reasonable soil that is not waterlogged, and does best in partial or full shade. If you want to improve the plant's shape or make a topiary, prune in late spring.

PROPAGATION Take cuttings in late summer.

PESTS AND DISEASES Generally trouble free.

COMPANIONS The soft pale colouring of the leaves makes it a good background shrub to strong coloured flowers: *Cistus x purpureus* for example, *Geranium psilostemon* or, in a group of pots, red pelargoniums or deep violet blue petunias.

RHAMNUS ALATERNUS 'ARGENTEOVARIEGATA'

RHEUM PALMATUM 'ATROSANGUINEUM'

Ornamental rhubarb, hardy perennial (China, 1763). Mature at 5 years: 1.8 x 1.8m (6 x 6ft).

This is a wonderfully dramatic plant if you have the space for it. The deeply-cut leaves are as large as those of the culinary rhubarb, and they emerge purple-red, fading to green on the top surface after flowering but remaining red on the underside. In early summer great stems carry branching plumes of deep pink or red bead-like flowers folllowed by translucent red seed heads.

USES Let it stand alone at the edge of a shrubbery in a large garden. In a small garden, break all the rules and make it the main attraction. The leaves are big enough to hide under when unwanted guests appear.

CULTIVATION Plant between autumn and early spring in ordinary garden soil and in a sunny position. The plants flowers more freely in rich soil, so mulch generously every spring with manure or good garden compost. In summer water during dry spells and give an occasional feed of liquid manure. Plants can be left undisturbed for several years. After flowering, cut the spikes down to ground level.

PROPAGATION Lift and divide established clumps in winter, making sure each piece has some roots and a dormant crown bud. Rheums can be grown from seed sown outdoors in early spring.

PESTS AND DISEASES Generally trouble free.

OTHER VARIETIES *Rheum x hybridum* is the culinary rhubarb. 'Champagne', 'Timperley Early' and 'Victoria' are all good varieties. For early, tender stalks, cover the plant in late winter with a clay rhubarb forcer or, less glamorous, an upturned bucket to blanch the stems. They should be ready to pick after some four weeks.

RHEUM PALMATUM 'ATROSANGUINEUM'

RHODODENDRONS AND AZALEAS

R

Evergreen and deciduous shrubs (Asia, Japan, N. America). Mature at 12 years.

Azaleas come under the botanical umbrella of 'rhododendron' so they are included here. Neither really qualify for inclusion as their flowering season is so short, but some have fine evergreen foliage or autumn colour to reinforce their claim, and they are an important and much-loved genus for gardens on acid soil. The plants range from small creeping shrubs to trees 18m (60ft) high, and most are evergreen. The leaves are oval or broadly lance-shaped; on some azaleas they are very small and densely packed on horizontal branches, giving the plants a distinctive shape. The leaves of some of the largest rhododendrons are huge with rusty fur on their underside; they droop in

RHODODENDRON 'HYNO-MAYO' (AZALEA)

RHODODENDRON AUGUSTINII

RHODODENDRON VIRGATUM SSP. OLEIFOLIUM

clusters on branches that are upheld like candelabras. The flowers, mostly blooming between late spring and early summer, are borne in clusters at the tips of the shoots and are bell- or funnel-shaped. A few species are fragrant, some strongly so. Colours range from an almost-lavender blue through every shade of purple, red, orange and yellow to white.

USES Rhododendrons and azaleas are at their best in naturalistic gardens, growing under trees, preferably on a steep slope to emulate their natural habitat. The smaller varieties do well in pots or tubs.

CULTIVATION There are a few exceptions, but it is best to assume that they will not tolerate alkaline soil. The ideal is a well-drained sandy loam. If you garden on chalk or limestone and you still want to grow rhododendrons, grow them in pots of lime-free compost or in raised beds of lime-free soil. Many species are sensitive to full sun and exposure to cold winds, and do best in woodland or other sheltered, semi-shaded positions. But avoid planting azaleas and rhododendrons under surface-rooting trees such as elms, limes, poplars and sycamores. Protect species that flower before the end of May from early-morning sun, to avoid damage caused by sudden thawing after frost. No regular pruning is needed but leggy plants can be cut hard back in spring. If a rhododendron has outgrown its position it can always be

RHODODENDRON OBTUSUM

RHODODENDRON 'BEAUTY OF LITTLEWORTH'

moved. They transplant easily because of their compact root system. Do it in mild weather between late summer and spring. When dead-heading, use your finger and thumb, as secateurs can easily damage the young shoots.

PROPAGATION Species can be grown from seed. Named forms can be increased by layering at any time of year or by grafting. Alternatively, take cuttings from hardy species and hybrids with small scaly leaves in late summer.

PESTS AND DISEASES There are many of these, but if the plants are grown in the right conditions, none of them should be too troublesome: rhododendron leafhopper, rhododendron bug, weevils, caterpillars, azalea gall, die-back, honey fungus, leaf spots, rhododendron bud-blast, rust and silver leaf.

GOOD VARIETIES There are thousands to choose from, and garden centres and general shrub nurseries usually have a wide enough selection to get you started, especially in areas of acid soil. If you become an enthusiast you will want to use specialist suppliers. Choose your first plants when they are in flower. For small gardens, evergreen rhododendrons of the Yakushimanum Group are free-flowering and have good dark leaves, often with light brown furry undersides. Among deciduous azaleas, *Rhododendron luteum* has yellow flowers, scent and good autumn colours. As scent and autumn colour are available, make sure you choose varieties that have them: Ghent hybrids are among the best in this respect. Evergreen azaleas are not all reliably hardy but Kaempferi hybrids and Vuyk hybrids should be all right.

soil

| ACID | | ALKALINE |
| DRY | | WET |

| J | F | M | A | M | J | J | A | S | O | N | D |

RHODODENDRON MUCRONULATUM

R

RHUS TYPHINA 'DISSECTA'

Syn. **R. hirta, R.t. *'Laciniata'* stag's horn, sumach, deciduous shrub or small tree (Eastern USA, early 17th century). Mature at 20 years: 3 x 2m (10 x 6ft) after 10 years; 4 x 4m (12 x 12ft) at maturity. AGM**

The 'stag's horn' epithet is earned by the plant's gaunt, forked winter branches covered in velvety hairs. But the main attraction is the autumn colour of the large finely dissected leaves, which turn deep red, orange and yellow. Stubby flower spikes appear in late summer covered in tiny fluffy dark pink flowers, changing in autumn to burgundy plush. At all seasons the plant is striking rather than beautiful.

USES Plant *Rhus typhina* as part of a scheme concentrating on autumn colours, or in a spot where the sculptural effect of the branches in winter can be enjoyed. It is a good plant for areas of industrial pollution, and will grow on ground that has been consolidated by machinery.

CULTIVATION *Rhus typhina* tolerates a wide range of soils on the dry side, including chalk and sand. Pruning is not necessary, but if you get bored with the plant you can cut it to the ground in late winter. It will then give a terrific display of large leaves but will not flower for a year or two. If the foliage is what you want, you can prune in this way every year.

PROPAGATION Take 10-13cm (4-5in) cuttings of half-ripe shoots with a heel in late summer, or detach rooted suckers in autumn. Shoots layered in early spring should be ready after one or two years.

PESTS AND DISEASES Generally trouble free. It is resistant to honey fungus.

OTHER VARIETIES Avoid the species *R. typhina* as it throws up suckers all over the place. The variety 'Laciniata' does not have this vice.

RHUS TYPHINA 'DISSECTA'

RHUS TYPHINA 'DISSECTA'

RIBES ODORATUM

Syn. **R. aureum, buffalo currant, deciduous shrub (Central USA, 1812). 2 x 2m (6 x 6ft).**

A much-branching plant making a dense mass of stems. The leaves are pale green, three-lobed and coarsely toothed. They turn red and purple in autumn. The flowers appear in spring, in hanging clusters. They are golden yellow and have a spicy scent. They are followed by round dark purple or purple-black currant-like berries.

USES Like the other flowering currants, this shrub is useful where quick results are needed. I prefer this one's golden flowers to the murky pinks and reds of *Ribes sanguinem* varieties, and this one has the bonus of autumn colour. Branches of the pink forms, if cut in bud and put in water indoors, will open palest pink or white.

CULTIVATION Plant between autumn and spring in ordinary soil in sun or light shade. Mulch with manure or compost every spring. Prune every year after flowering to keep the bushes compact and to encourage flowers: cut out one stem in three and, if necessary, shorten the remaining stems.

PROPAGATION Take hardwood cuttings during the autumn.

PESTS AND DISEASES Generally trouble free but susceptible to honey fungus.

OTHER VARIETIES *R. speciosum* AGM is the most attractive of the currants, very different from the rest, with long, sparse, arching branches hung with very slender red fuchsia-like flowers in spring; it is hardy in the open but does well and looks good against a wall. The ever-popular flowering currant *R. sanguineum* has a yellow-leaved form 'Brocklebankii' AGM but pink flowers with yellow leaves are not to everyone's taste.

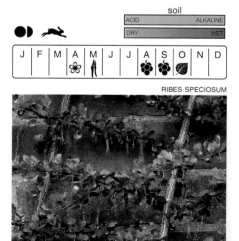

RIBES SPECIOSUM

ROBINIA HISPIDA

Rose acacia, deciduous shrub (Southeastern USA, 1743). 2.5 x 2.5m (8 x 8ft). AGM

The sparsely branching, bristly stems carry dark green divided leaves like those of an ash tree. In late spring and early summer hanging clusters of large deep rose-pink pea flowers appear. The stems are very brittle and liable to snap in the wind. In the wild the plants increase by sending out suckering roots, but commercially-grown plants are nearly always grafted on to a single stem.

USES *R. hispida* looks very attractive trained against a wall.

CULTIVATION Because of its brittle branches, it needs shelter from strong winds. Otherwise it is easily suited in a sunny place in any soil that is not waterlogged, including poor dry soil. Plant in spring. Wall-trained plants can be pruned in winter, cutting back outward pointing shoots to 2.5cm (1in).

PROPAGATION On non-grafted plants, detach rooted suckers. Otherwise graft on to *R. pseudoacacia* stock.

PESTS AND DISEASES Generally trouble free. Tolerant of honey fungus.

OTHER VARIETIES *Robinia pseudoacacia*, the locust or false acacia, is too big for most gardens at 25 x 15m (80 x 50ft), although *R. p.* 'Frisia' is a popular choice for small gardens. It has the soft multiple leaves of its parent, but they open bright golden yellow, turn greenish later and flare into orange yellow in autumn. It grows to 6m (20ft) in ten years, 15m (50ft) at maturity, but remaining narrow (about 7m, 23ft).

RODGERSIA PINNATA 'SUPERBA'

Hardy rhizomatous perennial (China, 1902). Mature at 5 years: 90 x 60cm (3 x 2ft). AGM

The rodgersias are a family of handsome foliage plants for moist and boggy ground. This one has large leaves divided into long oval leaflets held in pairs. They are bright green suffused with red-bronze and are held up on strong stalks. In summer established plants produce tall, multi-stemmed spikes of fluffy pink flowers.

USES Rodgersias make imposing ground cover for the margins of ponds and streams, or for damp woodland.

CULTIVATION Plant in spring and mulch well with manure or compost. Choose a position in sun or light shade in any soil that does not dry out, including bog. In very cold areas protect the crowns of the plants in winter by covering them with bracken or fern fronds.

PROPAGATION Divide and then replant the rhizomes in spring.

PESTS AND DISEASES Generally trouble free.

OTHER VARIETIES There are several other rodgersias with the same bronzed colouring but different leaf shapes. *R. aesculifolia* AGM has large crinkled leaves, held in fingers like chestnut leaves, and creamy flowers; *R. podophylla* AGM has huge broad lobed leaves and cream-white flowers in loosely branched clusters.

COMPANIONS In large-scale planting schemes, bold groups of rodgersias can hold their own with gunnera and lysichiton. Where space is more limited their handsome leaves set off the flowers of astilbes and primulas.

ROMNEYA COULTERI

Californian poppy, deciduous perennial or subshrub (Southwest California, 1875). Mature at 7 years: 1.8 x 1.2cm (6 x 4ft).

This is one of the loveliest grey-leaved plants, with large, deeply cut leaves of light bluish-grey and strong pale blue-grey stems. The stems branch to produce smooth blue-grey round buds. The flowers are huge white single poppies with silky crumpled petals and a large boss of yellow stamens at the centre. They appear in late summer and early autumn and have a sweet scent. They are unpredictable plants and slow to establish but if well-suited they will put out long suckering roots that pop up even in the narrowest of gaps between flagstones.

USES Romneya is usually grown against a wall but will grow in an open border in mild areas.

CULTIVATION Plant romneyas in spring in full sun in a position sheltered from cold winds. Avoid frost pockets and for the first few winters protect with a covering of bark mulch or bracken. They appreciate good, moisture retentive soil, so mulch them after planting and every spring thereafter. The stems usually die down in winter. Any that remain should be cut right down to the ground in spring.

PROPAGATION Detach rooted suckers.

PESTS AND DISEASES Generally trouble free.

OTHER VARIETIES *Romneya c.* 'White Cloud', syn. *Romneya x hybrida* is more compact and bushier, and may be somewhat hardier.

COMPANIONS It needs some solid, dark foliage to set it off: *Cistus x corbariensis*, perhaps. For flowers, the airy heads of gypsophila make a lovely contrast.

R

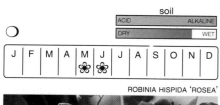

ROBINIA HISPIDA 'ROSEA'

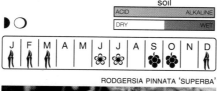

RODGERSIA PINNATA 'SUPERBA'

ROMNEYA COULTERI

R

ROSA

There is only space to give a rough indication of the variety of roses available and their versatility. There are ground cover roses, shrubs, climbers, ramblers, standards and weeping standards. Some creep along the ground at a height of 30cm (1ft), others rampage to the top of 12m (40ft) trees. The flowers can be single or double, 2.5cm (1in) across or 12cm (5in), borne singly or in clusters, and some have a wonderful sweet scent. Many roses have ornamental hips in the autumn and some shrub roses have very pretty foliage.

USES Very few gardens have space for the traditional separate rose garden. Instead roses are grown in mixed borders, as shrubs in grass, as ground cover, climbing up trees and on walls, trellises, arches or pergolas.

CULTIVATION Plant roses bought in containers at any time. Bare-rooted roses will be delivered between autumn and spring and should be planted as soon as possible. Roses are hungry plants and plenty of manure dug into the planting hole will pay dividends. Make sure you bury the joint where the branches join the roots two centimeters or so under the surface. When planting cut back the stems of all roses to about 15cm (6in). Every spring apply a granular fertilizer or mulch with manure. After the first flush of flowers, feed again to ensure a good second crop on repeat flowering roses. Pruning is not the tricky, skilled business it used to be. Research has shown that if you run over your roses with an electric hedge-trimmer in early spring

ROSA 'JUST JOEY'

ROSA 'KORRESIA'

the results will be as good as using more careful methods.

PROPAGATION Professional growers propagate by budding, but you will get quite a good strike rate from hardwood cuttings taken in autumn.

PESTS AND DISEASES Aphids and sawfly are the pests, blackspot, mildew and rust the diseases that attack roses. You can prevent them by spraying at fortnightly intervals, starting when the leaves first unfurl in spring. Well-fed healthy plants are less

susceptible and some varieties are more disease resistant than others. Most suppliers fail to include this invaluable information in their catalogues. Roses are also susceptible to honey fungus.

GOOD VARIETIES The best way to choose is to visit a good collection. An instructive time to go is after midsummer when the once-flowering roses are past their best. You can spot and avoid those with thin, straggly growth or flowers too heavy for their necks or flowers that rot in the bud in wet weather. If they are disease-prone it will be starting to show. Here I describe just one of each category, but of course there are very many others just as good.

PROSTRATE GROUND COVER: 'Snow Carpet' slowly makes a dense mound 30 x 75cm (1 x 2ft6in) with small glossy dark green leaves and masses of small double white flowers all summer and into autumn.

ROSA 'APPLE BLOSSOM'

ROSA 'CHARLES DE MILLS'

ROSA 'PINK BELLS'

ROSA 'ALEC'S RED'

R

GROUND COVER SHRUB: 'Bonica' 1.2 x 1.5m (4 x 5ft) makes a spreading mound of healthy, disease-resistant glossy leaves and clusters of soft pink double flowers. 'Pink Bells' is similar with pink pompon flowers.

SPECIES SHRUB: *R. x cantabrigiensis* is a graceful shrub with ferny leaves and arching branches smothered with pale yellow single flowers in early summer. The white-flowered *R. pimpinellifolia*, the Scottish rose, is good for poor soil.

OLD ROSE: 'Maiden's Blush' 1.5 x 1.2m (5 x 4ft) is an Alba rose, dating back to the Middle Ages. The leaves are grey-green and the flat rosette flowers are blush-pink and richly scented. Albas flower only once at midsummer but they are robust and will grow in poor soil and partial shade. The Gallica rose, 'Charles de Mills' has large rich crimson flowers.

FLORIBUNDA (CLUSTER-FLOWERED): 'Korresia' 75cm (2.5ft), plant 60cm (2ft) apart. This is a healthy, disease-resistant yellow variety with scented flowers. 'Just Joey' has stunning coppery-pink blooms.

HYBRID TEA (LARGE-FLOWERED): 'Deep Secret' 60 x 60cm (2 x 2ft) has large, very dark velvety red flowers with a rich scent. 'Alec's Red' is deep red and highly scented.

CLIMBER: 'Mme Alfred Carrière' grows to 6m (20ft) and is the most reliable all-purpose climbing rose. It is strong and disease-resistant and grows in any aspect including north. The flowers are white tinged with pink and sweetly scented. 'New Dawn' has silvery-pink flowers and fresh glossy foliage.

RAMBLER: 'Veilchenblau' 5m (15ft), has clusters of small blue-magenta flowers fading to dusky mauve. It is thornless and highly scented. 'Apple Blossom' has masses of pink flowers with crinkled petals.

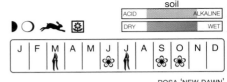

soil

| ACID | | ALKALINE |
| DRY | | WET |

| J | F | M | A | M | J | J | A | S | O | N | D |

ROSA PIMPINELLIFOLIA

ROSA 'NEW DAWN'

R

ROSMARINUS OFFICINALIS

Rosemary, hardy evergreen shrub (Mediterranean region, prior to 16th century). Mature at 7 years: 2 x 2m (6 x 6ft).

Rosemary is a much-loved herb. It is a low-branching shrub with upright stems covered in small narrow, dark blue-green leaves. They are aromatic, releasing their scent when rubbed or brushed against. The pale blue-mauve lipped flowers are borne all the way up the stems. Flowering is in early spring, but a few flowers will sometimes appear in mild spells in winter, and intermittently throughout the summer.

USES Rosemary has a strong position in the mythology of herbs as the plant for remembrance: to grow a cutting from a friend's garden is to reinforce the friendship. It is an important flavouring herb for meat and vegetables.

CULTIVATION Rosemary needs sun and good drainage; on heavy soil add gravel to the planting hole. It thrives on chalk or sandy soil or in containers and by the sea. Plant in spring; for hedges set plants 60cm (2ft) apart. In very cold areas grow rosemary in a pot and bring it into an unheated greenhouse in winter. Prune in spring to prevent plants becoming leggy. Clip all growth to within 10cm (4in) of the main framework. Annual plants can be kept small by pruning.

PROPAGATION Take cuttings in late summer or early autumn.

PESTS AND DISEASES Generally trouble free.

OTHER VARIETIES 'Miss Jessopp's Upright' AGM is the best for hedges, being compact and upstanding.

COMPANIONS Rosemary always looks happy with other herbs and makes a good structural shape among old roses.

soil		
ACID		ALKALINE
DRY		WET

J	F	M	A	M	J	J	A	S	O	N	D

ROSMARINUS OFFICINALIS

RUBUS 'BENENDEN'

Syn. R. tridel, deciduous shrub. A cross made in the 1950s, between R. trilobus (S. Mexico) and R. deliciosus (Rocky Mountains). Mature at 14 years: 1.8 x 1.8m (6 x 6ft) after 10 years; 3 x 3m (10 x 10ft) at maturity. AGM

This graceful shrub has arching stems with cinnamon brown peeling bark; they rise from the base of the plant. The leaves are shallowly lobed with serrated margins; they turn gold in autumn. Large slightly scented white flowers resembling single roses are borne in early summer.

USES Plant it as a specimen shrub where its arching shape can be appreciated, in grass or in a border surrounded by low plants. It tolerates pollution.

CULTIVATION Plant in any reasonable soil including chalk or clay, in sun or light shade. If stems are overcrowded remove some of the oldest from the base.

RUBUS COCKBURNIANUS

PROPAGATION Increase by layering in spring.

PESTS AND DISEASES Generally trouble free but susceptible to honey fungus.

OTHER VARIETIES *R. cockburnianus* AGM is grown for its prickly winter stems – purple overlaid with a dense white bloom. The leaves, grey-green above and white underneath, are fine cut and ferny. It spreads quite aggressively so chop out the suckers regularly to keep it under control. *R. tricolor* is a mile-a-minute, shade-tolerant ground cover plant sending out long, thick red bristly stems that root as they go. It has glossy green leaves and single white flowers followed by red raspberry-like fruit, edible but not delicious.

soil		
ACID		ALKALINE
DRY		WET

J	F	M	A	M	J	J	A	S	O	N	D

RUBUS TRICOLOR

RUBUS 'TRIDEL'

RUDBECKIA FULGIDA

Black-eyed susan, hardy perennial (N. America, 1760). Mature at 3 years: 60 x 30cm (2 x 1ft).

The bright golden-yellow daisy flowers have narrow petals pointing outwards and downwards to display prominent black cones at the centre. They are borne prolifically in late summer and autumn on strong stems above a clump of narrow green leaves.

CULTIVATION Plant in autumn or spring in any reasonable soil in full sun. After flowering cut the stems down to the ground.

PROPAGATION Divide congested clumps, plant rooted pieces and throw away the tired centre.

PESTS AND DISEASES Generally trouble free.

OTHER VARIETIES The form usually planted is 'Goldsturm' 75 x 30cm (30 x 12in). 'Goldquelle', 1.5m x 60cm (5 x 2ft), has double flowers that have green buttons at their centre.

COMPANIONS I find these bright hard yellows difficult to place. A background of dark coppery foliage helps, and the rusty autumnal colours of *Helenium* and *Gaillardia* blend well.

RUMEX ACETOSA

Sorrel, hardy perennial (Europe including Britain). Mature at 3 years: 45 x 30cm (18 x 12in).

This is not by any stretch of the imagination an ornamental plant; it is better suited to the kitchen garden or border, tucked in unobtrusively between shrubs. Strong upright stems carry juicy bright green arrow-head leaves with a sharp lemony flavour, which increases as the leaves mature. Taller stems bear close clusters of small green-pink flowers like those of the weed dock. In fact the whole plant can easily be mistaken for a dock.

USES You cannot buy sorrel at the supermarket so if you like sorrel soup or sauce you have to grow the plant yourself. Finely-shredded sorrel tossed in hot herb butter makes a delicious accompaniment to salmon. The juice from the leaves is said to remove stains from ink, rust and mould that discolour linen.

CULTIVATION Set plants out 30cm (12in) apart in lines or groups in the vegetable plot, herb garden or mixed border, in sun or light shade and in any reasonable soil provided it does not dry out. On light soils, mulch with manure or compost. Harvest the leaves on a cut-and-come-again basis and cut off the flower stems before they have a chance to flower, to keep a fresh supply of leaves coming.

PROPAGATION Divide the roots and replant about every five years or grow afresh from seed sown in spring.

PESTS AND DISEASES Slugs and snails may eat the leaves.

RUTA GRAVEOLENS 'JACKMAN'S BLUE'

Rue, herb of grace, evergreen shrub (S.E. Europe, pre-16th century). Mature at 5 years: 60 x 60cm (2 x 2ft). POISONOUS: Some people are allergic to the leaves and develop a serious skin rash on contact.

This form of common rue is a compact bushy shrub densely covered in smooth bright blue-green leaves, deeply divided with rounded tips. From midsummer onwards, clusters of small dark yellow flowers open at the tips of the stems.

USES Although the leaves contain an irritant, rue has always been used in herbal medicine and still is. It is also used as a homeopathic remedy. In the garden it can be clipped into simple topiary shapes and its distinctive colour makes it useful for contrasting with other foliage in knot garden patterns.

CULTIVATION Plant rue in spring in any well-drained soil in sun or partial shade. It prefers alkaline soil and will be hardier if grown in rather poor soil, so do not feed the plants. If you are planting a group, set them 45m (18in) apart. For edging or knots, plant at 20cm (8in). Some gardeners like to remove the flowers before they bloom, as they are a rather harsh shade of yellow. They can be clipped over closely using shears in spring and at any time during the summer. Wear gloves when handling the plants.

PROPAGATION Take cuttings during the late summer.

PESTS AND DISEASES Generally trouble free.

OTHER VARIETIES *R. graveolens* 'Variegata' has blue-green leaves splashed with cream but often reverts to all green.

COMPANIONS The blue leaves harmonize with almost any flower colour, especially the pure orange of pot marigolds.

R

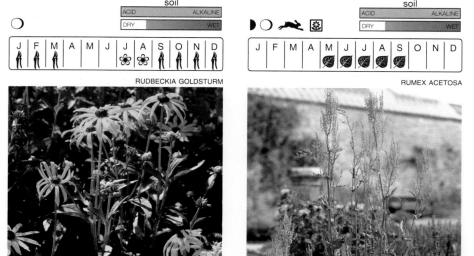

RUDBECKIA GOLDSTURM

RUMEX ACETOSA

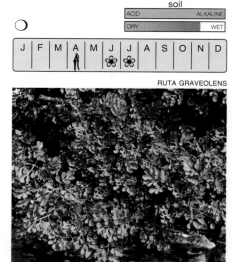

RUTA GRAVEOLENS

S

SAGITTARIA SAGITTIFOLIA

Syn. S. japonica. Arrowhead, hardy perennial water plant (Europe including Britain). Mature at 5 years: 45 x 30cm (18 x 12in).

This deciduous plant grows at the water's edge in ponds and lakes, in mud or in water up to 23cm (9in) deep. The glossy green leaves are carried upright and are a beautiful arrowhead shape. It is a plant worth growing for the effect of its leaves alone, but in summer there are also spikes of white flowers with three petals and dark purple centres. The double flowered variety 'Flore Pleno' is the one to go for: it increases slowly, whereas the single-flowered species can be invasive. They start flowering after midsummer.

USES Even the invasive species has its uses; it will hold a mud bank together and prevent erosion where ducks go in and out of the water.

CULTIVATION In late spring or early summer either plant the rhizomes directly into the mud at the water's edge or plant them in plastic mesh containers lined with hessian or other porous material. Lower the containers into position in shallow water next to the bank.

PROPAGATION Divide the rhizomes of large established clumps.

PESTS AND DISEASES Generally trouble free.

OTHER VARIETIES *S. s.* 'Flore Pleno' has double flowers (see above).

COMPANIONS *Butomus umbellatus*, the flowering rush, will provide contrasting slender upright leaves and pretty umbels of pink flowers.

J	F	M	A	M	J	J	A	S	O	N	D

SAGITTARIA SAGITTIFOLIA

SALIX ALBA

White willow and its varieties, deciduous trees (W. Asia and Europe including Britain). Mature at 30 years: var. sericea AGM, 15 x 8m (50 x 25ft) S.a. vitellina 25 x 10m (80 x 30ft) AGM, S.a. vitellina 'Britzensis' AGM, 25 x 10m (80 x 30ft).

Salix alba var. *sericea* is a fast growing tree with delicate, narrow silvery lance-shaped leaves, very beautiful when ruffled in the wind. *S. a. vitellina* has yellow stems and green leaves, and 'Britzensis' has orange-scarlet stems. These two are more often seen hard pruned as large shrubs than grown to their full size. Nevertheless, as mature trees they can be very striking when seen in a winter landscape.

USES These and other willows are great standbys for wet ground or heavy clay soil. Although they lose their leaves in winter they are invaluable when a quick screen is needed, and when they outgrow their space they can be pollarded or stooled.

CULTIVATION Plant willows in autumn or spring in a sunny position in any soil that is not too dry, including waterlogged soil. But *Salix caprea* and *S. purpurea* will grow in dry soil. Prune plants grown for their coloured stems in early spring, cutting them back to within a few centimetres of the main stem. This may be done every year, every two years or every three years.

PROPAGATION Willows are incredibly easy to grow from cuttings. You just cut off a few shoots 60cm (2ft) or more long and stick them in the ground. Rows of cuttings can be interwoven lattice fashion to make leafy live trellises or willow cabins.

PESTS AND DISEASES Aphids, caterpillars and gall mites may attack willows, and they may suffer from fungal diseases, including honey fungus.

OTHER VARIETIES *Salix x sepulcralis chrysocoma*, the weeping willow, although very lovely, is only for the largest gardens. *S. purpurea* 'Pendula' AGM is a pretty weeper just 5m (16ft).

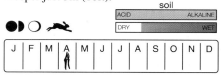

J	F	M	A	M	J	J	A	S	O	N	D

SALIX X SEPULCRALIS CHRYSOCOMA

SALIX ALBA 'CHERMESINA'

S

SALVIA OFFICINALIS

Sage, evergreen shrub (S. Europe, probably introduced by the Romans). Mature at 5 years: 60 x 90cm (2 x 3ft).

An ancient culinary herb, sage is also a handsome foliage plant, densely clothed with aromatic grey-green, downy wrinkled leaves, oval and pointed. Some forms carry spires of small mauve-blue hooded and lipped flowers after midsummer, but the flower stems tend to be sparse or non-existent because existing clones have been bred to produce leaves, not flowers.

USES Sage used to be an important medicinal herb and is still important in the kitchen, particularly for flavouring fatty meats. Sage leaves are delicious fried. In the garden sage makes excellent ground cover and can be used as infill in knots and parterres.

CULTIVATION Plant sage in spring in sun or partial shade in light, preferably alkaline soil. For quick ground cover or for edging, set the plants 45cm (18in) apart. Every spring cut all shoots hard back. Even so it will probably be necessary to grub them up and start again every five years.

PROPAGATION Cuttings in summer.

PESTS AND DISEASES Generally trouble free.

GOOD VARIETIES *S. o.* 'Icterina' has leaves with butter yellow variegation, and *S. o.* 'Purpurascens' has leaves with soft purple-grey colouring.

	soil	
ACID		ALKALINE
DRY		WET

J	F	M	A	M	J	J	A	S	O	N	D

SALVIA OFFICINALIS (FLOWERING FORM)

SALVIA OFFICINALIS 'ICTERINA'

SALVIA X SUPERBA

Hardy perenial (S.E. Europe, 1900). Mature at 3 years: 90 x 45cm (3ft x 18in). AGM

A clump of mat, dull green crinkled, pointed leaves throws up erect branching spikes of small violet-blue lipped flowers with red-purple bracts giving an overall effect of vibrant violet-purple. The bracts remain when the flowers have faded, extending the season of colour from midsummer to early autumn.

USES A valuable component in herbaceous and mixed planting schemes.

CULTIVATION Plant in groups of three or more 45cm (18in) apart in any reasonable soil in sun or partial shade, but salvias do flower more prolifically in full sun. If you dead-head regularly, new stems will keep coming. The alternative is to cut the whole plant to the ground in late summer to stimulate new growth for autumn colour.

PROPAGATION Divide congested clumps during the spring.

PESTS AND DIEEASES Generally trouble free.

GOOD VARIETIES *Salvia* x *sylvestris* 'Mainacht' ('May Night') is similar to *S. x superba* but at 45cm (18in), half as tall. *S. x sylvestris* 'Blauhügel', 50cm (20in), and *S. pratensis* Haematodes Group AGM, 90cm (3ft), are pale blue and pale mauve-blue respectively.

COMPANIONS All these herbaceous salvias contrast beautifully with yellow flowers – potentillas, achilleas and hemerocallis. In stronger colour schemes *S. x superba* and *S. x sylvestris* 'Mainacht' add richness and depth to crimson peonies or scarlet *Papaver orientale*.

	soil	
ACID		ALKALINE
DRY		WET

J	F	M	A	M	J	J	A	S	O	N	D

SALVIA FARINACEA 'VICTORIA'

SALVIA NEMOROSA 'OSTFRIESLAND'

S

SAMBUCUS RACEMOSA 'SUTHERLAND GOLD'

Golden cut-leaved elder, deciduous shrub. Mature at 10 years: 2 x 1.2m (6 x 4ft) after 10 years, 3 x 3m (10 x 10ft) at maturity. AGM

This robust shrub is grown for its foliage. Its habit of growth it similar to that of the wild elder, with stout soft light green stems maturing to greyish wood. The leaves are large and deeply divided. In bud they are pinky bronze, and open to golden yellow in sun, lime green in shade.

USES Plant elders for a quick and colourful effect, or to lighten dark corners in almost any soil. They tolerate industrial pollution and are useful when reclaiming derelict ground. The scented flowers and the berries of *Sambucus nigra* are used medicinally and as flavouring agents.

CULTIVATION Plant between autumn and spring in any soil including heavy clay, chalk and other very alkaline or acid soils. Elders will also grow in badly drained and waterlogged sites. Plant in sun or shade. In sun, make sure the site is sheltered from scorching winds. To prevent the plants becoming straggly and to keep a constant supply of fresh foliage, prune hard every year in early spring.

PROPAGATION Take hardwood cuttings in late winter.

PESTS AND DISEASES Generally trouble free. Tolerant of honey fungus.

OTHER VARIETIES *S. racemosa* 'Tenuifolia' AGM is a choice form slowly building up a mound of finely cut foliage, in the style of a Japanese acer. There is also a beautiful cut-leaved form of the wild elder, *Sambucus nigra* 'Laciniata' AGM; white and yellow variegated forms ('Marginata' and 'Aureomarginata'); and a dark-leaved form 'Guincho Purple' AGM.

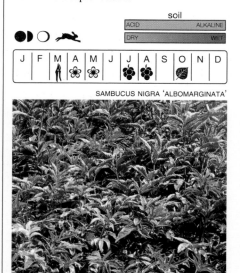
SAMBUCUS NIGRA 'ALBOMARGINATA'

SANTOLINA PINNATA SSP. NEAPOLITANA 'EDWARD BOWLES'

Cotton lavender, evergreen shrub (Italy, mid 16th century). Mature at 5 years: 80cm x 1.2m (2ft 6in x 4ft).

This fast-growing Mediterranean shrub makes a dense mound of light silvery blue-grey thread-like feathery leaves. After spring pruning the new leaves start green then gradually turn silver. After midsummer, straight wiry bare stems carry at their tips fluffy little cream-yellow button flowers. In some species and varieties of santolina the flowers are such a brassy shade of yellow that most gardeners prefer to cut the stems down before the flowers can open. But in the case of 'Edward Bowles' the flowers make a real contribution.

USES Santolinas are a mainstay of planting schemes on hot, dry sites, specially by the sea. The more compact varieties can be used to make threads in knot gardens, specially *S. chamaecyparissus* var. *nana* (syn. var. *corsica*). The larger kinds can be used for low hedges dividing the garden, and can be clipped into simple topiary shapes. All make excellent ground cover.

CULTIVATION Plant in full sun in any free-draining soil, especially chalk. For ground cover, plant *S. chamaecyparissus* and *S. pinnata* 45cm (18in) apart. For edging and hedges plant 30cm (12in) apart. To prevent the plants becoming leggy in spring, as soon as new young shoots show at the base cut the whole plant down to 5cm (2in) high. Trim hedges and edgings in spring and again at flowering time.

PROPAGATION Cuttings taken in late summer root easily.

PESTS AND DISEASES Generally trouble free.

OTHER VARIETIES *S. chamaecyparissus* AGM and *S. c. nana* AGM both have tighter, denser silver leaves than *neapolitana* and brassy yellow flowers best removed. *S. rosmarinifolia* 'Primrose Gem' is a pretty green-leaved form with attractive pale yellow flowers.

COMPANIONS Artemisias, lavenders, senecio and other grey-leaved plants provide textural contrasts. Dark red antirrhinums are terrific with the pale yellow flowers and silvery leaves.

SANTOLINA NEAPOLITANA

SANTOLINA PINNATA SSP. NEAPOLITANA 'EDWARD BOWLES'

SAXIFRAGA MOSCHATA

SAXIFRAGA FORTUNEI

Hardy perennial (China, Japan, 1863). Mature at 5 years: 30 x 30cm (12 x 12in). AGM

There are hundreds of different saxifrages, most of them requiring the special conditions that only alpine enthusiasts can provide. But some are easy and very worthwhile. *S. fortunei* makes a rosette of broad, glistening green leaves with undersides suffused with red. The flowers do not appear until early autumn; they are small and white, held in airy sprays on slender branching stems.

USES This and the other saxifrages listed below are good ground cover plants. Mossy saxifrages do well on or among rocks provided they are shaded from midday sun.

CULTIVATION Plant *S. fortunei* in drifts of five or more, 23cm (9in) apart, in a sheltered position in partial shade and moist cool soil. Mulch every spring with leaf mould or garden compost until the plants are making total cover.

PROPAGATION Divide established clumps during the spring.

PESTS AND DISEASES Generally trouble free.

OTHER VARIETIES *S. f.* 'Wada' and 'Rubrifolia' both have redder leaves than the species. *S. umbrosa* and *S. x urbium* (London Pride) AGM and its variegated form are evergreen and will make good ground cover in dry shade. Their evergreen rosettes of smooth rounded leaves slowly spread to form ground-hugging carpets with open sprays of tiny pale pink flowers in early summer. The mossy saxifrages are named varieties of *S. moschata* and are

SAXIFRAGEAX ARENDSII

good rock plants. They make springy cushions of much divided and crimped foliage with the appearance of moss, bright green or golden, according to the variety chosen. The flowers, fragile and star-shaped, appear in late spring, in white or shades of pink or crimson.

soil	
ACID	ALKALINE
DRY	WET

J	F	M	A	M	J	J	A	S	O	N	D

SAXIFRAGA FORTUNEI 'WADA'

SCABIOSA CAUCASICA

S

Scabious, hardy perennial (Caucasus, 1803). Mature at 5 years: 60 x 45cm (2ft x 18in).

These reliable herbaceous plants flower over a long period. The flowers have wide slightly frilled petals around a pincushion centre. They are carried on slender, almost leafless branching stems above a basal rosette of slightly greyish-green leaves. The colour range is white, cream, mauve and violet-blue.

USES Plant this scabious where you need to have a continuous display of flowers (and butterflies) all summer. They are excellent, long-lasting cut flowers, and the leaves make weed-smothering ground cover.

CULTIVATION Plant in groups of five or more in an open sunny position in well-drained limey soil. If lime is not naturally present it can be added, but don't attempt to grow scabious on heavy clay. Set the plants 30cm (12in) apart. If you cut the flowers regularly for flower arranging, more will follow. If not, dead-head regularly to ensure a succession. Divide every few years.

PROPAGATION Divide clumps in spring.

PESTS AND DISEASES Generally trouble free.

GOOD VARIETIES *S. c.* 'Clive Greaves' AGM is a tried and trusted favourite with large light lavender-blue flowers. Another old friend is the cream-white 'Miss Willmott'. Both have been going since the 1930s. The modern 'Stäfa' has darker violet-blue flowers. *S. lucida* is a smaller, front row plant, 20 x 15cm (8 x 6in), with mauve pincushion flowers like a wild scabious. *S. columbaria* var. *ochroleuca* has masses of small, pale yellow flowers on wiry branching stems.

COMPANIONS Mauve-blue scabious have a softening effect with scarlet and orange crocosmias.

soil	
ACID	ALKALINE
DRY	WET

J	F	M	A	M	J	J	A	S	O	N	D

SCABIOSA CAUCASICA

S

SCHIZOSTYLIS COCCINEA

*Kaffir lily, rhizomatous perennial
(S. Africa, 1864). Mature at 3 years:
60 x 15cm (2ft x 6in).*

From slim clumps of grassy leaves, flower stems emerge rather like miniature gladioli, but more elegant. They flower very late in the gardening year when autumn is already well under way. The silky textured flowers are crimson, white, or various shades of pink.

USES They are decorative indoors as cut flowers as well as outdoors at a time when not many flowers are left in the garden.

CULTIVATION Schizostylis need a sheltered, sunny site. They are shy of flowering in dry conditions, so are best suited by soil that remains moist. Give them a good mulch in spring and be prepared to water in dry spells. Plant them in spring in groups of five and wait for them to spread.

PROPAGATION Divide the rhizomes in spring when they become congested, which will be every few years.

PESTS AND DISEASES Generally trouble free.

GOOD VARIETIES *S.c.* 'Major' AGM has big crimson flowers, *S. c. alba* is white. 'Mrs Hegarty' is pale pink and 'Sunrise' has large flowers of a soft but intense blush pink. 'Viscountess Byng' is also pink.

soil

ACID		ALKALINE
DRY		WET

J	F	M	A	M	J	J	A	S	O	N	D
									✿	✿	

SCHIZOSTYLIS COCCINEA

SCILLA SIBERICA

*Siberian squill, hardy bulb (Asia Minor).
Mature at 2 years: 10 x 5cm (4 x 2in). AGM*

One of the most cheerful signs that winter is coming to an end is the arrival of the vivid Prussian blue squill flowers. With or very soon after the snowdrops and winter aconites they often push up through a thin layer of snow. A small clump of strap shaped, glossy green leaves splays out around short spikes of bell-shaped flowers.

USES Scillas are great colonizers and will naturalize in short grass or gradually make a blue carpet when grown between roses and other shrubs.

CULTIVATION Plant in late summer or autumn in any reasonable soil, 5cm (2in) deep and approximately the same distance apart. If you are planting them in grass, lift an area of turf 5cm (2in) thick, fork lightly over the surface underneath and scatter the bulbs at random. Then replace the turf and tread it down firmly. The bulbs should not need any further attention. If, in the fullness of time, their performance is disappointing, it probably means the clumps have become congested and need dividing.

PROPAGATION Lift and divide established clumps. Scillas seed themselves and can be raised from seed, but it takes three or four years for a seedling to reach flowering size.

PESTS AND DISEASES Generally trouble free.

OTHER VARIETIES There is a white flowered form, *S. s.* 'Alba'. *Scilla bifolia* is very similar to *S. siberica*. *S. bifolia* 'Rosea' is a pink form.

COMPANIONS It would be a mistake to mix these little scillas with other bulbs. Let them colonize a patch of shrubbery or make a blue pool under silver birch trees.

soil

ACID		ALKALINE
DRY		WET

J	F	M	A	M	J	J	A	S	O	N	D
	✿	✿									

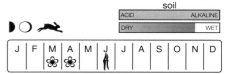

SCILLA SIBERICA ATTOCOERULEA

SEDUM SPECTABILE

Ice plant, hardy perennial (China). Mature at 3 years: 45 x 45cm (18 x 18in). AGM

Sedums look good for most of the year. This one starts in spring when a clump of chubby grey-green buds emerges, pushing up erect stems with leaves symmetrically arranged along their length. The leaves are fleshy, smooth, rounded and pale green with a grey-white bloom. After midsummer flat heads of tiny green-white buds develop and the plants are prettiest in late summer when the buds gradually flush pink. In full bloom the flowers are a rather murky shade of pink, becoming rusty maroon in late autumn.

USES This is a good ground cover plant but its main function is to bring butterflies into the garden: when it is in full flower tortoiseshell and peacock butterflies love it.

CULTIVATION Plant in autumn or spring in a sunny position in any well-drained soil. The flower stems fade to a warm brown and can be left on the plants until spring.

PROPAGATION Divide established clumps during the spring.

PESTS AND DISEASES Generally trouble free.

OTHER VARIETIES *Sedum* 'Herbstfreude' ('Autumn Joy') AGM is a dramatic plant with very large flower heads starting strong pink, turning coppery-red. Low-growing *S. spurium* and *S. kamtschaticum* have star-shaped flowers, the former deep purple to white, the latter yellow tinged with orange. *S. spurium* is a mat-forming plant; *S. kamtschaticum* forms a rosette.

COMPANIONS Sedums with purplish leaves look wonderful with plants of similar colouring such as *Rosa glauca* or *Dicentra* 'Adrian Bloom'.

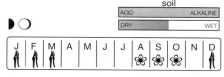

	soil	
ACID		ALKALINE
DRY		WET

J	F	M	A	M	J	J	A	S	O	N	D

SEDUM KAMTSCHATICUM

SEDUM 'AUTUMN JOY'

SEDUM SPURIUM

SIDALCEA

S

Hardy perennial (California, 1838). Mature at 3 years: 60-120 x 45cm (2-4ft x 18in).

This is a plant like a mallow or a small hollyhock, with flowering spires growing from a clump of rounded green leaves after midsummer. The flowers are shaped like wide funnels and the petals are silky in texture. They range from pale to deep pink.

USES Sidalceas make a pretty vertical show in borders and are good for picking.

CULTIVATION Plant in autumn or spring in a sunny position in any reasonable soil. If you cut the stems to the ground after the first flowering you may get a second crop in autumn.

PROPAGATION Divide established clumps in autumn or spring. Do this every three or four years to keep up a supply of vigorous young plants.

PESTS AND DISEASES Generally trouble free.

GOOD VARIETIES 'Sussex Beauty' reaches 1.2m (4ft) and has pale shell-pink flowers. 'Elsie Heugh' is pale pink with fringed petals and 'William Smith' AGM has salmon pink flowers.

COMPANIONS For a pale and pretty colour scheme plant sidalceas with blue and white *Campanula persicifolia*, *Geranium* 'Mrs. Kendall Clark' and gypsophila.

	soil	
ACID		ALKALINE
DRY		WET

J	F	M	A	M	J	J	A	S	O	N	D

SIDALCEA 'ELSIE HEUGH'

S

SILENE DIOICA

Red campion, catchfly, hardy perennial (N. Africa, Asia and Europe including Britain). Mature at 3 years: 45 x 30cm (18 x 12in).

This is one of the prettiest wild flowers in hedgerows, on road verges and in woodland clearings. The flower stems rise from a clump of pointed oval leaves that are hairy and sticky, hence the name 'catchfly'. The flowers are not really red but crimson-pink. They are five-petalled and carried at the tops of branching stems from late spring until the late summer.

USES If you are making a wild flower garden or border this would be an essential part of it. It also deserves inclusion in herbaceous and mixed borders along with exotic perennials. The flowers last well in water.

CULTIVATION Plant in well-drained soil neither excessively acid nor alkaline, in sun or light shade. In wild parts of the garden the plants can be set directly into thin grassland. In that situation, allow the plants to seed themselves before mowing or strimming after midsummer.

PROPAGATION Divide in spring or autumn or sow seeds in early autumn or early spring to transplant in autumn. Plants will usually seed themselves quite freely.

PESTS AND DISEASES Generally trouble free.

OTHER VARIETIES The red campion usually grown in gardens is the double flowered form, *Silene dioica* 'Flore Pleno'. *Silene schafta* 10 x 10cm (4 x 4in) AGM is a low, spreading rock plant with sprays of magenta-pink flowers from late spring to late autumn. Another rock plant is the sea campion, *S. uniflora* (syn. *S. maritima*), a sprawler 20cm (8in) high with small grey-green leaves and masses of white flowers from late spring until midsummer.

COMPANIONS Red campion's flowering time coincides with bluebells.

SILENE DIOICA

SILYBUM MARIANUM

Our Lady's thistle, hardy biennial (Mediterranean). Mature at 2 years: 1.2m x 60cm (4 x 2ft).

The main attraction is the spreading rosette of large dark green leaves netted with conspicuous white veins and edged with spines. In the second summer purple-pink thistle flowers are produced from spiny green buds. They continue in flower well into the autumn.

USES *Silybum marianum* is an easy-going plant providing eye-catching ground cover over a long period.

CULTIVATION In spring or summer plant out seedlings in an open, sunny position in any reasonable soil. Self-sown plants are usually big enough to move to new positions by midsummer. Water young seedlings until they are growing strongly.

PROPAGATION Sow seeds in spring or allow existing plants to seed themselves.

PESTS AND DISEASES Slugs and snails are fond of the leaves.

OTHER VARIETIES There are none.

SILYBUM MARIANUM

S

SINARUNDINARIA MURIELIAE

Syn. Fargesia murieliae. Bamboo, evergreen shrub (China, 1907). Mature at 12 years: 2.5-4m (8-13ft) tall, spreading indefinitely.

There have always been problems about the naming of the woody stemmed grass-like plants we know as bamboos. After several name changes in the past, the genus described here is now called *Fargesia* but most nurseries are still listing it as *Sinarundinaria* or *Arundinaria*. This slow spreading bamboo is one of the most graceful. It produces a thicket of yellow canes which are erect and leafless in their first year, but laden with foliage and arching outwards in subsequent years.

USES In time a belt of these bamboos will make an impenetrable barrier. They make weed-smothering ground cover, are tolerant of air pollution and will grow in containers in city yards. The canes are very useful for supporting runner beans and other plants.

CULTIVATION Bamboos will grow in sun or light shade but they appreciate shelter from cold winds. They do best in rich moisture-retentive soil, neither too light nor too heavy. Plant or transplant them in late spring or early autumn. Mulch in spring with manure or compost. When established clumps become congested, remove some canes, cutting them out at the base.

PROPAGATION Detach rooted canes from established clumps.

PESTS AND DISEASES Generally trouble free.

OTHER VARIETIES *Sinarundinaria nitida* (*Fargesia nitida*) is similar with purple-green stems and grows to 8m (10ft).

COMPANIONS They look best with plants of strong architectural form – Japanese acers, ivies, *Mahonia x* 'Charity', bergenia.

SISYRINCHIUM STRIATUM

Semi-evergreen hardy perennial (Chile, 1788). Mature at 3 years: 45 x 30cm (18 x 12in).

This plant makes strong, upright tufts of light grey green, slim sword-shaped leaves. The flowers are a pale straw yellow, single and open-faced with darker yellow centres. They are carried in small clusters all the way up the leafy stems at midsummer.

USES Plants with vertical leaves and flower spikes are always useful to contrast with more rounded plant shapes. This sisyrinchium's self-seeding habit makes it a good plant to grow informally in paving or gravel. It is also good for picking.

CULTIVATION It does best in a sunny position but will also grow in partial shade and any ordinary soil. Plant in autumn or spring in groups, setting the plants 23cm (9in) apart. If you grow them in poor soil, feed with manure or general fertilizer in spring. If you do not want the plants to self-seed, make sure you remove the flower stems as soon as the flowers fade.

PROPAGATION Dig up self-seeded seedlings and move to new positions. Or divide established clumps in early spring.

PESTS AND DISEASES Generally trouble free but the leaves may turn black at the tips, which does spoil the look of the plants.

OTHER VARIETIES *S. s.* 'Aunt May' has leaves that are attractively striped with cream at the margins.

COMPANIONS The grey-green leaves and soft pale yellow flowers combine to enhance bright or dark red, purple or blue flowers. For a bold effect try planting the plain or variegated form with magenta *Geranium psilostemon*.

SKIMMIA JAPONICA

Evergreen shrub (Japan, 1838). Mature at 7 years: up to 1.5 x 1.5m (5 x 5ft).

Skimmias are valued for their tidy, glossy evergreen leaves, their scented flowers in early spring and above all for their display of red berries in autumn. But, except for one subspecies, the berries only develop on female plants and then only if there is a male plant to pollinate it. The oval pointed leaves are borne on dense rounded bushes. The pink or white flowers are in tight clusters and their scent is strongest and sweetest on the male plants.

USES Skimmias make good ground cover. They are tolerant of industrial pollution and can be grown in containers.

CULTIVATION Skimmias prefer partial or full shade and neutral or slightly acid soil, but they will grow in alkaline soil provided it is fertile. In full sun or poor dry soil they will struggle. Plant in early autumn or late spring in groups with one male plant to pollinate up to six females. Mulch with manure or compost in spring every year or every other year. No pruning is necessary but tired old plants may be restored by cutting them almost to the ground.

PROPAGATION Take cuttings in late summer or layer the plants in autumn.

PESTS AND DISEASES Generally trouble free. If leaves become sickly and yellow the soil may be too alkaline.

GOOD VARIETIES *S. japonica* 'Rubella' 1.5 x 1.5m (5 x 5ft) is the male plant usually grown. Its stems and flower buds are reddish and the flowers have more impact than others, remaining in bud all winter. 'Fragrans' 1.2 x 1.2m (4 x 4ft) AGM is a male with very sweet scent. Female varieties include 'Veitchii' (syn. *S.* Foremanii,) 1.5 x 1.5m (5 x 5ft).

soil

ACID — ALKALINE
DRY — WET

J F M A M J J A S O N D

SINARUNDINARIA MURIELAE

soil

ACID — ALKALINE
DRY — WET

J F M A M J J A S O N D

SISYRINCHIUM STRIATUM 'AUNT MAY'

soil

ACID — ALKALINE
DRY — WET

J F M A M J J A S O N D

SKIMMIA JAPONICA

GARDEN PLANTS MADE EASY

S

SOLANUM CRISPUM 'GLASNEVIN'

Evergreen woody climber (Chile, Peru, 1830). Mature at 7 years: up to 6m (20ft) high and wide. AGM

This glamorous cousin of the potato gives very quick results, making leafy cover and from midsummer to autumn producing loose clusters of bright mauve-blue star-shaped flowers with prominent yellow centres. The leaves are green, lance-shaped and pointed and the young stems are green and vigorous.

USES This climber gives quick cover on a trellis, pergola, wired wall or low building. It needs to be tied in to its support on a fairly regular basis.

CULTIVATION Plant in spring in a position facing south or west in any reasonable soil. Poor chalky soil is as good as, or even better than any other. If the soil is too rich you will get lots of lush, leafy growth and fewer flowers. If it is to go up a wall, set the plant 45-60cm (18in-2ft) out from the wall and tie the shoots to a cane or canes leaning against the wall. Every spring prune out weak shoots and tie in new growth, cutting out any unwanted shoots. If hard frost cuts the plant to the ground in winter, it will usually recover, shooting again from the base.

PROPAGATION Take semi-ripe cuttings in summer or layer the lowest shoots.

PESTS AND DISEASES Generally trouble free.

OTHER VARIETIES *Solanum jasminoides* 'Album' AGM is not nearly as hardy as *S. crispum*, but is worth planting in mild areas if you can provide wall protection. It climbs by twining and has more papery leaves and flowers than *S. crispum*. The flowers of 'Album' are white.

SOLIDAGO 'GOLDENMOSA'

Golden rod, hardy perennial (N. America). Mature at 3 years: 75 x 60cm. (2ft 6in x 2ft). AGM

The plant described here is not the coarse and aggressive golden rod that has, in some areas, escaped from gardens and colonized railway embankments and waste ground. The yellow of 'Goldenmosa's' flowers is on the harsh side but in the right company this short-coming hardly shows. The flowers appear in late summer and autumn in fluffy mimosa-like plumes at the tops of strong, erect stems covered in lance-shaped yellow-green leaves. The whole plant slowly forms a dense well-behaved clump.

USES Any plant that flowers so late in the season is useful in herbaceous and mixed planting schemes. This one also attracts butterflies and lasts as a cut flower.

CULTIVATION Ordinary soil in sun or shade suits these obliging plants. Plant them in groups of five or more in autumn or spring. Some people find the dead stems and seedheads attractive enough to leave all winter, but they can look rather mournful and I prefer to cut them down to ground level as soon as flowering is over.

PROPAGATION Divide up the clumps during the spring.

PESTS AND DISEASES Generally trouble free.

OTHER VARIETIES 'Cloth of Gold' is free flowering and, at 45cm (18in), shorter; 'Queenie' is just 30cm (12in) high. X *Solidaster luteus* 'Lemore' is a hybrid of softer colouring than the solidagos. It grows to 75cm (2ft 6in) and produces pale cream-yellow flowers.

COMPANIONS Blue and white Michaelmas daisies will prevent the solidagos from appearing brassy.

SORBARIA TOMENTOSA

Syn. S. aitchisonii, deciduous shrub (W. Asia, 1840). Mature at 12 years: 3 x 3m (10 x 10ft). AGM

This handsome quick-growing suckering shrub has arching red-brown stems clothed in large ferny multiple dark green leaves with serrated margins. Pale undersides of the leaves are revealed in the wind. They often turn yellow in winter. After midsummer there are large fluffy plumes of tiny cream-white flowers. The effect is slightly spoiled by the browning of fading flower spikes, but nevertheless the shrub is worth growing if you have the space and need a quick effect.

CULTIVATION Plant in autumn or spring in ordinary soil in a sunny position. In winter prune established plants by removing some old stems from the base and shortening the rest to encourage flowering. If necessary chop out suckers in order to keep the plant within bounds.

PROPAGATION Detach rooted suckers and replant them.

PESTS AND DISEASES Generally trouble free.

OTHER VARIETIES *S. sorbifolia* is similar but only grows to 1.8m (6ft) and has smaller flower heads. It is more invasive than *S. tomentosa*.

SOLANUM CRISPUM 'GLASNEVIN'

SOLIDAGO

SORBARIA TOMENTOSA

SORBUS ARIA, SORBUS AUCUPARIA

Whitebeam, rowan or mountain ash, deciduous trees. Mature at 50 years: 6m (20ft) after 20 years, 15 x 8m (50 x 25ft) at maturity.

The two main groups of sorbus are very versatile, producing a number of gardenworthy small trees, and there are some other very attractive species too.

S. aria, the whitebeam, is a native of chalk and limestone areas of Europe including Britain. It forms a spreading irregular dome. The leaves are silvery when young and from a distance the opening leaf buds look like magnolia flowers. Later they become dark green above, remaining silver underneath. Broad clusters of small cream-white flowers in late spring are followed by round red berries.

S. aucuparia, the rowan or mountain ash, is a very hardy native of Asia and Europe including Britain, especially Scotland. Its gracefully spreading branches have multiple leaves like those of the ash but smaller. Clusters of cream, fluffy flowers hang down in late spring or early summer, followed by orange berries. In some varieties the berries are yellow. Other species have white or pink berries.

USES Both *S. aria* and *S. aucuparia* are tough, tolerant trees and will survive in most conditions.

SORBUS 'JOSEPH ROCK'

CULTIVATION Plant in autumn in any reasonable soil that is not waterlogged, in sun or light shade. *S. aria* is a better choice for alkaline soil although it tolerates acid conditions. The opposite is true of *S. aucuparia*.

PROPAGATION The species can be grown from seed; other forms are increased by budding or grafting.

PESTS AND DISEASES Fireblight is a risk and sorbuses are susceptible to honey fungus.

OTHER VARIETIES *S. aria* 'Lutescens' AGM has particularly good pale green-white spring leaf colouring. *S. aucuparia* 'Fructu Luteo' AGM has yellow berries. *S. hupehensis* (syn. *S. discolor*) has white flowers, with white pink-tinged berries and orange-red foliage in late autumn, and *S.* 'Joseph Rock' AGM has red and purple

SORBUS CASHMIRIANA

autumn leaves and yellow berries. Another for brilliant autumn leaves is *S.* 'Embley' with plentiful orange-red berries.

Sorbus cashmiriana AGM is a very elegant smaller tree with fine-cut ferny leaves, pale pink flowers, red autumn leaves and large white to pale pink berries retained late in the year.

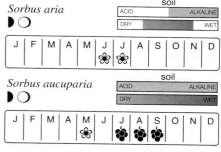

Sorbus aria

	soil	
ACID		ALKALINE
DRY		WET

J	F	M	A	M	J	J	A	S	O	N	D
						✿	✿				

Sorbus aucuparia

	soil	
ACID		ALKALINE
DRY		WET

J	F	M	A	M	J	J	A	S	O	N	D
				✿		✿	●	●			

SORBUS HUPEHENSIS

SORBUS ARIA 'LUTESCENS'

S

SPARTIUM JUNCEUM

*Spanish broom, deciduous shrub
(S. Europe before 1548). Mature at 12
years: 2.5 x 1.5m (8 x 5ft) after 10 years,
3 x 3m (10 x 10ft) at maturity. AGM*

Easy and fast-growing but short-lived,
Spanish broom has a long flowering season
from early to late summer. The honey-
scented flowers are pure bright yellow and
shaped like those of a pea. Dark green,
almost leafless shoots give the plant the
appearance of an evergreen in winter.

USES Plant *Spartium junceum* for quick and
colourful results in a sunny dry spot; it is
especially good at the seaside. It tolerates
industrial pollution but not cold winds.

CULTIVATION Plant in spring in a sunny,
fairly sheltered position. Spartium will
grow in any well-drained soil, including
chalk and sandy soil. It can become leggy
and gaunt after a few years. In the right
circumstances this may be attractive, but it
can be prevented by cutting back the new
shoots immediately after flowering to a few
centimetres away from the old wood. Do
not cut into the old wood or you may kill
the plant. Pruning can also be done in early
spring. If you do not want to interfere with
its habit of growth by pruning, plant it at
the back of a border where smaller shrubs
will hide its bare legs.

PROPAGATION Sow seeds in early spring.

PESTS AND DISEASES Generally trouble free.

COMPANIONS For a strong colour contrast
to gaze at through the summer rain from the
window of a seaside villa, plant this yellow
broom with red fuchsias.

SPARTIUM JUNCEUM
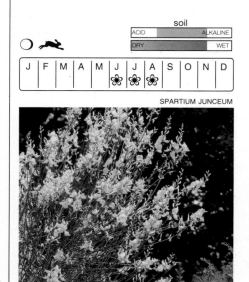

SPIRAEA 'ARGUTA'

*Bridal wreath. Hybrid, deciduous shrub
(1880s). Mature at 10 years: 1.2 x 1.2m
(4 x 4ft) after 5 years, 2.5 x 2.5m (8 x 8ft)
at maturity. AGM*

There are two distinct groups of spiraeas:
S. japonica varieties are small late summer-
flowering shrubs. The spring-flowering
group includes *S.* 'Arguta', one of the best.
It is one of the first shrubs to break in
spring, covering its slender flexible arching
stems with soft, rounded bright green
leaves. A little later the plant is weighed
down with a white foam of flowers along
the upper side of each branch.

USES These spiraeas are unfussy plants,
tolerating poor soil and industrial pollution.
After their splendid performance in spring
they do nothing for the rest of the year, so
plant them where they can become a
background to summer flowering plants.

CULTIVATION Plant spiraeas in sun or
partial shade, in any reasonable soil.
Immediately after flowering prune by
removing one-third of the branches at the
base. If it is necessary to reduce the shrub's
size, shorten the rest of the branches.

Straggly plants can be renovated by cutting
to the ground.

PROPAGATION Take cuttings in autumn or
increase by layering.

PESTS AND DISEASES Generally trouble free.

OTHER VARIETIES *S. x cinerea* 'Grefsheim'
AGM is similar but smaller, 1.5 x 1.5m
(5 x 5ft) and flowers a little earlier.
S. thunbergii AGM is low growing at
90 x 120cm (3 x 4ft) and early. Its leaves
turn yellow in autumn. *S. nipponica*
'Snowmound', 90 x 90cm (3 x 3ft), flowers
much later at midsummer. *S. japonica*
(syn. *S. x bumalda*) varieties are small,
60 x 60cm (2 x 2ft) on average, and have
dusky pink flowers in flattish clusters.
'Anthony Waterer' AGM is an old
favourite with cream and pink streaked
leaves. 'Goldflame' AGM and 'Gold
Mound' AGM have yellow-gold leaves
with pink flowers.

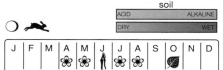

SPIRAEA THUNBERGII

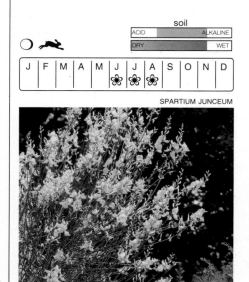

S

STACHYS BYZANTINA

Syn. S. lanata, S. olympica. Lamb's lugs, lamb's tongue, bunnies' ears, rabbits' ears, evergreen perennial (Caucasus to Persia, 1782). Mature at 3 years: 30 x 60cm (1 x 2ft).

This is one of those helpful plants that is easy to grow and increases quickly yet is easy to pull out where it is not wanted. It forms an impenetrable mat of wide lance-shaped grey leaves covered in short white fur. They are very tactile. After midsummer upright white flower stems appear with mauve-pink flowers half-hidden in the fur.

USES This is a five-star ground cover plant for any sunny position.

CULTIVATION Plant in groups at the front of sunny borders or between shrubs, setting the plants 45cm (18in) apart in any well-drained soil. To stop the plants getting straggly cut them right back in spring.

PROPAGATION Divide in spring.

PESTS AND DISEASES In a wet summer the rabbits' ears get bedraggled, just as those of a real rabbit might, and sometimes they rot. But though unsightly, this does not harm the plants. The non-flowering variety 'Silver Carpet' is said to suffer from mildew but I have not had that problem.

OTHER VARIETIES *S. b.* 'Silver Carpet' is more compact and does not flower, which makes it a very neat and labour-saving ground cover and edging plant. *S. b.* 'Primrose Heron' has a yellow-grey tone underlying the fur of its young leaves, becoming grey as they age.

COMPANIONS This is a good plant for marrying incompatible colours, for cooling harsh oranges, reds and magentas and for contrasting with other grey leaves of different texture. It is lovely planted under old roses.

soil	
ACID	ALKALINE
DRY	WET

J	F	M	A	M	J	J	A	S	O	N	D

STACHYS BYZANTINA

STACHYURUS PRAECOX

Deciduous shrub (Japan). Mature at 3 years: up to 2.5 x 1.5m (8 x 5ft). AGM

This shrub is perfectly hardy and worth growing for its winter beauty. Masses of hanging flower stems develop in autumn on bare branching stems with red-brown bark, and remain in bud until late winter when, in mild weather, they will flower. The flowers are pale yellow and cup-shaped, the whole flower stalk rather like an upsidedown yellow lily-of-the-valley. The long, oval leaves come later.

USES Any winter-flowering plant is especially welcome, and cut branches of stachyurus can be brought indoors.

CULTIVATION Plant stachyurus in late autumn. They need a sheltered position in light shade, and plenty of leaf mould or peat dug into the planting hole. This is particularly important on alkaline soil. They are said to be lime tolerant, but the more organic material you can incorporate the better. To keep the plant strong and healthy and encourage plenty of flowers, remove one-third of the stems at ground level or close to it every spring when the flowering period is over.

PROPAGATION Take semi-ripe cuttings in summer and grow them in a cold frame.

PESTS AND DISEASES Generally trouble free. Hard frost following mild winter weather may damage the flowers, but the plant will not be permanently harmed.

soil	
ACID	ALKALINE
DRY	WET

J	F	M	A	M	J	J	A	S	O	N	D

STACHYURUS PRAECOX

S

STEPHANANDRA INCISA 'CRISPA'

Deciduous shrub (a dwarf variety of a species native to Japan and Korea, introduced 1872). Mature at 15 years: 60 x 80cm (2 x 2ft 6in).

If you are only interested in plants with pretty flowers, ignore this one. Its tiny white flowers are quite insignificant, and it is grown for its attractive arching habit and its fresh green leaves in summer, orange-yellow autumn colour and network of warm brown twigs in winter. The leaves are oval, deeply lobed and toothed and lightly frilled.

USES This plant makes excellent ground cover, either under trees and between taller shrubs, or towards the front of beds and borders. It is suitable for urban areas as it is tolerant of industrial pollution.

CULTIVATION Plant stephanandra in autumn in sun or light shade in any ordinary soil that does not dry out. For weed-smothering ground cover set the plants 45cm (18in) apart. No aftercare or pruning is necessary unless the plants outgrow their site or become straggly. If that happens, they can be cut back as hard as you like.

PROPAGATION Dig up rooted suckers in autumn and transplant them, or take hardwood cuttings, also in the autumn.

PESTS AND DISEASES Generally trouble free but scale insects sometimes infest the leaves. Cut and burn the infested branches.

COMPANIONS The fresh green leaves make a good quiet foreground to flowers of any colour, but it is worth thinking about plants to complement the orange and yellow autumn leaves. Blue or soft lavender Michaelmas daisies seem to be the answer, and *caryopteris* or *ceratostigma* may still be in flower when the leaves turn colour.

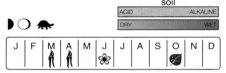

STEPHANANDRA INCISA

STIPA GIGANTEA

Golden oat, evergreen perennial grass (Spain). Mature at 5 years: 1.8m x 90cm (6 x 3ft).

This majestic grass forms a clump of narrow leaves 45cm (18in) long, and out of this clump numerous tall stiff stems arise carrying large loose heads of dangling spikey flowers on arching thread-like stems, which last all summer. The flowers open purple but change to golden buff.

USES Plant *Stipa gigantea* for weed-smothering ground cover, as a windbreak or simply as a beautiful specimen plant to be enjoyed for its own sake. This is a good container plant for a sophisticated city courtyard planting scheme. The stems are a magnificent addition to either fresh or dried flower arrangements.

CULTIVATION Plant in any reasonable soil in sun, and in a position open enough for you to enjoy seeing the flower heads catch the light when the sun is low in the sky. When the clump becomes congested, thin it in spring by cutting out one-third or half the stems, or cut the whole plant to the ground and let it start again.

PROPAGATION Divide established clumps during the spring.

PESTS AND DISEASES Generally trouble free.

OTHER VARIETIES S. *tenuissima* needs to be in full sun and well-drained soil. It has narrow thread-like leaves and delicate silver-green flower heads 60cm (2ft) high. S. *calamagrostis,* 90 x 45cm (3ft x 18in), makes an arching tuft of blue-green leaves with loose feathery flower clusters lasting all winter. It likes dry soil.

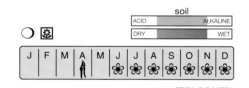

STIPA GIGANTEA

S

STOKESIA LAEVIS

Syn. Stokesia cyanea. Evergreen perennial (N. America, 1766). Mature at 3 years: 45 x 45cm (18 x 18in).

Strap-shaped mid-green leaves form ground-hugging rosettes, which remain through the winter. In summer large lavender-blue cornflower-like flowers with cream centres are borne for many weeks.

USES The plants are low enough to provide colour and interest in front of shrubs or other herbaceous plants.

CULTIVATION Plant in spring in ordinary garden soil in sun or light shade. In an exposed position the plants may not survive a hard winter; if you cannot give them a sheltered spot, it is a wise precaution to cover them or to lift them and pot them up indoors, putting them out again in spring.

PROPAGATION Divide the roots in early spring or sow seeds in warmth in late winter or early spring.

PESTS AND DISEASES Generally trouble free.

GOOD VARIETIES The flowers of *Stokesia laevis* 'Blue Star' and 'Wyoming' are a deeper shade of blue than the species. 'Alba' is a white-flowered form.

COMPANIONS The small pale yellow pokers of *Kniphofia* 'Little Maid' make a good contrast in both colour and form.

SYMPHORICARPOS X DOORENBOSII

Snowberry, deciduous shrub (Dutch hybrid, 1940). Mature at 7 years: 1.5 x 1.5m (5 x 5ft).

These useful shrubs are improved, non-suckering forms of an invasive plant introduced to Britain from North America in the eighteenth century and now naturalized. They are twiggy bushes covered in soft smooth rounded green leaves. The small pink or white flowers are hardly noticeable: it is the berries in autumn and winter that are the main feature. They are large round and smooth, pure white or pink, according to the variety chosen. Children love to pop the juicy berries but they are poisonous.

USES This is a plant for ground cover or hedging on difficult sites. It will grow anywhere in shade.

CULTIVATION Plant snowberry in autumn or spring in any soil including chalk, heavy clay and bog, in sun or light shade. Pruning is optional: to improve the shape and encourage the production of flowers and berries you can remove one stem in three from the base in late winter, and shorten the rest of the branches if you want to reduce the overall size.

PROPAGATION Take hardwood cuttings in autumn or winter, or remove rooted suckers.

PESTS AND DISEASES Generally trouble free.

GOOD VARIETIES Avoid the species *S. albus* and *S. orbiculatus*, they are too invasive. *S. x doorenbosii* 'Mother of Pearl' has pink-flushed white berries, 'White Hedge' is of upright habit with pure white berries, 'Magic Berry' has pink berries and *S. x chenaultii* 'Hancock' has orange-red autumn leaves and pink berries. It makes extensive low ground cover, 60cm x 2.5m (2 x 8ft), and is useful on problem soils.

SYMPHYTUM IBERICUM

Comfrey, hardy evergreen perennial (Caucasus, late 18th century). Mature at 3 years: 30 x 60cm (1 x 2ft).

Avoid *Symphytum caucasicum*, *S. officinale* and *S. x uplandicum*, all gross, invasive plants. *S. ibericum* is much better behaved, making tidy, dense mounds of broad, lance-shaped, hairy dark green leaves. Small cream-white flowers from reddish buds hang down from branching stems in spring and intermittently until early autumn. Like the others it spreads by underground shoots but is not a nuisance.

USES This and the other varieties described below are trouble-free groundcover plants for the light shade of woodland or shrubberies. The leaves are greatly valued by herbalists for treating a wide range of ailments. In the garden the cut leaves make a good mulch after being left to wilt for two or three days. They are high in potash and can be soaked for about four weeks to make a liquid feed for tomato and other plants.

CULTIVATION For ground cover, plant symphytum 45cm (18in) apart in sun or shade in any moisture-retentive soil. Mulch with manure or compost for the first season after planting. After that it should be able to look after itself.

PROPAGATION Divide the plants in spring.

PESTS AND DISEASES Caterpillars.

GOOD VARIETIES *Symphytum* 'Hidcote Blue' and 'Hidcote Pink' each grow to about 45cm (18in). *S. grandiflorum*, 25cm (10in), has creamy flowers. *S. x uplandicum* 'Variegatum' 90 x 60cm (3 x 2ft) has cream margins to its leaves.

COMPANIONS Keep comfreys away from more choice plants, placing them as ground cover in swathes under trees and between ornamental shrubs.

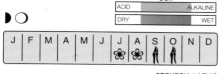

STOKESIA LAEVIS

SYMPHORICARPOS X CHENAULTII 'HANCOCK'

SYMPHYTUM GRANDIFLORUM

S

SYRINGA X JOSIFLEXA 'BELLICENT'

Lilac, deciduous shrub (Canada, 1940s). Mature at 15 years: 3.5 x 1.8 (12 x 6ft).

This lilac, bred from a Chinese species, is a graceful alternative to the usual garden lilacs which, although the flowers are lovely and deliciously scented, are rather ungainly, suckering shrubs and only flower for three weeks, which ought to disqualify them from this book. 'Bellicent' has a more graceful, arching habit and its flower heads, blooming in early summer, are less densely packed with flowers, therefore more elegant. They are a good clear pink for a lilac, and set off by dark leaves.

USES Lilacs have little to contribute once their flowers have faded, so plant them where they become part of a green background to later-flowering shrubs and tall perennials, or in a front garden as a barrier between house and road.

CULTIVATION Lilacs will grow in any soil that is not too acid, and do well on chalk, in sun or very light shade. Feed them with an annual mulch of manure or compost and an occasional dressing of bonemeal. Remove all the dead heads you can reach. If you need to restrict the size of the plant, prune immediately after flowering. In winter old neglected lilacs can be cut hard back, leaving just a few vigorous stems.

PROPAGATION Take semi-ripe cuttings in late summer.

PESTS AND DISEASES Plants can suffer from leaf miners and lilac blight. They are susceptible to honey fungus.

OTHER VARIETIES *S. microphylla* 'Superba' AGM is a neat little lilac growing to 1.5 x 1.5m (5 x 5ft) with mauve-pink scented flowers in early summer and a second flowering in late summer or early autumn. S. 'Souvenir de Louis Spaeth', 5m (15ft), has masses of scented flowers in late spring.

COMPANIONS Do not plant mauve, purple or pink lilacs next to laburnum.

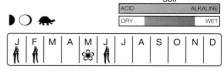

soil	
ACID	ALKALINE
DRY	WET

J	F	M	A	M	J	J	A	S	O	N	D

TANACETUM COCCINEUM

Syn. **Chrysanthemum coccineum, pyrethrum.** *Hardy perennial (Middle East, 1804). Mature at 3 years: 60 x 45cm (2ft x 18in).*

These coloured daisy flowers are old fashioned florists' flowers, still much grown commercially for that purpose and still known in flower shops as pyrethrum. They grow from a base of bright green divided feathery leaves, holding their faces to the sun on long clean stalks, and are available in white, red and all intermediate shades, constantly in flower from early to late summer.

USES They are excellent long-lasting cut flowers. In a mixed florist's bouquet the pyrethrums will still be fresh for a week after the rest of the flowers have faded.

CULTIVATION Spring is the best time to plant *Tanacetum coccineum* varieties, in good soil and in full sun. Keep picking the flowers to ensure a long succession.

PROPAGATION Divide the roots in late summer as soon as flowering is finished; otherwise leave the job until spring. The quality and quantity of flowers will be best if this is done every two or three years.

PESTS AND DISEASES It is a wise precaution to protect the young plants against slugs.

GOOD VARIETIES Tried and tested favourites include 'Brenda', bright rose red; 'Eileen May Robinson', pale pink; and 'James Kelway', crimson. Others have self-explanatory names such as 'Salmon Beauty', 'Scarlet Glow' and 'Snow Cloud'. A very different plant is *Tanacetum parthenium* 'Aureum', the yellow feverfew which happily seeds itself without ever becoming a nuisance. Its clusters of small white daisies and fresh yellow fine-cut leaves are always welcome.

TANACETUM COCCINEUM

TANACETUM PARTHENIUM 'AUREUM'

TANACETUM

T

TAXUS BACCATA 'FASTIGIATA'

Irish yew, evergreen tree (Ireland, early 19th century). Mature at 50 years or more: 1.5m x 60cm (5 x 2ft) after 10 years, 10 x 4m (30 x 12ft) or more at maturity.

This upright yew is as hardy and easy to please as the ordinary yew. It gradually forms a broad column with multiple irregular spires, a shape full of character.

USES Irish yew's vertical shape is distinctive and invaluable in groups of evergreen shrubs. Use Irish yews as sentinels either side of a path or flight of steps in a formally laid out garden. Ordinary *Taxus baccata* is indisputably the best plant for hedges and topiary.

CULTIVATION Yews are natives of chalk woodlands but will tolerate any except poorly drained soil. They will grow in sun or light shade. For hedges plant yew in a single line 60cm (2ft) apart using plants not more than 60cm (2ft) high. It is tempting, if you can afford it, to start with bigger plants, but the bigger they are the longer they take to establish, and the little ones will catch up in a few years. Yew hedges that are fed and weeded grow at least 15cm (6in) a year, reaching 1.5m (5ft) in less than ten years. Cut hedges and topiary in late summer. For a really immaculately tailored effect trim at midsummer as well.

PROPAGATION *Taxus baccata* grows easily from seed sown outdoors in early spring.

Cuttings of named varieties can be taken in early autumn.

PESTS AND DISEASES Generally trouble free. Yews are tolerant of honey fungus.

OTHER VARIETIES *Taxus baccata* 'Fastigiata Aureomarginata' AGM has yellow-tipped leaves, cheerful in winter. 'Standishii' is like a smaller, golden Irish yew, slow growing and excellent for small gardens, and 'Summergold' is a semi-prostrate variety.

TAXUS BACCATA 'SUMMERGOLD'

TAXUS BACCATA 'FASTIGIATA'

TELLIMA GRANDIFLORA

Evergreen hardy perennial (N. America, 1826). Mature at 3 years: 60 x 60cm (2 x 2ft).

A good ground cover plant with mounds of vine-shaped, scalloped hairy leaves, bright green in summer, bronzed in winter. Slender spikes of small cream bell-shaped flowers bloom from spring to early summer. It spreads quite quickly.

USES Plant tellima to keep weeds at bay under trees and between shrubs.

CULTIVATION Plant in autumn or spring, setting the plants 45cm (18in) apart. Tellima's ideal conditions are those of cool, semi-shaded woodland, but they will grow in any reasonable soil and in full sun.

PROPAGATION Divide the clumps in sprng.

PESTS AND DISEASES Generally trouble free.

OTHER VARIETIES *Tellima grandiflora* Odorata Group has yellow-green flowers with a scent similar to that of pinks. *T. g.* Rubra Group has winter colouring of a stronger red-purple and the flowers are pinkish green.

COMPANIONS Plant tellimas in interlocking drifts of other woodland ground cover plants: epimediums, hellebores, lamiums, tiarellas, and vincas.

TELLIMA GRANDIFLORA

THALICTRUM DELAVAYI

Syn. **T. dipterocarpum**. *Meadow rue, hardy perennial (China, 1890). Mature at 3 years: 1.5m x 60cm (5 x 2ft). AGM*

This plant has the prettiest leaves of any herbaceous plant. They are pale fresh blue-green and delicately divided like maidenhair fern. After midsummer tall slender stems appear, branching at the top to support a cloud of tiny nodding blue-mauve flowers with cream stamens.

USES This thalictrum is lovely at the back of a border in front of a dark hedge, but it is a pity to relegate the leaves to the back row, so plant it in a triangular group going from the back to the centre, or from the centre to front of a bed.

CULTIVATION Provide good rich soil in a sunny or lightly shaded position. If it can be sheltered from the wind the flower stems will not need staking. Plant in autumn or spring and mulch every spring.

PROPAGATION Divide roots in early spring, but not until a really good clump has built up as mature plants flower best.

PESTS AND DISEASES Generally trouble free.

OTHER VARIETIES *T. d.* 'Hewitt's Double' is similar but with double flowers like fluffy little balls. *T. aquilegiifolium* has grey-green leaves, much less finely cut, and branching heads of mauve-pink powder-puff flowers in early summer. There is also a yellow thalictrum with beautiful blue-grey leaves, *T. flavum* ssp. *glaucum*; it flowers from mid to late summer.

COMPANIONS *T. aquilegiifolium* needs a background of coppery leaves like those of purple hazel or cotinus as antidote to its slightly murky mauve-pink colouring. Plant *T. delavayi* with the burnt orange *Crocosmia* 'Emily McKenzie' or *Crocosmia masoniorum*.

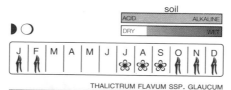
THALICTRUM AQUILEGIIFOLIUM

THALICTRUM FLAVUM SSP. GLAUCUM

THALICTRUM DELAVAYI

THUJA PLICATA

Western red cedar, evergreen coniferous tree (Northwest N. America, late 18th century). Mature at 40 years: 6m (20ft) after 10 years, 20 x 5m (70 x 15ft) or more at maturity.

A fast-growing tall columnar conifer, this is the best thuja for our climate. It is loosely branched but densely covered in dark rich green scale-like leaves on drooping branchlets. Downward-curving branches ensure that the tree gives cover right down to the ground.

USES Where there is space it makes a splendid solo specimen, but it is also a good hedge plant, giving quick results. As it is shade tolerant it can be used to thicken up existing windbreaks that have become straggly at ground level.

CULTIVATION Plant in late spring or early autumn, preferably in moist but well-drained soil of neutral pH, although it will tolerate alkaline soil and dry conditions. For a hedge, plant a single line 60cm (2ft) apart using trees up to 1.5m (5ft) tall. Mulch in spring for the first few years and water during dry spells.

PROPAGATION Sow seeds under glass in early spring or take cuttings in late summer.

PESTS AND DISEASES Generally trouble free, but susceptible to honey fungus.

GOOD VARIETIES *Thuja plicata* 'Atrovirens' is reliable either for hedges or as a single specimen.

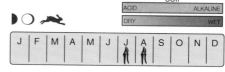

THUJA PLICATA

T

T

THYMUS

Thyme, evergreen shrub or subshrub (Asia and Europe including Britain). Mature at 5 years: from 2.5 x 20cm (1 x 8in) to 25 x 30cm (10 x 12in).

Thyme is a dense creeping plant with tiny oval aromatic leaves, smooth on some species, downy on others. Clusters of small lipped flowers cover the plants in summer, in shades of pink or purplish-red or white.

USES In the garden thyme is an outstanding ground cover plant, so robust that if it is planted as a lawn it will survive occasional foot traffic. Bees love it, so it is best to avoid walking barefoot on a thyme lawn. Thyme grows happily in paving cracks, at the sides of gravel paths and terraces, and as edging to sunny borders. In the kitchen it would be unthinkable to do without thyme as a flavouring for stocks and stews, and it has its place in the herbal medicine cupboard too.

CULTIVATION Plant thymes in full sun in any well-drained soil. They are particularly at home on alkaline soils. For ground cover on a bank or to make a lawn, set young plants 23cm (9in) apart. To make a tapestry carpet choose plants that will grow to roughly the same height. The main problem with thymes is their tendency to become leggy. To postpone this, as soon as they have flowered clip them over with shears. If the centre of the plant dies and all the leaves are on the perimeter, replace that plant with a fresh one.

PROPAGATION Detach rooted stems and replant them.

PESTS AND DISEASES Generally trouble free.

GOOD VARIETIES Thymes under 2.5cm (1in) for carpets: *T. caespititius,* bright green leaves, pink flowers; *T. ciliatus,* grey woolly leaves, pink flowers; *T. serpyllum* 'Pink Chintz' AGM, grey leaves, pale pink flowers; *T. s. coccineus* AGM, dark green leaves, dark pink flowers. *T. s.* var. *albus,* white flowers, *T. pulegioides,* grey woolly leaves, purple flowers. Upright shrubs, about 25 x 25cm (10 x 10in): *Thymus x citriodorus,* purple flowers; *T. x c.* 'Silver Queen' AGM, silver-white variegated leaves, mauve-pink flowers; *T. x c.* 'Golden King', yellow-edged leaves; *T. vulgaris,* mauve-pink flowers, the best thyme for culinary use.

	soil	
ACID		ALKALINE
DRY		WET

J	F	M	A	M	J	J	A	S	O	N	D

THYMUS

THYMUS CARPET

TIARELLA CORDIFOLIA

Foamflower, evergreen hardy perennial (Eastern N. America, early 18th century). Mature at 3 years: 23 x 60cm (9in x 2ft). AGM

Tiarella is a woodland plant making a dense mat of pale clear green leaves, shallowly lobed and toothed. In winter the leaf veins are bronze-red. It flowers in late spring and early summer producing masses of fluffy white flowers on spikes. The plants quickly increase by means of runners.

USES An indispensable plant for ground cover in shade. Plant it in generous drifts.

CULTIVATION Plant in autumn or spring, setting plants 60cm (2ft) apart. On the ground this looks very far apart but they will soon join up. The ideal site is in light shade in moist soil with plenty of humus, but tiarella will tolerate dry conditions and quite heavy shade. To get the plants off to a good start mulch thoroughly after planting. No further action is required except to pull out the occasional weed. If you like a very tidy garden run a strimmer over established groups after flowering.

PROPAGATION The plants do this for you, as they send out runners that root down into the ground. You can also divide the roots of large established clumps.

PESTS AND DISEASES Generally trouble free.

OTHER VARIETIES *T. wherryi,* 10 x 15cm, (4 x 6in) AGM, is a smaller, more compact and slower growing plant than *T. cordifolia.* The leaves are soft red-green and heart-shaped. Feathery spikes of pinkish-white flowers appear in spring.

COMPANIONS Keep it simple and allow *T. cordifolia* to spread on its own making a carpet under trees or shrubs.

	soil	
ACID		ALKALINE
DRY		WET

J	F	M	A	M	J	J	A	S	O	N	D

TIARELLA

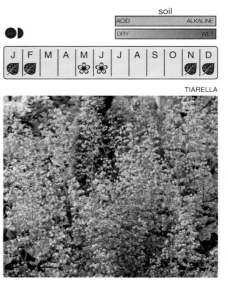

T

TILIA X EUCHLORA

Caucasian lime, Crimean lime, deciduous tree (of uncertain origin, 1860). Mature at 50 years: 8-10m (25-30ft) after 20 years, 20 x 10m (70 x 30ft) at maturity.

If you can accommodate a lime, this is the one to choose. Unlike most others it does not suffer the aphid attacks which cause sticky honeydew to drip from the leaves. *T. x euchlora* is a spreading tree with lower branches that droop as it ages. The leaves turn yellow in autumn and the fragrant yellowish-white flowers are loved by bees.

USES All limes except *T.* 'Petiolaris' and *T. tomentosa* (both toxic to bumble bees) are excellent bee plants. *T. x euchlora* is very hardy and will tolerate industrial pollution and most soil types. If you do not have room for a lime tree, you might like to consider using pleached limes on your garden's boundary, or as a division within the garden. *T x euchlora* and *T. platyphyllos* 'Rubra' AGM, the red-twigged lime, are the best kinds for pleaching.

CULTIVATION Plant in autumn in any reasonable soil, in sun or semi-shade. For those who want and can afford instant results, limes can be successfully transplanted in large sizes. For pleaching, plant young standard or feathered trees between 2.2 and 3m (7 and 10ft) apart and train to a frame made from timber, or angle iron with strong galvanized wire.

PROPAGATION Grow from seed, but hybrids must be grafted in late summer.

PESTS AND DISEASES Except for *T. x euchlora*, all limes are at risk from aphids. They infest the leaves in summer, making the sticky dripping honeydew.

OTHER VARIETIES *T.* 'Petiolaris' AGM, the weeping silver lime, is very beautiful with graceful hanging branches.

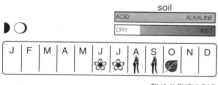

TILIA X EUCHLOAR

TOMATO

Lycopersicon esculentum, tender perennials treated as half hardy annuals (S. America). Mature at 1 year: from 20cm (8in) high to 2.5m (8ft) or more.

Tomatoes taste so much better straight off the vine than they do after a spell on the supermarket or greengrocer's shelf. 'Bush' tomatoes are compact plants useful for outdoor culture because they can easily be covered with cloches or mini-tunnels.

USES Home-grown tomatoes can be cooked but their flavour is best enjoyed by eating them raw immediately after picking.

CULTIVATION Outdoors, choose a sheltered sunny site in front of a wall or windbreak on good neutral or alkaline soil. Dig in manure or compost and add a general fertilizer. In pots use John Innes No. 3. Set out the plants when any danger of frost is past, tall varieties 45cm (18in) apart. Tie them in to canes as they grow and remove all side shoots. Pinch out the growing tip when four of five trusses of fruit have set. Set bush plants 45-60cm (18in-2ft) apart, preferably in slits in fabric mulch to keep the fruit clean. Water all plants regularly in dry weather. Plants grown in pots or in the green house should be fed with a good proprietary tomato food.

PROPAGATION Sow seeds indoors in early spring in pots, thinning to leave one per pot. Harden off before planting out.

PESTS AND DISEASES Tomatoes grown outdoors have fewer problems than those grown in greenhouses.

GOOD VARIETIES These are chosen for their good flavour: 'Gardener's Delight' and 'Sungold' are both tall cherry types. 'Red Alert' is a bush cherry tomato. 'Tumbler' is a trailing cherry tomato for containers.

TOMATO 'TUMBLER'

TRACHELOSPERMUM JASMINOIDES

Syn. Rhyncospermum jasminoides. Confederate jasmine, evergreen twining climber (China, Japan, 1844). Mature at 15 years: 1.8 x 1.8m (6 x 6ft) after 10 years, 9m (28ft) high at maturity.

This slow climber has oval pointed, very glossy dark green leaves. The white flowers bloom in late summer. They are tubular, opening at the ends into five-petalled stars like jasmine flowers, and they are every bit as sweetly scented as the sweetest jasmine.

USES Plant it where you can enjoy its wonderful perfume, near a place where you sit outside on a summer evening, or beside a door or a window.

CULTIVATION *Trachelospermum* will grow in full sun or semi-shade but it does need to be sheltered from harsh cold winds, so the safest position is against a south- or west-facing wall with wires or a trellis which it can twine around. Give it good, rich soil with added compost, and mulch the root area thickly. For the first few years guide the stems horizontally along the supporting structure to get wide coverage. Pruning need only involve tidying up the plant from time to time by cutting out weak straggling branches in spring.

PROPAGATION Take cuttings throughout the late summer.

PESTS AND DISEASES Generally trouble free.

OTHER VARIETIES *T. asiaticum* is very similar but the leaves are smaller and the flowers become yellowish as they age.

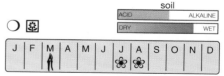

TRACHELOSPERMUM JASMINOIDES

T

TRADESCANTIA X ANDERSONIANA

Spiderwort, hardy perennial (hybrids of T. virginiana, N. America, late 17th century). Mature at 3 years: 60 x 45cm (2ft x 18in).

These plants are staunch components of the traditional herbaceous border. They make dense clumps of broad rush-like leaves untidily splayed at the ends. In bad weather they can look very bedraggled. However the flowers are pretty and unusual and appear over a long period from midsummer until early autumn. They are borne in small clusters and each flower has three broad petals. Colours are white, pale and dark blues, purple and palest pink.

USES The flowers are best appreciated close up, so plant tradescantias near the front of the border.

CULTIVATION Plant in autumn or early spring in an ordinary soil, in sun or partial shade. As with almost all herbaceous plants, regular dead-heading prolongs the flowering season. Cut the flower and leaf stems right down to the ground in autumn, winter or spring.

PROPAGATION Divide large established clumps in spring.

GOOD VARIETIES If possible, see the plants in flower before you buy. It is important to choose forms that carry the flowers above the leaves: with some they are half-hidden. 'Isis' AGM is a good true Oxford blue; 'J.C. Weguelin' is pale mauve-blue, and 'Osprey' white with a blue centre.

COMPANIONS The flowering time overlaps with that of border phloxes and the colours harmonize well.

soil

ACID				ALKALINE
DRY				WET

J	F	M	A	M	J	J	A	S	O	N	D

TRADESCANTIA 'PURPLE DOME'

TULIPA

Tulip (Europe and W. Asia, late 16th century). Mature at 3 years: from 10cm (4in) to 70cm (28in).

In the bulb category tulips are as varied and versatile as roses. The earliest flower as soon as the winter snow melts, the last overlap with the first of the species roses in early summer. Every colour is represented except blue, and some of the mauve-purples are not far off it.

USES There are tulips for naturalizing in grass, tulips for the rock garden, for informal groups in beds and borders, for formal bedding, for tubs and urns. Many can also be forced in pots for winter decoration indoors.

CULTIVATION Tulips are planted in late autumn, later than other spring bulbs, to reduce the risk of disease. They do best in full sun and in free-draining soil. Plant them about 15cm (6in) apart and 10cm (4in) deep, 15cm (6in) deep on very light soil. When gardeners had more time they used to lift the bulbs after flowering and store them for planting out again in the autumn. Nowadays most people leave them in the ground and hope they will come up again. They tend to flower for a few years in succession and then disappear. Cutting down the spent flower stems to stop the seeds maturing helps conserve the bulb's strength so that it will last longer. I keep up a supply by growing two or three dozen in pots each year and planting them out in the garden in the autumn.

PROPAGATION Detach offsets from the bulbs and plant them in pots or line them out in a nursery bed. They will flower in three or four years.

PESTS AND DISEASES Mice, slugs and eelworm can destroy the bulbs and they are susceptible to various fungal diseases including tulip fire.

GOOD VARIETIES Choose from the illustrated catalogue of a reliable supplier. If your garden is exposed to strong winds avoid tulips with long stems as the flower heads may snap off.

COMPANIONS In formal beds, tubs and pots, forget-me-nots and wallflowers are traditionally planted with tulips. In informal borders, plant between herbaceous plants. Peonies, for example, will grow up and take over when the tulips leave off.

soil

ACID				ALKALINE
DRY				WET

J	F	M	A	M	J	J	A	S	O	N	D

TULIPA 'FRINGED BEAUTY'

HYBRID TULIPS

V

VACCINIUM CORYMBOSUM

Highbush blueberry deciduous shrub (Eastern North America, 1765). Mature at 7 years: up to 1.5 x 1.5m (5 x 5ft). AGM

The fruit used in blueberry muffins or blueberry pie grows on this dense, bushy shrub, ripening in late summer. Vacciniums are also grown for their clusters of small pale pink or white urn-shaped flowers and stunning autumn colour; bright green, shiny, oval pointed leaves turn scarlet and bronze.

USES Vacciniums are a valuable component of shrubberies on acid soil but nowhere else. The berries, now available in supermarkets, look and taste good mixed with other summer fruits. *V. vitis-idaea* makes good low ground cover.

CULTIVATION Vacciniums will only grow on acid, lime-free soil. Damp and even boggy peat suits them, and although they prefer partial shade, they will grow in sun or total shade. No pruning is needed except occasionally to remove any dead branches.

PROPAGATION Take semi-ripe cuttings in summer or layer the plants in autumn; it may take two years for the layers to rot. Prostrate forms can be divided in autumn, winter or early spring.

PESTS AND DISEASES Generally trouble free.

OTHER VARIETIES *V. vitis-idaea* Koralle Group AGM is an evergreen prostrate form growing up to 15cm (6in) high and spreading indefinitely. Extremely tough and hardy, the species is plentiful on peat moorland in Scotland, Wales and Devon. The leaves are tiny, the pink flowers appear from early summer until autumn and the red berries are edible.

COMPANIONS Use vacciniums interplanted with rhododendrons and azaleas.

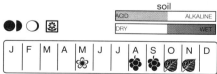

VACCINIUM CORYMBOSUM

VERBASCUM BOMBYCIFERUM

Mullein, hardy evergreen biennial. Mature at 2 years: 1.2-2m x 60cm (4-6 x 2ft). AGM

In a dramatic group of plants this is the most dramatic of all. Towards the end of summer in its first season *V. bombyciferum* makes a 60cm (2ft) wide rosette of large oval light green leaves. They are densely felted over with tiny white hairs giving a soft, overall silvery effect. The following summer a stout white woolly stem rises up, studded all the way along with yellow flowers.

USES Use it wherever you need an exclamation mark in the garden, preferably in the front row where its beautiful leaves can be enjoyed.

CULTIVATION Verbascums are lovers of chalk and limestone and prefer full sun, but they will also grow in any ordinary soil in partial shade. Plant them into their permanent positions when they are sturdy enough to survive. Do not bother to stake them. If they fall down new flower spikes will rise up all along the prostrate stem.

PROPAGATION Sow seeds of biennials in spring. Divide perennials in early spring.

PESTS AND DISEASES Mildew is the big enemy. In a dry summer it can ruin the appearance of the leaves.

OTHER VARIETIES Perennial verbascums are short-lived but very worthwhile. 'Helen Johnson' AGM, 60-75cm (24-30in) tall, is a beautiful recent introduction. Verbascums of the Cotswold Group are lovely but not always easy: 'Gainsborough' AGM has branching spires of soft pale yellow flowers, 1.2m (4ft) high; the flowers of 'Pink Domino' AGM are soft rose pink.

COMPANIONS The perennials are good grouped in borders with hardy geraniums and with other herbaceous plants.

VERBASCUM BOMBYCIFERUM

VERONICA AUSTRIACA

Syn. V. teucrium, hardy perennial (Europe, N. Asia 1596). Mature at 3 years: 30 x 45cm (12 x 18in).

V. a. ssp. *teucrium* 'Crater Lake Blue' AGM is the easiest variety to find and one of the best. It makes a tidy ground-hugging clump of green lance-shaped pointed leaves. In midsummer masses of tiny flowers of brilliant deep true blue are borne on upright spikes.

USES Plant veronicas in traditional herbaceous borders, among shrub roses or in mixed planting schemes.

CULTIVATION Plant in autumn or spring in any reasonable soil in sun. Cut the flower stems to the ground when they fade, and you may get a good second crop.

PROPAGATION Divide and replant the roots of established clumps. Do this for the health of the plants every three or four years.

PESTS AND DISEASES Generally trouble free.

OTHER VARIETIES 'Royal Blue' AGM is similar but a little shorter: 25cm (10in). *V. prostrata* AGM makes an ever increasing mat of short royal blue spires. When you are choosing prostrate veronicas, beware of *V. chamaedrys,* the wild germander speedwell, and its close relations; they are pretty but can easily become ineradicable weeds. *V. gentianoides* AGM and its variegated form are taller, 45cm (18in), but more low-key, with graceful stems of widely-spaced pale blue-grey flowers above ground-hugging leaf rosettes, in early summer. If you want a taller veronica, the flower spikes of *V. longifola* 'Blauriesin' or 'Foerster's Blue' top 90cm.

COMPANIONS Try Beth Chatto's combination of *V. gentianoides* with *Geum* 'Borisii'. Royal blue veronicas also contrast well with pale yellow irises.

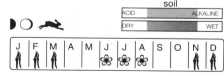

VERONICA LONGIFOLA

V

VIBURNUM

This important family has a lot to offer: evergreen or deciduous shrubs varying in height and spread from 3 x 3m (10 x 10ft) down to 1 x 1.5 (3 x 5ft). Mature at 15 years.

You can find one or another viburnum in flower or in fruit every day of the year, and many of the flowers have a wonderful scent.

USES There is also a viburnum for most positions in the garden, with the exception of dry shade. For which to plant where, see the individual descriptions.

CULTIVATION Most viburnums are happy in ordinary soil that does not dry out, in sun or partial shade. For special requirements, see the individual descriptions.

PESTS AND DISEASES Generally trouble free, but susceptible to honey fungus.

EVERGREEN VIBURNUMS They all thrive in sun or light shade in soil that remains permanently moist. A few flowers open on the species *V. tinus* in autumn and it continues in flower through until early spring – up to twenty weeks in all. The clusters of pink buds open into white flowers. *V. t.* 'Gwenllian' AGM is similar with pale pink flowers and prolific blue-black berries. 'Eve Price' AGM starts to flower in late winter, continuing into spring. They make hardy bushy shrubs to about 3 x 3m (10 x 10ft), but appreciate shelter from cold winds. They do well in pots.

V. x burkwoodii 'Park Farm Hybrid' AGM is open-branched with glossy leaves and large balls of waxy-looking very fragrant white flowers in spring. It reaches1.5 x 2m (5 x 6ft); more if grown against a wall.

V. davidii AGM is grown for its handsome, shiny ribbed oval leaves and its strong shape. It makes a low mound 1 x 1.5m

(3 x 5ft) after ten years. If you plant male and female plants (one male will serve up to five females) the female plants will bear a crop of unusual berries with a turquoise bloom. *V. cinnamomifolium* AGM, up to 5 x 5m (15 x 15ft), is an unusual large version of *V. davidii*.

DECIDUOUS VIBURNUMS *V. x bodnantense* 'Dawn', 2.5 x 1.5m (8 x 5ft), bears sweet-scented clusters of small pale pink flowers on bare branches all winter. 'Deben' is similar with white flowers. The dull green leaves are bronze when young. Next into flower are two highly-scented shrubs: *V. x burkwoodii* 'Anne Russell' AGM, 1.5 x 1.5m (5 x 5ft), with round clusters of white flowers; and *V. carlesii* 'Aurora' AGM, 1.2 x 1.2m (4 x 4ft), with pale pink clusters

opening from red buds. Of the summer-flowering varieties, *V. plicatum* 'Mariesii' AGM, 1.8 x 1.8m (6 x 6ft), has a beautiful tiered habit of growth, the horizontal branches being smothered in a layer of flat lacecap flower clusters in early summer. The leaves turn red-purple in autumn. It does best in full sun.

V. opulus 'Notcutt's Variety' AGM is a form of the native guelder rose, 3.5 x 2.5m (12 x 8ft), with large maple-like leaves that turn orange red in auutmn. The lacecap flowers eventually develop into a heavy crop of translucent red berries. The variety *V. o.* 'Xanthocarpum' AGM has yellow berries and *V. o.* 'Compactum' AGM 1.2 x 1.2m (4 x 4ft) is the one to choose if you are short of space.

VIRBURNUM PLICATUM MARIESII

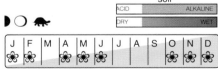

	soil	
ACID		ALKALINE
DRY		WET

◗ ○ 🐢

J	F	M	A	M	J	J	A	S	O	N	D
✿	✿		✿	✿					✿	✿	✿

VIRBURNUM X JUDDII

VIRBURNUM OPULUS

VIBURNUM DAVIDII

VINCA MINOR

Lesser periwinkle, evergreen shrubby perennial (Europe including Britain). Mature at 5 years: 20 x 60cm (8in x 2ft).

Dark green, smooth pointed leaves make a dense clump from which long stems grow and root down to form new plants. In this way a complete leafy mat develops over a wide area. Short stems at the centre of each clump carry tubular flowers opening out into five flat petals, blooming from mid spring to early summer and occasionally, if pruned after flowering, repeating later on.

USES Periwinkles are among the easiest of ground cover plants for sun or shade.

CULTIVATION Plant between late summer and spring in any reasonable soil, acid or limy. The plants are shade-tolerant but they will produce more flowers in a sunny position. They take a few years to establish as ground cover. Thereafter, to keep the foliage dense and tidy, clip over the plants with shears in early spring.

PROPAGATION Detach rooted runners or dig up and divide clumps in winter.

PESTS AND DISEASES Generally trouble free.

GOOD VARIETIES The variety *Vinca minor* 'Argenteovariegata' AGM has leaves with a silvery margin and blue flowers; 'Atropurpurea' AGM has plum-purple flowers; 'Azurea Flore Pleno' AGM has double blue flowers; 'Alba Variegata' yellow variegated leaves and white flowers; 'Gertrude Jekyll' AGM is also white but with small plain green leaves. The greater periwinkle, *V. major* and its forms are quite aggressive colonizers, and can get very straggly, but it is useful for difficult sites. It needs clipping over each year to keep it tidy.

COMPANIONS Vincas are best allowed to make an extensive carpet on their own.

VINCA MINOR 'ARGENTEOVARIEGATA'

VIOLA

Pansy, viola, violet, annuals and hardy perennials (Europe, Asia, N. America). Mature at 1 year: 10-15 x 20cm (4-6 x 8in).

Between shy violets and cheeky pansies there is a wide range of intermediate flower sizes, shapes and colours. The leaves vary from heart-shaped and kidney-shaped to broadly or narrowly lance-shaped. They form a dense central clump from which long stems straggle with secondary clumps at their ends. Flowers can be of uniform colour or multi-coloured, and the texture of dark coloured petals is sometimes very velvety. They bloom all the year round, depending on the species grown.

USES Pansies and violas are good edging plants and will seed themseves in paving or at the sides of gravel paths. They were used to underplant rose beds in Edwardian gardens, and are still effective when used in that way.

CULTIVATION Plant in spring in any reasonable soil that does not dry out. Mulch established plants in spring to conserve moisture and water them in dry spells. Ideally the flowers should be dead-headed regularly but this is hardly practicable in most gardens. However, it is worth finding time to clip over the plants after their first flush of flowering, usually soon after midsummer, cutting back the long straggly stems. This encourages new growth of both leaves and flowers. Winter pansies can be planted in autumn.

PROPAGATION Many pansies and violas can be grown from seed, but the germination rate is not high; this is surprising since they self-seed freely around the garden. The plants can also be divided in autumn.

PESTS AND DISEASES Generally trouble free.

GOOD VARIETIES *Viola labradorica* is a violet rather than a viola or pansy. It has pale violet flowers in spring and heart-shaped dark purple leaves suffused with green when grown in shade, spreading quickly to make dense ground cover. 'Bowles' Black' is a pretty self-seeding viola with little black velvet flowers, and 'Molly Sanderson' AGM has larger black flowers. *V. cornuta* AGM, *V. c.* Alba Group AGM and *V. c.* Lilacina Group are all easy, making mats of fresh green leaves or weaving their way up into the lower branches of roses or other shrubs. Other good violas include 'Huntercombe Purple' AGM, 'Maggie Mott' AGM, pale blue and a very old favourite; and 'Moonlight', pale yellow. There is such a vast choice of pansies for summer and winter bedding that it is best to choose plants in flower from a nursery at the appropriate season.

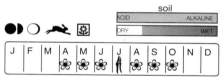

VIOLA 'PRINCESS CREAM'

VIOLA MIXED

V

VITIS 'PURPUREA'

Syn. **Vitis vinifera** *'Purpurea'. Claret vine, deciduous woody climber (Europe, Asia). Mature at 15 years: to 7m (23ft). AGM*

This grape vine climbs by means of twining tendrils. It is grown for its leaves rather than its fruit; its grapes are small and sour but the leaves are beautiful. They are three- or five-lobed and covered with fine white hairs when young. As they mature they become red-purple, darkening in autumn.

USES This vine will grow on a wall of any aspect or on a pergola or arch. The juice of the grapes of *V.* 'Brant' (see below) can be drunk fresh or made into wine.

CULTIVATION Plant *V.* 'Purpurea' in sun or light shade, in any reasonable soil. It is particularly happy in limestone or chalk. Provide a trellis, arch, or wires against a wall to support it. In the early stages, tie the shoots in to the support several times during the growing season until a wide-spreading framework has been made. Prune ornamental vines like this one in early winter, cutting back side shoots to two or three buds from the main stems.

PROPAGATION Take cuttings in late autumn.

PESTS AND DISEASES Generally trouble free.

OTHER VARIETIES *Vitis* 'Brant' is the best hardy outdoor fruiting grape. The green leaves turn bronze-red in autumn, the veins remaining green. *V. coignetiae* is grown for its large, handsome, rounded leaves which turn red-brown in autumn. It is a vigorous twining climber up to 15m (50ft) but can be kept in order by strict pruning. *V.* 'Incana', the dusty miller grape, has light grey-green leaves, which are covered in white down, and black grapes.

WEIGELA

Deciduous shrubs (garden hybrids of E. Asian species). Mature at 10 years: mostly 2.5 x 2m (8 x 6ft).

The weigelas are easy and popular shrubs, flowering from early to mid summer. The leaves are oval, pointed and deeply veined. In some forms they are variegated. The flowers, which are held in loose clusters, are shaped like long bells, white, pale or darker pink or red.

USES Plant weigelas at the back of a mixed border, or group them with other shrubs. They are tolerant of industrial pollution.

CULTIVATION Plant between autumn and spring in any reasonable soil including chalk, in sun or light shade. Variegated forms should be planted in light shade. Prune out one stem in three from the base each year.

PROPAGATION Take softwood cuttings during the summer.

PESTS AND DISEASES Generally trouble free.

GOOD VARIETIES 'Bristol Ruby' has the darkest colouring with crimson red flowers from darker buds. 'Newport Red' is similar but a little smaller. 'Eva Rathke' is a smaller red-flowered variety 1.5 x 1.5m (5 x 5ft). 'Abel Carrière' AGM at least 2 x 2m (6 x 6ft) has a more elegant, arching habit than the rest and soft rose-pink flowers. 'Candida' has white flowers. The best variegated form is *W.* 'Praecox Variegata' which has green and cream leaves and pink flowers.

WISTERIA SINENSIS

Deciduous woody climber (Central China, 1816). Mature at 30 years: up to 30m (100ft).

This wisteria, and the Japanese wisteria, *W. floribunda*, are similar, but the stems of *W. floribunda* twine clockwise and those of *W. sinensis* anticlockwise. The elegant light green leaves emerge in early summer and consist of eleven narrow leaflets, covered with silky down. The scented mauve pea flowers are carried in long hanging tassels and appear at the same time as the leaves.

USES Wisterias need plenty of space to climb: the wall of a substantial two or three storey house, a long and sturdy pergola, or a good sized tree. Use them on a metal frame to make a shady roof over a terrace. *Wisteria floribunda*, the less vigorous of the two, can also be grown as a standard at about 2.5m (8ft) high.

CULTIVATION Plant wisterias in full sun in ordinary soil. Some plants take up to ten years before they flower. Unpruned plants deteriorate into a tangle of intertwining, non-flowering stems. Start a twice-yearly pruning regime two or three years after planting. In late summer to make and maintain the framework, tie in any shoots needed to extend the framework and shorten all others back to five or six leaves out from the parent stem. In winter shorten the stems again to two or three buds from the main stems, to encourage flower buds to form.

PROPAGATION Layering is the most likely method to succeed.

PESTS AND DISEASES Generally trouble free.

OTHER VARIETIES *W. floribunda* 'Alba' AGM and *W. f.* 'Rosea' AGM have white and pink flowers respectively. *W. f.* 'Multijuga' AGM should be trained to hang from overhead not against a wall.

VITIS 'BRANT'

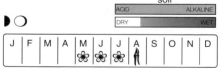

WEIGELA

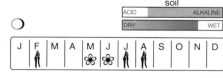

WISTERIA

YUCCA FILAMENTOSA

Adam's needle, evergreen shrub (Southeastern USA, 18th century). Mature at 7 years: 80 x 90cm (2ft 8in x 3ft) after 10 years; 1.8 x 1.5m (6 x 5ft) at maturity. AGM

Yuccas slowly grow into dramatic, architectural plants, with symmetrical rosettes of long, spikey sword leaves rising from the base. After several years (perhaps as many as ten) a tall strong flower spike will grow and bear large waxy looking, drooping bell-shaped cream flowers. *Y. filamentosa*'s leaves are edged with narrow white threads.

USES Yuccas make a dramatic statement wherever they are planted. They are especially useful for poor sandy soil in full sun; this one's native habitat is coastal sand dunes. A group of three or more in a seaside garden with the sea as backdrop is sensational. They also do well when grown in pots in town gardens.

CULTIVATION Grow yuccas in full sun in ordinary or poor well-drained soil including chalk, and shelter from cold winter winds. They are low-maintenance shrubs that do not need any pruning except to remove dead or damaged leaves occasionally and to cut down the flower stems.

PROPAGATION Remove and pot up any suckers that appear, or divide the plants in spring. This job is difficult and dangerous; beware of the sharp spines at the leaf tips.

PESTS AND DISEASES Generally trouble free.

OTHER VARIETIES *Y. filamentosa* 'Bright Edge' AGM and 'Variegata' AGM have yellow margins and stripes respectively. *Y. flaccida* 'Golden Sword' AGM has grey-green leaves striped with yellow. *Y. gloriosa* AGM is the largest in leaf and flower, and the most dramatic.

COMPANIONS Yuccas look like and are plants that enjoy near-desert conditions. To emphasize the theme plant them with *Cynara cardunculus*, *Euphorbia characias* ssp. *wulfenii* and sedums.

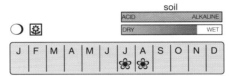

YUCCA FILAMENTOSA

ZANTEDESCHIA AETHIOPICA 'CROWBOROUGH'

Z

Arum lily, tuberous perennial (S. Africa, 1731). Mature at 5 years: up to 90 x 45cm (3ft x 18in).

The arum lily has the lush appearance of a waterside plant, and the species does like to have its roots permanently in water. But 'Crowborough' will thrive just as well on land provided it is not too dry. It is a marvellous foliage plant with glossy dark green arrow-shaped leaves growing from the base and elegantly poised. The flowers are held well above the leaves from early to midsummer. They have large pure white spathes and yellow spadices.

USES Zantedeschias provide sculptural emphasis in moist borders or at the margins of ponds and streams. They are excellent container plants indoors and out.

CULTIVATION Plant in spring placing the roots about 10cm (4in) deep in mud at the water's edge or in deep rich soil in a border. The plants are vulnerable to frost until they are well established, so cover them with a deep mulch in winter for the first few years. In cold areas grow them in pots and sink the pots in borders or pond margins in spring and summer, taking them into a frost-free greenhouse for the winter. In the greenhouse or indoors in winter, keep the compost just moist until early spring. Water freely and feed once a week during the flowering period.

PROPAGATION Divide plants in late summer or early autumn and pot up for use indoors or divide and replant outdoors in spring.

PESTS AND DISEASES Generally trouble free but plants grown at pond margins may need protection from ducks.

OTHER VARIETIES *Z. a.* 'Green Goddess' has flowers with green spathes splashed with white at the centres.

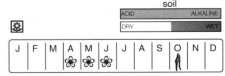

ZANTEDESCHIA AETHIOPICA 'CROWBOROUGH'

INDEX OF PLANT SYNONYMS AND COMMON NAMES

SYNONYMS

Acer dasycarpum ....Acer saccharinum

Aconitum fischeri...Aconitum carmichaelii

Actinidia chinensis...Actinidia deliciosa

Adiantum microphyllum ....Adiantum venustum

Aesculus octandra...Aesculus flava

Allium albopilosum ....Allium christophii

Allium bulgaricum ....Nectaroscordum siculum ssp. bulgaricum

Althaea rosea ....Alcea rosea

Amelanchier canadensis ....Amelanchier lamarckii

Ampelopsis 'Veitchii' ....Parthenocissus tricuspidata

Anchusa italica...Anchusa azurea

Anemone japonica ....Anemone x hybrida

Anemone pulsatilla..Pulsatilla vulgaris

Anthemis cupaniana....................Anthemis punctata ssp. cupaniana

Anthemis nobilis...Chamaemelum nobile

Aralia chinensis ....Aralia elata

Arundinaria murielae.................................Sinarundinaria murielae

Aster multiflorus ....Aster reicoides

Avena candida, A. sempervirens   Helictotrichon sempervirens

Azalea...Rhododendron

Campanula pusilla....................................Campanula cochlearifolia

Carex morrowii 'Varigata'.................Carex hachijoensis 'Evergold'

Carex oshimensis 'Evergold'   Carex hachijoensis 'Evergold'

Cheiranthus ....Erysimum

Chelone barbata..Penstemon barbatus

Chionodoxa gigantea......................Chionodoxa luciliae 'Gigantea'

Chrysanthemum coccineum ....Tanacetum coccineum

Cistus x corbariensis.......................................Cistus x hybridus

Convolvulus mauritanicus ....Convolvulus sabatius

Crataegus oxyacantha...................................Crataegus laevigata

Cyclamen neapolitanum ....Cyclamen hederifolium

                                                      Cyclamen ibericum

                                                      Cyclamen orbiculatum,

C. vernum ....Cyclamen coum

Dimorphotheca ....Osteospermum

Dracocephalum virginiacum   Physostegia virginiana

Endymion nonscriptus ....Hyacinthoides non-scripta

Fargesia murielae ....Sinarundinaria murielae

Helleborus corsicus.....................................Helleborus argutifolius

Hemerocallis flava........................Hemerocallis lilioasphodelus

Hydrangea petiolaris....................Hydrangea anomala ssp. petiolaris

Hydrangea sargentiana ....Hydrangea aspera ssp. sargentiana

Hydrangea villosa ....Hydrangea aspera ssp. Villosa Group

Iris kaempferi ....Iris ensata

Lippia citriodora ....Aloysia triphylla

Montbretia..Crocosmia x crocosmiiflora

Nicotiana affinis..Nicotiana alata

Oenothera missouriensis...............................Oenothera macrocarpa

x Osmarea burkwoodii...............................Osmanthus x burkwoodii

                                            Paeonia albiflora, P. japonica,

P. sinensis ....Paeonia lactiflora

Passiflora chinensis, P. mayana...........................Passiflora caerulea

                                 Phalaris arundinacea 'Elegantissima'

                                 Phalaris arundinacea var. picta

Phyllitis scolopendrium...............................Asplenium scolopendrium

Polygonatum multiflorum............................Polygonatum x hybridum

Polygonum affine ....Persicaria affinis

Primula acaulis...Primula vulgaris

Prunus amygdalus ....Prunus dulcis

Prunus 'Hillieri Spire' ....Prunus 'Spire'

Pyrethrum...Tanacetum

Rhus cotinus ....Cotinus coggygria

Rhus hirta 'Laciniata' ....Rhus typhina 'Dissecta'

Rhyncospermum jasminoides   Trachelospermum jasminoides

Ribes aureum..Ribes odoratum

Ribes tridel...Ribes 'Benenden'

Santolina neapolitana ....Santolina pinnata ssp. neapolitana

Scabiosa rumelica.......................................Knautia macedonica

Scilla nonscripta..............................Hyacinthoides nons-cripta

Scolopendrium vulgare ....Asplenium scolopendrium

Senecio monroi ....Brachyglottis monroi

Senecio 'Sunshine' ....Brachyglottis Dunedin Group 'Sunshine'

Spiraea x bumalda ....Spiraea japonica 'Burnalda'

Stachys lanata, S. olympica.........................Stachys byzantina

Stransvaesia davidiana ....Photinia davidiana

Thalictrum dipterocarpum...............................Thalictrum delavayi

Veronica teucrium..Veronica austriaca

Vitis henryana ....Parthenocissus henryana

Vitis quinquefolia ....Parthenocissus quinquefolia

Vitis vinifera 'Purpurea' ....Vitis 'Purpurea'

COMMON NAMES

PICTURE CREDITS

Original photography by John Freeman
who would also like to thank the following:

Keith Marshall, Hunt's Court Nursery; Greg Redwood, Royal
Botanic Gardens Kew; Mr and Mrs Thomas Messel, Alan Bloom,
Bressingham Gardens; Simon Hopkinson, Hollington Nurseries;
Clifton Nurseries Ltd; Mr and Mrs Michael Stone, Ozleworth
Park; Lynne Woods; Anthony Gardiner, Gardiner's Herbs,

Additional photography courtesy of the Harry Smith Horticultural
Photographic Collection: 61 c, 63 r, 64 c&r, 69 l&r, 78 l, 79 r,
84 c, 85 mr, 86 ml, 87 r, 88 bl,90 r, 91 l&r, 92 br, 94 r, 97 l,
98 l, 99 l, 100 r, 102 l, 104 mr, ml, bl&tr, 105 tl, ml, tr, cl, bc&br,
106 l&r, 116 r, 117 bl&c, 119 l&r, 120 l, 131 m&br, 136 r,
137 bl, 138 l, 140 r,141 r, 142 br, 144 l, 148 l, 151 l, 152 l,
153 l&r,154 l&r, 157 r, 162 bl, 167 r, 169 r, 170 tr, 171 tr, br,
178 bl, 179 r, 181 l, 182 r, 183 l, 184 r, 187 bl&r, 194 l, 196 l,
197 l, 200 r, 204 r, 206 br, 207 br&rc, 209 r, bl, 211 bl, tc, tr,
212 t, 214 l, 215 l, 217 r, 221 c, 223 l&r, 226 l, 227 l, 228 l,
230 bl, 231 l, 232 mc, tc, tr, br, 233 tr, 234 br, 236 br, 238 br,
239 c, br, 240 t, l, r, 241 r, 242 l, 243 l, 244 r, 245 l, 246 c,
247 r, 248 l, 249 l, 251 l, 252 r, 253 bl, 255 l, 257 l,